A NEW YOUTH?

A New Youth?
Young People, Generations and Family Life

Edited by

CARMEN LECCARDI and ELISABETTA RUSPINI
University of Milan-Bicocca, Italy

ASHGATE

Published by
Ashgate Publishing Limited
Gower House
Croft Road
Aldershot
Hampshire GU11 3HR
England

Ashgate Publishing Company
Suite 420
101 Cherry Street
Burlington, VT 05401-4405
USA

Ashgate website: http://www.ashgate.com

British Library Cataloguing in Publication Data
A new youth? : young people, generations and family life
  1.Youth - Social conditions. 2.Youth - Family relationships
  I.Leccardi, Carmen II.Ruspini, Elisabetta
  305.2'35

Library of Congress Cataloging-in-Publication Data
A new youth? : young people, generations and family life / edited by Carmen Leccardi and Elisabetta Ruspini.
     p. cm.
 Includes bibliographical references index.
 ISBN 0-7546-4422-7
 1. Youth--Cross-cultural studies. 2. Youth--Social conditions--21st century. 3. Youth--Attitudes. I. Leccardi, Carmen. II. Ruspini, Elisabetta.

 HQ796.N49 2005
 305.235'09'05--dc22

2005020423

ISBN 0 7546 4422 7

Printed and bound in Great Britain by Antony Rowe Ltd, Chippenham, Wiltshire.

Contents

PART III: TRANSITIONS TO ADULTHOOD, SOCIAL CHANGE AND SOCIAL EXCLUSION

List of Figures

List of Tables

List of Contributors

Helle Andersen trained as a psychologist (1981) and achieved a Ph.D. degree in Women's Studies in 1987. She was research coordinator for psychosocial research at The Danish Cancer Society from 1987 to 1995. Since 1995 she has been working as an associate professor at the Department of Psychology, University of Copenhagen. Her main research fields are women and family studies, coping and health studies, and general social psychology.

Andy Biggart is a lecturer in Social Policy/Sociology at the University of Ulster. His main research interests are in the areas of post-compulsory education and training and young people's transitions to the labour market, focusing on both national and European comparative contexts.

Manuela du Bois-Reymond is professor for Pedagogy and Youth Studies at the Department of Education, Leiden University/NL. She has conducted research in the field of youth transitions, the relationship between young people and parents and research on intercultural childhood. She has published widely in these areas. She is a member of the European network EGRIS and is in that framework especially concerned with new forms of learning and a European-based youth policy. She is a board member of several international journals, among others: *Journal of Youth Studies*, *Young*, *Childhood*, *Journal of Adolescent Research*.

Toby Daspit is assistant professor in the Department of Curriculum and Instruction at University of Louisiana at Lafayette, US. He is the co-editor (with Susan Edgerton, Gunilla Holm, and Paul Farber) of *Imagining the Academy: Higher Education and Popular Culture* (forthcoming), the co-editor (with John Weaver and Karen Anijar) of *Science Fiction Curriculum, Cyborg Teachers, and Youth Culture(s)* (2004), and the co-editor (with John Weaver) of *Popular Culture and Critical Pedagogy* (1998/2000). He is the co-editor of the 'Popular Cultural Matters' section of *JCT: Journal of Curriculum Theorizing*. His research focuses on the intersections of curriculum theorizing and popular cultural studies.

Arunachalam Dharmalingam is lecturer in Demography in the Department of Sociology and Social Policy and is Associate of the Population Studies Centre, University of Waikato, New Zealand. His research interests include family formation, ageing and retirement behaviour in New Zealand.

Ute Gerhard is professor of Sociology (since April 2004 Emeritus) and director of the Cornelia Goethe Centre for Women's and Gender Studies at the University of

Frankfurt/Main. Her research includes women's rights, social policy in a European comparison, the history of women's movement and feminist theory.

Helena Helve, Ph.D., is research professor at the University of Kuopio. She is president of the Finnish Youth Research Society and International Sociological Association (ISA) Research Committee of Youth Sociology (RC34) 2002-2006. She has written, co-authored and edited a number of books and scientific articles on youth including *The World View of Young People* (1993); *Youth and Life Management. Research Perspectives* with John Bynner (1996); *Unification and Marginalisation of Young People* (1998); *Rural Young People in Changing Europe* (2000); *Youth, Citizenship and Empowerment* with Claire Wallace (2001); *Arvot, muutos ja nuoret* (Values, Change and Young People) (2002) and *Ung i utkant. Aktuell forskning om glesbygdsungdomar i Norden* (2003).

Gunilla Holm is professor in the Department of Educational Studies and the Department of Teaching, Learning and Leadership, Western Michigan University, US. Her interests are focused on race, ethnicity, gender, and social class issues in education as well as the intersection of popular culture and education. She has published in numerous journals including *International Studies in Sociology of Education*, *Qualitative Studies in Education*, *Young*, and *International Journal of Educational Reform*. She is the co-editor (with Paul Farber and Eugene Provenzo Jr.) of *Schooling in the Light of Popular Culture* (1994), and co-editor (with Susan Edgerton, Toby Daspit, and Paul Farber) of *Imagining the Academy: Higher Education and Popular Culture* (forthcoming).

Sarah Hillcoat-Nallétamby is lecturer in Sociology and Population Studies in the Department of Sociology and Social Policy and is associate of the Population Studies Centre, University of Waikato, New Zealand. Her research interests include intergenerational relations, ageing and comparative social policy.

Allison J. Kelaher Young is associate professor in the College of Education at Western Michigan University, US. Her research interests involve motivational beliefs and self-regulated learning in the social contexts of secondary and post-secondary schooling, and epistemological beliefs and their relation to curriculum and instruction. Her work in the area of popular culture focuses on representations of sexual minorities in film and graphic narratives.

Carmen Leccardi is professor of Cultural Sociology at the University of Milan-Bicocca. She has researched extensively in the field of youth cultures, gender issues and time. Editor (with Mike Crang) of the journal *Time & Society*, she is a member of the advisory board of the ISA Research Committee Sociology of Youth and board member of *Young*. Her latest books include *Tra i generi (In Between Genders)* (edited) (2002) and, with Paolo Jedlowski, *Sociologia della vita quotidiana (Sociology of Everyday Life)* (2003).

Surya Monro is a senior research fellow at the Policy Research Institute, Leeds Metropolitan University, UK. Her research interests are gender and sexuality, social inclusion, citizenship and democracy. She has worked on a number of research projects, including projects on lesbian and gay equality in local government, on transgender, and on the voluntary sector and democracy. She has published a number of papers and chapters, particularly in the field of transgender studies, and has presented papers at numerous conferences. Her book *Gender Politics: Activism, Citizenship and Diversity* (2005) is published by Pluto Press.

Sven Mørch graduated in Sociology (1971) and took a doctorate in Youth Research in 1985. Since 1971 he has been working as an associate professor at the Department of Psychology, University of Copenhagen. His main research fields are youth social integration, youth educational theory and practice, and youth development and competencies. He has been engaged in action research and 'practice-research' among young people. In particular he has been writing about planning and evaluating youth projects. He is the Danish Educational Ministry youth research representative and a member of the Group of National Research Correspondents in The European Council. He is a member of the EGRIS group of social research.

Jane Parry is a qualitative sociologist and senior research fellow at the Policy Studies Institute (UK). Her research interests include labour market disadvantage, lifestyle transitions, and the significance of work for individual identities, in particular, how these are affected by class, gender and ethnicity. Before coming to PSI in 2000, she completed her Ph.D. at Southampton University. She has also worked as a Researcher at Swansea University, for Peter Hain MP, and for a local authority.

Yolanda te Poel is lecturer at the Institute for Higher Education in Eindhoven (the Netherlands), Center for Sustainable City and Environment Development.

Ken Roberts is professor of Sociology at the University of Liverpool. He is one of the UK's leading social scientists on young people's entry into the labour market and their life stage transitions more generally. Since 1989 he has coordinated a series of investigations into young people in East-Central Europe and the former Soviet Union. His books include *Youth and Employment in Modern Britain* (1995), *Surviving Post-Communism* (2000), and *The Leisure Industries* (2004).

Elisabetta Ruspini is associate professor of Sociology at the University of Milan-Bicocca, Faculty of Sociology. Between 2002 and 2005 she was a member of the editorial board of Sociological Research Online. Her research interests include: the gender dimension of poverty and social exclusion; lone motherhood and fatherhood; the social construction of gender identities; changing femininities, masculinities and sexual minorities. Within the methodological field: gender issues in social research; longitudinal research and analysis. Among her publications:

(with Angela Dale, eds.) *The Gender Dimension of Social Change. The Contribution of Dynamic Research to the Study of Women's Life Courses*, The Policy Press, Bristol (2002); *Introduction to Longitudinal Research*, London, Routledge (2002); *Le identità di genere (Gender Identities)*, Carocci, Rome (2003).

Monica Santoro is lecturer in Sociology at the Department of Social and Political Studies, University of Milan. Her research interests include the transition to adulthood, family change, young people and risk behaviours, risk and social change. She is author of: *A casa con mamma. Storie di eterni adolescenti (At Home with Mummy. History of Eternal Adolescents)*, Milan, Unicopli.

Nana Sumbadze is co-director of the Institute for Policy Studies, an independent think tank, and associate professor at the chair of Social Psychology of Tbilisi State University. She received her Ph.D. in social science at the Leiden University. Her fields of expertise include sociological and social-psychological research, public policy analysis, social integration processes, opinion surveys and focus groups, qualitative and quantitative data analysis. She combines research with teaching university courses in Social Psychology, Health Psychology and Environmental Psychology.

George Tarkhan-Mouravi, political scientist and policy analyst, is co-director of the Institute for Policy Studies. He specializes in Caucasian politics, democratic transition, social policies and development studies. He has been involved in developing the civic sector in Georgia, having initiated and/or headed a number of NGOs and research centres. He is a co-author of Georgia's Economic Development and Poverty Reduction Programme, and the author of the latest Human Development Report for Georgia (2003-2004, UNDP).

Andreas Walther, Ph.D. is researcher at the Institute for Regional Innovation and Social Research (IRIS) in Tübingen and holds also a part-time position in the Department for Social Pedagogy at the University of Tübingen. He has been coordinating the European Group for Integrated Social Research (EGRIS), a research network on young adults, since 1993. His research interests are youth transitions and policies for young people in comparative perspective.

Foreword

Andy Furlong

Balancing Change and Continuity

There has always been something of a tendency among youth researchers to claim to have identified significant social changes that are being revealed through the experiences of contemporary youth. In this respect, some of the earliest sociological work on youth can be linked to the emergence of the new forms of consumption and distinct youth cultures that began to emerge in the late 1950s and early 1960s. Changes in this era had a high visibility. Through fashion and music, young people were staking claim to a new society in which the tedium and greyness of the past era, in which people's concerns were firmly on making ends meet and keeping a roof over their heads, were gradually being cast aside. Although not everyone benefited to the same degree, full employment and the emergent affluence of the period encouraged people to see the world in new ways, to broaden their horizons and explore new possibilities. In the more affluent industrial societies, young people's entry to work was being delayed through more protracted engagement with full-time learning, the time available for leisure increased as did the personal resources that they had available for the enjoyment of leisure and for the establishment of distinct patterns of consumption.

In this context, much of the early sociological work on youth focused specifically on visible aspects of youth culture and consumption, while a smaller group of researchers were examining what can broadly be described as forms of economic socialization. Here researchers began to study linkages between education and work and the ways in which new generations of workers were incorporated into the workforces of industrial societies. In retrospect it can be argued that in this early era youth studies become stratified in ways that have remained entrenched to the present day. What we may call 'youth cultural studies' and 'transitional studies' largely developed along distinct lines; dialogue was restricted with open hostility emerging on a periodic basis (Cohen and Ainley, 2000; Bynner, 2001).

The stratification of youth studies has been damaging and, I would suggest, has diverted attention away from the most crucial sociological questions and led to a situation where processes of change are often exaggerated, especially by those whose interests do not include the economic spheres of life. Cultural representations can change while economic conditions remain static. In a nutshell, youth is the crossroads at which structured inequalities are reproduced. The life phase can become more protracted and fragmented, perceived and imagined in different ways with relatively little impact on the subsequent reproduction of inequality. In studying youth we need to remain aware of these crucial economic continuities and frame our interpretations accordingly. Unless we maintain a perspective on youth that is underpinned by a concern with structured processes of reproduction we risk falling into the arbitrary world of postmodernism where the diversity of life styles blinds us to the essential predictabilities of social life.

The problem we have is that although patterns of reproduction have remained intact, the protraction of the life phase does have implications for our understanding of youth. The experiences of young people have become individualized, young lives are being lived out in contexts that are more socially mixed and reflexive engagement with the social world has implications for processes of class formation. Our challenge is to reconcile these seemingly contradictory perspectives in ways that facilitate a reconceptualization of youth, an arena in which structured inequalities emerge from a context that can appear to be fluid and free of the constraints that characterized the old class society.

In part, the way forward involves the recognition that structures can become increasingly obscure and that people can lack class awareness – and may abandon the language of class – while membership of social class continues to exert an iron grip on the necks of youth. Biographies may be negotiated, but such processes occur within the constraints of structures based on factors like class, gender and 'race'. Individualization is a structured process and exposure to risk is dependent on socio-economic location.

But can we really argue that reflexivity and biographical negotiation is a product of late modernity? The tendency to focus on change at the expense of continuity has encouraged a few youth researchers to re-examine the models that we frequently see as being typical of Fordist transitions. A particularly good example here is Goodwin and O'Connor's (2005) reworking of data collected in Leicester in the early 1960s by a team led by Norbert Elias. They convincingly argue that transitions in this era were characterised by complexity rather than linearity. Similar conclusions emerged from work by Vickerstaff (2003). In other words, perhaps the evidence we have for radical changes in the lives of young people uses an unreliable historical benchmark and benefits from methodological advances. To take the argument one stage further, in a recent longitudinal survey carried out in the West of Scotland (Furlong *et al.*, 2003), it was argued that modern transitions are pretty equally divided by those that can be described as complex or non-linear and those that are best described as linear.

To highlight the essential continuities that govern young people's lives is not to deny the existence of change, but serves to identify more accurately the significance of those changes that have taken place. If the key continuity in the lives of young people is the maintenance of traditional structures of inequality, then the main change relates to the ongoing protraction of transitions – underlined by the recognition that many young adults are still in a more or less permanent state of 'transition' and may remain dependent on their families beyond the age of 30. Protraction of a process that, for many, has always been complex, has resulted in an increase in the period of time that young people feel their lives to be characterized by risk and uncertainty. Feelings of uncertainty permeate the social structure; privileged youth whose future advantages can be predicted with a high degree of reliability do not necessarily perceive the social world as devoid of risks (Walkerdine, 2001).

The purpose of a Foreword is to provoke debate and controversy and to set the scene for the research perspectives put forward by the authors whose work appears within this book. While focusing on different aspects of the youth experience, the chapters have a common concern with processes of change and with the ways in which people's lives unfold in the context of what may be referred to as late modernity. Some time ago Ken Roberts (1997) commented that we had reached a stage in youth studies where theoretical developments were beginning to run ahead of the empirical evidence. If that was true, then the contributions contained in this book will help us to redress this balance.

References

Bynner, J. (2001), 'British Youth Transitions in Comparative Perspective', *Journal of Youth Studies*, Vol. 4(1), pp. 5-24.

Cohen, P. and Ainley, P. (2000), 'In the Country of the Blind? Youth Studies and Cultural Studies in Britain', *Journal of Youth Studies*, Vol. 3(1), pp. 79-95.

Furlong, A., Cartmel, F., Biggart, A., Sweeting, H. and West, P. (2003), *Youth Transitions: Patterns of Vulnerability and Processes of Social Inclusion*, Scottish Executive Social Research, Edinburgh.

Goodwin, J. and O'Connor, H. (2005), 'Exploring Complex Transitions: Looking Back at the "Golden Age" of From School to Work', *Sociology*, Vol. 39(2), pp. 201-220.

Roberts, K. (1997), 'Structure and Agency: The New Youth Research Agenda', in Bynner, J., Chisholm, L. and Furlong, A. (eds), *Youth, Citizenship and Social Change in a European Context*, Ashgate, Aldershot, pp. 57-65.

Vickerstaff, S. (2003), 'Apprenticeship in the "Golden Age": Were Youth Transitions Really Smooth and Unproblematic Back Then?', *Work, Employment and Society*, Vol. 17(2), pp. 269-287.

Walkerdine, V., Lucey, H. and Melody, J. (2001), *Growing up Girl: Psycho-Social Explorations in Gender and Class*, Palgrave, Basingstoke.

Acknowledgements

This volume was developed from the International Conference 'Family Forms and the Young Generation in Europe' (University of Milan-Bicocca, 20-22 September 2001) jointly organized by European Observatory on the Social Situation, Demography and Family, Österreichisches Institut für Familienforschung (Vienna); International Sociological Association Research Committee 'Sociology of Youth' and University of Milan-Bicocca, Faculty of Sociology and Department of Sociology and Social Research.

A report of the Conference, bringing together the contributions of the plenary sessions, is contained in L. Chisholm, A. de Lillo, C. Leccardi and R. Richter (eds) *Family Forms and the Young Generation in Europe*, Heft 16, Österreichisches Institut für Familienforschung, Wien, 2003. This collection publishes a selection of the papers from the Conference, which have since been extensively reviewed and revised, together with other chapters that were explicitly commissioned for the volume. We would like to thank those who made the conference possible, in particular Sylvia Trnka.

We also must acknowledge the invaluable assistance provided by Giselda Rusmini in preparing the camera ready copy. A special thank you to Mary Rubick for her language revision and to Mary Savigar at Ashgate, for her support and assistance in the completion of this project.

Finally, we would like to thank Giovanna Rossi with gratitude for her collaboration.

Carmen Leccardi, Elisabetta Ruspini
Milan, November 2004

Introduction

Carmen Leccardi and Elisabetta Ruspini

The debate on the present and future of youth has aroused interest in western societies since the Second World War. The major youth movements of the nineteen sixties and seventies were of course the source of this renewed interest. Generally speaking, however, we may state that the investigation which the adult world dedicated to young people in those decades sprang from two main concerns. The first dealt with the issue of social control; the second with the widespread concern for the social inclusion of young people.

The functionalist theory may, to this regard, be seen as the first response which sociology gives to these concerns (Eisenstadt, 1956; Merton, 1968; Parsons, 1949; Parsons and Platt, 1970). As has in fact been highlighted (Zinnecker, 1987), adult concerns arose and developed with the emergence of autonomous youth cultures in the fifties – the first real young lifestyles spread in those years on both sides of the Atlantic and in a uniform fashion. Parallelly, what has aptly been called a youth 'protection culture' was also consolidated (Heinritz, 1985). On this basis, adult social institutions, from school to the family, were actively concerned with keeping the young world separate from the wider social universe. They attempted to prevent the overwhelming appeals of cultural modernization from cracking the protective wall built up around young people, seen as a pre-political world essentially needing pedagogical attention and care.

The tumultuous, conflicting relationship between the generations which was to develop in the following decades alongside the growth of youth cultures and sub-cultures – including political ones – originates to a considerable extent in young people's desire to free themselves from this restricting protection. The relations between young people and their families were thus to be marked for at least a decade, between the sixties and seventies, by the struggle of the former for independence: for free self-definition and for the control of their transitions in status.[1]

More recent history is written in a different register. The frame marked by the major clashes between generations for the control of social resources, which moulded most of the twentieth century and was seen in the social movements, has been replaced by a different scenario. It is characterized by fragmentation, the outcome of the lack of a true centre from which conflicts may radiate. The result of the great processes of change in the last few decades – from de-industrialization to the rise in education levels, from the transformation of gender and family models to the de-standardization and precariousness of labour and the explosion of the political crisis – this transformation has also led to a restructuring of inter-generational relations.

The new definition of relationships between generations, and in particular between parents and children, is also fostered by one of the most evident side effects of these powerful social processes: the change in life-course patterns (Heinz, 1991). This change, moving towards a de-standardization and growing contingency in life-courses and identity, today affects all generations, and creates new conditions of generalized uncertainty.

One of the consequences of this restructuring of biographical horizons, the outcome of the reshaping of the life sequences peculiar to the first modernity (Kohli, 1985), is however, in its way, positive. It has led to children and parents signing a new pact of solidarity. This pact is the result of the prolonging of youth (Cavalli and Galland, 1995; Wallace and Kovatcheva, 1998) and, in parallel, of a family support which is increasingly far-reaching in time and complex in the quality demanded by the new education levels of young people (Cicchelli, 2001). But it is also, in wider terms, the result of the growing unpredictability of the future and new responsibilities to 'protect' the younger generations, due to the risks associated with this unpredictability, which the adult generation is called upon to assume.

The future of young people is also made uncertain by the loss of those codified links between social and biographical time which until a few decades ago made it possible to identify (for males) clearly mapped-out, linear phases in life: firstly preparation for work through education; then employment, the central source of identity and undisputed hallmark of adulthood; lastly retirement (Kohli, 1985). For young people this new 'contingency of the life course' (Heinz, 2001, p. 9), which also brings with it the end of the concept of 'normal biography', involves the lack of an aspect which had previously been determining in reflection on youth: the identification of youth with a set of socially defined stages, which progressively lead to adulthood (Côté, 2000; Pollock, 2002). These stages, usually synthesized in the term 'transition', identified the young phase of life with a trajectory aimed at building an adult biography reaching increasing levels of existential autonomy and economic independence. As in the three biographical phases described by Kohli, here too the relationship between individuals and institutions was guaranteed by the entwining of life and social time, in a well-defined linear sequence. People became full adults once they had covered that path which involved a rapid succession of 'stages', such as the completion of studies, inclusion in the labour market, leaving the parental home for independent habitation, the construction of a relationship as a couple, and parenthood. Today, although these events are bound to happen sooner or later, both their order and the irreversibility and the frame which ensured their overall meaning are lacking.

Even more than of the sequence, linearity and rapid succession of the single stages, this frame of meaning was the outcome of the symbolic value, as a whole, they held in the life of the young individual. While the temporal aspect of the phase of young life was confirmed – youth was considered as a clearly recognizable stage, destined to end with the assumption of adult roles (Cavalli, 1980) – through these stages the two poles of (inner) autonomy and (social) independence could meet positively. Youth conceived as a transition phase, in short, made it possible to think of the relationship between individual identity and social identity as one between two dimensions which were not only complementary but also almost perfectly overlapping. The achieving of inner autonomy was ensured by the progressive transition to higher levels of independence. The whole process was made possible by the relation with sufficiently credible and non-fragmented social institutions.

The general scenario today has changed. Social institutions continue to mark the times of everyday life, but their ability to guarantee a fundamental dimension in the construction of individuality, the sense of biographical continuity, is lacking. Young people today no longer have the guarantee of gaining adult status with their inclusion in a pre-defined programme of transitions through different institutions. In the 'risk society' a socially ruled path towards adulthood has been lost (Bynner, Chisholm and Furlong, 1997; Chisholm, 1999; Cieslik and Pollock, 2002; Du Bois-Reymond, 1998; EGRIS, 2001; Furlong and Cartmel, 1997; Wallace and Kotacheva, 1998; Wyn and White, 1997). The arrival point of this pathway, in turn, is no less certain than the ways to achieve it. Adulthood has changed its meaning (Côté, 2000) symmetrically to match the changes which have affected all the ages in life in second modernity.

The enforced 'individualization' of biographies – in search of biographical solutions more suited to resolving the systemic contradictions of the times – characterizes the historical phase we are living in (Beck and Beck-Gernsheim, 2003). This involves a new emphasis on self-determination, autonomy and choice. But it does not, however, eliminate the profound furrows traced by differences in class, ethnic membership and gender. For young people, this means new paths to freedom and space to experiment, but also the loss of a positive relation with the biological time, because of the great difficulty in looking ahead in time and controlling, at least ideally, the future.

We may therefore state that its prolonging definitely constitutes the most evident aspect of youth, but perhaps not the most important one. The decisive transformation, in our view, lies in the lack of the possibility to anchor the experiences which young people make – in this phase, as we know, these experiences follow on with an existential intensity and at an almost unrepeatable pace – to the world of social and political institutions.

The 'new youth' which the title of this book refers to is the outcome of these powerful changes. It would be extremely reductive to focus attention exclusively on the aspects in the shade, on the 'losses' associated with this new condition. This is only, in reality, one side of the coin. The other side outlines a different picture. Within it the ways are shaped through which, at this turn of the century, the young generations interpret, tackle and hence transform the conditions of uncertainty of the 'world risk society' (Beck, 1998). The rich symbolic resources which contemporary Western societies make available render the repertoire of this re-processing highly varied. Youth cultures are a direct expression of it (Amit-Talai and Wulff, 1995; Bennett, 2000; McRobbie, 1993). It is through them, as we know, that young people 'negotiate structures' (Miles, 2002, p. 60), working out lifestyles

(Miles, 2000; Chaney, 1996) which respond in a creative way to the structural conditions laid down by the labour market, bureaucracy and the welfare system.

This book therefore does not only set out to contribute to general thinking on the 'new youth' by hinging on a comparative perspective. It also aims to focus on a particular aspect of the active negotiation process which young people today enact to re-define and restore order to the complexity of their existence. Relations with the family (see Catan, 2004) are an aspect which is frequently evoked but less often truly investigated by studies on youth.[2] In order to proceed in this direction, however, we must also discuss the ways through which the family, in the context of the 'society of uncertainty', restructures its relational codes and constructs new practices in its relations with its children. To this end we must bear in mind both the new cultural model informing what has been described as the 'post-familial family' (Beck and Beck-Gernsheim, 2003, chapter 6) – to indicate the central importance within it of forms of relationship and solidarity which are no longer discussable through reference to its traditional normative dimension – and the more material aspects of support to young people (forms of financial support, accommodation and so on). These two aspects, which may only be analytically separated, create a new 'family tree', as we may describe the world of relations between young people and their family which also emerges from the chapters in this book. This 'family tree' is not only a 'genealogical tree' in its traditional meaning, through which it is possible to highlight the ascending and descending relations. It is not a static frame, but a living organism. It is a 'real' tree: its trunk, branches, leaves, flowers and fruit give life to a living system of relations and inter-dependences. Between parents and children, but also, for example, between grandparents and grandchildren. In the 'foggy landscape' in which young people find themselves immersed (Abrams, 1982), this tree is essential so as not to lose the way, despite their many explorations and zigzagging, to obtain material and symbolic nourishment, to confirm their identity.

The sense of belonging and embeddedness which this 'tree' is today able to provide is seen to be essential on different levels. Not only relating to the objective extension of youth (paralleling the extension of the period of schooling), which demands further support by the family of origin whatever the specific nature of the single countries[3] and different welfare systems. Or to contain the risks of social exclusion and marginalization of young people in this historical period. But there is also a different, apparently paradoxical reason. The growth of the objective inequality between generations (Schizzerotto, 2002) – generally speaking the living standards of the older generations in the last decade have risen much more than those of young people, also due to their fewer opportunities within the labour force (Bien, 2003) – seems to facilitate, and not hinder, the relationship between parents and children. This absence of conflict is not due to purely instrumental reasons. It is rather caused by the entwining of these reasons and the increase in everyday exchanges between relatives, which are affective as well as communicative and practical (Galland, 2003).

As a result of this specific form of inter-generational inequality, young people's dependence and autonomy may increase in a parallel movement. The material and symbolic support they receive from the previous generations and from the family networks, while actually generating a return to forms of family 'protection' (and hence of 'dependence'), also favour the consolidation of their self-representation as autonomous subjects. This is also the reason why, unlike in the 1950s, these forms of protection are not opposed by young people, who do not see in them dangers for their self identity.

In other words, in societal contexts which no longer certify the asymmetry between generations on the level of agency potential, the increase in dependence of children in a family does not, in itself, seem to constitute the basis for the birth of inter-generational conflicts. Nonetheless, since the generation gap does not seem likely to close, at least in the short-medium term, the progressive ageing of the population is bringing the problems of distributional justice increasingly to the foreground – we may foresee that the issue of the relations between generations will end by having a growing importance in our affluent societies (Cavalli, 1994).

Seeking to focus, as this book does, on the young world – with the national, social, cultural and gender differences which distinguish it – *in interaction with adult generations*, may contribute, we consider, to sedimenting knowledge on an aspect with socially and ethically strategic consequences.

Outline of the Book

Within this analytical frame, the book sets out to reflect on the 'new youth' in the twenty-first century both in Europe (including Eastern Europe), the United States and New Zealand.

The first section 'Reconceptualizing Youth. New Perspectives and Challenges' aims to offer readers a discussion of the forces that shaped youth in the last decades; their impact on young people's lives and the role that young people played as actors in this change. This section also offers a comparative assessment of the relationship between the transition to adulthood and social change: change in living arrangements, in the organization of the labour market and in welfare policies, change in cultural models and in temporal experiences. It thus provides the conceptual framework for the theoretical and policy discussion contained in the subsequent chapters.

The section opens with a chapter by Carmen Leccardi, contributing to the understanding of the mechanisms by which young people today come to terms with the loss of an idea of the future. Also using information from a qualitative research study on the temporal experience of young adults, the chapter more particularly examines the ways in which social uncertainty and risk have become part of the biographical construction of young people. Although the case in question is the Italian one, and therefore has Mediterranean features (postponement of leaving the family, prolonging of education, major problems in the relationship with the labour market), the observations put forward on young 'temporal styles' and 'biographical subjectivization' have a value which goes beyond national boundaries. The chapter in fact emphasizes the need to avoid long-term commitments, to avoid fixity in favour of fluidity, to isolate the present both from the past and from the future.

The relation between impact of social change on the life courses of young men and women and the transition models to adulthood is further examined in the second chapter in this section, by Andy Biggart and Andreas Walther. Making use of a comparative perspective (necessary to represent the plurality and wealth of existing models), the chapter focuses on the de-standardization and complexification of the processes accompanying young people towards adult life and the consequent growing dependence of young adults on the family of origin. The chapter dwells in particular on the different forms which this dependence may assume and, therefore, on the growing risks connected with working life (precarious, badly-paid work careers), on the role of family networks and the response of the welfare systems.

Using a historical viewpoint, the chapter by Sven Mørch and Helle Andersen focuses on the important relationship between changes in individual and family lifes and processes of social construction of youth. After examining the peculiar nature of the process of socialization in the families belonging to traditional and modern societies, it dwells on the challenge posed by the growing individualization in life courses, a feature of contemporary societies, which lays the bases for a radical re-definition of the significance of the transition towards adulthood.

In the fourth chapter, Gunilla Holm, Tony Daspit and Allison J. Kelaher Young reflect on the cultural resistances which still prevent a complete, satisfactory definition of youth. The chapter analyses the dominant, generally unchanging public and research views of youth by reviewing the current ways young people are framed in the US with regard to schooling, sexuality, violence, consumerism and popular culture. The tension is also underlined between a 'static' view of the youth condition, on the one hand, and the recognition of young people's subjectivities and experiences (linked to ethnicity, social class, gender and sexuality) on the other.

Helena Helve's reflections on the relationship between cultural orientations of young people and social change end the first section. By using the data from empirical studies on attitudes, values and value structures of young Finns, the author analyses the relationship between young people, globalization and the complex construction of identities in the framework of multiculturalism. Young people learn cultural values in their own society but they also adopt different values from global (youth) cultures, the media and the Internet. Even in a modern 'mono-cultural' homogenous society like Finland, young people are thus free to change their national mono-cultural values to international multicultural values.

The aim of the second section 'Young People and Relations between Generations' is to offer the reader an overview of some of the most recent research experiences on the transition into adulthood, taking into account national variations and peculiarities. The relationship between social change and patterns of transition (accelerated social change has strongly contributed to the transformation of the significance of youth, making it more uncertain and unpredictable) are explored in different geographical contexts: Central-Northern European countries, Mediterranean countries and New Zealand.

The section opens with the chapter by Sarah Hillcoat-Nallétamby and Arunachalam Dharmalingam, exploring the crucial issue of solidarity across generations through the results of a survey on three generations carried out in New Zealand. In particular, the chapter examines the question whether young people in New Zealand continue to benefit from their parents' support once they have left the parental home and if so, whether the likelihood of receiving support will in any way be influenced by the presence of a third generation: their grandparents.

Within the context of the prolonging of the transition as a phenomenon shared by all Western countries, Monica Santoro focuses particular attention on the Italian context. The chapter specifically explores the descriptions – provided both by young people and by their mothers – of the extended stay of young Italian people in the parental home. These representations are analysed through the results of in-depth interviews carried out in Italy both on young adults living with their family and on their mothers.

A different slant on family cultural models is highlighted, this time related to the Netherlands, in the chapter by Manuela du Bois-Reymond and Yolanda te Poel. The two authors investigate a particularly interesting aspect for the analysis of the transformations which have affected the transition to adulthood: that of caring work. From a gender and generational viewpoint, the chapter examines the delicate negotiation processes between young women and men who are already parents or who are still postponing parenthood. These processes concern both the relationship between paid work and care work and the division of caring tasks between men and women. In the light of empirical data, the current co-existence among young adults of very different biographical orientations regarding the 'work-life balance' is also highlighted.

This section ends with the chapter by Ute Gerhard which takes into consideration young German women and their attitudes towards feminism in the light of inter-generational reflection. The profound processes of social and cultural change in the last decades, together with biographical options and lifestyles of young women, have also modified their vision of gender-linked issues. The analysis shows the considerable distance separating younger women from their mothers both from the point of view of the relation with the professional world and concerning relations with men. Even in their view of feminism, young women tend to distance themselves from those 'feminist issues' on which at least a part of their mothers identified with.

The third section 'Transitions to Adulthood and Social Exclusion' explores in a comparative perspective the issue of the distribution of resources and opportunities between generations together with the theme of young people's citizenship.

The chapter by Ken Roberts describes how young people in post-Communist Eastern Europe have been affected by the changes in their countries' economies and labour markets, the creation of multi-party political systems, and broader changes in gender roles. The chapter also discusses how young people have experienced these changes, by exploring how intra- and inter-generational relationships have been affected. It asks how the above relationships have differed between socio-demographic groups: young men and young women, young people from different kinds of family backgrounds and with different kinds and levels of education, in different regions of different countries.

Nana Sumbadze and George Tarkhan-Mouravi's chapter dwells on some crucial dimensions of the transition to adulthood in Georgia. More specifically, the chapter examines the impact of a different transition – the transition to a new political, economic and social system – on young people's life courses. After examining the new social reality in Georgia, hovering between tradition and modernity, the chapter reports the results of a survey on the youth condition. Particular attention is given to the analysis of the values and lifestyles of young people considered in an inter-generational key.

The theme of young people's citizenship and social exclusion is particularly investigated in the last three chapters in the volume.

Elisabetta Ruspini's chapter discusses the issue of young lone mothers in Italy, a social group through which light may be shed on a form of marginal, very 'swift' transition to adulthood. Within the small group of teenage sole mothers, tensions and contradictions emerge which are linked to the mixture of the needs of adult life and those of adolescence. Young lone mothers have considerably anticipated the reproductive function: motherhood precedes the conclusion of their education, their entry into the labour market, leaving their family and stable cohabitation with their partner. The aim of the chapter is thus to discuss the relationship between 'anomalies' in the transition process to adulthood and the development of inequality factors.

Jane Parry's chapter explores transitions to adulthood in terms of a group of young people in the United Kingdom who are variously disadvantaged and who have all experienced extended periods of unemployment. Drawing upon qualitative research conducted with young people at the lower end of deprivation (suffering from two or more 'disadvantages', including disability, criminal records and homelessness), the chapter looks at how structural disadvantage complicates the anticipated school-to-work, housing and domestic transition for young people. It also explores the strategies or coping mechanisms they invoke in negotiating these pathways.

Surya Monro, in the concluding chapter of the book, explores a very innovative issue: how young transgender people in the UK face a number of challenges during their transition to adulthood. The chapter addresses the social institutions which marginalize transgender young people, arguing for a social system which is more tolerant of gender diversity. It briefly indicates notions of citizenship as a means of moving beyond the individualizing, pathologizing models of transgender which have previously characterized the literature on transgender young people. In addition, it provides short case studies of transgender people's experiences of growing up adults.

Notes

1 It is therefore not surprising that a research study carried out by Frank Musgrove on inter-generational attitudes in Great Britain in the early sixties highlights an explicitly 'hostile and critical' attitude of parents towards their adolescent children. See Musgrove (1964, p. 102).
2 The international conference 'Family Forms and the Young Generation in Europe' (Milan, September 2001 – see Acknowledgements) on which this book is based constituted a rare opportunity to examine in greater depth the inter-generational nexus within the family. The European research work 'Family Forms and Transitions in Europe', coordinated by Andy Biggart and concluded on December 2004 (in which team Carmen Leccardi took part), is the direct expression of this new interest of the scientific community in the young people-family issue.
3 On the different European youth scenarios in relationship to national systems, see Iacovu and Berthoud (2001) and IARD (2001). For reflection on European youth and entering adulthood, see Cavalli and Galland (1995).

References

Abrams, P. (1982), *Historical Sociology*, Open Books, West Compton House.
Amit-Talai, V. and Wulff, H. (eds), (1995), *Youth Cultures: A Cross-Cultural Perspective*, Routledge, London/New York.
Beck, U. (1998), *World Risk Society*, Polity Press, Cambridge.
Beck, U. and Beck-Gernsheim, E. (2003), *Individualization. Institutionalized Individualism and its Social and Political Consequences*, Sage, London.
Bennett, A. (2000), *Popular Music and Youth Culture. Music, Identity and Place*, St. Martin's Press, New York.
Bien, W. (2003), *Generational Relations, Distributive Justice and Patterns of Exchange,* in L. Chisholm, A. de Lillo, C. Leccardi and R. Richter (eds), *Family Forms and the Young Generation in Europe*, Österreichisches Institut für Familienforschung, Wien.
Bynner, J., Chisholm, L. and Furlong, A. (eds), (1997), *Youth, Citizenship and Social Change in a European Context*, Ashgate, Aldershot.
Catan, L. (2004), *Becoming Adult: Changing Youth Transitions in the 21ˢᵗ Century*, TSA, Brighton.
Cavalli, A. (1980), 'La gioventù: condizione o processo?' ('Youth: A Condition or a Process?'), *Rassegna Italiana di Sociologia*, Vol. 4, pp. 519-542.
Cavalli, A. (1994), *Generazioni*, Enciclopedia delle Scienze Sociali, Vol. IV, Istituto della Enciclopedia Italiana Treccani, Rome.
Cavalli, A. and Galland, O. (1995), *Youth in Europe*, Pinter, London.
Chaney, D. (1996), *Lifestyles*, Routledge, London/New York.
Chisholm, L. (1999), 'From Systems to Networks: The Reconstruction of Youth Transitions in Europe', in W. Heinz (ed.), *From Education to Work: Cross National Perspectives*, Cambridge University Press, Cambridge.
Cicchelli, V. (2001), *La construction de l'autonomie. Parents et jeunes adultes face aux études*, PUF, Paris.
Cieslik, M. and Pollock, G. (eds), (2002), *Young People in Risk Society. The Restructuring of Youth Identities and Transitions in Late Modernity*, Ashgate, Aldershot.

Côté, J. (2000), *Arrested Adulthood. The Changing Nature of Maturity and Identity*, New York University Press, New York/London.

Eisenstadt, S. N. (1956), *From Generation to Generation*, The Free Press – Macmillan, New York.

du Bois-Reymond, M. (1998), '"I Don't Want to Commit Myself Yet": Young People's Life Concepts', *Journal of Youth Studies*, Vol. 1(1), pp. 63-79.

EGRIS (2001), 'Misleading Trajectories. Transition Dilemmas of Young Adults in Europe', *Journal of Youth Studies*, Vol. 4(1), pp. 101-118.

Furlong, A. and Cartmel, F. (1997), *Youth and Social Change. Individualization and Risk in Late Modernity*, Open University Press, Buckingham – Philadelphia.

Galland, O. (2003), 'Comments on Walter Bien's Paper', in L. Chisholm, A. de Lillo, C. Leccardi and R. Richter (eds), *Family Forms and the Young Generation in Europe*, Österreichisches Institut für Familienforschung, Wien.

Heinritz, C. (1985), 'Bedrohte Jugend – drohende Jugend? Jugend in fünfziger Jahre im Blick des Jugendschutzes', in A. Fischer, W. Fuchs, J. Zinnacker, *Jugendliche und Erwachsene '85. Generationen im Vergleich. 10. Jugendstudie der Deutschen Shell*, Leske + Budrich, Opladen, Band 2.

Heinz, W. R. (ed.), (1991), *The Life Course and Social Change: Comparative Perspectives*, Deutscher Studienverlag, Weinheim.

Heinz, W. R. (2001), 'Work and the Life Course: A Cosmopolitan-Local Perspective', in V. W. Marshall, W. R. Heinz, H. Krüger and A. Verma (eds), *Restructuring Work and the Life Course*, University of Toronto Press, Toronto-Buffalo-London.

Iacovu, M. and Berthoud, R. (2001), *Young People's Lives: A Map of Europe*, University of Essex, Institute for Social and Economic Research, Colchester.

IARD (2001a), *Study on the State of Young People and Youth Policy in Europe. Final Reports, vol. 1: Executive Summary and Comparative Reports*, IARD, Mimeo/Milan.

IARD (2001b), *Study on the State of Young People and Youth Policy in Europe. Final Reports, vol. 2: Country Reports. Youth Conditions in European Countries, Italy*, IARD, Mimeo/Milan.

Kohli, M. (1985), 'Die Institutionalisierung des Lebenslaufs', *Kölner Zeitschrift für Psychologie und Sozialpsychologie*, Vol. 37(1), pp. 1-29.

McRobbie, A. (1993), 'Shut up and Dance: Youth Culture and Changing Modes of Femininity', *Cultural Studies*, Vol. 7(3), pp. 406-426.

Merton, R. K. (1968), *Social Theory and Social Structure*, The Free Press of Glencoe, New York.

Miles, S. (2000), *Youth Lifestyles in a Changing World*, Open University Press, Philadelphia, Pensylvania.

Miles, S. (2002), 'Victims of Risk? Young People and the Construction of Lifestyles', in M. Cieslik and G. Pollock (eds), *Young People in Risk Society. The Restructuring of Youth Identities and Transitions in Late Modernity*, Ashgate, Aldershot.

Musgrove, F. (1964), *Youth and the Social Order*, Lowe & Brydone, London.

Parsons, T. (1949), *The Kinship System of the Contemporary United States. Essay in Sociological Theory Pure and Applied*, The Free Press of Glencoe, New York.

Parsons, T. and Platt, G. M. (1970), 'Age, Social Structure and Socialization in Higher Education', *Sociology of Education*, Vol. 43, pp. 1-20.

Pollock, G. (2002), 'Contingent Identities: Updating the Transitional Discourse', *Young*, Vol. 10(1), pp. 59-72.

Schizzerotto, A. (2002), *Vite ineguali. Disuguaglianze e corsi di vita nell'Italia contemporanea* (*Unequal Lives. Inequalities and Life Courses in Contemporary Italy*), Il Mulino, Bologna.

Schizzerotto, A. (2003), 'The Transition to Adulthood in Three European Countries as an Empirical Test of Various Theories on the Condition of Today's Youth', in L. Chisholm, A. de Lillo, C. Leccardi and R. Richter (eds), *Family Forms and the Young Generation in Europe*, Österreichisches Institut für Familienforschung, Wien.

Skelton, T. (2002), 'Research on Youth Transitions: Some Critical Interventions', in M. Cieslik and G. Pollock (eds), *Young People in Risk Society. The Restructuring of Youth Identities and Transitions in Late Modernity*, Ashgate, Aldershot.

Wallace, C. and Kovatcheva, S. (1998), *Youth in Society. The Construction and Deconstruction of Youth in East and West Europe*, Palgrave, Houndmills – Basingstoke.

Wyn, J. and White, R. (1997), *Rethinking Youth*, Sage, London.

Zinnecker, J. (1987), *Jugend Kultur 1940-1985*, Leske + Budrich, Opladen.

PART I:
RECONCEPTUALIZING YOUTH.
NEW PERSPECTIVES
AND CHALLENGES

Chapter 1

Facing Uncertainty.
Temporality and Biographies
in the New Century[1]

Carmen Leccardi

Introduction

By now the international scientific community should have been convinced that the era we are living in is substantially transforming the fundamental coordinates of the relationship with time constructed by modernity (Adam, 1995; Bauman, 2000; Harvey, 1990; Nowotny, 1994; Sennett, 1998; Zoll, 1988). Contributing to these profound changes in contemporary temporal experience are both the new information and communication technologies, which construct experiences of simultaneity capable of casting doubt upon the principles of sequential and linear causality (Adam, 1992) and, in parallel, the crisis of the temporal model of industrial society. This model revolved around the centrality and regularity of working time, its corollary of the rational use of time linked to scarcity, its ability to coordinate social rhythms and to impose the idea of an abstract time controlled through internalized discipline (Sue, 1994).

The crisis of industrial time brings with it a crisis in the 'normal' biography that constructs itself around this time: youth as preparation for work, adulthood as work performance, old age as retirement (Kohli, 1994). Today, biographical narrative seems to have lost its anchorage in this form of institutionalization of the life course, and the dimension of continuity associated with it. More and more often, this narrative is fragmented into 'episodes', each of which has its own past and future, limited in range and depth (Bauman, 1995). The repercussions of these processes on models of action and on the ways of interpreting reality have been amply stressed and concern the trajectories of identity (Melucci, 1996) as well as lifestyles, relationships to politics and ethics and to institutions generally.

These new characteristics of social time and their reflections on the construction of biography reverberate directly on the condition of youth. By definition, youth has a dual connection to the time dimension not only because it is 'limited', destined inevitably to reach a conclusion, but also because young people are asked by society to delineate the course of their own biographical time, to build a meaningful relationship with social time. This means constructing significant connections between an individual and collective past, present and future (Cavalli, 1988). In this process, meaning is given to overall living time.

The planning dimension is central to this. As has been pointed out (Berger and Luckmann, 1966), the formation of identity in a modern sense is guaranteed by adherence to the logic of the plan. It is the life plan in the context of modernity that constitutes the organizing principle par excellence of biography. Thanks to planning, the future is bound to the present as well as to the past and is anticipated in daily activities, which in turn are strictly planned (Bergmann, 1981).

Starting in the post Second World War period in Western society, the connection between planning and the future gradually went into crisis, in tandem with the waning of the ideology of progress. The image of a future progressive, controllable planned time, both for society and individuals, grew weaker. The term 'future crisis' (Pomian, 1981) describes well this widespread social malaise. This crisis, which underwent an acceleration in our 'world risk society' (Beck, 1999), is today incorporated in the biographical narratives of young people. In other words, these narratives are shaped by the understanding of the unpredictability of the future and the constant flexibility that this requires.

The reflections proposed in the following pages intend to contribute to the understanding of the mechanisms by which young people today come to terms with the loss of the idea of a future and plan that is specifically part of the 'second modernity' (Beck, 1998). In particular, this chapter will focus on ways in which contemporary social uncertainty is part of the biographical constructions of young people, and how it is metabolized and transformed as an eventual resource for action.

With these aims in mind, the results of a recent qualitative study of the temporal experience of young people in Italy (concluded in 2003) will be considered. Now several decades old (having been commenced in the early eighties), the itinerary of analysis within which this research is located focused on the condition of young people on the one hand, and on the transformations of time on the other.

Before giving an account of the results that come from this research, some background is necessary. In the first place, the specificity of the condition of young people in Italy must be considered, if only in broad strokes, and posited in the context of the more widespread transformations of young people's biographical constructions in Europe. In the second place, it is opportune to offer some general information about the methods of research and some of the specifics governing the criteria that guided the choice to concentrate attention in this chapter exclusively on one of the cohorts included in the investigation, that of young adults between 26 and 29 years old. After having presented a part of the material obtained in the research and using this as reference, the chapter will conclude with some theoretical reflections on the subject of contemporary transformations of temporal and biographical coordinates.

The Uncertain Transition to Adulthood and Young People in Italy

Changes in the transition to adulthood are evident today. In the first place, it takes longer – the time necessary in order to enter adulthood has increased – and it is more discontinuous: the different milestones that characterize this entry, from the end of schooling to leaving home, to the stable entry into the world of work and the construction of an autonomous family, tend to be de-synchronized, that is, to abandon the traditional, ordered temporal sequence. This order facilitated the planning for the practically perfect superimposition of three crucial moments for the transition: abandoning the parents' home, entering the world of work and forming one's own family (Galland, 1991). Today, not only is the average age in which these milestones are reached older, but between one stage and another there may be frequent interruptions, slowdowns or pauses: as the Italian title of the book edited by Cavalli and Galland (1995) states, 'there's no rush to grow up'. The trend to extend and especially de-standardize the transition (Walther and Stauber, 2002), fragmenting it into discontinuous phases without clearly delineable connections between one phase and another, which are furthermore reversible, is common in European societies,[2] although as we will see shortly, European countries also show certain specific characteristics.

Likewise gaining in importance are biographical models, increasingly distant from linear trajectories of life (Wyn and White, 1997), which refer to the so-called *choice biography* (Beck, 1992; du Bois-Reymond, 1998; Fuchs, 1983) that is characterized by strong individualization and at the same time by an accentuation of 'risky' traits. 'Risk biography' has been spoken of in this sense (Furlong and Cartmel, 1997), connected to the need to make decisions in a social context characterized by great uncertainty.

On the whole, therefore, this reality emphasizes aspects of 'biographical subjectivization', which ascribes great importance to individual responsibility in defining choices and generally assigning a leading role to the ability to work out autonomous projects. However, this latter aspect seems contradicted by another characteristic of our time, which is tied to the contraction of collective temporal horizons: the need to avoid long-term life projects, to elude fixity in favour of fluidity, to isolate the present as much from the past as from the future.

So young people live their phase of life in a social climate in which the right to decide what one wishes to become is accompanied by the difficulty of finding reference points in one's biographical construction so as to avoid indetermination (Bynner, Chisholm and Furlong, 1997; Reiter, 2003). Generally, it may be said that the imperative to choose does not go hand in hand with the certainty that personal decisions will be able to weigh effectively on future biographical outcomes.

If this is the overall framework that today distinguishes European young people, what are the specific characteristics that pertain to Italian young people? First of all, it is advisable to keep in mind the typology of models of transition to adulthood proposed by Cavalli and Galland (1995) to understand these specifics. In this perspective, Italy together with Greece, Spain and Portugal would typify a transition model (called 'Mediterranean') whose specific traits may be synthesized thus: extended schooling; a phase of accentuated professional precariousness at the end of studies; a long cohabitation with the parents – even after entering the labour market – that nevertheless provides young people ample space for autonomy; leaving the parents' home when getting married. This model is contrasted by the one defined as 'Nordic',[3] with an early leaving of the parental home and later marriage and procreation. Great Britain would constitute a sort of autonomous model that is polar with respect to the Mediterranean model: early conclusion of studies, early entry to the labour market, also early in leaving the parental home and in marrying.[4]

In order to concisely illustrate the profile of Italian young people in the context of this Mediterranean model, let us take into consideration three crucial dimensions for the transition to adulthood: schooling, work and the family.

Schooling. In line with the European context, even in Italy the great majority of young people study: the condition of young people and the condition of students coincide. A relative discrepancy persists however between the European data and Italian data: in Italy, 69.8 per cent of 15-19 year-olds study, while the European average is 76.3 per cent (OECD, 2000). According to the data of the national survey on young people conducted by IARD on a sample of young people between the ages of 15 and 34,[5] 60.9 per cent of the 15-29 year-olds completed a high school diploma (the percentage was ten points lower in the previous survey done in 1996) while one in four attended university (Gasperoni, 2002, p. 75). Female participation is of particular importance in Italy – as it is in the rest of Europe: not only do girls comprise the majority among students, but their scholastic itinerary presents a greater degree of excellence whatever the level or nature of the cultural and material resources of their families. However, there is still a rather large gap persisting between young people of Northern and Central Italy, areas of economic advantage, and those of the South and the islands of Sicily and Sardinia. Thus, for example, while young people possessing only a middle school degree comprise between 14 per cent and 18 per cent in Northern and Central Italy, in the South and the islands, this percentage oscillates between 23 and 24.6 per cent.

Work. A central problem for Italian young people today is less unemployment – a traditional Italian problem especially as regards the South, young people and the female segment of the population – than precarious/insecure employment. Although lack of employment has been a traditional Italian problem, especially as regards the South, young people and the female segment of the population, the central problem for Italian young people today is precarious, insecure employment. According to the data of the IARD survey (Chiesi, 2002, p. 123), the number of young people who neither work nor study decreased in four years from 19.2 per cent (1996) to 13.8 per cent (2000), because there are fewer people looking for a first job and there are fewer young housewives. Even if in principle, the entrance into the world of work is easier today, young people not only continue to enter it on average at a later date with respect to their European counterparts, but they must frequently be satisfied with marginal or less secure employment (Chiesi, 2002, p. 150). This happens especially in the regions of Southern Italy where the labour market remains very precarious (according to the IARD data related to the 2000 inquiry, among young people employed in the North, almost 65 per cent have a stable job as a regular employee, as opposed to 38 per cent in the South). In a service-oriented society, in other words, the number of young people performing atypical jobs with flexible hours and without guarantees of continuity over time is on the rise. In this regard, the generational discrepancy is particularly marked. Young people looking for a first job run up against the rigidity of the 'official' labour market, where mostly male workers in the central age bracket (35-60) find employment, at the expense of young people and women (Cavalli, 2002, p. 515). The latter continue to have, in any case, a weaker position on the labour market even with respect to young men. According to the Eurostat data (Labour Force Survey 1998 and 2000, quoted in IARD 2001b, p. 8), while among young people in the labour market between the ages of 15 and 24 years old the percentage of men is 25.4 per cent, the percentage of women is 10.1 points lower. Young women are, on the other hand, over-represented (4.2 percentage points higher) among those who study (IARD, 2001b, p. 8).

Family. As mentioned previously, long cohabitation between parents and children constitutes perhaps the strongest feature of the Mediterranean model of the transition to adulthood. According to the latest IARD inquiry, 70 per cent of young people between 25 and 29 still live at home, a percentage that is even higher than that registered in 1996 (6 percentage points higher). A third of the 30-34 year olds still live with their parents (Buzzi, 2002, pp. 23-24).[6] In fact, from the beginning of the nineties, this figure has constantly continued to grow. The extension of schooling (and the tendency on the part of those who go to university to choose schools in the same city where they reside or a city very close by); the difficult relationship between young people and the labour market; the lack of university housing together with the high cost of housing together certainly constitute a constellation of dimensions that contribute to explaining this phenomenon. But these explanations remain insufficient. The cultural propensity to continue living with one's parents is an example demonstrated by those who have already concluded their studies and who have already found stable work in the labour market. Moreover, in principle this tendency lacks clear-cut divisions in class or gender (even if there is a slight tendency for a more extended stay in the family among young people belonging to upper classes and for young men).

If it is true that the family plays a central role in the economic support of children,[7] the link that unites the latter to their parents – and vice versa – seems to pass through dimensions that are not just economic. For children, the family represents a shield against social uncertainty, an existential and emotional anchor capable of blocking anxiety about the future. Prolonged living together with parents allows them more easily to construct biographical itineraries by trial and error, or to start existential experiments, leaving aside at least for the moment, existential decisions of a non-reversible character (among them that of bringing children into the world). For parents, in turn, continuing to have children to care for means putting off the unknowns of a phase of life – that of 'the empty nest' – which would impose a radical restructuring of daily rhythms and biographical time. Thus, for parents and children, extending cohabitation is transformed into a question of identity. This aspect reinforces the cultural model, characteristic of Mediterranean countries, at the basis of which it is marriage that gives full legitimacy to the choice of leaving parents' home.

Along with the increased propensity of young people to prolong living with their parents, over the past few decades the family has acquired a more open, flexible and negotiable nature. The great majority of young people enjoy ample space for freedom within the family, and live fairly harmoniously with their parents, thus experiencing the privileges connected to a lack of responsibilities connected with the organization of daily life. It is significant, in this regard, that in the research done at the end of the nineties (ISTAT, 2000), 40 per cent of the sample of young people between the ages of 18 and 34 years old judged their remaining in their families as 'a normal situation' (31.7 per cent of the cohort of 30-34 year olds give this evaluation). The less positive point of view expressed by young women (4 percentage points lower) should be underscored, however; the latter, correlatively express a greater need for independence with respect to young men (27.6 per cent of young women express this need as opposed to 19.9 per cent of young men). Thus, the theory of young women's more ambivalent feelings about the 'long term family' with respect to young men is confirmed – linked also to girls' more contained freedom of movement within the family (Facchini, 2002, pp. 175-176).

In concluding this brief reflection on the relationship between young people and their families, it is fitting to at least mention the most significant changes in the socio-demographic profile over the past few decades that relate to the prolonged cohabitation of parents and children under the same roof. The reference is to the increase in age at the time of the first marriage and for the first child;[8] the progressive drop in marriage rates (which for 25 to 29 year olds passes from, for example, between 1996 and 2000, 32 to 24 per cent – see Buzzi, 2002, p. 24); to fertility rates among the lowest in the world (1.2 children per woman); finally to the rate of living together among young people that, despite a slight increase, still remains quite low in relation to the European average (4.3 per cent of young people between the ages of 25 and 34 live with a partner, according to the IARD data – see Sartori, 2002, p. 196).[9]

Overall, the profile of Italian young people delineated above shows a picture marked by great uncertainty. To the general social uncertainty that pervades Western societies, in Italy we may add specific factors of uncertainty linked, for young people, in the passage from schooling to work and from the family of origin to autonomous living conditions. These factors negatively affect the transition to adulthood and sharpen the fear of the future.[10]

The Research

The research from which results will shortly be presented has its origins at the end of the seventies, when an inquiry on young people and time was begun. The first objective was an analysis of the experience of young men and their use of time (summarized in Cavalli, 1985). Subsequently, in the late eighties, this was expanded into an exploration of the temporal experiences of young women (Calabrò, 1996; Leccardi, 1990, 1996; Rampazi, 1991; Tabboni, 1992). It should be underlined that this initial research considered time essentially as an instrument for focusing on changes in the condition of young people. The relationship with time, how it is lived and its use constitute a litmus test for revealing changes that had taken place in the youth phase. The reference to the temporal dimension indeed allowed for unifying different dimensions in the world of young people – the relationship with school, with work, with the family, with politics and so on – usually considered separately. In other words, it guaranteed a comprehensive look at a constellation of changes that were radically transforming the meaning and ways of being young.

In 2001, twenty years after the initial study,[11] new research was begun, which in the framework of a broader examination of the changes in contemporary society's relationship to time, once again concentrated on the world of young people. In this case, however, the reflection on the condition of young people constituted a point of arrival, so to speak, rather than a point of departure for the research. In other words, the study concentrated on the transformations of ways in which to experience time, in the light of changes that had taken place over the past few decades in the temporal organization of society (acceleration and compression of time, fragmentation and contraction of temporal horizons, growth in a feeling of scarcity). The young people were considered a privileged subject for making these transformations transparent, keeping track of the centrality of the relationship to time – biographical and daily – in the construction of an identity.

The research, financed jointly by the Ministry of Education and individual universities, involved various academic institutions: in the North, the University of Milan-Bicocca and the University of Pavia; in central Italy the Universities of Florence and of Perugia; and on the islands, the University of Cagliari (Sardinia). While Milan-Bicocca, Pavia and Perugia took into consideration the relationship between young people, biographical time and daily time, Cagliari and Florence restricted themselves to looking at how daily time was used and experienced. The principal instrument of the inquiry was in-depth interviews. Perugia also made use of focus groups; Cagliari and Florence used diaries as well as the interviews (and avoided time budgets, considered unsuitable for the study of subjective representations connected to the use of daily time).

The interviews, performed in 2002 in the cities where the participating universities are located, involved two hundred young people of both sexes between the ages of 18 and 29 (students, manual and non-manual labourers, young people who study and work, unemployed and drop-outs). The interviews, lasting between forty minutes and an hour and a half, were accurately transcribed and interpreted. The interpretation of the material gathered utilized both techniques linked to content analysis as well as methodologies of a hermeneutic nature (Hitzler and Honer, 1997). A specially privileged reference was the method worked out by Rainer Zoll (1989): a 'collective hermeneutics', a re-elaboration of 'objective hermeneutics', the methodology of research constructed in Germany in the seventies by Ulrich Oevermann (Oevermann et al., 1979).[12] The results of the research are still being worked on.

In this chapter I will present some of the initial results of interpreting the interview material, with specific reference to the topic of biographical time. Special attention will be paid to the ways through which young Milanese people re-elaborate the uncertainty that characterizes the times of their transition to adulthood, constructing forms of biographical narrative that are subjectively meaningful.

Having to make a selection from the rich material available (more than a thousand pages of transcription of the fifty interviews gathered in Milan and environs), I decided to focus on the twenty interviews involving the cohort of 26 to 29 year olds, the oldest of those considered in the research. This deals with a group of young Italian women and men (no foreigners), who belong to all social classes, who have finished or are about to finish their studies. Some have job experience, but they still appear to be far from complete involvement in adult roles (as may be seen by the fact that many of them still live with their parents). For them, reaching adulthood still seems far off. They live a prolonged transition to adulthood and, as we shall see, they experiment with biographical solutions capable of controlling or attenuating the fears associated with the idea of the future.

All those interviewed, as has been stated, live in Milan or its environs. The choice to use material exclusively from interviews with Milanese young people is tied to two ways of reasoning. First of all, the specific nature of the urban situation in Milan, probably the Italian city with the most metropolitan, post-modern characteristics, where the pace of life is particularly fast and the social climate extremely dynamic. Secondly, the possibility, thanks to this choice, of making some comparisons with the results of the research carried out in Milan twenty years earlier during the first research on young people and time (Cavalli, 1985).

Dealing with Uncertainty

Uncertainty as a constitutive dimension of the *Zeitgeist* (and its corollaries: temporariness, the irrationality of making long-term plans, the need to be ready to review set goals in the light of evolving events) has become part of the cognitive baggage of young people in the twenty-first century. One could say that it constitutes the other side of the coin in the growth and pluralization of life's opportunities that young men and women perceive as an epochal trait. How do our interviewees re-elaborate this dimension? How do they neutralize the restraints on their actions that this brings about? How do they think about their own future in this scenario?

As is obvious, the reactions vary. One tendency emerging from the interviews is that the idea of planning that we are accustomed to – a medium to long-term plan of action able to deeply influence everyday life – can be replaced with that of *guidelines*, a sort of compass for action that is not, however, binding from the standpoint of measurable results. Alongside these guidelines, a sort of 'existential direction' to which one refers for an orientation in the rapid changes that take place, 'little' projects may appear, designed on shorter temporal scales (and therefore, if necessary, easy to reverse and transform). It is mostly the young people capable of good subjective control over their own biographical time, who choose to pursue this strategy. For instance, to the question 'Have you got any projects for the future?' Sergio (engineering degree, consulting work, age 29, lives alone) responds:

> I have no projects... maybe overall plans... but it's better to call them guidelines rather than plans... I don't like having plans because I wouldn't like not being able to follow through on them. Having a project means having a goal, which for me means pursuing it and if, the times being what they are, I don't succeed, that means frustration. Instead, not having projects, but living calmly with guidelines, having a basic direction, but one that has little to do with what I will do concretely in life, seems better to me... I can have only short-term goals, so I decide something and do it within six months (...). I know that life has so many ups and downs... that it's practically by chance if you manage to achieve your goals.

And a little further on he adds:

> What I try to do is not to force things, to go a bit with the tide, and so the directions, the real trajectory I can take at a given time can change... so I don't have projects, I don't want to have them... I can't answer the question about how I see myself in two years, two years are really ten, twenty, fifty.

For other interviewees, the reference to 'guidelines' tends to disappear. Here the main motif is 'chance', viewed as an unexpected occurrence to work out reflexively, to transform into a resource for action. In this framework the biography becomes a (difficult) work-in-progress, constructed in a highly uncertain context. Berenice, 28, with many temporary jobs, currently works for a number of publishing houses and lives with her parents. Asked to describe her ideal job, she emphasizes that:

> I don't have an ideal job, that's too big a question, I haven't got one... like I don't have plans, precisely because I've always gone by trial and error, I have no goal... a goal is built step by step.

And in another part of the interview she specifies:

> [In my life] everything is fairly casual... then yes, yes I do see that we create ourselves and so we have to be able to work on whatever chance brings us (...). I believe pretty much in human potential, you become aware of and pick up on certain things and then you work on them...

Biographical construction requires skill, flexibility and the ability to 'sniff the air', to not miss an occasion, a chance, the unexpected; to transform the latter, when it appears, into an opportunity from which to benefit. Even if chance is referred to as a biographical arbiter, in reality time-of-life is governed, and the ability to turn chance into an existential opportunity is highly valued.

Instead of 'guidelines', Berenice tends to emphasize 'minimum objectives': a way of not making plans, yet keeping the tiller of decisions in hand. To understand this way of building a biography it is important to keep in mind her protracted situation as a temporary worker and the continual need to change that derives from this – at an age when, traditionally, the first needs for stability begin to be felt. To the question about future projects Berenice laughingly replies:

> What a question!... In the situation I'm in right now... I don't know... that is, I'm sort of revolutionizing my existence and so, well, I really couldn't say... if you ask me something specific like, 'Do I want to do this...' I wouldn't know what to answer... Naturally, I have minimum aims that could be, say, I like to work here, I'd like to keep on working here rather than someplace else, and with these people...

In a third group of people interviewed, the idea of control over biographical circumstances that are objectively hard to control – also due to fairly unusual biographical and career routes – tends to intertwine with that of 'luck'. Here, too, 'luck' is viewed more as the ability to reap opportunities than as a total submission to events. A good example of this type of biographical narration comes from Fabiana, 25, a ballet-dancer who spent a number of years studying dance in the United States (and now lives at home). About projects she says:

> I have lots of plans... a whole list even... but it's one thing to think about them and another to carry them out. Yeah, well, my main project is my career as a ballet-dancer, let's say that that's the big thing for now... then there are small ones, like traveling, yeah, I'd love to travel, start traveling around Europe. Next year I think I'll pack my bags again and travel around Europe... to dance, to look for work, to look for artists, to meet artists, dancers... chance will play a big part in this because even in being a ballet-dancer, chance and luck count a lot (...). I hope to meet thousands of people, go thousands of places, see thousands of things, live thousands of experiences... and I need luck on my side. I think that up to now maybe there was a lucky star protecting me, maybe I even ran risks, but I've always been fortunate... I think I'm really terribly fortunate, but because I want to be.

And so in the last analysis, recourse to 'chance' in biographical narration – to 'pure' chance, or in Fabiana's case interwoven with luck – represents for this portion of young people interviewed a cognitive trick for actively coping with the dimension of uncertainty and with fear of the most distant future. Their strategy for dealing with such fitfulness is completed through an increase in rationality that is expressed through projects concentrated on the areas contiguous with the present (the so-called 'extended present').[13]

A good example of this trend, by now widespread in the world of young people (and not only young people), is provided by Alessandra, 26, who is getting her degree in education and lives at home. Asked to talk about her plans for the future, she stresses:

> For right now, nothing, I'm off to London. My mind goes as far as these next five months and then we'll see. Ideally, yes (I have some projects) for work, and I would also like to live in Amsterdam with Stefano but: a) I don't know how it will go with Stefano after five months of being apart; b) I don't know what I'll be like when I get back from London, maybe I'll come back traumatized... I don't know... I mean for the time being I'm doing this, then we'll see... actually, this business of having the near future tied up is a relief, because that's what I wanted... but the long-term future is really misty, foggy because I haven't graduated yet, because I still haven't figured out how to do what I

want to do... and therefore the steps to take... I'm taking one thing at a time and then I'll see.

Recourse to the extended present, to the temporal space in which present undertakings are brought to conclusion, therefore always ends up by producing a reassuring effect on the representation of a biographical time increasingly forced to cope with discontinuity – and therefore, in general, hard or impossible to plan.

Another two forms of biographical narration, which can be considered polar attitudes in the contemporary construction of time-of-life, also emerge from the interviews. The difference in the quantity and quality of social and cultural resources available to the two young people personifying such attitudes is food for thought. The first, that embodies the impossibility of a positive attitude towards time, is well summarized by Luigi, 26, a supermarket stock-boy who lives at home. About projects Luigi says:

No, I haven't the vaguest idea, absolutely none... I try to live in the present as best I can, to have fun... I could do other things, but I don't know... maybe I'll change when I'm older, but for now that's how it is.

The same orientation emerges – and the same expression is used – even when Luigi is asked to describe his ideal job:

I haven't the vaguest idea what it could be. Even when I was in school, my friends who are the same age had an idea of what they wanted to do with their lives. But when they asked me, I didn't know what to answer, and I still have no idea.

In another part of the interview, Luigi contextually uses the expression 'inner uneasiness' in reference to the feeling with which he looks at his time-of-life. He is aware of living in a social time that is fast – 'time is getting faster, you don't know where it goes', he says – but at the same time, he experiences his own time as inordinately 'slow':

You realize that a month's gone by, a year... it's been two years since I started this job... actually, it's like time never passes, while the days go by one by one, they just slip past you, almost as if you had no chance to live them...

The comparison between speed, change perceived as incessant, the plurality of options that remain in the background and the slowness of the present that escapes control, constitutes the imprint of Luigi's biographical experience. The existential balance sheet here is totally negative. In parallel, the dimension of extended present as planning time disappears, replaced by the reference to a vacuous present devoid of temporal depth.

An opposite experience is that of Francesco, 28, who lives at home, has a degree in physics, is taking a post-grad course in cooperation and development, is an activist in one of the networks of the Italian no-global movement, and is town councillor for the small town outside Milan where he resides. His existential horizon is full of initiatives: 'I have so much to do, my day is always super-full, my evenings are super-full... I can't stand having nothing to do... maybe six more hours a day would be needed for an ideal one.' He also has long- and medium-term projects: 'You need both: a general framework of long-term plans in order to work out the medium ones.' It is interesting to note the biographical strategy that Francesco works out to successfully cope with the uncertainty of the context:

> I have a lot of projects, yes, yes, perhaps too many. Too many, okay, but having too many is important because any plan can change, can run into insurmountable difficulties and if you bet everything on just one and it doesn't work out, what do you do? So I have a lot of different projects that can be integrated with one another – for work, for my love life, for politics.

He lists these projects in other parts of the interview. What should be specifically underscored is the conviction which pervades Francesco's biographical narration: whatever happens, whatever unexpected event emerges on the horizon, he makes it clear that he will be able to recoup a planning dimension, a control over time-of-life. While quite distinct from the first group of interviews analysed (that is, those characterized by a reference to 'guidelines' and 'chance') because of greater biographical structuring, here, too, appear those 'principles of action' that serve as a general tool of orientation – and hence as an antidote to uncertainty. Asked to clarify how he envisions himself ten years from now, Francesco says:

> [Ten years from now] I don't see myself with a specific job, with anything specific, that's not what I'm aiming for. If I see myself, I see myself with a method, with intentions, with a desire to do, with general things at stake. What these general things will be, what they will lead to, will depend on what I decide to do.

Taking an overall look at the content of the interviews considered thus far, it could basically be stated that most of the young adults interviewed were able to work out biographical strategies adequate for actively coping with the 'new uncertainty' of the twenty-first century. However, to draw a fuller picture it is necessary to dwell on another aspect: the pervasive feeling that time today has accelerated its pace, that everything goes faster (beginning with experience), while transition times are slower and slower, almost snail-paced. What derives from this is an insoluble contradiction, generating a feeling of 'belatedness' in regard to steps that in turn have lost their link to clearly recognizable temporal milestones (the conclusion of studies, entry into the working world, construction of an independent family, procreation). Many of those between the ages of 25 and 30, both young men and young women, seem today to be suffering from this kind of widespread angst.

But before reflecting on this aspect, I would like briefly to dwell on the generalized perception of time's acceleration as revealed in the interviews. In fact, this feeling influences one's view of self and of one's time-of-life, stimulating an orientation – sometimes anxious – toward doing and producing (in the present). Twenty years ago, at the time of the first research on young people's representation and use of time, this feeling was unknown:[14]

There are two aspects: on the one hand we have many more opportunities to go fast, technology helps us to in many, many ways; and then there is forced acceleration, you go fast, and faster and faster, but you can't keep up with what you're doing. In any case, there's been a speed-up in work, everything is much more frenetic, much quicker. Personally, I'm always in a rush (Giorgio, 28, IT expert, lives alone).

Time is too pressured, pressured... like, when you're talking to people it seems that everyone is in a rush but don't really know where they're going. There's a general sort of production logic, so that any time you're not producing something, you're not doing something useful, you feel guilty... it's a social thing, not personal (Paolo, 29, unemployed, lives at home).

Today there's so much more to do in the same amount of time. And since you can do many more things than you could before, it seems that there's less time, that time goes faster... there are more possibilities, many more economic possibilities to do things than before, more physical possibilities, more offers of entertainment in the broadest sense, and this leads you to having to choose, and having to choose leads you to feeling that there's not enough time. You'd like to be able to choose everything (Chiara, 28, white-collar worker, lives alone).

Time goes too fast, life goes too fast... I wish there was more time, more time to do all the things I'd like to during the day, I wish a day had 48 hours (Matteo, 26, law student, lives at home).

In many young people, the perception of speeded-up social rhythms ends up accentuating the sensation of not being personally fit for the times, of not being able to keep up with the fast pace of collective living, of being too 'slow' in relation to what is necessary to satisfactorily construct one's own biography. This is, for example, what Mary says (26, architecture student, lives at home):

If I measure myself against Milan, against these people who manage to do a million things at the same time, I feel, especially lately, that I've done too little... I've lived calmly in a city where I could have done a million things... and so I feel that, compared to other people, I've wasted my time.

This feeling of 'wasting' time – even though, as in Mary's case, there is no specific plan to fulfil, which means effectively no compulsion to reckon time – is increasingly widespread, especially among the many people having to cope with temporary work. Michela, 28, lives with her parents, has done quite a number of jobs ('cashier, maid, set designer, I worked at a tourist resort, now I decorate ceramics, do stuff on the computer...'), has no degree ('I'm not the studious type, I need practical things to do') and greatly feels the pressure of time that passes unproductively:

I feel I'm wasting my time... I have time and I'm not taking the best advantage of it, I'm angry about it. On the other hand I feel blocked by events, by the things around me... in the past four years I turned my life topsy-turvy working as a cashier, a routine job, for me it was time wasted, especially there I wasted my time (...). It's important to make use of time doing special things that make you feel good (...). I still don't know what I want to do, I haven't figured it out... but I would definitely like to live my time in another way, with a faster pace...

The same anxiety, if possible even more intense, torments Daniela, 29, a free-lance journalist with a recent degree in political science, who lives at home. Her days are hectic ('continually on the go, from city hall to the police station, from the theater to the central square'):

> Often, there you are writing until three a.m., in your room with the computer on, and then you e-mail it to the paper – sometimes they're surprised (by the time). My pace used to be slow, but now it's frenetic, really crazy...

Not having made good use of her time, as underscored frequently in the interview, is linked primarily to the ten years she took to get her degree (not such a rare situation in Italy):

> I threw away ten years for university, really just tossed them out... I should have finished much earlier, because getting a degree at 29 when you start out at 19 (...). So if I look back all I see is a waste of time, a great waste of time, time wasted doing things that had a beginning and an end, not following-up... I wasn't able to manage the time available to me, I didn't fill it up as it should have been filled (...). Now I'm unhappy, no one can give you that time back.

Today she is trying to make up for lost time through extremely fast existential rhythms ('I have to fill time, there can't be any empty spaces') and plans to work full-time at the paper where she is now free-lancing. Overall, her interview reveals the close relationship between temporal anxiety and biographical anxiety: the latter is an anxiety linked to the feeling of 'not being in step' with transition times.

The same problem bothers Elena, 29, who lives with her fiancé, studies philosophy and at the same time works in a shop. Elena, too, has been studying for her degree for the past ten years and still hasn't finished ('What have I accomplished in the past ten years? Little, basically very little (...) I didn't study when I should have, at the right age for it, and I regret that very much.') It is interesting to report her thinking in its entirety, indirectly linked to this overly 'long' time, with respect to which she feels 'out of sync':

> Nowadays it's the fact of having so many opportunities that makes you unable to decide. Having so much available and then not knowing how to take advantage of it, because it's as if you're mind-boggled by what's out there.

And comparing her own situation to that of her parents, she stresses:

> If our parents had had the same possibilities [of choice] the same things would have happened to them. Instead, if you have a narrower horizon, a more obligatory road, then you say: 'I have to go forward, I can't stop.' Whereas we stop sooner, at the crossroads... and now what?

Knowledge about the greatly reduced range of options at the basis of the biographical constructions of their parents (and even more so for grandparents) in relation to their own emerges in a number of interviews. Paradoxically, the advantages in relationship to the future that previous generations' situation, if seen with the eyes of the present, could bring (the selection of options would not be necessary, the choices would be simplified, ambivalence would dissolve by itself) seems to be understood as well. The attention and passion with which the majority of young people compare their own time-of-life with that of their parents is surprising for many reasons.[15] An unexpected capacity to understand the profound nature of intergenerational social changes thus comes to light, and how these changes influence the construction of a biography. The testimony of Gabriella (26 years old, degree in law, apprentice in a law firm for six months, lives with parents) appears significant on this point:

> The phases for growth, let's say, once upon a time were more clearly marked… now there's more confusion… instead, in the previous generation it was all more defined, there were many more rules, childhood, adolescence and maturity were more pronounced… now I see people thirty years old who are there every day asking themselves what to do (…). The turning points were stronger before, more pronounced… I see many people in my condition… a lot… it's not just a question of the difference between who studies and who works… think of being twenty-four, twenty-five, twenty-six years old and not knowing which way to turn every day… this is something earlier generations didn't experience.

Young Women: Uncertainty, Time for Themselves and Multiplicity of Times-of-Life

This understanding of the intergenerational differences over the course of a lifetime is particularly widespread among young women. They know well, for example, that their biographical choices, constructed on a vision of equality in the 'weight' of various existential times, and with a strong emphasis on 'time for themselves', separate them from their mothers' generation sometimes in a radical way. The latter, in fact, did not enjoy the possibility of constructing a biography *à la carte* as their daughters did. At most, they dealt with the double burden, putting up in silence with the constraints, or improvising and juggling their time to get around them. And they did this, in any case, always within a vision that foresaw for women a biographical 'main road'. This road leads us to the existence of a substantially unchanged hierarchy that is the fundamental underpinning of the women's biographical construction, a hierarchy structured around private time for the family and its priorities which change over time. These are the priorities that give a comprehensive significance to time-of-life. In contrast to their daughters, the mothers were not able to choose to entirely escape these priorities – unless they opted for radical existential decisions at a very high social and personal cost. As Stefania explains (29 years old, with a degree in political science, she does odd jobs researching for the university and lives at home):

My mother got married at twenty... and... I don't know... my mother's life at twenty was a life that had already assumed a very definitive shape, aside from the changes in time management once we were grown up... from twenty to thirty years old she lived like she is still living now.

And then she adds, shortly after:

I don't think my mother ever grew up, she never became an adult as I mean it... because until she was twenty she lived with a father who was extremely authoritarian who imposed on the family everything that was to be done... she married a man fourteen years older than herself without ever having lived on her own and... with a very deep love between them, I think, but I think that in a certain sense my father was not just a companion but also another father a little bit ...

To this biographical construction, organized all around a single temporal order, that of the private sphere, and structured around a profound gender asymmetry, Stefania contrasts her own life experience – that is to say, the plurality of experiences that have up to now marked her biography. The distinguishing feature, in marked contrast with the mother, is the total openness (but also uncertainty):

Between the age of twenty and thirty, I changed universities with all the related problems, and then there was the end of university studies, the masters, I changed jobs a million times... I lived all these experiences, but today I don't know... the future... who knows...

Even Nicoletta (26 years old, with a degree in education, lives at home) underscores the differences between her life and her mother's life. In this case, she brings to light the different ways in which they think about what it is to be a woman:

[If I had children] I am sure I wouldn't leave my job... in the sense that with all the effort I'm putting into it now... absolutely not... but I would want to have time to be with them, to play (...). For my mother it was different, my mother is a housewife, she stayed at home for the children and never worked again...

If in a certain sense, the comparison with preceding women's generations may be a great comfort for mitigating the weight of uncertainty – showing without a shadow of a doubt the advantages of being a woman in the twenty-first century with respect to fifty years earlier – things may get complicated when one looks at one's present condition. Some young women who have not yet built a stable relationship as a couple and who are therefore still far from reaching adult roles, may for example perceive a sort of social stigmatization. They end up feeling like they are 'late': it is as if a social calendar was weighing upon them (albeit in the background), continuing to prescribe the principal biographical markers and their times. Caterina (27, studies sociology, lives alone) affirms, for example:

No, I don't have sentimental plans... I live very egotistically... I'm in love with love...

more in love with love than with people... it's an abstract thing... very detached... I don't see love concretely... marriage... maybe children, yes... that's what gives me the pulse of life... that's where I realize that time is passing, it warns me that I am twenty-seven... the outside reminds me of these things, society reminds me of my sentimental duties... but I don't have a plan, I could have eternal loves, but not something more concrete.

This pressure is even more encumbering in that for Caterina, like for several other young women in this cohort, the absence of a plan for their love lives becomes part of a more general refusal in the area of a 'life plan' (on this subject, Caterina affirms: 'No, I don't have a life plan, like I want this career, I want to do this or that, I don't have this type of a plan... I don't want to say I live day to day... but anyway with a future that is very limited... from today to a few months from now, more or less, then little by little, I see...'). But is it possible, as women, not to want a plan for your love life? One part of the ambivalence that the girls express with regard to the future comes from this radical doubt that splits gender identity for some.

However, it should be said that there are those who elaborate this absence as an extra possibility for freedom, like a chance for widening the field of one's own experiences. The absence of plans for one's love life is transformed in this new frame into an instrument of self-expression:

Not having any ties in terms of one's heart, let's just say, I can get up and go when I want... maybe travelling tomorrow or in a few years, maybe working some more... even if it's in Australia, you take your things and go (Federica, 27, non permanent employment, lives with her parents).

The same young woman insists on the equation between the sentimental and family tie and the temporal tie also in another place in the interview where, when talking about marriage, she makes clear how in the final analysis getting married means seeing your time stolen. Federica thus brings up the idea of sacrifice, which for the moment, she has no intention of accepting:

I see my girlfriends who are married... anyway, things change, in that they change for sure. That is, when someone is only going steady to when they decide to live together or then they get married, let's say, everything changes completely (...). Of course it's hard [getting married] because exactly that, there isn't enough time. There isn't enough time to do everything. I see my married girlfriends, they have even less time than I do (...) It's the idea of having your own home, that you have to keep clean, in order... if you live alone that's one thing, but if there are already two of you the responsibilities are doubled (...) Because the hours are what they are, you can do somersaults all you want.

The theme of time as a resource, time as wealth to be protected and defended from outside 'attacks', is very widespread in the young women's interviews. At the basis of this is the knowledge that existential autonomy is inseparable from a substantial reserve of time for oneself. In other words, for many young women in their biographical construction, it is not just simply a matter of 'reconciling' time

for professional activity with time for the family. It is more about safeguarding –
alongside, and one might say above, these two times – a time for oneself: for
expressing oneself, one's passions, one's need for self-realization, for
'authenticity'.[16]

For some, maintaining this positive relationship with the 'time for oneself'
without however giving up on investing in a job and the family represents a real,
true biographical perspective. At the basis of this is a vision of existential time in a
multiple key, as time that is not hierarchical but open. A vision that, for the
moment, is as widespread among young women as it is little or not at all present on
a societal level (Leccardi, forthcoming). Gabriella's reflections (26 years old,
employee in a law firm for six months, lives with parents) on this topic are
interesting:

> Today I flit from one flower to another without finding the pollen ... the honey (...). But
> I want to have a family, I was thinking about it just today. I want to have a family, a
> home, take care of my own affairs... with my children, my husband... a classic
> picture... but surely I do not want to give up on my interests, those that involve only
> me... like going to take this trip, painting... no, I wouldn't give up on that for anyone...
> in the Gabriella of the future, the wonder woman of the future, these things are all inside
> and equal.

The knowledge of the pluralistic nature of existential time therefore reinforces
the need to focus on biographical constructions in which space is provided for the
many faces of women's identity, where the 'equal value' of these different times is
accepted and made socially legitimate. With respect to preceding generations of
women – even only with respect to the generation of the mothers – this means a
cultural revolution.

Concluding Remarks

The research conducted in the eighties on young people and time had identified
'biographical uncertainty' as a characteristic of the condition of young people in
the last decades of the twentieth century. The term was meant to refer to the great
difficulty – sometimes a refusal, sometimes the inability – to project oneself into
the future by means of decisions made in the present (Cavalli, 1985; Leccardi,
1999). Among the elements generating biographical uncertainty, twenty years ago
were an initial lengthening and a transformation of the transition to adulthood,
together with the gradual spread of a social climate of uncertainty (related
especially to the rise of juvenile unemployment). But above all, what counted then
for young people was the disappearance of the lengthy and intense season of
movements that in Italy had spanned the entire decade of the seventies (Lumley,
1994; Melucci, 2001, pp. 259-283). And with this disappearance went the chance
to give meaning to one's own present by working on broad projects able to unite
the individual and the collective dimensions.

Within the frame of our present-day 'society of uncertainty', whose social institutions are marked by a general precariousness and instability – think, for example, of the de-standardization of work and its consequences for personal life – biographical uncertainty tends to assume new features. In the relationship between time and biography as presented in this article, one element appears of paramount importance in order to understand the transformations: temporal acceleration.

In an in-depth analysis of this phenomenon, Hartmut Rosa (2003, p. 10) defines as 'accelerated' the society in which '*technological acceleration and a growing scarcity of time (i.e. an acceleration of the pace of life) occur simultaneously, i.e. if growth rates outgrow acceleration rates*'. An 'acceleration society' is founded on three different levels, which complement each other. The first is technological acceleration, which generates a complex set of processes of spatial-temporal compression (Harvey, 1990). The contemporary positive value assigned to speed is also abetted by hastening the processes of social change, which first and foremost affect work and family, the institutions of production and social reproduction. This accelerated rate of change has striking consequences, not only for the life of institutions but also for individual biographical constructions, forced into continual mixings. Finally, and a pivotal dimension for our theme, there is the acceleration of the pace of life. This aspect *per se* refers to the temporal compression encountered in our daily lives. It is the process through which the number of acts that a given amount of time can contain tends to increase. A corollary to this type of acceleration is being pressured by a lack of time and the feeling (which the interviews clearly bring out) of being overwhelmed by an uncontrollable number of potential courses of action, within which it is impossible to trace an itinerary but which have to be dealt with daily. As Bauman has amply shown in his works (for example 1995; 1999; 2000), one has to be mobile, ready to reap opportunities, deft in appropriating new possibilities as soon as they arise, but also skilful in abandoning them should more fruitful ones appear on the horizon. The real possibilities of being able to meet these new biographical obligations are limited. And the result is frequently a sense of personal inadequacy, an uneasiness generated by the gap between what is real and what is possible. At the same time, a faster pace of life favours the growth of short-term plans, replaced each time by new 'experiments' able to certify that those performing them are able to deal with changing situations as they arise.

The particular cognitive style accompanying this form of temporalization and reverberating in the contemporary trend towards biographical construction *sans projet*, recalls rather closely the concept of *bricolage* proposed by Lévi Strauss (1962) – an emblem of magical and archaic thought. For Lévi-Strauss the *bricoleur* is a person who performs work with her/his own hands in an experimental fashion, utilizing tools different from those used by a person of the *métier*. What is striking is the ability of the *bricoleur* to adapt her/himself to the materials available, to construct for her/himself, step by step, the equipment she/he needs. Lacking a previously delineated project, the equipment is created on the spur of the moment. No element of the whole on which the *bricoleur* works is tied to a predetermined use; the outcome of the work is linked to the conditions and means with which she/he deals with the here-and-now. The initial intention may easily become extraneous to the final product. In a certain sense the *bricoleur*, guided by an essentially 'practical' logic, personifies the separation between rationality and intentionality.

'Nomads of the present' (Melucci, 1989) is an appropriate metaphor for contemporary biographical trajectories. The 'nomads of the present' do not pursue an end, they explore, enveloped in impermanence. They do not concern themselves with the idea of a frontier, with the idea that links time and space to something that 'is in front' and thus needs to be 'confronted' (Cassano, 2003, p. 53). In the mass media universe in which we live, frontiers have been thrown open. The 'nomads of the present' construct biographies where links may eventually be identified not on the basis of a project but as the result of reflection *ex post facto*. Temporal experience and biographical experience interweave exclusively around a series of presents, generally with few reciprocal relations (Bauman, 1996).

In this context, a tendency to experiment arises – not viewed, however, in the traditional reference to an itinerary of trial and error, whose purpose is to find the most suitable ways of reaching a given goal. The process is inverted: one tries 'different applications of the skills, talents and other resources which we have, suspect we have or hope to have', attempting to discover 'which result brings most satisfaction' (Bauman and Tester, 2001, p. 90). The result is a basic orientation in which 'the secret of success is not to be unduly conservative, to refrain from habitualizing to any particular bed, to be mobile and perpetually at hand'. In a word, to be always and above all 'flexible' (Sennett, 1998).

The interviews conducted among Milanese young people underscore strategies of adaptation to the highly uncertain context of contemporary society that come close in a significant way to the picture drawn by the above-mentioned authors. As conveyed in the analyses of these writers, for the young people interviewed the idea of stable commitments of long-term duration – and as a consequence of long-term responsibilities – has been eroded. Existence is, as it were, de-temporalized. '(L)ife is no longer planned along a line that stretches from the past into the future; instead, decisions are taken from "time to time" according to situational and contextual needs and desires' (Rosa, 2003, p. 19). In this sense, it may be asserted that the young men and women interviewed represent the emblem of a way of constructing biography that is more and more widespread among young Europeans, especially among those who possess high levels of education (as was the case in the majority of those interviewed). Within the Italian context considered here, this form of 'situationalism' is in a certain sense reinforced both by the long cohabitation with the parents, a trend that accentuates the de-responsibilization of young people, and the specificity of the accelerated Milanese context in which the interviews were gathered.

At the same time, however, the interviews also allow us to glimpse aspects that may spoil the consistency of a vision that is homogeneously 'de-temporalized' in the contemporary biographies of young people. Let's dwell for a moment on two principal aspects: again the relationship with the family and the connection of past-present-future.

Even if in Italy it has also exhibited a growing tendency towards instability (Barbagli and Saraceno, 1997; Zanatta, 1997), the family can still guarantee for young people a certain anchorage, a reference point that is not risky. Thus it creates forms of *temporal continuity*, capable of counterbalancing the discontinuity by which the biographical constructions of the young people are explicitly marked. These 'new families' that welcome and sustain young people in their long periods of transition, recall very closely the profile of institutions of the second modernity recently traced by Scott Lash (2003, pp. xi-xii): institutions that 'regulate' individualization processes not through regulative rules (of a prescriptive nature), but through rules that allow for free play of individual choices. Something analogous happens today within the 'long-term families' of young Italians. In fact, young people's commitment to the best expression of their own potential, and their taking the time to decide in which direction to proceed, is made possible more often than not by the support of these families. In short, if evading responsibility is one side of the coin, the other side can be an open and 'experimental' vision of biography.

The second aspect that the interviews take on is a problem regarding the relationship that takes place between the crisis in the connection of past-present-future and the so-called 'presentification' understood as a tendency to identify in the present the temporal area of reference for action. 'Presentification' (Rampazi, 1985; Leccardi, 1990) causes difficulties in projecting oneself into the future of a medium-long term, through planning (projection into this type of future may then happen on the level of imagination and day-dreaming). In contemporary reflection, the two aspects are usually linked and superimposed, sending us back to the crisis of the temporal experience of the first modernity. Actually, the 'presentification' that emerges in the interviews does not automatically imply a cancellation of the connection past-present-future. In other words, as has emerged clearly when the young Milanese men and young women were asked to illustrate their own point of view about the relationship between past and present biographical constructions (their parents' generation compared to their own), the understanding of the nexus between past and present appears to be well-rooted in their reflections. The same thing may be said about the relationship between present-future. Many young people reason along the line that the first is linked to the second, reflecting for example on the possible (or desired) outcomes of present actions. Even the nexus between past and future, more delicate and less self-evident, comes to light (for example, when in the interviews one speaks of existential turning points, touching in an explicit way on the theme of identity). One may therefore affirm that the privileged reference to the present or to the areas immediately adjacent – the extended present of Nowotny (1994) – in the relationship with time seems more to be the fruit of a privileged strategy of biographical construction, a pragmatic way to come to terms with the speed of change and the uncertainty that accompanies it, rather than as one of the aspects of a 'syndrome of de-temporalization' characteristic of the second modernity.

One last point should be mentioned as a specific contribution of the research on the nexus between time and biography. As has been seen, by making this nexus interact with gender, it is possible to produce a significant redefinition of the coordinates of analysis – in our case for example, including the understanding of the multiplicity of existential time as a strategic factor in the biographical construction. Ambivalence as an inescapable characteristic of the biographical narrative is a corollary to this understanding. Young women, in this way, increase their own cognitive capacity for dealing with uncertainty – for example, by showing themselves to be aware of the fact that their choices are not always and not necessarily able to reduce ambivalence. In a society that makes the continuous obligation to choose a new imperative, this awareness generates, among other things, a positive familiarity with the dimension of doubt. What remains open for them still, however, is the problem of the complete social recognition of a biographical time, in principle without hierarchies and with many focal points. The difficulty in constructing a personal narrative that is completely satisfying is still tied, for many young women, to the insufficient level of this recognition.

Notes

1   A version of this chapter is published in Young, *Nordic Journal of Youth Research*, Vol. 13(2), 2005.
2   Commenting on this tendency to extend the times of the phases in the transition and its parallel de-structuring, Giovanni Sgritta (1999, p. 2) writes: 'Studies and research carried out during the last decades show that this has happened in all advanced societies. In tune with the process of (…) the restructuring of the production systems and the globalization of markets, the behaviour, the choices and the opportunities which distinguish the transition to adulthood have changed almost everywhere. Marriage is taking place later, fertility is decreasing, studies are continuing to a greater and greater age and therefore the employment rates in correspondence with the younger ages have gone down; the same thing has happened, although to a lesser degree, as far as concerns the average age of leaving home which has increased in most Western countries'.
3   According to Cavalli and Galland (1995), France is included in this second model.
4   For a different analysis of the British model that disassociates itself from the emphasis on earliness, see Iacovou (1999).
5   In Italy, IARD is the most important research institute on the condition of young people. This institute, which is private, with headquarters in Milan, has been conducting a survey on the condition of young people every four years for two decades. On the subject of the age of the sample, it should be noted that the progressive extension of the transition to adulthood in Italy forced the institute to extend the age of the sample from 15-24 years old at the beginning of the eighties to the present 15-34 years old.
6   According to ISTAT (Italian Central Statistics Institute) 59.1 per cent of the young people between 18 and 34 live at home (ISTAT, 2000).
7   Among Italian youths aged 15-25, 68 per cent are economically dependent on their original family – as compared, for instance, to half that figure among young Swedes (34 per cent). In Nordic countries, as we know, a large number of youths meet their need for autonomy thanks to state subsidies, while in middle-European countries the source of income comes both from the labour market and the family. In the United Kingdom, the main source of income is the labour market (IARD, 2001a, p. 43). On a more general plane, one may state that in Italy the family functions as a 'social shock-absorber', substituting in large part for welfare policies.
8   On this subject, it should be remembered that children born out of wedlock in Italy are five times less with respect to Scandinavian countries and Great Britain, and less than a third of those born in France (Cavalli, 2002, p. 514).

9   In fact, as has been underscored (Sabbadini, 1997, p. 86), in Italy, living together constitutes 'a transition toward marriage and not an alternative model to marriage'.

10 It is not surprising, therefore, that almost 60 per cent of the young people interviewed in the IARD survey in 2000, without distinguishing age, declare that having interesting experiences in the present is more important than planning for the future (Buzzi, 2002, p. 34).

11 The research team in 2001 had a different composition from that of 1980. Two people, the present author and Marita Rampazi, constitute the link between the old and the new teams.

12 For a general presentation of the method, see Flick (1998, pp. 207-213).

13 For reflection on this temporal dimension, increasingly central in the contemporary context, see Nowotny (1994, pp. 45-74) and, in regard to biographical planning, Cottle (1976).

14 In fact, in the Eighties the difficulty in projecting oneself forward in time through an existential project was fundamentally related to problems in the assumption *per se* of roles connected to the public sphere, work and political action in particular (Cavalli, 1988; Leccardi, 1999). Increased social acceleration and contingency did not play a relevant role in this respect. Handling life on a day-to-day basis, for example, was more a personal strategy than a kind of social requirement related, as happens today, to 'the speed and flexibility demands of the social and economic world' (Rosa, 2003, p. 18). We will come back to a reflection on these longitudinal aspects in the conclusion.

15 The question asked at the interview was the following: 'If you compare the turning points in your life to those in your parents' lives, what impression do you have?'

16 The time for oneself constitutes the emblem of this decisive change in the biographical construction of women. See Beck-Gernsheim (2003).

References

Adam, B. (1992), 'Modern Times: The Technology Connection and Its Implications for Social Theory', *Time & Society*, Vol. 1(1), pp. 175-192.

Adam, B. (1995), *Timewatch. The Social Analysis of Time*, Polity Press, Cambridge.

Barbagli, M. and Saraceno C. (eds), (1997), *Lo stato delle famiglie in Italia (Families in Italy)*, Il Mulino, Bologna.

Bauman, Z. (1995), *Life in Fragments. Essays in Postmodern Morality*, Blackwell, Oxford.

Bauman, Z. (1996), 'From Pilgrim to Tourist – or a Short History of Identity', in S. Hall and P. du Gay (eds), *Questions of Cultural Identity*, Sage, London, pp. 18-36.

Bauman, Z. (1999), *In Search of Politics*, Polity Press, Cambridge.

Bauman, Z. (2000), *Liquid Modernity*, Polity Press, Cambridge.

Bauman, Z. and Tester, K. (2001), *Conversations with Zygmunt Bauman*, Polity Press, Cambridge.

Beck, U. (1992), *Risk Society. Toward a New Modernity*, Sage, London.

Beck, U. (1998), 'Misunderstanding Reflexivity: the Controversy on Reflexive Modernization', in U. Beck, *Democracy without Enemies*, Polity, Cambridge, pp. 84-102.

Beck, U. (1999), *World Risk Society*, Polity Press, Cambridge.

Beck-Gernsheim, E. (2003), 'From "Living for Others" to "A Life of One's Own"', in U. Beck and E. Beck-Gernsheim (eds), *Individualization*, Sage, London, pp. 54-84.

Berger, P. and Luckmann, T. (1966), *The Social Construction of Reality*, Doubleday, New York.

Bergmann, W. (1981), *Die Zeitstrukturen sozialer Systeme*, Duncker & Humblot, Berlin.

Bynner, J., Chisholm L. and Furlong, A. (eds), (1997), *Youth, Citizenship and Social Change in European Context*, Ashgate, Aldershot.

Buzzi, C. (2002), 'Transizione all'età adulta e immagini del futuro' ('Transition to Adulthood and Images of the Future'), in C. Buzzi, A. Cavalli and A. de Lillo (eds), *Giovani del nuovo secolo (Youth in the New Century)*, Il Mulino, Bologna, pp. 19-39.

Buzzi, C., Cavalli, A. and de Lillo, A. (eds), (2002), *Giovani del nuovo secolo (Youth in the New Century)*, Il Mulino, Bologna.

Calabrò, A. (1996), *Una giornata qualsiasi (Any Day)*, Ripostes, Salerno/Rome.

Cassano, F. (2003), 'Pensare la frontiera' ('Thinking about the Frontier'), in F. Cassano, *Il pensiero meridiano* (*Meridian Thought*), Roma-Bari, Laterza, pp. 53-66.

Cavalli, A. (ed.), (1985), *Il tempo dei giovani (Time of Youth)*, Il Mulino, Bologna.

Cavalli, A. (1988) 'Zeiterfahrungen von Jugendlichen', in R. Zoll, *Zerstörung und Wiederaneignung von Zeit*, Suhrkamp, Frankfurt a. M., pp. 387-404.

Cavalli, A. (2002), 'Giovani italiani e giovani europei' ('Young Italians and Young Europeans'), in C. Buzzi, A. Cavalli and A. de Lillo (eds), *Giovani del nuovo secolo (Youth in the New Century)*, Il Mulino, Bologna, pp. 511-521.

Cavalli, A. and O. Galland (eds), (1995), *Youth in Europe*, Pinter, London.

Chiesi, A. (2002), 'La trasformazione del lavoro giovanile' ('The Transformation of Young People's Work'), in C. Buzzi, A. Cavalli and A. de Lillo (eds), *Giovani del nuovo secolo (Youth in the New Century)*, Il Mulino, Bologna, pp. 121-155.

Cottle, T. (1976), *Perceiving Time: A Psychological Investigation with Men and Women*, Wiley & Sons, New York.

Du Bois-Reymond, M. (1998), '"I Don't Want to Commit Myself Yet": Young People's Life Concepts', *Journal of Youth Studies*, Vol. 1(1), pp. 63-79.

Facchini, C. (2002), 'La permanenza dei giovani nella famiglia di origine' ('Young People's Stay in the Family'), in C. Buzzi, A. Cavalli and A. de Lillo (eds), *Giovani del nuovo secolo (Youth in the New Century)*, Il Mulino, Bologna, pp. 159-186.

Flick, U. (1998), *An Introduction to Qualitative Research*, Sage, London.

Fuchs, W. (1983), 'Jugendliche Statuspassage oder individualisierte Jugendbiographie?', *Soziale Welt*, Vol. 34, pp. 341-371.

Furlong, A. and Cartmel, F. (1997), *Young People and Social Change. Individualization and Risk in Late Modernity*, Open University Press, Buckingham/Philadelphia.

Galland, O. (1991), *Sociologie de la jeunesse. L'entrée dans la vie*, Armand Colin, Paris.

Gasperoni, G. (2002), 'I processi formativi fra vecchie disuguglianze e nuove trasformazioni' ('Educational Processes between Old Inequalities and New Transformations') in C. Buzzi, A. Cavalli and A. de Lillo (eds), *Giovani del nuovo secolo (Youth in the New Century)*, Il Mulino, Bologna, pp. 73-96.

Harvey, D. (1990), *The Condition of Postmodernity*, Blackwell, Oxford.

Hitzler, R. and Honer, A. (eds), (1997), *Sozialwissenschaftliche Hermeneutik*, Westdeutscher Verlag, Opladen.

Iacovou, M. (1999), 'Young People in Europe: Two Models of Household Formation', paper presented at the 'International Conference on Youth Transition', Philadelphia, 9-10 April.

IARD (2001a) *Study on the State of Young People and Youth Policy in Europe. Final Reports, Vol. 1: Executive Summary and Comparative Reports*, IARD, Mimeo/Milan.

IARD (2001b) *Study on the State of Young People and Youth Policy in Europe. Final Reports, Vol. 2: Country Reports. Youth Conditions in European Countries, Italy*, IARD, Mimeo/Milan.

ISTAT (2000) *Le strutture familiari. Indagine Multiscopo sulle famiglie 'Famiglia, soggetti sociali e condizione dell'infanzia' (Family Structures. Multiscopo Family Survey 'Family, Social Actors and Childhood')*, ISTAT, Rome.

Kohli, M. (1994), 'Institutionalisierung und Individualisierung der Erwerbsbiographie', in U. Beck and E. Beck-Gernsheim (eds), *Riskante Freiheiten*, Suhrkamp, Frankfurt a. M., pp. 219-244.

Lash, S. (2003), 'Foreward: Individualization in a Non-Linear Mode', in U. Beck and E. Beck-Gernsheim, *Individualization*, Sage, London, pp. vii-xiii.

Leccardi, C. (1990), 'Die Zeit der Jugendlichen: Was heisst männlich und weiblich in der Zeiterfahrung?', in M. du Bois-Reymond and M. Oechsle (eds), *Neue Jugendbiographie. Zum Strukturwandel der Jugendphase*, Leske + Budrich, Opladen, pp. 95-114.

Leccardi, C. (1996), *Futuro breve. Le giovani donne e il futuro (Short Future. Young Women and the Future)*, Rosenberg & Sellier, Turin.

Leccardi, C. (1999), 'Time, Young People and the Future', *Young*, Vol. 7(1), pp. 3-18.

Leccardi, C. (forthcoming), 'Junge Frauen und die Vielfältigkeit der Zeit in der 'Gesellschaft der Unsicherheit'', in I. Sabelis, K. Geißler and K. Kümmerer (eds), *Kultur der Zeitvielfalt*, Hirzel, Stuttgart/Leipzig.

Lévi-Strauss, C. (1962), *La pensée sauvage*, Plon, Paris.

Lumley, R. (1994), *States of Emergency. Cultures of Revolt in Italy from 1968 to 1978*, Verso, London.

Melucci, A. (1989), *Nomads of the Present: Social Movements and Individual Needs in Contemporary Society*, Temple University Press, Philadelphia.

Melucci, A. (1996), *The Playing Self: Person and Meaning in the Planetary Society*, Cambridge University Press, Cambridge.

Melucci, A. (2001), *Challenging Codes. Collective Action in the Information Age*, Cambridge University Press, Cambridge.

Nowotny, H. (1994), *Time: The Modern and Postmodern Experience*, Polity Press, Cambridge.

OECD (2000), *Education at a Glance: OECD Indicators. 2000 Edition*, OECD, Paris.

Oevermann, U., Allert, T. et al. (1979), 'Die Methodologie einer 'objektiven Hermeneutik' und ihre allgemeine forschungslogische Bedeutung in den Sozialwissenschaften', in H.G. Soeffner, *Interpretative Verfahren in den Sozial- und Textwissenschaften*, Metzler, Stuttgart, pp. 352-434.

Pomian, K. (1981), 'La crisi dell'avvenire' ('The Crisis of the Future'), in R. Romano (ed.), *Le frontiere del tempo (Time Frontiers)*, Il Saggiatore, Milan, pp. 97-113.

Rampazi, M. (1985), 'Il tempo biografico' ('Biographical Time'), in A. Cavalli (ed.), *Il tempo dei giovani (Time of Youth)*, Il Mulino, Bologna, pp. 149-263.

Rampazi, M. (1991), *Le radici del presente (The Roots of the Present)*, Angeli, Milan.

Reiter, H. (2003), 'Past, Present, Future: Biographical Time Structuring of Disadvantaged Young People', *Young. Nordic Journal of Youth Research*, Vol. 11(3), pp. 253-279.

Rosa, H. (2003), 'Social Acceleration: Ethical and Political Consequences of a Desynchronized High-Speed Society', *Constellations*, Vol. 10(1), pp. 3-33.

Sabbadini, L.L. (1997), 'Le convivenze "more uxorio"' ('Living Together "More Uxorio"'), in M. Barbagli and C. Saraceno (eds), *Lo stato delle famiglie in Italia (Families in Italy)*, Il Mulino, Bologna, pp. 86-94.

Sartori, F. (2002), 'La giovane coppia' ('The Young Couple') in C. Buzzi, A. Cavalli and A. de Lillo (eds), *Giovani del nuovo secolo (Youth in the New Century)*, Il Mulino, Bologna, pp. 187-228.

Sennett, R. (1998), *The Corrosion of Character*, Norton and Company, New York/London.

Sgritta, G. (1999), 'Too Slow. The Difficult Process of Becoming an Adult in Italy', paper presented at the Jacobs Foundation Conference 'The Transition to Adulthood: Explaining National Differences', Communication Centre, Marbach Castle, 28-30 October.

Sue, R. (1994), *Temps et ordre social. Sociologie des temps sociaux*, PUF, Paris.

Tabboni, S. (1992), *Costruire nel presente (Constructing in the Present)*, Angeli, Milan.

Walther, A. and Stauber, B. (eds), (2002), *Misleading Trajectories – Integration Policies for Young Adults in Europe?*, Leske + Budrich, Opladen.

Wyn, J. and White, R. (1997), *Rethinking Youth*, Sage, London.

Zanatta, A.L. (1997), *Le nuove famiglie (New Families)*, Il Mulino, Bologna.

Zoll, R. (ed.), (1988), *Zerstörung und Wiederaneignung von Zeit*, Suhrkamp, Frankfurt a. M.

Zoll, R. (1989), *Nicht so wie unsere Eltern! Ein neues kulturelles Modell?*, Westdeutscher Verlag, Opladen.

Chapter 2

Coping with Yo-Yo-Transitions. Young Adults' Struggle for Support, between Family and State in Comparative Perspective

Andy Biggart and Andreas Walther

Introduction

Over the past few decades socio-economic change has resulted in labour market restructuring and there has been an associated rise in youth unemployment, which has not only contributed to a prolongation of young adults' transition to employment but has also increased the risks within these transitions (see Furlong and Cartmel, 1997; Chisholm and Kovacheva, 2002). Today, young people not only have to cope with a longer period of financial dependency, they also have to cope with uncertainty over the suitability of their occupational choice in relation to whether it will provide them not only with an income but full social recognition as an adult member of society. In short, for a growing proportion of the younger generation the need for support has become increasingly necessary as transitions have become more prolonged and complex. While the need for support is increasing, the availability of formal support is in decline and therefore informal sources of support (material and emotional) through families, friends and wider social networks are regaining importance (Dey and Morris, 1999).

This chapter argues that in the context of increasingly de-standardized transitions, reducing transitions to a simple dichotomy between dependency and autonomy fails to account for the emergence of a variety of states of *semi-dependency* that can be found within young people's biographies. While the two concepts are often inter-related it is useful to distinguish between dependency as a socio-economic concept and autonomy as a concept that is related to identity processes such as experiencing one self as able to act, take decisions and to develop an independent lifestyle. Young men's and women's career decisions may be interpreted as strategies to deal with dependency as a way of maintaining an autonomous self-concept (van de Velde, 2001). Gender studies in particular have contributed to the demystification of the ideology of independence as a result of modern (labour market) individualization by highlighting the reproductive dependency of apparently independent (male) breadwinners (Fraser and Gordon,

1994). The issue of semi-dependency and the assumption of varieties in this regard seems particularly salient as the differences between Northern and Southern Europe, that have been highlighted by transition research, are most often explained by reference to dependency on 'the family'. Whilst the family has been used as a means to explain these differences it has tended to be left in a black box in terms of what family support means and to what extent it implies intergenerational control restricting young people's – especially young women's – autonomy. In trying to explore some of these issues in further depth we draw on a series of (completed as well as ongoing) primarily qualitative European research projects that explore the changes in youth transitions and the challenges for transition related policies that emerge from these changes. These studies have been carried out in the framework of the EGRIS network (European Group for Integrated Social Research) and have been funded by different EU programmes. Their shared concern is to investigate youth transitions in a more holistic perspective, which also takes young people's subjectivities as a dimension of social integration into account.[1]

We begin by providing an outline of the concept of *de-standardization* and the increasing 'yo-yo' nature of transitions as they have become less linear, more complex and also reversible. This section is primarily based on the results of the *Misleading Trajectories* project that examined the unintended risks of social exclusion arising from policies aimed at the integration of young adults (Walther, Stauber et al., 2002). The second part of the chapter takes a comparative perspective and relates this general trend to the contexts of different *transition regimes* (social, economic and institutional structures as well as the various cultural assumptions of 'normal transitions'). Here we refer primarily to the study *Integration through Training* a comparative analysis of national youth unemployment policies in the context of the European Employment Strategy (Furlong and McNeish, 2001; McNeish and Loncle, 2003). Third, we discuss the implications of the different transition regimes in terms of the autonomy or dependency of young men and women in constructing their biographies. This is based on a secondary analysis of reports produced in the context of the project Families and Transitions in Europe (FATE) which has been concerned with the role of family support on young people's transitions to work (see Biggart et al., 2004). Drawing on the cases of Denmark, Germany, United Kingdom and Italy we will show a range of *constellations of semi-dependency* whereby the state and the family play very different roles: constellations that not only differ cross-nationally but are also stratified according to family resources, education, gender and ethnicity. In this section we will also draw on some more quantitative indicators provided by the European 'Study on the State of Youth and Youth Policy' (IARD, 2001). We conclude by highlighting the consequences and possible new directions for family and transition research, arguing that there is a greater need for these two distinct areas of research to become integrated.

De-Standardized Transitions of Young Adults: The Yo-Yo-Metaphor

Research and policy related to young people and their integration into society has traditionally referred to the transition process from youth to adulthood as one that can be defined by a series of markers, among which completing education or training, entering a stable occupation and gaining financial independence are seen as central (Eisenstadt, 1967; Musgrove, 1964). This is primarily due to the fact, or at least a dominant assumption that in labour societies paid employment is the main gateway to other wider aspects of social integration. As a result the transition to adulthood has tended to become synonymous with the transition to work while the completion of other transitions in terms of leaving the family, partnership, parenthood, housing or lifestyles has been interpreted as consequences of entering the labour market. Although the limitations of such a perspective have been highlighted by the significant prolongation in young people's transition from school to work that has been observed across Europe since the 1980s, the concept of linear transitions continues to predominate (see Cavalli and Galland, 1995; Dwyer and Wyn, 2001). In terms of the 'standard' biography the completion of education equals labour market integration, which in turn equals social integration. Whilst this remains true for many young adults, for a significant minority transitions have become increasingly complex and more contradictory than that expressed simply by the 'prolongation of youth'. Concentrating on the education to employment axis both research and policy increasingly fail to describe, explain and address the reality of young people's biographies:

- young people pursue transitions in different life spheres (education, work, lifestyle, family, sexuality, civil life etc.) with different rhythms and logics which are still *interlinked* but have to be reconciled within the context of the individual biography (see also the Chapter by Holm and others in this volume);
- transitions to adulthood are *reversible* either through personal choice or forced through unemployment: from dependency to autonomy and back to dependency (EGRIS, 2001);
- young men's and women's *self-concepts* differ from how the institutions of the state classify them or are contradictory in themselves: rather than clearly describing themselves as 'young' or 'adult' they more and more locate themselves somewhere between youth and adulthood (see Plug et al., 2003; Westberg, 2004);
- *gender roles* have become less rigid although the structure of education and training and segmented labour markets often force young people into conventional gendered pathways (Leccardi, 1996; Stauber, 2004);
- changes in youth transitions may reflect more *fundamental changes in the conventional status of adulthood* and in the process of social integration in general.

In order to take account of this changing context of transitions we prefer the term *young adults* rather than *youth* and the metaphor of 'yo-yo'-transitions to refer to the ups and downs of young people living adult and youth lives simultaneously (EGRIS, 2001). A driving factor behind this 'yo-yo-ization' of transitions is the re-structuring of labour societies both in terms of flexibilization and individualization. However, it is important to highlight that while some young people may be forced into yo-yo-trajectories, others actively choose them, a distinction that is often based on economic, social and personal resources. We can also witness an increasing mismatch between young people's biographies and the institutional structures of transition systems. Most programmes and policies in Europe are still based on the idea of the standard biography, a concept of full employment and a linear smooth transition from education to work. This mismatch is reinforced by a trend towards the withdrawal of welfare benefits available to young people making their transitions, and a corresponding increase in the conditions attached to 'activation' or 'workfare' policies (see Lødemel and Trickey, 2001; van Berkel and Hornemann Møller, 2002). As a result, this increases the risk of what we have called 'misleading trajectories' which we define as structured by policies that:

- do not take account of young adults' subjective perspectives with a conflation of social integration with labour market integration,
- function simply as 'containers' (to keep young people off the street) that lead to 'scheme careers' rather than being part of a flexible individual career,
- individualize and 'pedagogize' the structural problem of labour market competition by constructing problem groups according to an individual deficit model,
- de-motivate individuals,
- exclude young men or women according to formal criteria regardless of their actual needs (see Walther, Stauber et al., 2002; see also chapter by Ruspini in this volume).

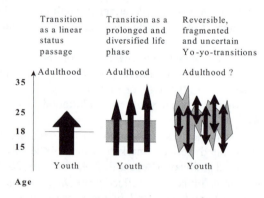

Figure 2.1   The 'yo-yo-ization' of transitions between youth and adulthood

Source: Walther, Stauber et al., 2002.

The de-standardization of transitions includes a trend of individualization where young people have increased personal responsibility for their education and career decisions (see also the chapter by Leccardi in this volume). Not only do they have to take more decisions, but they are also made more accountable for the consequences of their decisions, however differential access to resources and opportunities continue to be structured according to social, spatial and ethnic origin, education, and gender.

In conceptualizing the risks associated with the social integration or social exclusion of young adults in transition, in order to take account of both structural and subjective dimensions, we make a distinction between two different components of risk, which we call subjective and systemic risks. 'Systemic risks' are the risks that are inherent in particular pathways, which exist irrespective of individual perceptions. They can be linked to individual characteristics (gender, class and ethnicity); labour market characteristics (local opportunity structures, gender segmented labour markets); the linkages between education and the labour market or in-built within the systems architecture of specific educational programmes or schemes. 'Subjective risks' on the other hand arise from the individual negotiation of transitions, that is, young adults subjective perceptions of their transitions and whether achieved outcomes lead to what they themselves consider social integration, especially if adapting to the labour market requires a downgrading of individual aspirations and consequent loss of motivation or if participation in special training measures has a perceived stigma attached. Whilst the two components of risk are closely linked and some young people experience both systemic and subjective risk, we would argue that a trajectory could be characterized as misleading when only one of them is present. For example, a young person may be following a trajectory that quite clearly leads towards the unskilled and less stable sections of the labour market may correctly anticipate the outcome with without experiencing subjective discomfort because the immediate need of money subjectively is more urgent than access to a potentially more stable career. In this sense, a young person whose view of the world incorporates the idea that work is inherently unstable and unsatisfying may be following a trajectory that is characterized by systemic risk but which carries little subjective risk (EGRIS, 2002).

The perspective developed by the concepts: 'young adults', 'misleading trajectories' and the image of yo-yo-transitions highlights a situation where young men and women increasingly find themselves in pending situations of uncertain duration in which they try to develop their 'own lives' while still being in a state of economic dependence (see van de Velde, 2001). Within this constellation of semi-dependency the question of support becomes crucial: what kinds of support are available to young people and how do they manage the different kinds of support? It is clear that the cultural and structural specifics of how different societies conceptualize and institutionalize transitions are an important aspect of differentiation.

Comparing Transition Regimes in Europe

If one tries to compare social policies one necessarily reflects on the work of Esping Andersen's and his typology of welfare regimes (1990; 1999). In his work Esping-Andersen distinguished 'Three Worlds of Welfare Capitalism', the social-democratic (Scandinavian), the conservative (Continental) and the liberal (Anglo-Saxon), a model that has experienced a number of modifications, two of which we highlight due to their importance for the development of our own typology of 'transition regimes':

- the distinction between strong and weak male breadwinner welfare states refers to the degree to which women have access to social security separately from that of men. This only partly coincides with the model of Esping-Andersen. While social-democratic welfare regimes can be considered as weak male breadwinner welfare states, the conservative and the liberal regimes tend more to the strong male breadwinning type; with the exception of France where family-oriented policies allow for a more independent position of women. They also distinguish between strong male breadwinner countries such as the UK and Germany, where there are considerable differences in the way they deal with single mothers: placing obligations on them to enter employment in the liberal regime while keeping them away from the labour market in conservative ones (Lewis and Ostner, 1994; Sainsbury, 1999).
- Gallie and Paugam (2000) have also developed Esping-Andersen's model in terms of the high degree of divergence within the conservative regime, which they split into the employment-centred and the sub-protective welfare regime typified by Mediterranean countries with the particular role of the family and informal work (see Ferrera, 2000).

Table 2.1   The model of welfare regimes

Regime	Characteristics of coverage	Examples*
Universalistic	Comprehensive and high	Denmark, Sweden
Employment-centred	Variable and unequal	Germany, France and Netherlands
Liberal/minimal	Incomplete and low	United Kingdom and Ireland
Sub-protective	Very incomplete and very weak	Italy, Spain, Portugal

*countries included in at least one of the studies mentioned in Note 1.

Source: Gallie and Paugam (2000).

It needs to be said that this model represents ideal types with many 'hybrid' cases (van Berkel and Hornemann Møller, 2002) and that it is restricted to 'Western'

European welfare states while Eastern European countries have yet to be considered. 'Post-socialist' regimes may be characterized by a shift from a socialist past mixing universalistic and employment-centred aspects towards an employment-centred or a sub-protective structure (see Wallace, 2002).

In order to adapt a typology of welfare regimes, which is based on social security compensations for employment income to one suitable for a comparative analysis of youth transitions it is necessary to enlarge and adapt this perspective (see Walther, 2000). While social security remains an important aspect of differentiation, structures of education and training have also to be included in addition to employment regimes, taking account of both concepts of work and structures of employment. A combination of these structures results in the particular design of programmes for the unemployed which have underlying assumptions of the cause of youth unemployment and of 'disadvantaged youth', either being ascribed to individual deficits or alternatively due to structural segmentation. Policies also depend on, and reproduce context-specific notions of youth, influenced by the main expectations of society for this age group, the nature of labour market structures and also gendered in different ways and extents. Drawing on the materials and findings provided by the research projects introduced above we construct this typology in the following way (Furlong and McNeish, 2001; Walther, 2002; Walther et al., 2002):

The *universalistic* transition regime in Scandinavian countries such as Denmark or Sweden is based on a comprehensive school system in which general and vocational education are integrated at the post-secondary level. Three out of four school leavers achieve a post-compulsory certificate which permits progression to higher education. Vocational training is regulated according to nationally set standards, is increasingly diverse according to individual learning and training plans, and is school-based but includes practical elements such as internships. Social assistance is available to young people from the age of 18 and is linked to their citizenship status, whilst those who are within formal education or training receive a comparable income in the form of an educational allowance. Counselling is widely institutionalized throughout all stages of education, training and the transition to employment and aims to primarily reinforce individual personal development and motivation, which is the societies' primary definition of youth. Within this constellation 'youth unemployment' is a paradox because young people are not expected to be on the labour market but to be in education, albeit education in the wide sense of personal development. This is reflected within youth unemployment programmes, which have been re-structured as 'activation' with rights tied to obligations while individual choice remains of central importance in order to ensure individual motivation remains high. Disadvantage is ascribed to the individual in the form of not being ready for an individualized choice biography, with most programmes aiming to (re)open access and develop the individual's orientation towards regular and recognized options. Individual rights and responsibilities are regulated collectively by social responsibility. The labour market is characterized by considerable opportunities due to the extended public sector. This is reflected in the very high rates of employment among females, which is also facilitated by the widespread system of public childcare allowing the reconciliation of family and employment. As long as young adults remain within the system they are encouraged and supported in experimenting with yo-yo-transitions, which are provided for with individualized education and welfare options.

The *liberal* transition regime stands for the model developed in the United States and in the British Isles (more accentuated in the UK rather than in the Republic of Ireland) which values individual rights and responsibilities much more than collective provision. Although regional variation needs to be taken into account, education is predominantly organized along comprehensive lines until the age of 16. Over the last few decades the post-compulsory stage has been developed towards a flexible system of vocational (school and employer based) and academic options with a variety of entry and exit points. The mass expansion of the post-compulsory stage has been accompanied by the postponement of benefit entitlements to age 18 as up until the early 1980s a majority of young people entered the labour market directly after compulsory school at the age of 16. Social benefits, as in the case of universalistic regimes, are tied to citizenship status and open to all. However benefit levels are low and increasingly time-limited so that universal access does not contradict the high level of emphasis placed on personal responsibility in the compensation of social risks. The assumption of youth as a transition phase that should be completed as quickly as possible is still generally reflected within youth unemployment programmes with labour market entrance as the main objective, while education and training options tend to be short-term and of variable quality. Individual responsibilities are claimed through workfare policies like the New Deal in the UK. Involvement in counselling and the choice between options (employment, training, voluntary or environmental work) are obligatory in so far as non-participation results in benefit sanctions. The labour market is characterized by a high degree of flexibility and is weakly regulated in terms of qualifications. Diversity of access has resulted in a high rate of female employment and female unemployment rates lower than among men. However, the trend from (male) full-time manufacturing jobs to (female) part-time service jobs has increased precarious conditions in particular in the case of women. Women also bear the main responsibility for childcare, which is mainly organized through the private market while in the Republic of Ireland this is aggravated by the heritage of a strong catholic family ethic. In the context of the liberal transition regime it is parallel process of a flexible system coupled with individualized risks that leads to yo-yo-transitions.

Table 2.2   Transition regimes

Regime	Countries	School	Training	Social security	Employment regime	Female employment	Concept of youth	Concept of youth unemployment	Concept of dis-advantage	Focus of transition policies
Universalistic	**Denmark** Sweden	Not selective	Flexible standards	State	Open Low risks	High	Personal development Citizenship	'Not foreseen'	Mixed (individual-/structure-related)	Education Activation
Employment centred	**Germany** France Netherl.	Selective	Standard-ized	State / family	Closed Risks at the margins	Medium	Adaptation to social positions	Disadvan-tage (deficit model)	Individualized	(Pre-)vocational training
Liberal	**United Kingdom** Ireland	Not selective	Flexible, low standards	State / family	Open, High risks	High	Early economic independence	Culture of dependency	Individualized	Employability
Sub-protective	**Italy** Spain Portugal	Not selective	Low standards and coverage	Family	Closed High risks Informal work	Low	Without distinct status	Segmented labour market, lack of training	Structure-related	'Some' status: work, education or training

Continental countries such as Germany, France and the Netherlands are indicative of the *employment-centred transition regime.* In these countries secondary education is typically organized on a selective basis that sorts and allocates young people to occupational careers in different segments. Vocational training which can be school-based in the case of France, company-based like the German dual system or mixed in the case of the Netherlands, is relatively standardized and therefore reproduces a highly regulated employment regime. In Germany, the concept of work is particularly rigid due to its vocational structure where the labour market is divided into a highly standardized and protected core with a precarious periphery and women are clearly under represented. This is reflected in the structure of the social security system that distinguishes between high levels of compensation for those who have paid sufficient social insurance contributions and a residual system of social assistance that provides a basic safety net. This is true with the exception of the Netherlands, where young people are not automatically entitled to benefits unless they have paid sufficient contributions through employment. The concept of youth is seen as principally about the allocation and socialization of young people into social and occupational positions. Youth unemployment is therefore interpreted as a breakdown in the process of socialization due to deficits in educational attainment or social skills. Programmes are designed to tackle such deficits and reintegrate young people into regular training and employment; the exception to this is the *emploi-jeunes* programme in France that creates a significant amount of regular jobs in the public sector. Yo-yo-transitions in this regime can be seen in terms of young adults that have to navigate between the strong demands and implications of standard trajectories and the construction of an individual career, a process of reconciliation that they have to pursue individually against the normative power of institutional assumptions. Among these countries the Netherlands has to be considered as the most hybrid, with traits of both the liberal and universal regimes. This hybrid combination consists of a flexible education and training system, a citizenship based social assistance model, workfare policies, and a very high share of (female) part-time employment.

The model of *sub-protective* transition regime applies primarily to the Southern European countries such as Italy, Spain and Portugal. Due to a low percentage of standard work places and a high rate of unprotected living conditions the family and informal economy both play a significant role. Up to the end of compulsory education school is structured along comprehensive lines. Until recently the rate of early school leaving was nevertheless high with the continued existence of child labour especially in the case of Portugal. Vocational training is not well developed and largely provided through professional schools with low levels of company involvement. Due to the economic weakness of many regions and the orientation of employment law towards (male) breadwinners youth transitions are particularly prolonged. Young people are not entitled to social benefits and therefore tend to be employed in unstable jobs, either in the informal economy in the case of Italy, or through the use of fixed-term contracts that are widespread in Spain. Segmentation and structural deficits contribute to the highest rates of youth unemployment, particularly among young women. With minimal public childcare provision young women with children tend to face particular difficulties in developing their own personal career. Higher education plays an important role in providing young people with a status in this waiting phase, although many drop out before completing their degree (for example in Italy) or alternatively find themselves over-qualified (such as in Spain). Policies that address youth transitions can be characterized by the discrepancy between comprehensive reform and structural deficits in implementing them. The policy objectives with the highest priority are to prolong school participation, the integration and standardization of vocational training, labour market policies that provide incentives for employers, and the development of career guidance and assistance encouraging self-employment. The objective behind such policies can be characterized as providing youth with some form of recognized status, be it education, training or employment. Unlike other regimes yo-yo-transitions do not develop against dominant assumptions of youth but through a social vacuum that is compensated by a prolonged dependency on the family.

Autonomy and Independence Across Different Transition Regimes

In this section we want to discuss the implications of different transition regimes for young people's biographical construction in terms of the institutionalization of resources and opportunities. We will refer to four examples: Denmark for the universalistic transition regime, the UK for the liberal, Germany for the employment-centred and Italy for the sub-protective type. We will deal with three specific aspects: indicators of economic and residential dependency or autonomy and independence, the role of 'cooling out' processes in young people's transitions and states of semi-dependency.

Sources of Income and Living Arrangements

To give an overview of the four countries we highlight some quantitative indicators on the economic and residential status of young people provided by the 'Study on Youth and Youth Policy in Europe' (IARD, 2001) that appear to confirm the typology of transition regimes:

- in the case of *sources of income* we find a high rate of economically independent young people in the UK either through employment or social benefits with the lowest proportion of economic support from parents. Parental support is highest in Italy as is income from informal and casual work whilst support from benefits is almost non-existent. In Germany employment, parents and training allowances play a significant role without reaching the highest rate among the countries concerned in any category. Finally, in Denmark young people primarily live on income from employment or training allowances, although it has to be taken into account that this only refers to the

major source of income while there is no information about 'typical' combinations between different sources;
- in terms of *living arrangements* these correspond to the broad shape of transition regimes with young Italians showing the highest rates remaining in the parental home while cohabitation is most common in Denmark.

Of course, young people's living arrangements are not only influenced by their respective economic resources, but other factors such as the affordability and availability of housing (Bendit et al., 1999) or whether the availability of education or training opportunities are within travelling distance from the family home or require young people to move to avail of such opportunities.

Table 2.3   Economic and residential indicators of young people's autonomy/dependency in the UK, Italy, Germany and Denmark

	UK	Italy	Germany	Denmark
Major source of income in % (1997)				
Regular employment	56.8	26.1	51.2	**64.9**
Informal and casual work	6.7	**19.1**	18.2	7.7
Benefits	**18.3**	0.1	7.8	8.5
Training allowance	2.8	1.3	5.8	**28.2**
Parents	17.3	**67.6**	37.7	18.7
% of 20/24 year-olds living with parents (1995) or cohabiting (1994)				
Living with parents	47.0	**87.0**	55.0	n.a.
Cohabiting	19.0	1.0	13.0	**37.0**

Source: IARD (2001).

Balancing Subjective and Systemic Risks Against Mechanisms of 'Cooling Out'

While statistics provide a structural overview of young people's transitions from dependency to autonomy they fail to explain under what conditions young people in the different contexts feel autonomous, or the subjective experience of dependency or autonomy. Both have a potential impact on young people's decisions over how they construct their biographies, that is decisions by which young men and women try to appropriate and to reconcile their fragmented lives in a subjectively meaningful way: career decisions, decisions related to partnership and lifestyles, or decisions to remain in or leave the parental home. In the following section we will try to outline a range of biographical constellations that arise from the structures of different transition regimes. We are especially interested in the types of mechanisms that aim to adapt young people's aspirations to the demands of the labour market. For this we draw on the findings of the

Misleading Trajectories and the FATE projects (Walther et al., 2002; Biggart et al., 2004).

By *cooling out* we refer to the processes of transition systems that result in the adjustment of individual aspirations according to the structure of labour markets. It was Erving Goffman (1962) who introduced this concept to refer to the fundamental contradiction between the principle of equal opportunities and the scarcity of recognized social positions; this is the paradox of democratic market societies per se. Apart from being a fundamental democratic right, equal opportunities are functional for the competition and meritocracy on which capitalist labour markets are based. However, individual efforts do not pay off for all and the losers in the race have to be persuaded that it is not the injustice of the system that was the cause of their failure but their unrealistic aspirations compared to their abilities. Cooling out mechanisms may operate in a number of ways: they can be institutionalized, applied by professional gate-keepers according to 'objective' criteria and procedures; arise as a result of local labour market opportunities or alternatively resisted through utilizing the resources of the family in order to wait until an occupational position corresponding to one's own aspirations arises.

In the *United Kingdom* the traditional expectation is that after leaving education young people enter into employment and leave the family home soon afterwards. Although they can access social assistance independently from their parents and use benefits as an aid for the positive construction of biographies this has become increasingly difficult, for example through the introduction of the New Deal programme (see above). Concerns have however been raised over the compulsory element of the New Deal as it may undermine young people's motivation and career initiative. There is also some evidence that faced with limited opportunities in employment or training a proportion of young people opt out of the system altogether and become involved in crime or the informal economy. With the contraction of the youth labour market, protracted periods of education or training and high pressure on benefit recipients from the state, the role of family support is becoming increasingly important. However, with a strong tradition of leaving home at an early age and gaining independence after completing initial education, young people's attitude towards education tends to be rather instrumental, in so far as it will help them gain a good job or a well paid one. As young people increasingly invest in education the potential for subjective risk increases, but in general, there are few mechanisms that allow for the maintenance of aspirations (Biggart and Cairns, 2002; Biggart et al., 2004).

In *Italy*, young people's transitions to work lack clear institutional structures and extended periods of unemployment are common. Young people are not entitled to social assistance if they have not yet been in regular employment and few families would compel their offspring to work at a level below their education, they therefore rely on the family to provide for them during the prolonged period of transition. Living in the so-called 'long family' (see the chapter by Santoro in this volume) is no longer considered a moratorium in the sense of postponed independence but a condition of living, which is reproduced by both parents and young adults alike at an emotional as well as economic level. The 'long family' is also characterized by very low rates of cohabitation in comparison to other European countries as moving out for both genders still tends to coincide with marriage and family formation.

There are of course, considerable regional, gender and class differences in the extent of family support and the expectations placed on young people to contribute to the family in kind. In Southern Italy, and especially in the case of young women, this is normally through domestic chores or informal work in the family business where aspects of parental control tend to predominate. In the more affluent North-East families often act as an unconditional 'resource network' for their adult children. This is reflected in higher rates of satisfaction with family life in the North where young people do not necessarily leave the parental home when they find stable employment. Therefore in the North family dependency is to a large extent the result of young adults' choices while in the South young people's dependency is due to a lack of other alternatives. For young Italians systemic transition risks are generally high and with the increasing investment in education we would also expect high levels of subjective risk, however this is not the case. Due to the widely shared experience of unemployment among young people in Italy there is little stigma attached to an extended period of unemployment. In addition, the family provides a cushion that allows them to maintain their aspirations in the light of adverse labour market conditions. In terms of 'cooling out' this means that it is the combination of local labour market structures and family resources that determines whether young adults have to trade down their occupational aspirations or play a waiting game which has increasingly become the dominant model (Leccardi and Santoro, 2002; Biggart et al., 2004).

In the case of *Germany* there is a high level of stigma attached to claiming social assistance. The nature of the system ensures young people are highly committed to the 'normal biography' based on regular qualified work. As a result, young people are willing to trade down their aspirations as a way of avoiding unemployment at any cost. Those who fail to find qualified employment or regular training willingly enter pre-vocational programmes and training schemes even when they offer few genuine opportunities in terms of either qualifications or employment and where there is also a high stigma attached to participation. Independence from the family of origin is not expected quite as early as in the UK, but rather to be attained on the completion of education and training. Therefore families still have to provide financial support to compensate for insufficient levels of benefits and education allowances to allow for personal autonomy. Although families may be willing to support an extended period of dependency, to prevent young adults entering unqualified work, the strong orientation towards the normal biography among young people and parents alike means this is associated with individual failure. Family support for and the dependency of young adults are rarely considered an issue by policy makers, research or by young people themselves and therefore have to be negotiated and coped with at the individual level. This includes the moral dilemma of being both a burden for one's parents and unable to care for oneself. While this is not typically the case for male dual system apprentices, due to their younger age and the training wage they receive, it is more common among higher education students, young people who are unemployed or in casual employment and female apprentices due to lower allowances in 'female professions'. The rigidly structured nature of the German system requires a heavy investment in education or training. Within the context of a selective school system, standardized training and a differentiated system of remedial schemes, individual qualifications are the key mechanism for 'cooling out' while the adjustment of aspirations results in high subjective risks. Those who enter the core sectors of segmented training and employment gain a high degree of autonomy, while those who fail to do so are kept in a state of dependency with few options for the development of an individual pathway (Goltz et al., 2002; Biggart et al., 2004).

In *Denmark*, as we have seen, young people are able to achieve independence at an earlier stage than in the other countries. This is due to the abundant opportunities for paid employment with a prospering economy, combined with generous state funding for those in education or training or alternatively through state benefits. State funding is not in itself sufficient to cover the costs of independent housing, but provides a solid basis for independent life, especially if combined with other sources of income. As it is the individual that is the main focus of social policies, and with an education system that prioritizes personal choice and development, young people appear to be free to take their own decisions. This is also the case in respect of gender as both the labour market and the education and training system are only segmented to a limited extent. The high level of public childcare provision means that young women can plan their lives with few perceived difficulties in reconciling employment and starting a family. In this case parents seem to play only a minor role in young people's transitions, however in recent years we have also witnessed an increase in the age young people move out of the parental in Denmark. This can be interpreted as stemming from two complementary processes: an increase in the necessity of support due to extended and more uncertain trajectories and a change of family relationships towards individualized support networks that are subject to individual negotiation and the link with other support networks such as peers. At first sight, it seems as if the Danish transition regime is characterized by low unemployment, individual access to welfare, and education and training focused on personal choice and development, and therefore by a low level of both systemic and subjective risks with no cooling out mechanisms. However, the phenomenon of early school leaving persists, especially among ethnic minority youth. This may be interpreted as a cultural model of participation and biographical construction, which needs to be accepted and internalized to profit from the generous resources and opportunities provided by the state (Mørch and Os Stolan, 2002; Böhnisch et al., 2002).

If we take a comparative perspective we can see that these cooling out mechanisms work in different ways cross-nationally as well as the ways in which family support varies in its contribution to the maintenance of aspirations. Transition regimes play a role in so far as they can support delayed transitions and lead to the maintenance of strong aspirations. This is especially clear when looking at the Danish case, whilst the conditions attached to social security benefits in the UK or in Germany can be linked to a more rapid 'cooling-out' process. These examples demonstrate that the differences between 'Northern' welfare state regimes and the role of family support for young adults have often been underplayed, but also one that is regaining importance due to heightened risks and the increasingly restrictive nature of welfare policies. In contrast, Southern family regimes have typically been reduced to backward constellations of control and dependency; however in some contexts the family has experienced processes of modernization towards becoming an important resource for post-fordist network economies.

Our analysis is supported by the findings of another European study. The YUSEDER project examined the relationship between young people's unemployment and their risks of social exclusion in six countries by qualitative research methods. Six aspects of exclusion were assessed and three levels of risk from low to high were distinguished. Those who were found to have the highest level of risk were in Germany and lowest risk was found in Italy. The main differentiating features were social isolation and institutional exclusion (for example stigmatization) these affected unemployed young German's much more than young Italians (Kieselbach et al., 2001).

Comparisons however also demonstrate some more general structures that are not so easily ascribed to a single transition regime. One is *gender* and the gender-specific relationship between dependency and autonomy and its impact on leaving the parental home. Across all countries young women leave the parental home at an earlier age than their male counterparts although this is most evident in the Southern countries. One important aspect for interpretation is that they are also younger when they start to cohabit and they marry younger than is the case for men. Another aspect highlighted through qualitative research is that young women have a more limited time in their biographies during which they have the opportunity to develop an individual career and lifestyle. Leccardi (1996) calls this the 'short future' which on the one hand is determined by the 'biological clock' of motherhood; on the other hand young women realize that their options for a independent career are limited because they anticipate that in future they will carry the main responsibility for childcare and the family home with only partial assistance from their spouses. Although there is significant cross-national variation in most cases women have reduced opportunities to sustain independent careers once they become mothers (Geissler and Oechsle, 1996).

Constellations of Semi-Dependency

Another cross-national trend related to de-standardized transitions is the emergence of a diverse range of states of semi-dependency; this has replaced the dichotomy of dependency in youth and autonomy in adulthood. Traditionally youth was associated with dependency and adulthood with autonomy, and in Southern Europe youth are assumed to be more dependent than Northern youth. Notions of dependency and autonomy however, need to be analysed differently not only according to national context, but also in terms of the changing patterns of transition. Today processes of acquiring personal and social autonomy no longer develop in a linear fashion from total dependence to total independence, a situation which in traditional societies with gender-specific normal biographies was also more ideological than real, in so far as it neglected the dependency of working males on the reproductive work of their wives and mothers (Fraser and Gordon, 1994; du Bois-Reymond, 1998). In the current context biographies switch between dependency and autonomy within what we have called yo-yo movements, young adults may achieve legal or civic autonomy, but still remain economically dependent on the state, the family or both. In a similar vein they may move out of the family home only to return after a failed relationship, or become unemployed with few immediate prospects to reverse their situation. Alternatively they may become economically independent, but still depend on their family in terms of cultural-emotional support. Young people may live autonomously in cultural terms while remaining dependent in economic terms. There are two issues that are central to the understanding of young adults' yo-yo-transitions: definitions of dependency and autonomy need to move beyond the sole criteria of income and housing and there is a need to recognize that there are an increasing number of forms of *semi-dependency* (EGRIS, 2002). Such constellations are less clear-cut when the general features that are relevant to all European countries are mixed together with country-specific elements:

• Young people combine their own money with family resources. This can be through a regular salary, income from informal work, or social benefits; and it is quite probable that this configuration is quite significant in all European countries. However the combination of family resources and informal work is more widespread in Southern Europe, while the combination of state support like welfare benefits or educational grants coupled with family resources is more dominant in Northern Europe.

• Another form of semi-dependency is where young people leave the parental home, but still receive economic support in order to compensate for low wages or to assist with housing costs. In particular, this applies in the case of university students who live on their own or share a flat with others – more pronounced in the Northern countries but not exclusively – but it can also be the case for couples in Southern regions who marry because of parenthood before achieving stable independence.

• A phenomenon more typical in the South is young people who continue to live at home despite having achieved full economic independence, but have not found a long-term partner.

• In both the Southern and Northern contexts there is a large proportion of young people who have casual or part-time jobs and use their money for an independent social life of leisure and consumption related to their sub-cultural identities.

The examples given above were intended to at least partially de-construct ideologies related to autonomy and dependency and one-dimensional assumptions regarding the potential of gaining autonomy through welfare and the bonds of dependency on family support. This analysis helps to clarify what we mean by semi-dependency; the strategies are the context for the decisions they take, for example, in the case of education, training or work, despite being economically dependent, young people have their own independent lifestyle and take their own decisions in shaping their biography. Often risk-laden decisions such as dropping out from a scheme may be seen as an active choice as a way of maintaining a sense of being in control. While this more often seems to be the case among young men, young women may not invest enough into their own career as they often burdened with caring responsibilities – be it for younger siblings or for their parents, particularly in the case of divorce (du Bois-Reymond et al., 2002; see Geissler and Oechsle, 1996).

Conclusions

In this chapter we have tried to demonstrate the increasing necessity of support for young people in order that they may cope with the risks they encounter in their transitions to adulthood and the role that their families play in this respect. It has been argued that these risks have been increasing at the same time as the availability of support is in decline. For those young men and women who are backed by sufficient resources transitions tend to be experienced as spaces in which they can navigate and construct their own personal biographies, while for others with limited resources they are more likely to be pushed towards reversible and precarious careers.

Although there is a general trend towards the de-standardization of transitions, they take different forms according to the different institutional and cultural contexts in which transitions are embedded. These differences not only shape trajectories differently according to the linkages between education, training and employment or the timing of leaving the parental home, they also result in a different set of relationships between subjective and systemic risks.

Research findings across Europe highlight increased periods and forms of semi-dependency during which time young people try to achieve personal autonomy while still remaining dependent on their parents (or the welfare state). However, knowledge in this area remains fragmented especially in terms of how young people cope with semi-dependency and how they experience it at the subjective level; how they balance and reconcile autonomous identities whilst remaining dependent, or the way in which extended periods of semi-dependency influence their future lives. It is also unclear what the consequences are for families both in terms of their willingness and ability to provide the support needed by their adult children. In the context of welfare states that are retreating from their responsibility for young people's integration into society combined with the growing insecurity and uncertainty of family stability with increasing divorce rates, there is the risk that parents become overburdened, a risk which is particularly relevant in the Mediterranean countries (Sgritta, 2001; see the chapter by Ruspini in this volume).

This close interrelationship between individuals, families and the state has for a long time been neglected by both transition and family research. On the one hand, youth and transition research have tended to reduce families to the economic and cultural capital they pass down to their offspring, while family research has been primarily concerned with the issues of child poverty and the reconciliation of paid employment and childcare for women. More qualitative aspects of the relationships between young adults and their families have tended to be neglected while the 'family' has often used to explain differences in North-South-comparisons within the EU. The family is often related to traditional social structures and is interpreted primarily in terms of an obstacle for young people's biographic construction, such a 'stereotype' fails to address both the modernization of Southern family regimes and the changing context in the Northern countries where young adults increasingly have to rely on family support as a means of either replacing or supplementing state support.

We have examined the issue of support for young people in their transition to work in terms of the relationship between the welfare state and the family and it is quite probable that again this represents a reductive dualism. If we look at research on youth cultures, lifestyles and peer relations, we can see that young people develop their own strategies and support, whether this is in terms of counselling, networking for jobs, education and training opportunities and even material support.

To conclude, in terms of youth transitions strong support has become ever more crucial as young men and women, during their transitions, experience life stages that are not simply subsumed under a prolonged youth phase, but show these reversible and fragmented structures between youth and adulthood. However, simple dichotomies between welfare and the family, and Northern and Southern Europe, not only fail to account for the changing shifts between the public and the private that have been occurring in a number of Northern European countries but also fail to account for the extent of diversity that exists both within the North and South.

Note

1   'Misleading Trajectories' has been funded by the 4th Framework Programme from 1998 to 2001; 'Integration Through Training?' has been funded by the Leonardo da Vinci programme from 1999 to 2001; the 'Families and Transitions in Europe' and 'Youth Policy and Participation' has been funded by the 5th Framework Programme; see: www.iris-egris.de/egris; http://www.socsci.ulster.ac.uk/policy/fate/fate.html.

References

Bendit, R., Gaiser, W. and Marbach, J. (eds), (1999), *Youth and Housing in Germany and the European Union. Biographical, Social and Political Aspects*, Leske + Budrich, Opladen.

Biggart, A. and Cairns, D. (2002), *Families and Transitions in Europe. UK National Report*, working paper, University of Ulster.

Biggart, A., Cuconato, M., Furlong, A., Lenzi, G., Stauber, B. and Walther, A. (2002) 'Misleading Trajectories between Standardisation and Flexibility. Misleading Trajectories in Great Britain, Italy and Germany', in A. Walther, B. Stauber et al. (eds), *Misleading Trajectories – Integration Policies for Young Adults in Europe?*, Leske + Budrich, Opladen, pp. 44-66.

Biggart, A., Bendit, R., Cairns, D., Hein, K. and Mørch, S. (2004) *Families and Transitions in Europe: State of the Art Report*, European Commission, Brussels, (http://www.cordis.lu/citizens/publications.htm#stateoftheart).

Böhnisch, L., López Blasco, A., Mørch, M., Mørch, S., Errea Rodríguez, J. and Seifert, H. (2002), 'Educational Plans in Segmented Societies. Misleading Trajectories in Denmark, East Germany and Spain', in A. Walther, B. Stauber et al. (eds), *Misleading Trajectories – Integration Policies for Young Adults in Europe?*, Leske + Budrich, Opladen, pp. 66-94.

Cavalli, A. and Galland, O. (eds), (1995), *Youth in Europe. Social Change in Western Europe*, Pinter, London.

Chisholm, L. and Kovacheva, S. (2002), *Exploring the European Youth Mosaic. The Social Situation of Young People in Europe*, Council of Europe, Strasbourg.

Dey, I., Morris, S. (1999), 'Parental Support for Young Adults in Europe', *Children and Youth Services Review*, Vol. 21(11-12), pp. 915-935.

Du Bois-Reymond, M. (1998), '"I Don't Want to Commit Myself Yet". Young People's Life Concepts', *Journal of Youth Studies*, Vol.1(1), pp. 63-79.

Du Bois-Reymond, M., Stauber, B., Pohl, A., Plug, W. and Walther, A. (2002), *How to Avoid Cooling Out*, YOYO Working Paper, Vol. 1, www.iris-egris.de/yoyo.

Dwyer, P. and Wyn, J. (2001), *Youth, Education and Risk: Facing the Future*, Routledge-Falmer, London.

EGRIS (European Group for Integrated Social Research) (2001), 'Misleading Trajectories – Transition Dilemmas of Young Adults in Europe', *Journal of Youth Studies*, Vol. 4(1), pp. 101-119.

EGRIS (European Group for Integrated Social Research) (2002), 'Leading or Misleading Trajectories? Concepts and Perspectives', in A. Walther, B. Stauber et al. (eds), *Misleading Trajectories – Integration Policies for Young Adults in Europe?*, Leske + Budrich, Opladen, pp. 117-153.

Eisenstadt, S.N. (1967), *From Generation to Generation*, Free Press, New York.

Esping-Andersen, G. (1990), *The Three Worlds of Welfare Capitalism*, Cambridge University Press, Cambridge.

Esping-Andersen, G. (1999), *Social Foundations of Post-Industrial Societies*, Oxford University Press, Oxford.

Ferrera, M. (2000), 'Reconstructing the Welfare State in Southern Europe', in S. Kuhnle (ed.), *Survivial of the European Welfare State*, Routledge, London, pp. 166-181.

Fraser, N. and Gordon, L. (1994), '"Dependency" Demystified: Inscriptions of Power in a Keyword of the Welfare State', *Social Politics*, Vol 1(1), pp. 4-31.

Furlong, A. and Cartmel, F. (1997), *Young People and Social Change*, Open University Press, Buckingham/Philadelphia.

Furlong, A. and McNeish, W. (eds), (2001), *Integration through Training? Comparing the Effectiveness of Strategies to Promote the Integration of Unemployed Young People in the Aftermath of the 1997 Luxembourg Summit on Employment*, Final Report to the European Commission, University of Glasgow.

Gallie, D. and Paugam, S. (eds), (2000), *Welfare Regimes and the Experience of Unemployment in Europe*, Oxford University Press, Oxford.

Geissler, B. and Oechsle, M. (1996), *Lebensplanung junger Frauen. Zur widersprüchlichen Modernisierung weiblicher Lebensläufe,* Juventa, Weinheim/München.

Goffman, E. (1962), 'On "Cooling the Mark Out": Some Aspects of Adaption and Failure', in A. Rose (ed.), *Human Behaviour and Social Processes*, Houghton Mifflin, Boston, pp. 482-505.

Goltz, J., Menz, S., Stauber, B. and Walther, A. (2002), *Families and Transitions in Germany. National Report for the Project 'Families and Transitions in Europe' for Germany*, working paper, Tübingen/Dresden.

IARD (2001), *Study on the State of Youth and Structures of Youth Policy in Europe*, Report to the European Commission, http://europa.eu.int/comm/youth/whitepaper/index_en.html.

Kieselbach, T., Heeringen, K. van, La Rosa, M., Lemkov, L., Sokou, K. and Starrin, B. (eds), (2001), *Living on the Edge. An Empirical Analysis on Long-Term Youth Unemployment and Social Exclusion in Europe*, Leske + Budrich, Opladen.

Leccardi, C. (1996), *Futuro breve. Le giovani donne e il futuro (Short-term Future. Young Women and Future)*, Rosenberg & Sellier, Torino.

Leccardi, C. and Santoro, M. (2002), *Families and Transitions in Europe. National Report Italy*, working paper, University of Milan-Bicocca, Milan.

Lewis, J. and Ostner, I. (1994), 'Gender and the Evolution of European Social Policies', ZeS working paper 4/94, Centre for Social Policy Research, University of Bremen.

Lødemel, I. and Trickey, H. (eds), (2001), *An Offer You Can't Refuse. Workfare in an International Perspective*, Policy Press, Bristol.

McNeish, W. and Loncle, P. (2003) 'State Policy and Youth Unemployment in the EU: Rights, Responsibilities and Lifelong Learning', in A. López Blasco et al. (eds), *Young People and Contradictions of Inclusion. Towards Integrated Transition Policies in Europe*, Policy Press, Bristol, pp. 105-126.

Mørch, S. and Os Stolan, L. (2002) *Families and Transitions in Europe. National Report Denmark*, working paper, University of Copenhagen, Copenhagen.

Musgrove, F. (1964), *Youth and the Social Order*, Routledge, London.

Plug, W., Zeijl, E. and du Bois-Reymond, M. (2003), 'Young People's Perceptions on Youth and Adulthood. A Longitudinal Study from The Netherlands', *Journal of Youth Studies*, Vol. 6(2), pp. 127-144.

Sainsbury, D. (1999), *Gender and Welfare State Regimes*, Oxford University Press, Oxford.

Sgritta, G. (2001), 'Family and Welfare Systems in the Transition to Adultshood. An Emblematic Case Study, in Family Forms and the Young Generation in Europe', in L. Chisholm, A. de Lillo, C. Leccardi, R. Richter (eds), *Report on the Annual Seminar of the European Observatory for the Social Situation, Demography and Family*, ÖIF, Vienna, pp. 59-87.

Stauber, B. (2004), *Junge Frauen und Männer in Jugendkulturen. Selbstinszenierungen und Handlungspotentiale*, Leske + Budrich, Opladen.

van Berkel, R. and Hornemann Møller, I. (2002), *Active Social Policies in the EU. Inclusion through Participation?*, Policy Press, Bristol.

van de Velde, C. (2001), 'Autonomy Construction in a Dependence Situation. Young Unemployed People and Family Relationships in France and Spain', paper presented at the International Conference on 'Family Forms and the Young Generation in Europe', University of Milan-Bicocca, Milan, 20-22 September.

Wallace, C. (2002), 'Households, Work and Flexibility. Critical Literature Review', Project Households, Work and Flexibility, Research Report 1, www.hwf.at.

Walther, A. (2000), *Spielräume im Übergang in die Arbeit. Junge Erwachsene im Wandel der Arbeitsgesellschaft in Deutschland, Italien und Großbritannien*, Juventa, Weinheim/München.

Walther, A. (2002), 'Benachteiligte Jugendliche: Widersprüche eines sozialpolitischen Deutungsmusters. Anmerkungen aus einer europäisch-vergleichenden Perspektive', *Soziale Welt*, Vol. 53(1), pp. 87-106.

Walther, A., Stauber, B. et al. (eds), (2002), *Misleading Trajectories. Integration Policies for Young Adults in Europe?*, Leske + Budrich, Opladen.

Westberg, A. (2004), 'Forever Young? Young People's Conception of Adulthood: the Swedish Case', *Journal of Youth Studies*, Vol. 7(1), pp. 35-52.

Chapter 3

Individualization
and the Changing Youth Life

Sven Mørch and Helle Andersen

The Challenge of Late-Modernity and Individualization

Today, many issues in everyday life are understood from the perspective of the
change from modern to post- or late-modern society. We talk about how things
were before and how they have developed today. We also focus on how child and
family life have changed and how people's lives and self-identities have been
influenced by these changes. Post- or late-modern life (or 'modernistic' life as we
prefer to call it here) has become a basic concept, and Bauman, Beck and Giddens
especially have influenced the understanding of contemporary modernity in social
science, the media and current thinking in general (Bauman, 1998, 2001; Beck,
1992; Giddens, 1984, 1997).

The modernistic discussion is, of course, just one perspective among others for
understanding contemporary social development. It focuses on the challenges of
individual development or the issue of individualization and therefore the questions
of individual rights, participation, democratization and so on. Commitment to
understanding the individualization process follows from the fact that in
contemporary society, the individual has become important and influential both in
politics and working life, and therefore individual activities and the development of
individual functioning and social responsibility have become important issues.

In the 'early-modern' – bourgeoisie or industrialized – society, traditionally
thought to have begun in the late part of the 18th century and continuing until the
1950s, the challenge of the development of the 'modern individual' became
important. The modern individual, both for political and productive reasons, had to
become a knowledgeable agent in society. The individual became important and
influential and society became dependent on individual activities and individual
functioning and social responsibility. In particular, the educational system formed
and controlled the development of individualization. The construction of youth
through education towards the end of the 18th century illustrates the first step in this
development. Youth was created by education as an individualization phase in the
bourgeoisie (Gillis, 1981; Musgrove, 1964; Mørch, 1985). Individualization
followed education, and education both followed class lines and attacked them.
Individualization became a developmental opportunity for the bourgeois upper

classes, and later on, also an opportunity for the general population. In Denmark, for instance, schools in the 19th century screened children at the school gates according to social background, but opened their gates to all children regardless of social class from around the start of the 20th century. In the new school system, children were of course still differentiated according to social class and future social position, but they were all at least included in educational institutions and a basic individualization took place. The children were not streamed before they entered school, but differentiated within it according to their abilities for learning and their social capital, and according to the quality of individualization that was needed in their future lives.

Moreover, while this educational policy allowed for a broader development in all social classes, the policy was at the same time also responsible for a change in individualization. Especially after World War II, educational life was an opportunity for all and created 'individuals' within all educational institutions. Educational life focused on the individual as a subject not only in his or her own life, but in the societal world as well. With the growing economic opportunities in the welfare society, young people became subjects of their lives and were given the prerequisites for influencing not only their own lives, but the broader society as well. This, in particular, occurred in the mid and late 1960s. The youth revolt was especially a revolt of educated youth and students.

Educational policy, which was mostly the same in all first world countries, laid the ground for another 'modus' of individualization. In this new modus, individuality was seen more or less as an inherent personal quality, and as such, a quality that should be acknowledged in the further development of the individual within the educational system.

A change therefore took place, from a situation in which individuality was seen as the result of family life and later institutional development especially in the educational system, and in which socialization and formal education went hand in hand to control and regulate individual development, to a new situation in which individuals were seen as possessing the rights and means for at least influencing their own lives. Thus, they should not be controlled by adults, but rather supported into adult life.

This current individualization perspective is especially visible in the educational system. From around the 1970s, the Danish educational policies of 'equality through education' and 'education for all' delivered the last attack on educational class privileges. All young people should have the same opportunities for education, jobs and a future – and therefore equal opportunities for individualization. No social class or other dimensions of social inequality should block the road to individual development. Moreover, in Denmark, all students from the age of 18 are given a study grant, which is designed to encourage students to continue their education.

This change in the educational system followed a broad societal trend: a greater awareness of children's life perspective, and a focus on individual rights. Participation, autonomy and democratization became key issues. People are born as individuals with individual rights, which should be acknowledged from the very beginning. As a case in point, a mother in a televised discussion about maternity leave declared, without any reactions from the other discussants, that her one-year-old daughter had 'decided not to choose kindergarten'. This example illustrates how even the youngest of children are considered 'individuals' who are able to make choices in their lives.

This new situation, however, where subjectivity is seen as an inherent quality, creates a new social challenge. Subjectivity can become a very private and antisocial quality. Therefore, it is important not only to strengthen the subject, but also to influence him/her, maybe not openly but by more subtle means. The modern process of social integration tries to solve the challenge of making society work not in opposition to, but based on individuals, who are free to do whatever they like. And this process demands a change from the institutional perspective of learned individualization and control to an often non-formal learning influence and support of the individual.

The new demands for individual development explain the broad interest in the concept and issue of competence (Mørch, 2003). In the early modern educational system, the goals of education were to give the students qualifications, for example knowledge about different scientific disciplines and real life issues. In the late-modern or modernistic society, competence is seen as a personal quality, though valuable for societal engagement and involvement. Competence refers to 'real life demands', and individuals have to develop competence as some sort of individual qualification for engaging in and managing social life.

The modernistic individualization process and therefore the educational systems are caught in the following predicament: how to secure broad societal interests while simultaneously making the individual and his or her subjectivity the prerequisites of activity.

The solutions to this challenge go in several directions. On the one hand, children and young people must themselves learn to cope with the problems they are confronted with. It is in the interest of the individual him/herself to find his/her way in society, both in having an education and later on a job. As both Beck and Bauman point out, societal problems today should be solved in individual biography. But this is exactly the situation that also creates problems. Maybe there are too few jobs available. Maybe not all young people are able to develop adequate competencies and expedient behaviour. And maybe some young people mainly look out for their own interests, only look for 'what do I get out of it'. The individual solutions can be in opposition to more overall individual and societal interests, so that new forms of supervision in everyday life may become necessary to secure societal interests. And this is exactly what seems to be happening. State supported campaigns, information programmes and the number of police and security personnel are increasing rapidly in most late-modern societies.

On the other hand, a response to this new modus of individualization is to develop new forms of social integration in late-modernity. Here, participation and democratization become the leading perspectives, but media and advertising take part in this process as well. The consumer society makes consumption itself a new means of social integration. Individuals are free to choose, but they are at the same time guided by consumer interests, and thus 'societal' interests as well. Advertising companies urge consumers to buy their products, and even state TV includes commercials between programmes. These forms of integration, however, may also create problems. Consumer interests can become too 'narrowly'-business oriented. Business interests may sometimes conflict with general societal interests, making consumer protection popular and necessary. Also, participation and consumerism require competent persons, and often the competencies for being an agent in these integrative processes are not present.

If we sum up the central message that exists in the different writings about late-modernity, it seems to be that the state of individualization is both changing and should be changed. The development from the 'early' modern society to the (late-) modernistic society is about the challenge of existence and integration. We can talk about a shift in an individualization modus from an early 'modern' modus to a 'modernistic' or late-modern modus. This development can be summed up in the following figure:

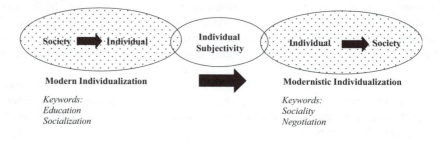

Figure 3.1   From modern to modernistic individualization

The point of this figure is to show the changing forms of individualization, from the first modern individualization process to contemporary late-modern or modernistic individualization praxis.

In the first, modern modus of individualization, society and social institutions were thought to be responsible for the construction or development of the individual. Qualifications, attitude formation, normative learning, upbringing and socialization were processes of individualization. The more long-term result of this first process was the creation of an individual as an agent of both society and his or her own life. Since World War II, the individual agent has increasingly been seen as an independent subject, which might even be seen as a contradiction to society or as suppressed in society. The resulting political and broad popular interest in supporting the subject can be seen in most theories in psychology and sociology from the 1960s and 1970s. Critical theory and other critical writings argued for the 'liberation' of the individual subject, for autonomy and for supporting individual subjective rights (Marcuse, 1964).

In the second, contemporary and modernistic or late-modern modus of individualization, this new position of the individual as a subject has been generally acknowledged both politically and in scientific writings. But this 'subjectivist society' creates a new challenge. Individualistic or egocentric individuals may threaten society. Social integration now has to support the individual subject but at the same time strengthen subjectivity as a socially responsible quality. The late-modern society is based on unique, autonomous and self-aware individuals, and therefore society must support not only the social but also societal qualities in the individual (Andersen and Mørch, 2000).

Consequently, the lesson from late-modern literature seems to be that late-modern individualization has increasingly become an issue of individual development inside a new paradigm of social integration. Social integration seems to have changed from 'controlling' the individual to 'supporting' individual subjectivity. In this new situation, family and youth life undertake different roles in becoming central agents of individualization. Family and youth are in a state of change.

The Construction of Youth

In the beginning of the 20th century, two quite different books were published that both attained a great influence on the understanding of young people and the formation and development of 20th century youth life.

Stanley Hall's well-known book had the impressive title *Adolescence. Its Psychology and Its Relation to Physiology, Anthropology, Sociology, Sex, Crime, Religion and Education* (Hall, 1904). A central idea of the book was to show that individual life course or individual biography should be seen as a repetition of the evolution of mankind. In this perspective, 'being young' was seen as a natural developmental stage in between childhood and adulthood, and with the concept of adolescence, Hall emphasized that 'being young' should be seen as a psychological phase. Young people were 'immature' and should be 'matured'.

The concept of adolescence and its psychological perspective gained tremendous popularity, probably for many reasons. Firstly, Hall was quite influential in American higher academia. Secondly, the concept referred to a real-life problem in the bourgeois world. Young people in the bourgeois and middle classes were spending progressively more time in school and educational activities and thus developed a special 'youthful' behaviour. The concept of adolescence made it obvious that their 'immature' behaviour was only natural. Thirdly, by claiming adolescence – noticeable as it was now in the bourgeois class – to be a 'natural' developmental stage, it became obvious that other social classes were less developed or underdeveloped and should be developed. This made psychology the natural home of this development. Psychology – and pedagogy – had a role to play.

More or less at the same time, Baden Powell's *Scouting for Boys* (Powell, 1908) was published in England. This book (originally a collection of journals) and the ideas it contained also had a tremendous influence on the development of young people and youth-life in the 20th century. *Scouting for Boys* became the bible for the Scout movement and was translated into most European languages within a few years. This book also told a story of developmental progress. By taking inspiration from his time in the Boer War, Baden Powell developed the concept of a Scout in the image of military scouts who reconnoitred the landscape. Young people should get to know the world and what is lying ahead of them.

But besides the pedagogical perspective of the book, it also drew a more specific picture of how youth should be understood. This understanding is visible in one of the most famous drawings in the book. It shows a magician standing with his magic wand in front of a magic box. From the left, a person enters the box and to the right a person leaves the box. The one who leaves the box is a Scout. He is in uniform, looking bright. He is, obviously, a bourgeois or middle class young person. The message is clear. The Scout movement is like a magic box creating well-functioning young people.

The amazing aspect of Baden Powell's drawing is that the person entering the box is not a child, which the scouting life or youth life should change into an adult person. The person entering the box is another young person, but from a lower social class. He is dirty, his clothes are ragged, and he is smoking a cigarette – the figure is well known in the book, in another drawing he is spitting in the street. Obviously he is a proletarian. Thus, the message of the book is quite unexpected. Youth is not a psychological phase of transition, of changing children to adults. It is a social construction for the creation of young persons, individuals for the social life. In contemporary language, we can say that the message of the Scout movement is that it aims to help individualize young persons to become well-integrated citizens in the bourgeois society. Its aim is to contribute to social integration.

These two books from the early 20th century each maintain a fact about youth. Youth is both a social construction and a psychological stage.

Now it is possible to combine these perspectives in the drawing of a general youth theory, which looks like the following:

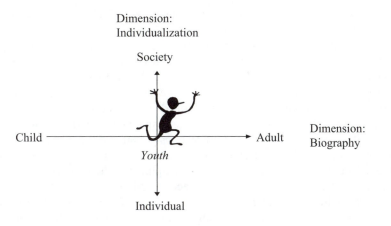

Dimension:
Individualization

Society

Child

Youth

Adult

Dimension:
Biography

Individual

Figure 3.2   Individualization in biography

The drawing reveals two dimensions. On the one hand, youth is a social construction that deals with the issue of social integration by focusing on the individualization process. On the other hand, youth also appears to be a transition phase, but as a biographical process, a psychological developmental period in which children are changed into adults. Both of these dimensions point to challenges that face the individual, the challenges of becoming integrated as an individual and of using and producing a biography. On this basis, we might make a general statement about youth: *youth concerns the social integrative challenge of individualization in biography.*

As such, youth is both an objective and subjective construction and, at the same time, a social and individual challenge. But as an objective and subjective challenge, youth and youth developmental demands are experienced and responded to subjectively. The individual may be more or less reflective about his or her own youth life situation.

This perspective makes it obvious that the creation, construction and challenges of youth are dependent on the changes of the two dimensions of individualization and biography: how they change over time and how they may correspond or be in conflict with each other. Youth as an individual or maybe psychological quality is always a result of or an answer to changing social or societal challenges.

These two dimensions are not static: the process of social integration changes with the changing of societal production and political reorganization, as this is one of the issues in late-modern discussions. But biography changes as well: from traditional biographies in the agricultural society where clear life-phases for children and adults existed, but where youth was not visible; through the industrial society in which institutionalization of biography developed in planned social contexts such as kindergartens and schools, and where youth became an important life phase; and to contemporary choice- or 'yoyo' biographies, which not totally but to some extent make youth and biography an individual choice, neither goals nor means being unequivocal (Walther, Stauber et al., 2002; Biggart, Walther and Leccardi in this book).

The analytic value of the perspective of 'individualization in biography' becomes clear if we briefly glance at the historical construction of youth. In contemporary social science, it seems a well-established fact that youth developed in European societies at the end of the 18th century as an objectively visible and a subjective experienced phase of life (Gillis, 1981; Mørch, 1985; Ariès, 1973; Stafseng, 1996). This of course does not imply that people until then were unaware of the different ages of the individuals, as when girls were seen as 'in the blossoming of their lives'. But the understanding of youth as a special stage in individual life was established with the development of the bourgeois society at the end of the 18th century. The bourgeois became individualized by the demands for skills and qualifications of modern business and industrial life and for political competencies by the new status of being in power in the modern democratic society (Mørch, 1985; Musgrove, 1964). Therefore, individualization became the task to be taken care of in education, and the individualization process in education constructed youth at its centre.

Family changes influenced the development of youth as well. In the bourgeois society, the family on the one hand became the sign of 'noblesse' of the bourgeoisie, taking the place of the primacy of the political powerful lineage of the aristocracy. And at the same time, the orderly bourgeoisie family presented itself at a distance from the poor and politically threatening masses, who had no means for living a family life. The bourgeois family became an active and responsible partner in the construction of the bourgeoisie society (Andersen, 1986; Donzelot, 1979).

But at the same time, family life became separated from everyday production. It was lived in private homes, and in the middle of the bourgeois home it placed its children. Mothers and nannies protected the children from 'real life' and in the nursery, they developed a special child life and childishness. So, an important part of family life became oriented to nursing the child, watching over his/her early steps toward the proper and healthy development to come (Badinter, 1980).

The development of youth followed this family model. Children had to be 'changed' from children to adults. And as, among others, Musgrowe pointed out, this change was brought about by education and school life (Musgrove, 1964).

Individualization therefore was created in biography. And the bourgeois identity became a developmental goal for the individual child and for family and school. School and educational rooms became the contexts of individualization.

However, the new democratic constitutions all over Europe in the 19th century made it necessary to widen the educational possibilities to broader parts of the populations. They needed competencies for their new democratic influence. But the social integrative challenge of the industrialization process also called for qualifications in the general population and in this way created a broad need for education as well (Mørch, 2003).

Changing Dimensions of Individualization and the Educational System

When discussing the challenges of late-modern youth, we must still focus on individualization in biography, but now according to the development of today. We have to look for changes within each of the two dimensions of integration and biography and for changes in between them.

In analysing the late-modern development, Giddens' book *Modernity and Self Identity* (Giddens, 1997) has become popular. In this book, Giddens draws a picture of how demands on individuals have changed. According to Giddens, one risk in late-modernity is for people to lose their self-identity and self-assurance. Late-modernity in itself may cause individual failures and therefore unintended differentiation among people. The answer is for people to develop social influence. In contemporary modern times, according to this theory, the individual is forced to take an active part in shaping the conditions under which he or she lives. The individual must participate actively in the 'structuration' process, as Giddens calls it (Giddens, 1984, 1997). The individual must become a – democratic – actor or subject in the world.

De-institutionalization calls for a new institutionalization based on a new individualized paradigm. Not only structures are called for. Giddens' concept of 'structuration' refers to this new demand for developing a relation between society and the individual, which recognizes the late-modern individualization process: *individualization takes place when the individual develops his or her own structural conditions.*

Giddens' analysis can be useful for pointing to general demands of competence for the individualization development in late-modern life: *self-identity, reflexivity, self-assurance, knowledgeability, participation, individual basic trust in the world and one's self.*

These late-modern requirements describe the general aspects of individual competencies in relation to an overall social integration perspective of late-modernity. They refer to our understanding of individual or personal competence, and they become important factors in the process of constructing oneself as a winner or loser in late-modernity. Young people, for example, who have a very high self-assurance but only a low degree of knowledgeability will only have low achievement in education and on the labour market. Therefore, Giddens' list points to singular items, but these should be seen as intertwined elements of a general structure.

The modernistic demands on individual subjects or actors also attack former traditions. Social class, ethnic background and gender are overruled by contemporary modernization processes. Late-modernity seems to be the new force that destroys all former privileges and traditions.

In Denmark, these changes of modernization have become most visible in youth life. As said before, already in 1970, the school model of 'education for all' created equal conditions for all young people. Individualization through education was seen as an equal opportunity for all, but also as having the same form for all young people. This optimistic picture of equality, however, has of course not succeeded in every respect. Social class is still visible in the Danish educational systems. For example, studies show that among students at the highest educational levels, there is an over-representation of those coming from academic or middle-long educational family backgrounds (Hansen, 1995). But the democratic educational system has certainly influenced the development of individualization in society.

The fact that an ideal of total equality within and through education is not accomplished may be due to several reasons. One obvious reason may be that endeavours towards giving all children the same opportunities run counter to some well-educated parents' ambitions for a higher education especially for their children. Interests in equality cannot compete with interests in the education of their own offspring, and many parents even move to special parts of the cities or place their children in private schools to avoid the risk of getting a lower educational standard in schools with general admission. However, the combination of welfare development and active school politics has actually changed the education pattern in Denmark. For example, the level of education has generally increased dramatically in recent years. In 1980, only 25.5 per cent of a youth cohort completed further education, while the corresponding number for 1998 was 40 per cent. It is expected that by 2010, 50 per cent of a cohort will complete further education. Statistics also show that 80 per cent of the Danish population have at least a 'youth education', and this means that the level of education is high compared to other countries in Europe where the average is 59 per cent. Only Germany reaches a higher level (Ministry of Education, 2000).

If we look at the 'new' challenge of ethnic individualization, this problem seems to be especially a product of a combination of parents' education and reigning traditional values. Immigrants in Denmark come from different educational backgrounds. Children from well-educated immigrant parents are performing almost as well as 'ethnic Danish youth' in the educational system. In contrast, children of immigrants with a lower school education, who have unskilled jobs or no jobs at all, more often have difficulties in meeting the expectations and demands of the modernistic Danish educational system. But it is worth noting that Danish research seems to demonstrate a stronger correlation between children's lack of educational attainment and traditional values, lifestyle and factors of 'lower social class' than between educational achievement and cultural diversity (Kyvsgaard, 2001).

'Foreign' or immigrant youth and especially second (and 'later') generations of immigrant youth generally do quite well in the educational system. The percentage of young people from immigrant backgrounds between the ages of 16 to 19 participating in youth education grew from 25 per cent in 1990 to 45 per cent in 1999. In particular, second (and later) immigrant generations of youth show a high percentage; 70 per cent of this group participate in youth education compared to 72 per cent of the general youth cohort. Though some young immigrants show marked difficulties in meeting the demands of the Danish school system, there is no simple correlation between these difficulties and an ethnic background other than Danish (Ministry of Education, 2000).

The question of gender differences is also complex. The general picture today is one of girls and women performing better throughout the educational system than boys and men. This development has been especially significant in the last 10 years. Some work areas have traditionally been and still remain occupied by men, but these work areas often consist of skilled or semi-skilled jobs. Within further education women are taking over, a shift that is central in a society where educational careers are becoming increasingly important: today 29 per cent of Danish women complete a medium length education compared to 14 per cent of the men (in 1980, the ratio was 19 per cent to 11.5 per cent). The growth in the proportion of women's education has especially occurred in the medium-long education of teachers, pedagogues and nurses, as the largest groups. But a growing proportion of women also complete longer, academic educations.[1]

At the same time as women are becoming better educated, they are also experiencing more disruption between occupational demands and the demands of family life and the upbringing of children. Many well-functioning families tend to become more and more like mutually supportive networks, meaning that both men and women become practically responsible for supporting the children's development and for daily family housework. But in many families, the picture of mutual responsibility towards the demands of family life is never put into practice. Women are still in general under more pressure to invest more of their commitment and time in family life, though this pressure is expressed in indirect and subtle ways. These ongoing processes of progressive development parallel to the coexistence of more traditional gender patterns create corresponding discourses in modernistic society, for example modernistic feminist debates. These have very different scopes: one end of the continuum shows endeavours to reconstruct and appreciate traditional women's values and qualities, while the other end has protests and political activity against gender inequalities regarding access to politically and economically influential appointments and jobs.

Changing Biographies

Just as the dimension of individualization changes continuously, so does biography. If we look back at history, we can see that the construction of youth and youth-life in the bourgeoisie changed the former traditional linear biography existing in agricultural societies with no specific youth life phase (Gillis, 1981). In the bourgeois society, youth developed within a specifically arranged youth life. From the beginning, young people were 'developed' by inclusion in educational contexts and by fulfilling the demands set within the repertoire of these contexts. From the start of the 20th century, school contexts were supplemented by social contexts such as youth clubs, sport clubs, Scout movements and so on. And from around the 1950s, the peer group or youth culture developed as a social frame of reference for young people, often influenced by music and the media. Youth individualization in its changing forms was constructed within the institutional processes in biography.

A general picture of youth trajectories and individualization can be seen in the following:

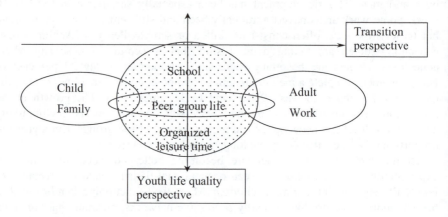

Figure 3.3   The institutional youth life model

In this figure, the two dimensions of individualization in biography point to qualities in youth life as these are organized in youth life transition.

What we might experience today is not only a change in individualization demands, but a change of the youth trajectory, too. The biographical trajectory of child – young – adult is changing. First of all, youth-life is prolonged: it starts early and ends late in life – or it never ends. We may not only talk about a 'disappearing of childhood' (Postman, 1982), but also talk about a 'disappearance of adulthood' (Côté, 2000). This development follows the popularity of youth and being young. Firstly, youth life and being – and looking – young has become so popular that children want to become 'young' very early. They are encouraged not only by the media and advertisement-interests, but also by parents and other adults who create 'youth' in children or early 'youthhood' by dress and lifestyle. This process is quite interesting. In former times, adults saw children as immature adults and they liked to dress children as adults (Ariès, 1973), but when youth took over popularity as a developmental goal, this also influenced children. They are made 'young' very early in life. Not only in dress, but in lifestyles, too.

Secondly, it has become popular to stay young. Youth lifestyles, looks and sexual behaviour have become popular goals for all. Nobody wants to become, look like or act like an adult, a tendency that also influences many people's relations to the labour market: jobs should be entertaining, provide secure continuous development and be 'sexy'. The popularity of youth changes the idea of transition. Youth is not something to get through; youth has become the wished-for life (Frønes and Brusdal, 2000; Côté, 2000).

In this situation, we may talk about the development of a new trajectory, though maybe not for all, and maybe not in all parts of life. It could be called a 'yoyo' trajectory, in which it is possible to change between being a child, a youth and an adult all the time, or a choice biography, which promises the opportunity to choose whatever seems fun (see also du Bois-Reymond and te Poel in this book).

The general structure of the modernistic trajectory, on the one hand, could be seen as a non-directed youth life trajectory. Youth life does not lead directly to adult life, and adult life in itself loses its former significant characteristics. This means that adulthood is more or less disappearing from young people's perspectives, and this situation makes it difficult to establish developmental perspectives.

The development of a non-directedness of modern youth life, on the other hand, may even require a total new understanding. Instead of specific stages of life, in the late-modern Western world we are confronted with new and shifting circumstances of 'fragmented contextualization'. This means that we live in a world in which all social contexts are formed within and influenced by the overall demands and conditions of late-modernity. And at the same time, more contexts are functioning as a network producing different aspects of development (Mørch, 1999). This fragmented contextualized world makes the trajectory a sort of choice biography in the sense that the individuals have to choose between different contexts and contextual demands; and the individuals themselves have to arrange and combine the different contexts in their own lives. They have to develop an individual or personal trajectory.

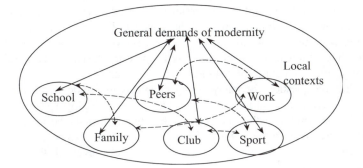

Figure 3.4   Fragmented contextualization

Today, therefore, social integration no longer points to one major trajectory or common trajectories between childhood and adult life. Many more routes or pathways may exist and become trajectories within and between different or fragmented social contexts.

This means that the real trajectory challenge falls back upon the individual. Individuals form their own trajectories and in this way contextualize aspects of development in their youth life by combining societal conditions and individual interests. Therefore, in a modernistic society, the primary trajectory challenge for young people is not merely to participate, but to decide what they should participate in and for what reason.

To understand this challenge, it is important to include a broader view of young people's lives, pathways and trajectories, especially for the young persons themselves. Logic and sense do not objectively exist nor are they visible in formal transition trajectories – the individual has to develop them. The individual has a new responsibility for making his/her own trajectory and this calls for a better understanding of how to cope with conditions, how to become empowered to make choices within youth and societal life, how to become competent in life. Therefore, the second new challenge of youth seems to be 'the construction of sense and competence' for manoeuvring in a more open world. Young people should learn to 'cope', or in other words, they should develop forms of 'expedient' life management (Mørch and Laursen, 1998).

But even in a 'fragmented contextualization' situation, some contexts may be 'reserved' for specific age groups. It is still possible for outsiders to observe youth and for young people to see themselves as youth. Youth still exists as an objective and subjective social category. But also, other 'reservations' appear, such as ethnic, educational, sports-groups, etc., and the new rooms of late-modernity may be very exclusive, with gatekeepers to screen people entering.

This new situation creates both great opportunities and difficulties for young people. They have to develop a subjective understanding of the youth challenge. They may commit themselves to and learn from the non-formal or non-educational contexts of late-modern youth life and reject 'irrelevant' formal education and they may gain new competence in a broad sense of the concept. But they may also lose their connection with further education and future access to relevant areas of influence in their own lives. Individual trajectories may become too 'private'. The problem of a 'choice trajectory' is that people may make the wrong choices.

The difficult question for many young people is to decide which activities and competencies are important in youth life for their future employment careers. One of the individual answers to this 'non-plannable situation' might be to get as 'much' education as possible. In the Danish educational system, for example, more and more young people choose to go on to grammar schools, even if their educational orientations are not academic.

The great challenge in modern 'fragmented contextual' youth life, on the one hand, seems to be the ability to manoeuvre amongst the different contexts and demands, but, on the other hand, the demand seems to be to construct one's own trajectory. When transition trajectories or pathways become an individual challenge, this demands from the individual that he or she become an agent of structuration. Young people have to make their own structures as they use the existing opportunities. But perhaps this challenge of 'structur-ation' should be supplemented by a challenge of 'competence-ation'. For young people, the overall demand seems not only to be to develop structures, but also to develop competencies for their lives, both as competencies for social life in a broad sense, but also as a sort of employability for being able to grasp work opportunities (Mørch and Stalder, 2003).

Youth and the Family

The broad theory of youth as *the social integrative challenge of individualization in biography* can now be made more precise. If the double challenge of both social integration and biography is not seen, we might misunderstand the essentials of youth. On the one hand, if we only look at biography – as often happens in psychology – it leads us to think that the 'challenge of youth' is about the development of identity. This may be either as a psychological phenomenon or as some sort of social identity, but identity does not point to the future, rather it points to itself. Maybe it is important to have a self-identity, as Giddens points out, but it is a prerequisite for engaging in the world, not a goal in itself. Self-identity, if this is focused on as a goal, may even be a hindrance to progressive change. If, on the other hand, we see the youth problem only as a question of social integration, we will miss the specific challenge of becoming a subject and an agent at the same time. The young person must develop in the structuration and competence-ation of a trajectory. Young people have to see themselves as planning their lives and as progressing from being an individual subject to becoming a societal agent as well. Individualization in biography points to the challenge of forming an individual trajectory. And here family support and guidance becomes most important.

The double challenge of both social integration and biography point to the relation between childhood and youthhood. They are both closely connected and at the same time quite different. Therefore, youth is also a break with childhood and childhood life, as this is often imbedded in and formed in the family. And the transition from child to youth takes place earlier and earlier, now in the midst of family life. Late-modernity in this way poses a challenge for the family. How should the modern family cope with the process of individualization when childhood is shortened, and youth becomes an ultimate goal?

The Family Perspective

Family life has developed with changing societal conditions as an active structuration process in the different social classes. At the same time that societal conditions have been basic to the possibilities for the creation of family life, family forms have also been influenced by current pictures of the family. Family seems to have developed in between traditions and has itself changed conditions of modern and late-modern life. Families reproduce former forms of family life and they develop new forms according to the general developmental demands of modernization.

Nevertheless, of course, it is possible to have and develop a variety of family types within the same society. Families may be influenced by tradition or may be organized according to different new coming societal life conditions. Therefore, contemporary families vary according to how they uphold traditions and how they cope with late-modernity.

Also families are defined and described from different perspectives, as 'nuclear/extended', 'conventional/non-conventional', middle class/working class and so on. In this context however, families are seen according to how they handle their functions, or how they become families.

From a family historical perspective (Anderson, 1980; Flandrine, 1980; Donzelot, 1979), we suggest that three basic structures of family exist today, as they have developed in history and also as they function today.

First is the traditional, kin-orientated family, which we call the *reproductive* family, both because it reproduces family forms from farming societies and makes the family in the sense of 'kin' the agent of history, but also because it 'reproduces' children. Children are brought up towards being as the adults were before. This does not mean, of course, that the family does not try to 'modernize', or that the parents do not want their children (especially boys) to be better qualified, for example, than they themselves are. But in this type of family, the family comes before the individual. Family 'honour' is more important than individual – developmental – freedom. In this family, the children may have problems keeping up with the many demands of late-modern life and education and, at the same time, engaging in their more traditional family life patterns. Not surprisingly, these types of problems may be most characteristic during youth, and especially among young immigrants whose families come from rural areas.

The second type is the *productive* family. It still has a traditional perspective, but the perspective is from the bourgeois family as it exists today, as the middle-class nuclear family or housewife family (Frønes, 1994; Frønes and Brusdal, 2000). The family is no longer seen as 'kin', but more as a close relation between parents and children. As such, it socializes children or produces children. It creates children and gives them prerequisites for a later individualization in youth and educational life. At the same time, however, this family form can produce personal problems for children and young people. The challenge of being 'good enough' and fulfilling parents' expectations may create psychological distress for the young people.

The third type is the *supportive* family. This family is trying to forget traditional family patterns in its orientation towards modernistic individual challenges. It is a transition from the modern family to a modernistic family, in which all family members are individuals in their own right (Beck and Beck-Gernsheim, 2002). This family may become a form of network or association that competes for influence with other networks that the family members engage in. The modernistic family is both a result of a changing world and also a partner in this societal change towards late-modernization. One of the central objectives of the late-modern family is its emotional support of its members and its support for children to exert themselves in society. The central objective is to further the development of the children's individuality as an inherent quality. The concept of 'children as a project' is an example of this orientation (Ziehe and Stubenrauch, 1984; Ziehe, 2001), though it appears as if there is little understanding of 'children' in a more traditional sense. Children or youth are only seen as individual subjects to be supported. Often it is not clear to parents – and pedagogues (teachers and youth workers) – how the late-modern challenges of individualization should be understood. Obviously the concern of the adults is not that children should be brought up to be strictly like their parents, or that the children are just adults to be. The children are seen as unique persons from the very beginning, strangers so to speak, whom the parents have to get to know and who have a claim on receiving support from parents and other adults for engaging in their future life. This situation of course also creates problems. Children may be misguided or – maybe more often – they may not be guided or supported at all. They may not be given conditions for developing 'ontological security' (Giddens, 1997), or they may be unable to participate competently in different institutional developmental practices. Some of these potential problems may be most visible during youth.

In this way, the supportive family becomes an active player in developing late-modernity. Not only in the sense that it 'produces children', but because it supports individuals and also because it adapts to shifting conditions of individualization in late-modernity. It creates new forms of social and organizational 'answers'. Thus, the late-modern developments of youth individualization and youth life also influence the life of the modernistic family. The family becomes a supportive network like other sorts of networks. Parents see themselves as friends or comrades to their children.

Changing Families and Youth

To sum up these perspectives, we point out that when youth is understood as the development of individualization in biography, it is closely connected to the general development of society and the forms of social integration. This societal development can be seen as a three-step process, which is historical, but a general integrative model as well. This means that all 'stages' can coexist while new modes of social integration develop:

1. A traditional society, which does not focus on individualization and therefore does not recognize a specific youth development or psychology. This situation still exists in rural-based societies.
2. A modern industrial society, in which individualization becomes the goal and the prerequisites of being an adult, job-oriented and politically competent person, a situation that still exists in societies engaged in an industrialization process.
3. A late-modern society, in which individual choice seems to be the prerequisite of both the direction of individualization and of consumer behaviour.

Individual biography clearly changes during this development. Biography is the individual life history, but it is always made possible by or being formed by societal organization.

In traditional society, (youth) biography follows a normative, traditionally organized status model. Norms exist as norms of family life. The young person should behave according to the ascribed status of being a child or an adult, a female or a male. In modern industrialized society, youth biographies become organized within families and social institutions such as schools and educational establishments. Here youth life is constructed as a time and stage for transition into qualified, individualized adulthood. And also youth life exists as a normative universe with rules and expectations for proper institutional behaviour. In today's late-modern society, youth biography seems to become more and more an individual construct in a fragmented contextual social world. Social norms does not function as guidelines for behaviour but rather seem to be some sort of tool-box from which young people can choose whatever is appropriate. In this situation, transition is dissolved and replaced by new strategies such as 'choice biography' (see also du Bois-Reymond and te Poel in this book).

Family life also changes during this development and as part of the individualization process. Family life occupies quite different positions in the different integrative or historical situations.

In the traditional society, families are gatekeepers of tradition. The *reproductive* family is concerned with the maintenance of existing, well-defined roles for each of the family members according to age and gender. The adults – in many respects primarily the fathers – have rather solid values, norms and goals from tradition, to pass on to their children. The adult teaches and the children learn. For young people, living in a family means staying 'a child'. In the family they are subordinate to the head of family while they maybe in other parts of their lives, in education and sports etc., are treated as youth.

In the industrialization – or modern society, the family is considered *productive.* Roles and rights are distributed according to developmental stages, but still with recognition of gender and age as basic parameters. Individuality is accepted as a personal quality to come and the adults are responsible for influencing its development. At the same time, this forming of individuality also guides the transition of young persons from family life to the outside world, and for the modern family, norms, values and proper behaviour in the outside world are rather important as guidelines of development. In the productive family also differences are produced between boys and girls. The perspective of socialization for coming adulthood especially makes gender differentiation natural in the family (Andersen, 1986; Haug, 1983; Gerhard, 1981). Construction of the individual biography as part of the integrative, societal process is a main concern, but the adult can still teach and the children learn. Young persons living in a family may react and become more or less rebellious or combatant during their developmental process, but the adults can make claim to knowing the societal structures and therefore the proper results of the development.

In the late-modern society, where the family could be called *supportive*, rules and roles are shifting, and neither age nor gender are clear means of distributing rights and authority. Individuality is presupposed as each single person's own quality, but now at the same time implying an open-ended result under conditions that are still being produced. The late-modern family has to support the production of individuality, but its main concern is to do so without having any stable guidelines. Norms for the family life or for its role in the production of individual behaviour do not exist as visible options. And at the same time, the families are engaged in changing their own conditions – and doing so knowledgeably. Basically, family life has become 'democratic'. Everyone, both parents and children, has a vote. The adults in this late-modern family generally cannot just teach and hope for their children to learn. Instead, they can occupy the role of *counsellor* for children and – primarily – youngsters within the family. In that respect, they can guide their children, and in some ways the family must be seen as a *network,* parallel to other networks the family members engage in within formal and informal groupings. However, it is obvious that the family occupies a specific role for children and youth as a network. For one thing, the adults in the family have a formal responsibility towards their children, and besides this, the emotional and other bonds between family members put the family's adults in a more visible, but also more difficult or widespread position as 'counsellors'. A young person's rebellion will not be understood solely as a natural consequence of his/her 'adolescence', behaviour to be dealt with suitably, hoping for a proper result. It will have to be negotiated to end without confrontation.

The supportive family may be seen as the friendly family in two respects. Relatives play a less important role compared to friends and the authoritative relation between parents and children is changed. Parents and children become friends. This situation however also weakens the role of family. They have to compete with other friends. In the friendly family also the gender perspective changes. Traditional gender differences do not exist or are not developed. Children are expected to be treated equally and given the same conditions. But late modern pictures of youth, and also gender expectations influences the family picture. Gender becomes an individualized psychological expectation to be supported by the consumer society.

From a cross-European and comparative perspective, these developments seem to exist in different forms and combinations. Youth development and individualization relates to both employability demands and family life and support. The different youth life challenges that follow modernization patterns create at the same time not only different biographies and opportunities, but also different forms of individualization and subjectivity.

The Family Today

Though families today vary all over Europe, the late-modern development and its challenge of individualization influence all family development. Families are under pressure to 'modernize'. Not necessarily to become the supportive family, but to support modernistic individualization in children and young persons. The picture is maybe not unambiguous. But all sorts of family life are under pressure to support youth individualization and the development of youth subjectivity.

The changing perspectives of individualization and biography are essential for the understanding of the impact of late-modern, societal challenges for children and youth. What we can observe today is that the fragmented contextualization of individualization leads to a network construction, which includes family life. Families are under pressure to become contexts like other contexts. This means that all aspects of life are influenced by the challenge of individualization. At the same time, we can see that the institutional biography is changing. Youth life has become the centre of individualization and tends to be seen as a primary aim to practise not only for persons from certain age groups, but for all kinds of persons. This focus on youth life has influenced all parts of society. As already said, not only are the media and business life focusing on youthhood as primary target groups and youth lifestyles as an ideal for other segments of the population to follow, but also parents more and more wish for and prompt their children to become youth, to look and act as youth. When treating their children like 'born individuals', they very early treat them like youth, both in dress, in activities and expectations for their knowledge and decisions. Young children are seen as subjects. This development is both supported and made possible by commercial and media interests. Song contests, beauty contests, sexy clothes are all part of a very early youth construction (see also Holm, Daspit and Kelaher Young in this book). Moreover, political life has this same perspective: children's parliament and other arrangements invite children and youngsters to contribute with their opinions.

The role of the family no longer seems only to prepare for individualization, but to be an active partner in the construction of individualization. Therefore, families are in the midst of a comprehensive change. They are changing according to socialization goals, to personal relations and to authority structure. But as families, they often have difficulties in both understanding and acting within these new developments and the new challenge of individualization. Children and youth may become strangers to parents, they become unique projects, who should find their own trajectories, which are radically different from the trajectories of their parents. Parents feel they are needed but not what they are needed for. Parents often see children and youth as 'friends' and 'equals' and have difficulties in finding ways of both securing value and normative support, but also in taking on their new role as counsellors for their children. They may easily support a very private subjectivity and in this way become partners in the construction of the most central modernistic problem: the individual's difficulties in meeting the demands of becoming not only an individual subject, but a societal agent as well.

Note

1   In 1980, 5 per cent of women and 6.5 per cent of men completed a higher education. In 1998, 13 per cent of women and 11.5 per cent of men completed a higher education. So, women have overtaken men in regard to higher education. There is a higher percentage of men only in the very highest academic education, the Ph.D. level (Ministry of Education, 2000).

References

Andersen, H. (1986), *Kvindeværd (Women's Worth)*, Rubikon, Copenhagen.
Andersen, H. and Mørch, S. (2000), 'Socialpsykologiens verdener' ('The Worlds of Social Psychology'), *Psyke og Logos*, Vol. 21(1), pp. 283-415.
Anderson, M. (1980), *Approaches to the History of the Western Family 1500-1914*, Sage, London.
Ariès, P. (1973), *Centuries of Childhood*, Random House, New York.
Badinter, E. (1980), *L'amour en plus. Historie de L'amour maternel*, Edition Flammanion, Paris.
Bauman, Z. (1998), *Work, Consumerism and the New Poor*, Open University Press, Philadelphia.
Bauman, Z. (2001), *The Individualized Society*, Polity Press, Cambridge.
Beck, U. (1992), *Risk Society: Towards a New Modernity*, Sage, London.
Beck, U. and Beck-Gernsheim, E. (2002), *Individualization*, Sage, London.
Côté, J. (2000), *Arrested Adulthood. The Changing Nature of Maturity and Identity*, New York University Press, New York.
Donzelot, J. (1979), *The Policing of Families*, Pantheon Books, New York.
Esping-Andersen, G. (1990), *Three Worlds of Welfare Capitalism*, Polity Press, Cambridge.
Flandrine, J.L. (1980), *Families in Former Times*, Polity Press, Cambridge.
Frønes, I. (1994), *Den Norske barndommen (The Nordic Childhood)*, Cappelen Akademisk Forlag, Spydebjerg.
Frønes, I. and Brusdal, R. (2000), *På sporet av den nye tid (On the Track of Modernity)*, Fakbokforlaget, Bergen.
Gerhard, U. (1981), *Verhältnisse und Verhinderungen. Frauenarbeit, Familie und Rechte der Frauen im 19. Jahrhundert*, Suhrkamp, Frankfurt a.M.
Giddens, A. (1984), *The Constitution of Society*, Polity Press, Cambridge.
Giddens, A. (1997), *Modernity and Self Identity*, Polity Press, Cambridge.
Gillis, J. (1981), *Youth and History*, Academic Press, New York.
Hall, S.G. (1904), *Adolescence. Its Psychology and Its Relation to Physiology, Anthropology, Sociology, Sex, Crime, Religion and Education*, Vols. I-II, D. Appleton, New York.
Hansen, E.J. (1995), *En generation blev voksen: Den første velfærdsgeneration (A Generation Grew Up: The First Generation of Welfare Society)*, Socialforskningsinstituttet, Rapport 95(8), Copenhagen.
Holter, H. (1975), *Familien i Klassesamfundet (The Family in the Class Society)*, Pax, Oslo.
Haug, F. (1983), *Frauenformen*, Argument-Verlag, Berlin.
Kyvsgaard, B. (2001), 'Kriminalitet, retshåndhævelse og etniske minoriteter' ('Crime, Justice and Ethnic Minorities'), *Juristen*, November, pp. 32-41.
Marcuse, H. (1964), *One Dimensional Man*, Beacon Press, Boston.
Ministry of Education (2000), *Facts and Figures*, Ministry of Education, Copenhagen.
Ministry of Education (2001), *Indvandere og efterkommere i uddannalsessystemet (Immigrants and Successors in the Educational System)*, Ministry of Education, Copenhagen.
Musgrove, F. (1964), *Youth and the Social Order*, Routledge and Kegan Paul, London.
Mørch, S. (1985), *At forske i ungdom (Studying Youth)*, Rubikon, Copenhagen.
Mørch, S. (1999), 'Informal Learning and Social Contexts', in A. Walther and B. Stauber (eds), *Lifelong Learning in Europe: Differences and Divisions*, Neuling, Tübingen, pp. 145-171.
Mørch, S. (2003), 'Youth and Education', *Young*, Vol. 11(1), pp. 49-73.

Mørch, S. and Laursen, S. (1998), *At lære at være ung (Learning to be Young)*, Ungdomsringen, Copenhagen.

Mørch, S. and Stalder, B. (2003), 'Competence and Employability', in A. Walther (ed.), *Trajectories and Politics*, Policy Press, Cambridge, pp. 154-172.

Postman, N. (1982), *The Disappearance of Childhood*, Comet, London.

Powell, B. (1908), *Scouting for Boys*, Horace Cox, London. (Later reprints)

Stafseng, O. (1996), *Den historiske konstruktion av moderne ungdom (The Historic Construction of Modern Youth)*, Cappelan, Oslo.

Walther, A., Stauber, B. et al. (eds), (2002), *Misleading Trajectories – Integration Policies in Europe?*, Leske + Budrich, Opladen.

Ziehe, T. and Stubenrauch, H. (1982), *Plädoyer für ungewöhnliches Lernen, Ideen zur Jugendsituation*, Rohwolt, Reinbek.

Ziehe, T. (2001), 'De personlige livsverdeners dominans'('The Dominance of Personal Life Worlds'), *Uddannelse*, Vol. 10, pp. 3-18.

Chapter 4

The Sky is Always Falling. (Un)Changing Views on Youth in the US

Gunilla Holm, Toby Daspit and Allison J. Kelaher Young

Familiar educational notions have traditionally identified young people as 'students' or 'pupils,' locating them in passive cultural roles where – under varying conditions of supervision – they are expected to serve a kind of apprenticeship, gaining the skills, dispositions, and knowledge that the adults of a given society deem important for them to possess. It is only at some later chronological point, after they have demonstrated a certain level of accomplishment, that youngsters are permitted to engage (albeit differently on the basis of ability, appearance, gender, color, and class) in the various tasks of cultural practice (Paley, 1995, p. 3).

'We Are Outraged' and We are Going to Hell

A recent full-page advertisement ran in our regional, fairly liberal, newspaper, *The Kalamazoo Gazette*. This newspaper serves a city with a population of about 80,000 residents as well as suburban and rural communities in five surrounding counties in Western Michigan. The advertisement proclaimed, 'We Are Outraged At What TV, Pop Music And Movies Are Doing To Our Children' (p. C4) and proceeded to decry contemporary youth. The ad, written by a group called 'Parents and Grandparents Alliance', declared that teen violence, drug use, and sexual activity were out of control. The primary reasons? Entertainment media, particularly television, movies, and music. The ad 'cited' various 'studies' and declared that 'A Horrendous Tragedy Is Happening In America. Children Are Being Led to Sex, Drugs, Violence, Killing and Suicide!'

Such an advertisement reflects and reinforces the dominant view of the public, and researchers as we'll soon see, that young people are becoming more uncontrollable and morally corrupt. The sense is that young people do not learn much in school, that they are becoming more criminal, and that their moral values and cultural interests are being corrupted by popular culture (including television, popular music and popular movies, and increasingly video games and the Internet). We argue that this view has been the predominant one for decades and is rooted in adult society's need to control young people as well as its fear of them being autonomous. Young people are framed as being irresponsible and incapable of being trusted with tasks that matter. This justifies diverse societal efforts to control them, including standardized testing regimes in school, bans on films and books, and tough punishments for various kinds of infractions. Furthermore, since in the US there is no official, national youth policy, public awareness tends to be closely connected to the research that is funded by the federal government and foundations Côté (2004) explains this connection:

> In the US, research tends to follow funding opportunities and funding tends to policy oriented, where a 'problem-to-be-rectified' is identified by individual researchers or government institutes and in turn massive funding initiatives are undertaken by government agencies (e.g., National Institute of Health or National Institute of Mental Health) or private foundations (e.g., William T. Grant Foundation). Moreover, there is no national youth policy in the US or a recognition of youth as an age category in need of special policies (in contrast to the elderly, for when massive reforms have been undertaken in the last 30 years). Hence, we find the focus on specific 'youth problems'... rather than on the overall situation confronting young people as an interest group or a disadvantaged group with special needs. This has tended to result in a 'psychologizing' of youth circumstances, where reactions to difficulties are seen to have individual rather than structural causes. (pp. 1-2)

This kind of research is mostly focused on contemporary problems such as drug abuse, teen pregnancy, and violence related issues. The public is thus regularly reminded that young people have a number of problems and are a problem themselves.

In addition, for more than a century positivist researchers have primarily examined youth as a unified group. This is exemplified by numerous studies that treat white males as a representative sample for all youth. Although youth have never been a monolithic group, it is even more difficult today to discuss youth as a group without qualifying which young people are being discussed. Drawing from post-modern and critical theoretical stances, we recognize that young people from different ethnicities, racial groups, genders, social classes and sexualities have entirely distinct experiences and therefore, multiple identities and experiences within such categories are hardly monolithic. Additionally, heeding Paley's (1995) exhortation, we understand that youth are not simply apprentices – they are active agents in society.

There is an emerging body of research that challenges modernist, positivistic paradigms. Youth cultures have been explored in depth from a variety of critical and post-modern perspectives in attempts to decenter such monolithic conceptions. For example, Hebdige (1979) and Willis (1981) examine specific working class 'subcultures.' Roman (1988) argues that this 'class essentialism... holds that subjectivity is unitary and homogenous, having been formed strictly out of *a priori* class interests' (p. 143). Instead, Roman examines the gender dynamics of 'ideologies of feminine sexuality' (pp. 143-184), while Walkerdine (1997) examines the complex intersections of gender and class. Stuart Hall in particular shifted the interests of cultural studies away from the meta-level of culture to the ambiguity and uncertainty of everyday life (in Grossberg, 1996) – and where the complex construction of identities is often enacted through popular cultural experiences.

Unfortunately, as McCarthy and Valdivia (in Dimitriadis, 2001) observe, most research on youth (especially with regard to popular culture) focuses exclusively on either textual analysis or ethnographic studies, thus ignoring richer understandings:

> Those emphasizing textual analysis in their work have tended to marginalize the lived experiential dimension of human endeavor in the realm of popular culture. Those pursuing ethnographic study of human dilemmas often emphasize interviews, participant observation, and cultural description to the point of abridging the rich possibilities for triangulation to be found in popular texts. (p. vii)

Though such perspectives offer serious challenges to dominant paradigms, both theoretical and methodological, popular perceptions of youth and most funded academic research remain firmly entrenched in the modernist framework. Such attitudes are, in a sense, a denial of the post-modern condition, which we find ourselves in. Or as Rushkoff (1996) might say, it is a refusal to allow ourselves to be taught by youth cultures, by youth who have been nurtured within post-modern contexts, and who are attracted to cultural forms which embody decentered, ruptured identities. We hope to offer possibilities for reconceptualizing youth studies that are more salient given the conditions of post-modernity.

We will discuss the dominant, generally unchanging public and research views of youth by reviewing the current ways youth are framed in the US with regard to schooling, sexuality, violence, consumerism and popular culture, viewing each as a 'snapshot' example of how the problem areas are seen within the dominant framework. We have chosen to focus on these four snapshots because they are the areas most often discussed and debated when issues related to youth enter the public debate. Additionally, these are often cited in education texts as areas of interest for pre-service teachers. Furthermore, these snapshots show very clearly why we cannot follow the positivist tradition of talking about youth as a monolithic unit. In each of the areas portrayed, these snapshots show that there are major differences among groups of young people. We will conclude by analyzing the implications of these unchanging views that 'we are going to hell'. We believe that by continuing to frame young people in these ways, we ignore the ways young people work in constructive ways in their communities and as producers of knowledge and entertainment. As Daniel Cavicchi observes, 'I'd argue that the act of applying theory is colonizing – it conquers realms of experience in the name of academia and completely ignores the values and ideas of the people who actually participate in those realms' (in Daspit, 2002, p. 96). Hence, we want to begin a conversation about how to theorize about youth without colonizing them, without denying their agency.

Snapshot One: Social Contexts of Schooling

Schools and students have traditionally been blamed for not doing as well as politicians and policy makers want them to do. In 1983 the national report *A Nation At Risk* claimed that students were failing in school and thereby the whole nation was at risk of failing. Books like Allan Bloom's (1987) *The Closing of the American Mind* fostered the notion that schools fail to fulfill their core intellectual function, passing on the Western canon with its concomitant values, and instead contribute to a rise in nihilism. The now common term 'at risk' is indicative of this view that young people are at the brink of failing and dropping out of school, falling prey to drug abuse, becoming gang members, etc.

Much of the public discussion during the nineties centered on efforts, mostly at the state and local school district levels, to tighten controls on academic achievement, especially by way of regimes of impersonal standardized testing with the purpose of holding teachers and schools accountable. This way of thinking has been further strengthened through the *No Child Left Behind* legislation in 2002. According to this legislation schools have to close the achievement gaps between different groups of students, at all age levels in schools, within a dozen years. All students have to reach proficient levels of performance in at least math and reading. Standardized tests analyzed according to 'poverty, race, ethnicity, disability, and limited English proficiency' ('No Child Left Behind', 2002, p. 1) will hold schools and teachers accountable so that no one is 'left behind.' This is of course an unattainable goal. The question thus becomes who is to be blamed for the 'failure' of the students who for a variety of structural and individual reasons do or will not perform at the prescribed level. For example, based on standardized tests 'in 2001, 77 percent of students in New York City did not meet state standards of proficiency in eighth-grade mathematics, and 70 percent failed in reading' (Tyack, 2003, pp. 125-126).

Interestingly, Tyack and Cuban (1995) argue there has never been a golden period when children have known more or done better in schools than they do today. According to the National Assessment of Educational Progress tests student performance was quite level between 1970 and 1990. However, 'both minorities and children from impoverished families... improved their performance on the tests, significantly narrowing the gap between them and Caucasian and middle-class children and youth' (Tyack and Cuban, 1995, p. 37). Thus, while the policy makers are decrying the efforts of students and schools, the data suggest that current performance levels are improving.

Because of the compartmentalized view of young people in the US, the issues about raising academic standards and making everybody proficient in reading and math is disconnected from larger structural inequalities. For example, the gap between the rich and the poor in the US has been increasing for many years. Since 1980, about 20 percent of children under the age of 18 have lived in poverty. In 1999 37 percent of the poor population in the United States were children and youth of which many were homeless (Forum on Child and Family Statistics, 1999). Though the popular perception is that these are urban youth of color, in fact the majority of impoverished youth is Caucasian and many live in rural areas. The US Department of Education estimated the number of homeless students in 1997 to be 630,000 (Stronge, 2000).

Children living in poverty do not only have a very different experience growing up, they also have many fewer opportunities to do well in school. Fewer than half of the 630,000 school aged children who are homeless were estimated to be attending school (National Center for Educational Statistics, 1997). Poor children go to poorly funded schools and are often subjected to what Haberman (1991) calls the pedagogy of poverty where the focus is on keeping students under control through busy work such as endless worksheets. Anyon (1980) showed that working class, middle class, and upper middle class students received a very different education. Poor and wealthy students are tracked into different career paths in high school (Oakes, 1985). However, social class is not discussed much in the US even though it is on everybody's mind. As bell hooks (2000) simply states 'class matters.' The achievement gap between on the one hand White and Asian American students and on the other hand Latino and African American students (Schuman, 2004) makes it almost impossible to talk about academic achievement for adolescents overall in the US Berliner (quoted in Tyack and Cuban, 1995) makes a good counterargument to the politicians' views on our failing schools by stating 'the public school system of the United States has actually done remarkably well as it receives, instructs, and nurtures children who are poor, without health care, and from families and neighborhoods that barely function,' (p. 37) and, we might add, the children with limited English proficiency.

In other words, students (and teachers and schools) are not doing as well as they could, but neither are they doing any worse than before. In fact, a new report found substantial improvements in reading and math among students in the big cities (Council of Great City Schools, 2004). However, because of the way schools and students are framed as failing by politicians and others, the public perception is one of failure. Likewise, we have pointed out the absurdity of testing, researching or establishing educational policies for young people in school as if they all had the same opportunities and lived similar lives. In this debate about failing students and schools, the voices of students are mostly absent. The agency of well over 100 million young people has been largely ignored. The assumption is that they do not know what works for them or what they need in order to get a good education.

Snapshot Two: Sexuality and Teenage Pregnancy

Another example of how public perceptions are influenced by how an issue is framed is teenage pregnancy and motherhood. Teenage pregnancy and motherhood are perceived as highly problematic in a country where people prefer to think of teenagers as not sexually active despite being immersed in a sex-saturated popular culture. Pregnancy, however, proves otherwise. The perception is that teenage pregnancy is a major problem. Interestingly despite the pessimistic reports about declining moral values (Damon, 1995; Mueller, 1999), the teenage pregnancy rate has decreased nationwide substantially. The pregnancy rate has dropped 28 per cent nationwide between 1990 and 2000 to the lowest level on record after peaking in the late 80s (Alan Guttmacher Institute Report, 2004; Kaiser Family Foundation, 2000). Interestingly this declining trend is reaching the media and the public only recently (Rimer, 2004; Kalamazoo Gazette, 2004). Furthermore, contradicting stereotypes about the birth rate for black youth, there was 'an impressive 46 per cent decline among non-Hispanic blacks' aged 15-17 compared to a 35 percent decline among all 15-17 year olds (Bernstein, 2004). Better employment and educational opportunities for poor girls, better birth control programs, and pregnancy prevention programs are credited for the decline.

Our point here is that both researchers and the media are reluctant to publicize positive aspects in young people's lives. Hence, the public is left with the impression that the young continue to live irresponsible and problematic lives. In addition, rarely in research do we hear the voices of teen mothers and fathers themselves. With a few exceptions where the research is focused on the teen parents' own voice (for example, Kelly, 2000 and Holm, 1997) most research on this issue is focused on large-scale data surveys. This methodological contrast is indicative of the tension between positivist views and post-modern perspectives on teenage pregnancy. We are arguing that we need to reconceptualize the way we look at, in this case, teen parents in order to understand and assist them more fully. We need to examine the situation more critically by listening to their voices while not losing sight of the fact that 'despite these declines in the past decades, US teenage pregnancy rates and birthrates are among the highest in the industrialized world' (Manlove, Ryan and Franzetta, 2003, p. 246).

Snapshot Three: Violence

Young people live not only in a culture saturated by sexual images but also saturated with violent images and acts. For example, 'by the end of elementary school, ... [a] student will have seen about eight thousand murders on television and a hundred thousand acts of violence' (Schuman , 2004, p. 306). Violence is considered part of the American everyday life whether in the form of entertainment or as a more generalized fear despite declining crime and murder rates. Young people, and especially African American and Latino males, are often framed as potentially dangerous. Their presence often causes tensions in neighborhoods and schools. Since schools are one of the major playing arenas for young people we will examine the framing of youth as potentially violent in schools.

The public's perception tends to be that schools are dangerous places, even though there are data showing that school violence is rare (Levin, 1998) and that schools are often the safest places for young people. Public perception is mainly due to a series of highly publicized school shootings in the 90s and the fact that gun-related murders increased sharply for young teenagers in the mid-90s (Fuentes, 1998). However, the schools' responses to these shootings have contributed to the violent image schools and young people have attained. Many schools responded by installing a technological armory with everything from metal detectors, bulletproof booths for checking identity cards to see-through backpacks and anticrime videos for students, and crime prevention professional development for school personnel (Devine, 1996). This techno-response 'advances and normalizes the perception that violence and the potential for violence are to be expected' (Farber, 1998, p. 539).

Public and academic debates lead us to believe that young people, especially boys but girls as well, are much more violent than before. Youth politics and policies are taking a punitive path even though research indicates that what students and young people need more than harsh punishment is for adults to know and care for them (Schlosser, 1992; Ladson-Billings, 1994; Devine, 1996). A prime example of these policies is how the regular police force in New York City is arresting students for misbehaving in class, for breaking dress codes, for special education students being unruly, etc. Only a minor number of cases involve actual assaults or weapons. Schools have suffered from severe budget cuts and have eliminated classroom teachers, mental health and social service personnel who normally would have explored the reasons for the misbehavior. Steinberg notes 'the idea that you try to find out why somebody did something or give a person a second chance or try to solve a problem in a way that's not punitive – that's become almost quaint now' (Rimer, 2004, p. 15).

Schools' zero-tolerance regulations are another example of how public and public institutions overreact when problems related to young people are portrayed and perceived as overwhelming. The zero-tolerance policies seemed like a good idea to most parents, teachers, and students when first introduced. Who would object to drug and violence-free schools? Once implemented, though, media have publicized and civil rights groups have vigorously protested the exaggerations of the zero-tolerance laws. One of the most well known cases is the so-called 'Midol-case' where an eighth-grade girl was expelled for giving a Midol tablet she had received from the school nurse to a friend who had menstrual cramps. Her crime was that she gave a drug to another student. However, despite the protests over the harshness of the policies and the fact that schools no longer honor their commitment to educating all children, most school districts now have zero-tolerance laws.

The zero-tolerance law in the State of Michigan is considered among the harshest in the US (Bogos, 1997). According to Polakow-Suransky (2000) this is due to 'its permanent-expulsion mandate, the absence of due process guidelines, the lack of alternative education, and the failure to mandate data collection and reporting' (p. 104). In addition,

> the state of Michigan has never developed a systematic monitoring mechanism to keep track of expelled students despite a federal mandate requiring expulsions to be reported (Gun Free Schools Act, 1994). Consequently, no one knows exactly how many children have been expelled, whether they have been readmitted, or where they have gone…[A] disproportionate number of African American students have been expelled in districts across the state, and in several districts the majority of students expelled are under the age of 16, the cutoff for compulsory attendance in Michigan…Moreover, data indicate that most students are neither reinstated following expulsion…nor are they provided with any form of alternative education. (Polakow-Suransky, 2000, pp. 104-105)

No distinctions are made between students committing assault and students being accused of crimes without evidence or students committing minor offenses by mistake (such as bringing to school a pen knife or scissors that the school considers a potential weapon). Everybody receives the harshest possible punishment (often a one-year expulsion) but no help for improvement or change by the way of alternative education is provided.

Viewing all young people as potentially violent places them in a distinctly threatening role vis a vis the public, and in this way dehumanizes them, further contributing to their lack of agency. Likewise the extreme attempts to control youth do not help young people grow into responsible citizens. With the exception of discussions about gangs, missing from public and research debates on violence in most cases are the voices of the young themselves. We know very little about how they see their schools and living environments in terms of violence. Instead we are left with the monolithic perception that large segments of young people are living in a violent culture without any hope for redemption.

Snapshot Four: Popular Culture, Consumerism and Technology

As we have observed in the first three snapshots of US youth culture, media and academia construct images of youth that imply, as Schuman (2004) observes, that 'the sky is falling' (p. 297), that youth are always in crisis. Youth interaction with popular culture, particularly as consumers, 'create(s) the image of young people as without complexity, as one-dimensional and evil' (Dimitriadis, 2001, p. 7). That is, youth are viewed as being especially susceptible to the manipulations and influences of the popular culture industry (see Weaver and Daspit, 2003). Our goal in this final snapshot is to explore some of the complexities of theorizing about youth without succumbing to tendencies to view youth as monolithic reactors, perpetually in crisis and subject to the whims of media culture. The inherent complexities of studying youth without following more traditional approaches are most evident in explorations of consumerism and technology.

Technology connects post-modern youth and the way they are viewed. Walcott (1997) argues that we are in an era 'when capital accumulation, globalization, and the export of particular erosions of youth culture from America are the basis from which much of the world understands both the rebelliousness of youth and the desire to morally regulate it' (p. 36). Young people themselves see popular culture as an important part of their lives, and rightfully so. Popular culture, and media especially, serves the purposes of entertainment, sensation seeking, coping mechanisms, identity formation, and youth culture identification (Arnett 1995). While adults, liberals and conservatives alike, have perennially held the belief that popular culture has a destructive influence on young people, the reality is that this oppositional stance is more a perception than a reality. This perception is exacerbated by a 'techno-gap,' where many youth are more technologically fluent particularly with computers than are adults, especially parents. This leads to a mutual mistrust and misunderstanding around the meaning of popular culture.

The production of popular culture generally is very youth oriented and its consumption is likewise driven by youth. In the US teenagers 'spend almost $ 100 billion a year and influence how more than $ 300 billion is spent' (Schuman, 2004, p. 304). The general perception among the public as well as among researchers again is that video games, television, and music are full of too much violence and sex. Already in the 1950s parents were horrified by Elvis and his sexually explicit moves (as well as the fact that he brought black music into the white world) and the young loved him! Parents were upset about the Beatles' long hair (and the generational divide it symbolized) and the Rolling Stones' more sexually explicit lyrics. In the 1990s 'gangsta' rap was criticized for targeting 'themes of sexual exploitation of women, violence, and racism' (Arnett, 2001, p. 392). However, not much research has been done on how these messages are interpreted by teenagers who listen to rap songs. Likewise, 'heavy metal music has been accused of promoting suicidal and violent tendencies. However, adolescent heavy metal fans generally report that the music has a cathartic effect on their anger' (Arnett, 2001, p. 392). Additionally, as Schuman points out, sex and violence in popular music are nothing new. There might be changes in nuances, types and degrees but sex and violence have always been part of popular culture and especially popular music. '[C]ountry music has always been violent and sexist. Listen to the music of Hank Williams Jr., or Johnny Cash or even Tennessee

Ernie Ford. Cash, for example, sings about shooting someone "just to see him die"' (Schuman, 2004, p. 305).

Academic researchers have unfortunately perpetuated the general public's perception of youth being manipulated by popular media. Many researchers (for example, Damon, 1995; Mueller, 1999; Berman, 2000; Giroux, 2000) claim the current generation of young people is manipulated by corporate interests or subjected to an increasingly amoral culture. Additionally, scholars have traditionally approached popular culture with suspicion, even disdain (see Weaver and Daspit, 2003). The consequence of such beliefs is that the manners in which popular culture are actually experienced by young people have been sorely undertheorized. In 1954 Robert Warshow declared that the 'unresolved problem of "popular culture" ... (is a) kind of nagging embarrassment to criticism, intruding itself on all our efforts to understand the special qualities of our culture and to define our own relation to it' (2001, xxxvii). Half a century later, Warshow's words still echo. In spite of increased attempts to understand the terrain of the popular and its significance to youth cultures, Warshow's insistence on articulating, and theorizing about, the 'lived experience' of interactions with popular culture has had little impact on dominant modes of cultural criticism. Cavicchi (2002) summarizes prevalent academic attitudes toward the popular:

> (W)ork on popular culture continues to be shaped by an older generation of professors whose understanding is based in either historical or critical analysis, which in both cases interrogate popular culture from an etic, or outsider, perspective. I don't get the feeling from my older colleagues yet that it is okay to actually like, and participate in, popular culture. Much of the current popular culture approach comes out of the cultural studies movement, which finds value in the political resistance of popular culture consumption but remains silent about any other value or role it might have in people's lives. Many of the people I know who study popular culture do so because it is useful in forwarding social change, not because they think the X-Files is cleverly crafted or Charlie Rich songs break their hearts. Stuart Hall's last few lines in his famous essay, 'Deconstructing the Popular,' sum it up: 'Popular culture is one of the sites where (the) struggle for and against a culture of the powerful is engaged. ... That is why popular culture matters. Otherwise, to tell you the truth, I don't give a damn about it' (in Daspit, p. 91).

We believe that popular culture matters, especially as we recognize themes that unify youth, even globally. Post-modern realities, where cultural forms can simultaneously be liberatory and reproduce oppressive structures, are highlighted in the following analysis of technology.

Currently, technological advances in the last half-century have been unprecedented. Provenzo (2000) argues 'Like the Gutenberg revolution, the contemporary computer revolution represents a cultural divide in which traditional models of knowledge, communication and learning have been transformed as a result of new forms of media and information transfer' (p. 5). The proliferation of personal computers and access to the Internet and World Wide Web have certainly allowed for connections across race, class, gender, and sexuality. By 1998, low-income students were equally likely to have access to computers in school as were high-income students (Becker, 2000). Thus, many students may have access to computers and technology while their parents or guardians do not.

But technology is not a neutral entity. The socio-political landscape of technologies is such that neither content nor access are value-free. In fact, Bowers (1988) argues that technologies subordinate all other cultural orientations to a technicist social order. More specifically, Provenzo (2000) argues that many computer simulations used in education make assumptions about power and control, and the need to direct others. This can be applied to other types of computer and video games, which he argues are wrought with racist, sexist and heterosexist assumptions. For example, male characters are portrayed as actors, while female characters are acted upon and viewed more for their secondary sexual characteristics. These kinds of assumptions influence who is likely to consume these games.

While technology seems to unify our sense of youth there is evidence that computer usage varies across youth cultures. Currently, there are a number of digital divides that reify the entrenchment of social and political structures that serve the dominant paradigm, as predicted by Weizenbaum (1976). Clearly, the question of who uses technology is an important one when we consider the role of technology on youth cultures. Social class and ethnicity are immediate and obvious facets of digital divides. While all socioeconomic groups have experienced an increase in computer usage in the home, in 1997 78 per cent of high-income students in grades 7-12 had computer access at home compared to 15 per cent of low income students (National Center for Educational Statistics, 1998). In addition, the quality of the home computer varied by socioeconomic status, with higher income households having higher quality hardware and peripherals (CD-ROM, printers, modems, etc.) than lower income households (Becker 2000). More startling than these data are the findings of a recent study which suggested that even when accounting for socioeconomic status, students of color were less likely to have access to home computers. In addition, this study suggested that students of color were less likely than were white students to access the Internet at a location other than home when a home computer was unavailable ('Dividing Lines', 2001). Hence, all youth are not consuming technology in the same ways.

Gender and sexualities are a second major facet of digital divides. Early on, girls are equally likely to want to interact with technology. Elementary-age girls are equally interested as same aged boys in playing computer and video games, but they would prefer different content (Provenzo, 2000). By high school, the field has shifted somewhat. Schofield (1995) presents an ethnographic study of computer usage in a high school which revealed that the computer lab in the school was claimed by the gifted white males who were both allowed the privilege of using the space in their free time as well as of assisting teachers in the set up and maintenance of the computers in the space. The interaction of content and access serves to disenfranchise women and people of color, thus essentially blocking them from entry into higher paying fields that require knowledge of computing. By the time they are in college, women are perceived as less adept at computing than are men and consequently, women tend to feel less efficacious about computing than do men (Margolis and Fisher, 2002). After twenty years of media that is unresponsive to their wants and needs, female youth still have a qualitatively different experience with technologies. While there is an expectation that this gender gap will decrease as the variety of computer applications increases, efforts to create and market non-sexist game content have been ineffective (Provenzo, 2000). In addition, there may be structural inequalities such as access to high quality computing resources that will drive this facet of the divide.

However, there are complex factors that remind us that such oppressive 'facts' do not tell the whole story, that the intersections of youth and technology do not always reproduce existing inequalities. Couture and Dobson (1997), for example, explore how students co-opt computer e-mail access in the classroom. They conclude that 'student use of the Internet is a playfulness that is most meaningful when it is outside the gaze of the school's sanctioned technology learning outcomes' (p. 35). Sherry Turkle (1995) explores the '(a)nonymous' nature of internet technology, where 'the self is multiple, fluid, and constituted in interaction with machine connections; it is made and transformed by language; (...) and understanding follows from navigation and tinkering rather than analysis. And (...) I meet characters who put me in a new relationship with my own identity' (p. 15). She contends, like Rushkoff (1996) and McRae (1996), that many youth are growing up in such a simulacra, where post-modern philosophies become lived experiences in an incipient apparatus of meaning. Turkle (1995) contends that we need to explore 'how a nascent culture of simulation is affecting our ideas about mind, body, self, and machine' (p. 10). Furthermore, Turkle argues, 'Indeed, in much of this, it is our children who are leading the way, and adults who are anxiously trailing behind' (p. 10).

Quite clearly the consumption of popular culture is an area that youth researchers need to follow closely due to the sheer amount consumed daily by young people. Today we simply do not know enough about how teenagers interpret and rework popular culture. Some research indicates that teenagers look at messages (about, for example, diets in teen magazines) cynically or use popular culture scenarios to try out alternative identities (Holm, 1997). We need to not focus only on the literal popular culture messages but on other more subtle affects. We need research on the possible displacement effect (Strasburger and Donnerstein, 1999) due to the number of hours per day young people spend on popular culture consumption instead of other activities but also on the new ways of communicating (playing video and computer games, chat rooms, instant messaging, systems, etc.) that the new forms of technology and popular culture have given birth to. However, it is also important to remember that adults are complicit in the perceived problems related to popular culture sources in the sense that most of commercialized popular culture is produced by adults. Focusing more on popular culture produced by teenagers themselves might give researchers a more complex and interesting picture of teenagers today.

Conclusions: Possibilities for Reconceptualizing Youth

> We face a cultural landscape that does not make sense in old ways or with old frameworks. (Dimitriadis, 2003, p. xiii)

Modernist perspectives on youth provided a relatively unified vision of youth. At the time, this vision helped to interpret a new and growing segment of the population. As industrialization and urbanization grew, youth were increasingly moved out of the workforce and into schools in order to make room for adult male wage earners (Fasick, 1994). This placed adolescents in the position of being more dependent on the family for a longer period of time as they were schooled. By the middle of the twentieth century, youth had their own culture, and as such, it began to run counter to the adult culture at the time (Coleman, 1961). Thus, in the modernist perspective, youth became defined largely by what they were not and were segregated from the rest of society into secondary schools and universities designed to prepare them for vocations. Youth became colonized by both popular perception and by researchers who argued that adolescents were not capable of authentic agency, but were instead manipulated by, and subject to the vicissitudes of, the popular culture industry (see Weaver and Daspit, 2003).

Post-modern approaches problematized this unified vision of youth and presented a more relativistic view of youth, focusing on the differences among youth experiences. By the latter decades of the 20th century, the discussion had turned to youth cultures, in acknowledgement of the variety of interactions between adolescents and their myriad social contexts. While this shift has been important and fruitful, it remains that youth, as a subject of study, are still colonized both by popular perception and by theoretical frameworks. Youth continue to be both demonized and romanticized by theorists and by adult culture. The federal government as well as foundations continue to support research and programs aimed at solving teenage problems or teenagers as a problem. A most telling example of this kind is a $ 273,000 grant given by the federal government to the city of Blue Springs, Missouri, 'to study the goths, with the intent of preventing kids involved in the subculture from inflicting harm on themselves or the community' (Kurutz, 2004, p. 76). The group of goths might have looked scary to their community because of their dark colors and piercings, and perhaps due to the legacy of the Columbine shootings, this look may have alarmed the community. However, there was no indication that this group was doing anyone any harm. Hence, this example of how influential public perceptions, built to a large extent by the media, of youth as dangerous, also shows the importance of including youth themselves in governing their lives instead of trying to control and change young people from a distance.

In order to avoid a unified and dichotomized view, we argue that as researchers, we need to reconceptualize 'youth' and to engage in more participatory research with youth. We argue that youth policies should not be established *for* youth but based on what we hear from them. We need to hear their voices, learn to understand how they interpret the world, and how they construct the world. As one example, Ruth Vinz (1996) argues that we should be 'more vigilant about what they (youth) are reading on the school bus or subway or in classrooms where they read away those periods between bells' (p. 23). Young people do not perceive, for example, schooling or popular culture in the same way as adults. Symbolic messages carry different meanings for young people. In addition, listening to young people has some methodological implications. It would mean that more research would have to be interactive, qualitative, and interpretative. Youth researchers need to be less problem based and prescriptive.

This does not imply that we accept the voices and actions of youth uncritically. Indeed, in attempting to understand phenomena emerging *from* youth (Daspit, 2000, p. 166), we need to be mindful of the complex ways, as exemplified in our discussion of technology, that youth can simultaneously reproduce socially unjust practices *and* find agency and empowerment. Such research can be found, for example, in Dimitriadis' (2001) explication of the 'unpredictable relationship between contemporary media texts and black youth reception' (McCarthy and Valdivia, in Dimitriadis, p. ix) or Malott and Carroll-Miranda's (2003) exploration of the 'PunKore' subculture and 'how youth have both empowered and contributed to their disempowerment though the PunKore scene' (p. 6).

Such work highlights the necessity of researchers and policy makers to enter, without colonizing, the world of youth before writing about or making policies for them. In his book *Holler if you can hear me* Michie (1999) discusses the necessity for him to listen to his students in order to even attempt to be a good teacher for them. Julio, one of his students, deftly expresses a point that youth researchers would do well to bear in mind:

> People just don't know
> that we are not all gangbangers or drugdealers
> We are people too
> We did not all cross the boarder
> for some of us the boarder crossed us
> We don't always go looking for truble
> truble sometimes comes to us
> So you can't say you know me
> cause you don't
> You don't know where I'm coming from
> and you don't know where I'm going.
> Julio, 14 (quoted in Mitchie, 1999)

References

Alan Guttmacher Institute Report (2004), *US teenage pregnancy statistics with comparative statistics for women aged 20-24*, 19 February, (http://www.guttmacher.org).

'A Nation At Risk', http://www.ed.gov/pubs/NatAtRisk/index.hml.

Anyon, J. (1980), 'Social Class and the Hidden Curriculum of Work', *Journal of Education*, Vol. 162, pp. 67-92

Arnett, J.J. (1995), '"Adolescents" Uses of Media for Self-Socialization', *Journal of Youth and Adolescence*, Vol. 24, pp. 519-533.

Arnett, J.J. (2001). *Adolescence and Emerging Adulthood: A Cultural Approach*, Prentice Hall, Upper Saddle River, New Jersey.

Becker, H.J. (2000), 'Who's Wired and Who's Not: Children's Access to and Use of Computer Technology', *The Future of Children: Children and Computer Technology*, Vol. 10, pp. 44-75.

Berman, M. (2000), *The Twilight of American Culture*, Norton, New York.

Bernstein, N. (2004), 'Young Love, New Caution: Behind Fall in Pregnancy, a New Teenage Culture of Restraint', *New York Times*, 7 March.

Bloom, A. (1987), *The Closing of the American Mind*, Simon and Schuster, New York.

Bogos, P.M. (1997), 'Expelled. No Excuses. No Exceptions – Michigan's Zero-Tolerance Policy in Response to School Violence: M.C.L.A. 380.1311', *University of Detroit Mercy Law Review*, Vol. 74, pp. 357-387.

Bowers, C.A. (1988), *The Cultural Dimensions of Educational Computing: Understanding the Non-Neutrality of Technology*, Teachers College Press, New York.

Christensen, P.G. and Roberts, D.F. (1998), *It's Not Only Rock & Roll: Popular Music in the Lives of Adolescents,* Hampton Press, Cresskill, New Jersey.

Coleman, J.S. (1961), *The Adolescent Society*, Free Press, New York.

Côté, J. (2004), 'Trends in Youth Studies in (English-Speaking) North America', unpublished paper.

Council of the Great City Schools (2004), Press Release Retrieved 25 March, http://www.cgcs.org.

Couture, J.C. and Dobson, T. (1997), 'Stamping Out: Student Use of E-mail in Public School', *JCT: Journal of Curriculum Theorizing*, Vol. 13(4), pp. 31-35.

Damon, W. (1995), *Greater Expectations: Overcoming the Culture of Indulgence in Our Homes and Schools*, Free Press Paperbacks, New York.

Daspit, T. (2000), 'Rap Pedagogies: Bring(ing) the Noise of Knowledge Born on the Microphone to Radical Education', in T. Daspit and J. Weaver (eds), *Popular Culture and Critical Pedagogy: Reading, Constructing, Connecting*, Falmer Press, New York, pp. 163-182.

Daspit, T. (2002), '"We Will Interpret Us": An Interview with Daniel Cavicchi', *JCT: Journal of Curriculum Theorizing*, Vol. 18(2), pp. 89-98.

Devine, J. (1996), *Maximum Security. The Culture of Violence in Inner-city Schools*, University of Chicago Press, Chicago.

Dimitriadis, G. (2001), *Performing Identity/Performing Cultures: Hip Hop as Text, Pedagogy and Lived Practice*, Peter Lang, New York.

'Dividing Lines' (2001), *Education Week*, Vol. 20(35), pp. 12-13, http://counts.edweek.org/sreports/tc01/tc01article.cfm?slug=35divideintro.h20.

Farber, P. (1998), 'J. Devine: Maximum Security', *Contemporary Justice Review*, Vol. 1, pp. 535-547.

Fasick, F.A. (1994), 'On the "Invention" of Adolescence', *Journal of Early Adolescence*, Vol. 14(1), pp. 6-23.

Forum on Child and Family Statistics (1999), *America's Children: Key National Indicators of Well-being, 1999*, US Government Printing Office, Washington DC.

Fuentes, A. (1998), 'The Crack Down on Kids', *The Nation*, 15-22 June, p. 20.

Giroux, H.A. (1997), *Channel Surfing: Race Talk and the Destruction of Today's Youth*, St. Martin's Press, New York.

Giroux, H. (2000), *Stealing Innocence: Corporate Culture's War on Children*, Palgrave, New York.

Grossberg, L. (1996), 'On Post-modernism and Articulation: An Interview with Stuart Hall', in D. Morley and K.H. Chen (eds), *Stuart Hall: Critical Dialogues in Cultural Studies*, Routledge, New York, pp. 131-150.

Haberman, M. (1991), 'The Pedagogy of Poverty Versus Good Teaching', *Phi Delta Kappan*, Vol. 73, pp. 290-294.

Hebdige, D. (1979), *Subculture: The Meaning of Style*, Methuen, London.

Henke, S.M. (2003), 'Urban Education, Broadcast News, and Multicultural Spectatorship', in G. Dimitriadis and D. Carlson, (eds), *Promises to Keep: Cultural Studies, Democratic Education and Public Life*, Routledge Falmer, New York.

Holm, G. (1997), 'Public Texts/Private Conversations: Readings of a Teen Magazine from the Girls' Point of View', *Young*, Vol. 5(3), pp. 20-29.

Holm, G. (1997), 'Teenage Motherhood: Public Posing and Private Thoughts', in J. Jipson and N. Paley (eds), *Daredevil Research*, Peter Lang, New York, pp. 61-81.

hooks, b. (2000), *Where We Stand: Class Matters*, Routledge, New York.

Kaiser Family Foundation (2000), 'Teen Sexual Activity Fact Sheet', www.kff.org/entmedia/upload/ 13722_1.pdf.

Kalamazoo Gazette (2004), 'Parents and Grandparents Alliance Advertisement', 30 January, p. C4.

Kalamazoo Gazette (2004), 'Teenage Births Drop Statewide', 12 January, pp. A1-A6.

Kelly, D.M. (2000), *Pregnant With Meaning*, Peter Lang, New York.

Kurutz, S. (2004), 'Village of the Darned', *Spin*, Vol. 20(3), pp. 74-79.

Ladson-Billings, G. (1994), *The Dreamkeepers. Successful Teachers of African American Children*, Jossey-Bass, San Francisco.

Levin, T. (1998), 'Study Finds No Big Rise in School Crime', *The New York Times*, 28 March, p. 20.

Malott, C. and Carroll-Miranda, J. (2003), 'Punkore Scenes as Revolutionary Street Pedagogy', *Journal for Critical Education Policy Studies*, Vol. 1(2), pp. 1-15, http://www.jceps.com/?pageID=article&articleID=13.

Manlove, J., Ryan, S. and Franzetta, K. (2003), 'Patterns of Contraceptive Use within Teenagers' First Sexual Relationships', *Perspectives on Sexual and Reproductive Health*, Vol. 35(6), pp. 246-255.

Margolis, J. and Fisher, A. (2002), *Unlocking the Clubhouse: Women in Computing*, MIT Press, Cambridge, Massachussetts.

McRae, S. (1996), 'Flesh Made Word: Sex, Text and the Virtual Body', in D. Porter, *Internet Culture*, Routledge, New York, pp. 73-86.

Mitchie, G. (1999), *Holler if You Hear Me. The Education of a Teacher and His Students*, Teachers College Press, New York.

Mueller, W (1999), *Understanding Today's Youth Culture, Revised and Expanded*, Tyndale House, Wheaton, Illinois.

National Center for Educational Statistics (1997), *Digest of Educational Statistics, 1997*, Government Printing Office, Washington DC.

National Center for Educational Statistics (1998), *The Condition of Education*, US Department of Education, Office of Educational Research and Improvement, Washington DC.

National Education Goals Panel (1994), *The 1994 National Education Goals Report*, US Government Printing Office, Washington DC.

'No Child Left Behind' (2002), http://www.ed.gov/nclb/landing.jhtml.

Oakes, J. (1985), *Keeping Track. How Schools Structure Inequality*, Yale University Press, New Haven.

Paley, N. (1995), *Finding Art's Place: Experiments in Contemporary Education and Culture*, Routledge, New York.

Polakow-Suransky, S. (2000), 'America's Least Wanted. Zero-tolerance Policies and the Fate of Expelled Students', in V. Polakov (ed.), *The Public Assault on America's Children*, Teachers College Press, New York.

Provenzo, E.F. (2000), 'Computing, Culture, and Educational Studies', *Educational Studies*, Vol. 31(1), pp. 5-19.

Rimer, S. (2004), 'Unruly Students Facing Arrest, Not Detention', *New York Times*, 4 January, pp. 1, 15.

Roman, L. (1988), 'Intimacy, Labor, and Class: Ideologies of Feminine Sexuality in the Punk Slam Dance', in L. Roman and L. Christian-Smith (eds), *Becoming Feminine: The Politics of Popular Culture*, Falmer, London, pp. 143-184.

Rushkoff, D. (1996), *Media Virus: Hidden Agendas in Popular Culture*, Ballantine Books, New York.

Schlosser, L.K. (1992), 'Teacher Distance and Student Engagement: School Lives on the Margin', *Journal of Teacher Education*, Vol. 43(2), pp. 128-140.

Schofield, J.W. (1995), *Computers and Classroom Culture*, Cambridge University Press, New York.

Schuman , D. (2004), *American Schools, American Teachers*, Pearson, Boston.

Strasburger, V.C. and Donnerstein, E. (1999), 'Children, Adolescents, and the Media: Issues and Solutions', *Pediatrics*, Vol. 103, pp. 129-139.

Stronge, J.H. (2000), 'The Education of Homeless Children and Youth in the United States: A Progress Report', in R.A. Mickelson (ed.), *Children on the Streets of the Americas*, Routledge, New York, pp. 66-76.

Turkle, S. (1995), *Life on the Screen: Identity in the Age of the Internet*, Touchstone, New York.

Tyack, D. (2003), *Seeking Common Ground*, Harvard University Press, Cambridge, Massachusetts.

Tyack, D. Cuban, L. (1995), *Tinkering Toward Utopia. A Century of Public School Reform*, Harvard University Press, Cambridge, Massachussetts.

Vinz, R. (1996), 'Horrorscapes (In)forming Adolescent Identity and Desire', *JCT: Journal of Curriculum Theorizing*, Vol. 12(4), pp. 14-26.

Walcott, R. (1997), 'Sounds/Songs of Black Post-modernity: History, Music, Youth', *Educational Researcher*, Vol. 26(2), pp. 35-38.

Walkerdine, V. (1997), *Daddy's Girl: Young Girls and Popular Culture*, Harvard University Press, Cambridge, MA.

Warshow, R. (2001), *The Immediate Experience: Movies, Comics, Theatre and other Aspects of Popular Culture*, Harvard University Press, Cambridge.

Weaver, J.A. and Daspit, T. (2003), 'Promises to Keep, Finally? Academic Culture and the Dismissal of Popular Culture', in G. Dimitriadis and D. Carlson (eds), *Promises to Keep: Cultural Studies, Democratic Education and Public Life*, Routledge Falmer, New York.

Weizenbaum, J. (1976), *Computer Power and Human Reason*, Freeman, San Francisco.

Willis, P. (1981), *Learning to Labour: How Working Class Kids Get Working Class Jobs*, Columbia, New York.

Chapter 5

Social Changes and Multicultural Values of Young People

Helena Helve

If it is right that some people die of hunger, so why do I have things so good? What privilege do I have with respect to it? I've often thought that I ought to suffer, too, but when I thought about this matter I thought that I can't really do anything about the poverty in the developing countries. Now I'm just thankful for what I've received and I pray that the poverty-stricken will get rich at some time. I don't know if that was thought out correctly. (Female, secondary school student from Helsinki)

Everyone wants money, it's so indispensable in today's society, it keeps you going physically and materially, without it you can't do anything. (Male, secondary school student from Helsinki)

The Greens have the right idea, but I'm somewhat critical of their system. They ought to organize, now a confused image has become associated with them…a little less fanaticism. I followed one of their meetings… Linkola[1] has been called ecofacist and that is certainly a correct characterization… (Female, secondary school student from Helsinki)

Introduction

This chapter uses the data of empirical studies of attitudes, values and value structures of young Finns.[2] The comparative and longitudinal data of 16-19 year-old young Finnish people was gathered for the first time during the economic boom in Finland in 1989, for the second time during the economic recession in 1992 and for the third time in 1995-96 when Finland was recovering economically. The article focuses on the social and economic impact on the attitudes and values of secondary school, vocational and business school students in rural (Ostrobothnia) and in urban (Helsinki) Finland. The differences in and essential features of the attitude and value structures were investigated. The results supported the research hypothesis that the values of young people were a reflection of deeper economic and social changes of society's values (Helve 2001, pp. 201-218). Factor analysis were used to summarize the attitude data, which embraced politics, environment, participation, work and family.

In this chapter the results will be analysed in the framework of multiculturalism. After raising the question of what 'multiculturalism' means in general usage and in youth research, the chapter argues that among some of the younger generation a new ecological biocentric perspective has emerged which challenges, for example, anthropocentrism. Focusing on research in Finland, the chapter analyses the significance of shifts in generational and gender values and uses a typology to differentiate young people's attitudes along a spectrum ranging from groups such as humanist – egalitarians and environmentalist – greens to racists.

The findings in 1995-6 showed that young people had different types of values when Finland recovered from the economic recession. It was possible to find among 16 to 19 year-old young people (N = 457) five value dimensions which were called: 1) Humanism 2) Traditionalism 3) Environmentalism 4) Political – Cynicism and 5) Globalism. Different attitudes and values arose from different educational backgrounds. There was also a difference in values between the sexes. The results are discussed in the broader context of values and attitudes of European young people.

Multiculturalism, Attitudes and Values

In this chapter I interpret 'multiculturalism' in the framework of the empirical data of attitudes and values of young people who live in a society which can be seen as culturally homogenous.[3] However the internet and new mass media have ignored the traditional Finnish values. Globalization challenges the new multicultural values, which are distinctive in our 'postmodern world' with postmaterialistic value worlds (Inglehart, 1997). Multiculturalism is associated with the process of the culturalization of people's everyday life, which it is possible to investigate in the interdisciplinary framework of linguistic discourses and textual writings, within academic disciplines such as sociology, anthropology and psychology, and cultural and media studies.

What is multiculturalism in young people's everyday lives? Is it cultural differences with equal rights as citizens (see Helve, 1998, pp. 211-221; 1997b, pp. 228-233)? Is it pluralism in values and ethical issues and neutrality in the public sphere? It should in these cases mean the rule of treating all people equally. Is it freedom of speech, thought, religion and association? It should mean here that no one should be manipulated to accept the cultural values of the majority.

Multiculturalism often seems to be among the concepts or slogans which have been generated by academics, politicians and the media. The concept of multiculturalism varies also in discussions. For example it is discussed in Finland in the terms on the assimilation of immigrant ethnic minorities (Vainikainen, 2003). Thus, the definition of multiculturalism seems to depend upon the context in which it is discussed. Also, the concept of multiculturalism is constantly changing.

In an interpretation of multiculturalism, the culture is recognized to include learned patterns of behaviour, traditions, ways of thinking and acting, attitudes, values and morals. In Nordic countries such as Finland, the debate about multiculturalism has been raised by multicultural education (see, for example, Suurpää, 1998). This demonstrates a concern among parents and educators about the ethnocentric and racist beliefs and attitudes of young people. The questions are: How multicultural are young people? Do they have racist beliefs, and if they do, how can we see it in their world views and values?

We can think about these questions by imagining two pictures of multicultural young people. First, imagine a picture of children from different cultural and also religious backgrounds standing together; this is an ideal view of educational multiculturalism, reflecting solidarity and tolerance – we hope that these children will be future cosmopolitans. In the second picture is a cosmopolitan of today – a young skinhead with a hair style which comes from England, a personal stereo from Japan, jeans and boots from the USA, music from Afro-Caribbean culture and thoughts maybe from an Austrian Adolf. He seems to be very multicultural. Should we respect his individualized identity and values of nationalism and racism (see Gutmann, 1994, pp. 21-22)?

Young people share many of the same experiences or information spread by the mass media with shared, global life experiences, exemplified by such things as fears of terrorism, war or environmental damage. These experiences awaken in young people different types of questions concerning life. The following question was used in my longitudinal study of worldviews (Helve, 1993a) to identify the problems in young people's lives: 'We sometimes think about some things which are difficult to understand. I have recently been thinking about something I have thought about before, and which I would like to understand. I have been thinking about…'. The question was evidently difficult, since many left it unanswered. The classification of the answers was also difficult. For example the answer could be something relating to the surrounded society and globe as well as the universe, death and suffering. Many also answered that 'I haven't thought about anything more serious which I don't understand' or 'I don't remember', and 'I can't say' were also added. Questions concerning the environment, society and the entire globe, the universe, death and suffering were most common for more than half of females (61 per cent). One example is: 'Why are there so many poor people, laboratory experiment animals, weapons and criminals?'. A third of males (28 per cent) had questions relating to their own lives such as 'What will I become when I'm an adult?' and 'How can I succeed in my life?'. Also questions concerning the home and parents were represented: 'Why do my parents always have to fight?' and 'Why don't I get along with my stepfather?'. Almost half thought about social and world problems: 'Why is it that some people in the world are doing all right, while others are in real distress, with famine and the like?', or 'Why is it that people may become handicapped, alcoholics, or drug abusers?'. Concrete problems presented were connected with earning a living, 'finding a solution to my lack of money'.

The young people conceptualized themselves both as part of humanity and the world. They kept up with world affairs. This could be seen in their attitude towards the future as well as in their fears. Their experiences and insights followed international trends. Concerns and speculation about the whole world did not, however, appear to play a role in their individual expectations and values concerning the future. Peace, for example, was not among the most important values. The values of females and males differed. The males emphasized the importance of health and of acquiring a good standard of living, while the females were interested in success and relationships with other people (Helve, 1993a, pp. 152-181).

It seems that young people today live in a reflexive modernity where they have to be flexible and adaptable (see Beck 1992; Fornäs 1995; Giddens, 1994; Helve, 2001). Does this mean that we accept the post-modern thesis about the death of great narratives like humanism, socialism, communism or Christianity (Fornäs, 1995, p. 214; Lyotard, 1984, 1985)? What is coming instead of those ideologies? My study (Helve, 1993a, 1993b) has given evidence that there is an ideological – maybe even a religious – base in the new ecological biocentric perspective which challenges, for example, anthropocentrism. There are young people who equally respect other life forms like animals, plants and ecosystems. In their view animals and plants even have the same moral rights as people.

Generational and Gender Value Shifts

The Dutch researchers Henk Vinken and Peter Ester have presented the hypothesis that the more modern a country and society is as a whole, the more progressive are the values which have spread among its people. Conversely, the less difference there is between the values of different generations, the less developed the country is in comparison with these modern societies (Vinken and Ester, 1992; see also Appiah, 1994, pp. 156-158). On the other hand, in modern societies there has been a change in adult roles that maybe makes the older generation more similar to the younger ones, and thus diminishes generation gaps (see the concept of arrested adulthood, Côté, 2000). This may therefore sometimes be the result of cultural modernization rather than an indication that it has not occurred (Fornäs, 1995, p. 247).

I think that animal rights activism can be classified as a sort of modern value system. Considering the differences in values between generations in advanced Western countries brings up another interesting question of gender: are girls more interested in animal rights (see the name 'fox girls') than boys? In my own research it has become apparent that girls are more willing than boys to compromise their standard of living in order to reduce pollution and environmental problems (Helve, 1997a, pp. 154-155).

European value studies (for example Friesl et al., 1993; Vinken and Ester 1992; Commission of the European Communities, 1991, 1993; see also Vinken et al., 2004) have also shown how young people's environmental awareness throughout Europe has increased since the 1980s and interest in ecological issues has grown. At the same time there has been an increase in gender equality within the younger generation. The fences protecting gender roles are coming down. Young people, both boys and girls, are more diversified than before in their goals in life and more willing to approve of alternative lifestyles. Comparative longitudinal studies (see Helve, 1993a) indicate that there is widespread distrust of societal institutions, such as political parties.

The content of mass media, for example television series which are alien to life, provides young people with unrealistic conceptions of life. These can be seen as improbable expectations and aspirations, regarding such things as choice of a profession. The mass media form the views that children and adolescents have of the world. On the other hand, the young people themselves are also aware of this, as we see from this quotation of a male (Helve, 1993a):

The American series are made with a purpose... that people just live and there are no troubles, and if some do pop up, they're solved with the snap of a finger. This is a completely deceptive device...the advertisements certainly do their thing...images which give a positive slant on life surely stimulate the greatest desire to buy things.

The mass media also provide young people with a picture of how political decision-makers take care of the problems of our society in addition to showing what kind of people they are, as demonstrated by the following interview of a male (Helve, 1993a):

I'm not generally able to get interested in anything political, what you see in TV is what they read directly from the paper, they don't have any opinions of their own...(politics) no longer holds any interest for me.

The attitudes of the young people studied to politics was sceptical and critical. This can be understood in term of their life situation, their uncertainty about employment, and the shortage of places to study. A diffuse, unstructured but positive attitude towards politics takes shape when an individual is satisfied with his living conditions, such as his/her education professional opportunities, and work. Unemployment also lowers young people's political activity (Helve, 2002).

The collective belief of young people during the sixties and seventies that together they could bring about a better world could still be seen in Finland in the peace marches of the early eighties, but these had faded by the middle of that decade. In place of this meta-narrative came a progressively growing concern with individual peace of mind and small scale micro-narratives (Helve, 1993a and 1993b; Helve, 2002).[4]

Multicultural Value-Systems of Young Finns[5]

This chapter combines the findings of the data of the longitudinal study with the data of the comparative study. The purpose is to describe attitudes and values of young people and their changes during the 1990s using these different data sets. The first data was collected in 1989-90 from 240 persons aged 16-17 and 19-20 in the Helsinki area and in some rural localities. The sample included 107 upper secondary school pupils, 52 vocational school pupils, 27 university students plus 54 working young people; the girls numbered 123 and boys 117. Of these young people, 165 participated in follow-up study three years later in 1992-93. A comparative data was gathered in 1995-96 from 457 aged 16-19 students of secondary schools, vocational schools and business schools in the same localities as six years before. The sample included 229 males and 228 females.

The following quantitative and qualitative methods of data collection were used: questionnaires, word association, and sentence completion tests, attitude scales and group-focused interviews which were complemented by pictures. The attitude scales were formulated in the same way as the attitude survey conducted by the Centre for Finnish Business and Policy Studies in 1989 (EVA, 1991). The interviews were videotaped. The results were analysed using multivariate statistical methods (for example the method of factor analysis) and by a content analysis. Different methods in the analysis of quantitative and qualitative data were used to complement each other.

The primary reason for using the factor analysis was to clarify the connections between the variables and to create a descriptive system which would be as simple as possible. The same technical solutions for the analysis were used in each of the three stages of the study. The same variables which were common to the entire set of 452 variables in the three stages of the study, covered issues concerned with politics, environment, science and technology, economics, nationalism, gender equality, human rights, participation, work and family values.[6]

The theoretical starting point of my empirical research project was the assumption that the evolution of post-industrial society has caused, and will presumably continue to cause, numerous changes that are first seen in young people. A three-phase study suggested that the following main attitude dimensions could be constructed by factor analysis: Humanism, Individualism and Traditionalism (see Tables 5.1, 5.2 and 5.3).[7]

Humanistic beliefs and values included such humanist ideas as respecting the beliefs of conscientious objectors; readiness to tolerate a reduction in one's own standard of living in order to reduce pollution and environmental problems; concern for the unemployed, sick, disabled and other disadvantaged groups; and the belief that the standard of living is so high that better care should be taken of the underprivileged in society. Such views show that the attitude structure of those who fall under this category stems from a Christian humanist set of values. Further evidence of this is a positive attitude towards foreigners arriving in the country and an unselfish willingness to increase foreign development aid irrespective of needs at home. The construction of a fifth nuclear reactor is not considered worthwhile, and there is little faith that science and technology will be able to solve the majority of today's problems. This belief system is also comprised of attitudes demonstrating a critical stance towards science, technology and continuous economic growth. The attitudes incorporated in this belief system may be regarded as progressive. They include attitudes to be found in the ideologies of, for example, the Green movement, Christian social action groups and the political Left. Many of these attitudes were already fashionable in the 1960s and 70s (see Tipton, 1984).

Comparing the humanistic belief system in the first phase of the study (1989), the position that development aid to foreign countries should be increased even if there are people in need of help in Finland was lower in the second and third phases of the study, when the Finnish economy (measured by per capita GDP) was no longer the third highest in the world (after Japan and Switzerland) but had slipped way down the rank. Unemployment rates for young people had grown rapidly. In the second phase (1992-93), when the economic crisis was deepest, the growth in the popularity of the beliefs that 'Science and technology are beginning to control people instead of serving them', and 'Economic growth is not the only possible basis for continuous social welfare', could be interpreted to show that there were more young people who were critical towards science and technology, believing that they have not helped the world (for example, because they are creating environmental problems) and that more young people were seeking other solutions than economic growth as the basis of a good life. In the third phase (1995-96) the beliefs that 'The construction of a fifth nuclear power plant should not be supported' and 'Science and technology are beginning to control people instead of serving them' had reached new heights. The critiques towards science and technology had grown among young humanists. Also the attitude towards developing economic welfare had become increasingly critical (Table 5.1).

Table 5.1   Factor 'Humanism'

	1989	1992	1995-96
We should have more respect for the conviction of a conscientious objector	.65	.58	.57
I am willing to lower my standard of living in order to decrease pollution and environmental problems	.55	.61	.71
Our standard of living is so high that we must have the means to care for the unemployed, the sick, the disabled and other people who are badly off	.54	.56	.68
If more foreign people came to Finland these contacts would be mutually beneficial	.52	-	-
Science and technology are beginning to control people instead of serving them	.44	.66	.77
Developing economic welfare even further will result in an illfare state	.41	.60	.72
Development aid to foreign countries should not be increased as long as there are people in need of help in Finland	-.70	-.56	-.60
Economic growth is the only possible basis for continuous social welfare	-.63	-.66	-.69
The building of a fifth nuclear power plant is to be supported	-.57	-.57	-.81
In the future, science and technology will solve most of today's problems	-.49	-.56	-.70

Young people's changed set of values and beliefs reflected the then current economic recession. The humanist youth's willingness to sacrifice their standard of living in order to solve environmental and pollution problems increased. More young people also subscribed to the notion that science and technology are becoming the master instead of the servant of human beings. For humanists the economic recession signified the need for a more critical look at the foundations of welfare for humankind. They believed that welfare could not depend solely on economic progress. It was also clearer to them that the progress of science and technology had not helped solve ecological problems or inequities in the distribution of income in society.

The *Individualistic* belief system represented highly pessimistic attitudes concerning traditional party politics. Attitudes based on an individualistic set of values expressed no personal interest in public political matters. This does not mean that at the personal and private level they are not interested in political matters (see Biorcio et al., 1995, pp. 35-36). Throughout all phases of the study their most common belief was that, 'People's opinions don't have much influence on social and political decisions'. According to this thinking, an individual cannot have faith in the fundamental political institutions of society, since they have no regard for the opinions of the ordinary citizen. No political party stands for matters of importance to them. Such values presumably imply that a person can trust only in himself or herself, because the institutions of society are far removed from him or her. It can also be assumed that those displaying attitudes belonging to this category are modern, critical young people who have not inherited the values and attitudes of traditional ideologies.

This individualistic attitude structure was manifested in an increasingly critical view of society which spread during the 1990s. The political cynicism and pessimism of individualists towards parties and party politics has increased in the wake of economic difficulties. They felt that parties had drifted away from the problems of ordinary people, and as a result, people have to cultivate individual happiness and navigate through life without political/societal systems (Table 5.2).

Table 5.2   Factor 'Individualism' or 'Political – Cynicism'

	1989	1992	1995-96
People's opinions don't have much influence on social and political decisions	.74	.74	.88
The political parties have become estranged from ordinary people and their problems	.65	.72	.84
None of the political parties advocate things that are important for me	.63	.65	.72
In modern society you have to be bold if you want to succeed	.36	-	-
It is a privilege to be Finnish	-.34	-	-

Traditionalism comprised traditional Finnish attitudes, behind which lay a conservative attitude structure. Examples include a desire to prevent depopulation of the countryside, belief that abusers of social benefits, idlers and 'spongers' have it too easy in Finland, a high regard for the Finnish 'fatherland', manifested in the belief that it is fortunate and a privilege to be a Finn. This nationalistic attitude loaded highest in the 1995-96 study. Also the attitudes towards foreigners had become stronger. These attitudes are evidently those of young people for whom the fatherland, religion, honesty and industry still constituted important values (Table 5.3).

Table 5.3   Factor 'Traditionalism'

	1989	1992	1995-96
Migration to Greater Helsinki should be controlled so that the whole country will remain populated and inhabitable	.69	.63	.68
People who take unfair advantage of the social services, idlers and spongers, are treated far too well	.51	-	-
Science and technology are beginning to control people instead of serving them	.50	-	-
It is a privilege to be Finnish	.52	.57	.74
You will always find a job if you are skilled and hard-working	.49	.47	-
If more foreign people came to Finland these contacts would be mutually beneficial	-	-.53	-.66
We should have more respect for the conviction of a conscientious objector	-	-	-.59

According to the findings of the 1995-96 survey, it was possible to divide young people into five different groups with regard to their values.[8]

Humanist – Egalitarians stressed gender equality, for example in working life, and also in family life. They were willing for a woman to be their boss and in their opinion it is equally important for a woman to go to work as for a man. Men and women both need to earn money and take care of the home and the family. In their opinion there should be more women bosses in important jobs and they think that there is not too much talk about gender equality. They would not mind if their children went to a school where half of the children were of another 'race'. In their mind it is very important to live according to one's conscience and everyone should have freedom to live as he or she likes but everyone has also an individual responsibility for example in environmental issues (Appendix 2; Table 5.7).

The most *Traditionalist – Conservative* values were found among secondary school boys and most urban girls were against such values. These values were very conservative, such as 'Couples who have children should not divorce', 'Marriage is for life' and 'Young people today don't respect traditional values enough'. They supported the opinion that 'Our country needs strong leaders who can restore order and discipline and respect for values'. Rural young people valued family values more than urban young people. With respect to gender differences, girls valued humanism and equality more than boys, who valued technology and economic welfare more (Appendix 2; Table 5.8).

The *Environmentalist – Greens* stressed environmental green values and were mostly female upper-secondary school students. In their opinion, the development of economic welfare should not be taken any further. Nuclear energy should be given up, even if this would result in a decrease in the standard of living. They believed that the continued raising of economic wellbeing only increases mental illness and that science and technology are beginning to control people instead of serving them. They were willing to lower their standard of living in order to decrease pollution and environmental problems. They also believed that 'Even young people can promote world peace by participating in peace work' (Appendix 2; Table 5.9).

Political – Cynicism was seen in statements such as 'Citizens' opinions don't have much influence on the decisions made in society' and 'The political parties have become estranged from ordinary people and their problems' (Appendix 2; Table 5.10).

A new group of values was global (see 'Generation Global', Watson, 1997). *Internationational globalists* thought that if more foreign people came to Finland these contacts would be mutually beneficial. In their opinion it was not a privilege to be a Finnish and 'East, West, home is best' was an obsolete phrase (Appendix 2; Table 5.11).

In the variance analysis, significant differences in the values of boys and girls were found.[9] Girls more than boys valued environmental issues, urban secondary school girls most of all. Boys (including most urban secondary school boys) valued technology and science more than girls. Vocational school urban girls were the most politically passive and critical of politics. The most active in politics were urban secondary school girls. Business school students mostly valued technology and economic welfare, whereas secondary school students were most critical about them. Green values were given as an alternative to technological and economic values. On the other end of the spectrum from International globalists were 'Racists', who were more often boys, the majority of them studying in vocational or business schools and colleges. The most humanistic values were found among secondary school girls.

Several studies have demonstrated that girls and boys perceive the world in different ways (Dahlgren, 1977; Helve, 1993a, 1996 and 2004; Rauste-von Wright et al., 1975). For girls the formation of both identity and perception of the world is effected by the framework of their gender. Many cultures regard 'soft' values as being feminine. The different values associated with the gender stereotypes created by a patriarchal society are evident. School, peer groups and commercial mass entertainment convey sexual stereotypes which guide the viewpoints held by young people and manifest themselves in matters such as their career choices.

The deteriorating economic situation in Finland was reflected in young people's more rigid attitudes regarding for instance refugees and development aid. Whereas in 1989 every other boy and every fifth girl were of the opinion that development aid should not be increased as long as people in Finland needed help, three years later (1992) almost every second girl (40 per cent) and a clear majority of boys (66 per cent) thought so. This has not changed since: in 1995-1996 40 per cent of girls and 57 per cent of boys were against increases in development aid as long as there is need in Finland (Table 5.4).

Table 5.4 'Development aid to foreign countries should not be increased as long as there are people in need of help in Finland' (comparison of 1989, 1992 and 1995-1996; percentage values)

			1989	1992	1995-96
Total	Agree		35.2	51.2	48.5
	Difficult to say		16.7	15.4	19.0
	Disagree		48.1	33.3	32.5
Sex	Agree	Girls	21.4	40.2	40.5
		Boys	50.0	65.7	57.1
	Difficult to say	Girls	15.7	17.4	16.4
		Boys	17.9	12.9	21.7
	Disagree	Girls	62.9	42.4	43.1
		Boys	32.1	21.4	21.2

In 1989 young people (84 per cent of girls and 73 per cent of boys) still considered the standard of living high enough in Finland for the country to afford to take better care of the unemployed and other disadvantaged population groups. These attitudes also grew more negative towards these groups, although well over half (78 per cent of girls and 59 per cent of boys) were still of the same opinion in 1992.

This shows that the decrease in the standard of living has affected young people's attitudes. Although in 1995-1996 more than half of them considered Finland's standard of living so high that it could take better care of the unemployed and the disadvantaged, nevertheless the overall figures had gone down (68 per cent of girls and 51 per cent of boys were of this opinion; Table 5.5).

Table 5.5 'Our standard of living is so high that we must have the means to care for the sick and other people who are badly off' (comparison of 1989, 1992 and 1995-1996; percentage values)

			1989	1992	1995-96
Total	Agree		79.0	69.8	59.8
	Difficult to say		12.4	17.9	27.4
	Disagree		8.6	12.3	12.8
Sex	Agree	Girls	84.3	78.3	67.5
		Boys	73.2	58.5	51.4
	Difficult to say	Girls	10.7	14.1	22.7
		Boys	14.3	22.9	32.4
	Disagree	Girls	5.0	7.6	9.8
		Boys	12.5	18.5	16.2

Most young people (66 per cent of girls and 77 per cent of boys) in 1989 thought that Finland was too indulgent with regard to people who abuse the social welfare system, the lazy and other 'spongers'. The most uncompromising attitudes in this respect were found among the young working population. In 1992 girls had grown more adamant regarding those who abuse social welfare (70 per cent), whereas boys had become more lenient (66 per cent).

The Finnish study showed that girls were not as aware of party politics as boys. For many of them politicians were, 'fat old men who lie to people'. This critical stance taken by many girls heralds the birth of a new type of political culture. Girls held attitudes which were more global than those held by boys. They were more willing to increase aid to developing countries, they were more willing to accept refugees and they were also more critical than boys with respect to the capacity of science and technology to solve the problems of our era. Most but not all of the girls expressed humanistic values. The space within which girls can move has expanded, and it has provided them with the possibility of being either 'soft' or 'hard'. Girls' perceptions of the world seem to be more varied and open than those of boys.

Collective consciousness of such things as the kinds of role expectations which are directed towards women arises within a social context. The situation experienced by mothers, sisters, and girl friends, for instance, indirectly provide girls with information about the essence and role of being a woman. Various theories of cultural influence claim that the media have a great influence on their audience. They create beliefs, attitudes and values according to which people interpret the world. The differences in girls' and boys' values and attitudes cannot be explained as simply biological. The only personality difference that can be shown to have biological roots, perhaps, is the level of aggressive activity (Campbell, 1993). Parents and society tend to respond to girls differently than to boys. These differences and social influences have to be considered. One social explanation is in terms of the divergent socialization of girls and boys. Another explanation is in terms of gender roles and culture.

Discussion

There are still insufficient empirical data to conclude that young people have core values. My studies have shown that most young people's attitudes and values are not anchored in any political, religious or other ideology. They feel free to change their views according to the situation. The attitudes and values of young people are in many cases contradictory and unanalytical. The same person can consider equality a good thing in a certain context, while expressing for example very racist opinions in another (see also Helve, 2001 and 2002).

Inglehart's comparative value study described contemporary changes using the categorical designations of 'materialist' and 'postmaterialist' values (Inglehart, 1977, pp. 27-28; 1990; 1997). Inglehart presented a hypothesis of scarcity, according to which people generally consider whatever resources are scarce enough to be important, and people's basic needs and values thus reflect the socio-economic situation of society (Inglehart 1977, 1990, 1997). He claims that the postmodern period is connected with the postmaterialist value world, which criticizes the modern and materialist value world. My results indicate that postmaterialist values are to be found among Finnish young people as well. They are found especially among humanists supporting gender and racial equality and among international cosmopolitans. These young people support cultural differences with equal rights as citizens. The greens also expressed postmaterialist ideas in their criticism of the raising of the material standard of living and in being willing to lower their standards of living in order to eliminate nuclear power.

However, people's multiple needs, attitudes and values form a more conflictual value world than for example Inglehart's typology suggests. One person may have very different needs, attitudes and values, a portion of which are materialist and a portion of which are postmaterialist. For example, my study of Finnish young people's value systems indicates a decline in postmaterialist values among young people during the recent period of economic recession. Although a proportion of young people can be described as humanist multiculturalists, among them attitudes to poor people and foreigners became sharper as the result of the recession, just as they did among the individualists. Economic scarcity can thus be seen in the increase in materialistic values and xenophobia. Young people, however, do value things other than material goods. Most young people are tolerant and ready to compromise their own standard of living, among other things, in order to protect the environment and help those less fortunate.

According to Inglehart, those who are postmaterialists in their value world are more ready to give economic help to poor countries and are also more concerned about women's rights (Inglehart, 1977, p. 30). We can interpret that young people's values are generally postmaterialistic and multicultural (see also Inglehart, 1977, 1990, p. 76). Recent research, however, has indicated that traditional attitudes of nationalism and racism are still widespread (see Inglehart, 1990, p. 3; Vinken and Ester, 1992, p. 411). Not all the new national political movements within Europe – with such diverse concerns as environmental issues, peace or human and animal rights, fighting poverty or promoting equal rights for developing countries or between genders – can be considered expressions of postmaterialist values and multiculturalism.

The attitudes and values in the framework of multiculturalism are difficult to discuss because there is not a clear concept of multiculturalism. Anyway I think that multiculturalism stems from a learning process. According to this way of thinking, multiculturalism is a part of the values of the culture of a society or social group.[10] Young people learn cultural values in their own society but they also adopt different values from global (youth) cultures, the media or the internet. In a modern 'monocultural' homogenous society (like Finland) young people seem to be free to change their national monocultural values to international multicultural values according to the situation.

Appendix 1

Table 5.6   The phases and methods of the research

1989	**Phase 1**	**Methods**
	16-19 year olds	• Questionnaires
	123 girls, 117 boys (n = 240)	• Word association and sentence completion tests
		• Individual and group focused interviews (video taped)
		• Attitude scales
1992-93	**Phase 2**	**Methods**
	Follow-up study	• Questionnaires
	19-22 year olds	• Word association and sentence completion tests
	93 girls, 72 boys (n = 165)	• Attitude scales
1995-96	**Phase 3**	**Methods**
	Comparative study	• Questionnaires
	16-19 year olds	• Word association and sentence completion tests
	228 female, 229 male (n = 457)	• Attitude scales

Appendix 2 Factors and loadings

Table 5.7 Factor 1: 'Humanism – Egalitarians'

	F 1	F 2	F 3	F 4	F 5
I would not want a woman to be my boss	-.62				
It is less important for a woman to go to work than it is for a man	-.60				
A man's job is to earn money and a woman's job is to take care of the home and the family	-.58				
It's very important to me to live according to my conscience	.51				
There should be more women bosses in important jobs in business and industry	.51				
I would not mind if my child went to a school where half of the children were of another race	.40				(.39)
There is too much talk about gender equality	-.40				
Saving is an obsolete virtue	-.39				
Everyone should have the freedom to live as one likes	.37				
Individual person's acts have no mentionable effect on the state of nature	-.36				
I am willing to lower my standard of living in order to decrease pollution and environmental problems	.30		(.44)		
The building of a fifth nuclear power plant is to be supported	-.30		(-.40)		
There are situations where military action is allowed, for example, when a country defends its independence	.30				

Table 5.8   Factor 2: 'Traditionalism – Conservatives'

	F 1	F 2	F 3	F 4	F 5
Couples who have children should not Divorce		.61			
Marriage is for life		.55			
Young people today don't respect the traditional values enough		.51			
Divorce is too easy to get these days		.50			
Our country needs strong leaders who can restore order and discipline and the respect of right values		.44			

Table 5.9   Factor 3: 'Environmentalism – Greens'

	F 1	F 2	F 3	F 4	F 5
Further development of economic welfare should not be carried out			.56		
Nuclear energy should be abandoned even if it would cause a decrease in the standard of living			.54		
The continued development of economic well-being only increases mental ill-being			.53		
Science and technology are beginning to control people instead of serving them			.48		
I am willing to lower my standard of living in order to decrease pollution and environmental problems	(.30)		.44		
Even young people can promote world peace by participating in peace work			.40		
The building of a fifth nuclear power plant is to be supported	(-.30)		-.40		
Economic growth is the only possible basis for continuous social welfare			-.39		
Development aid to foreign countries should not be increased as long as there are people in need of help in Finland			-.35		
We should have more respect for the conviction of a conscientious objector			.32		(.39)
Our standard of living is so high that we must have the means to care for the unemployed, the sick, the disabled and other people who are badly off			.31		

Table 5.10   Factor 4: 'Cynicism – Political Passives'

	F 1	F 2	F 3	**F 4**	F 5
Citizens' opinions don't have much influence on the decisions made in society				.65	
The political parties have become estranged from ordinary people and their problems				.59	
None of the existing political parties advocate things that are important for me				.49	

Table 5.11   Factor 5: 'Internationalism – Globalists'

	F 1	F 2	F 3	F 4	**F 5**
If more foreign people came to Finland, we would benefit from useful international influence					.49
It is a privilege to be Finnish					-.46
'East West, home is best' is an obsolete phrase					.44
I wouldn't mind if my child went to a school where half of the children were of another race	(.40)				.39
We should have more respect for the convictions of a conscientious objector			(.32)		.39

Notes

1   Pentti Linkola is a controversial personality in Finland. A fisherman, he has gained some notoriety by advocating unmitigated Darwinism as the solution to ecological problems.
2   See Appendix 1, Table 5.6.
3   Finland is religiously a coherent country: 85.3 per cent of all Finns belong to the Evangelic – Lutheran church, 1.1 per cent to the Orthodox Church and 1 per cent to other religious communities; 12.6 per cent are not involved to religious communities. Being a member of the church and using its services, as rites of passage at the special occasions of life are part of Finnish culture. Most children are baptized as church members, and over 90 per cent of 15-year olds are confirmed in the Lutheran church (Statistics of Finland, 2000).
4   See, for example, Bourdieu, 1987; Fraser and Nicholson, 1991, pp. 373-394. Lyotard (1985) theoretically categorizes as postmodern those contemporary western countries in which meta-narratives no longer legitimize issues. Some examples of these sorts of narratives, which directed the value worlds of previous generations, were the development of rationalism and liberalism by the philosophy of the Enlightenment, and the Marxist theory of class conflict culminating in revolution. With the help of these narratives various

facts, policies and ideologies qualified as true and legitimate paradigms, according to which actions could also be judged to be right (see also Van Dijk, 1998).

5   My chapter is based upon two empirical longitudinal studies of world views (Helve, 1993a) and attitudes and values of young Finns (Helve, 1993b, 1995, 1996 and 2002). Over the last few years I have led the project, Values, World views and Gender (Helve, 1997). Now I'm carrying out a project on social capital and identity formation of young people financed by the Academy of Finland. In the project we have also examined trends in the values of young people in Finland and elsewhere in Europe.

6   The 19 variables used to measure attitudes principal components followed by varimax rotation produced a comparable three-factor result in the different phases of the study. Also factor scores were computed for each subject on these three factors. Because of the generally high level of the factor loadings a minimum cut off for significance was set at .40. Each individual was given a factor score to show the extent to which he or she displayed the characteristics of each factor. An individual was regarded as being characteristic of the attitude structure represented by a factor if the deviation from zero was more than 1.5 (Bryman and Craemer, 1990, pp. 253-265) .

7   Factor 1 was bipolar. It accounted for 24.4 per cent of the total variance in 1995-96 data. There were in the first phase of the study (1989) 12 variables loading over .40, in the second phase (1992) 9 and in the third phase 9. Factor 2 accounted for 15 per cent of the total variance of the third phase of the study. The factor loadings were also higher than before. Factor 3, accounting for 11.5 per cent of the total variance in 1995-96 study.

8   In the survey of 1995-96 together 22 attitude statements were derived mainly from the earlier studies (Helve, 1993a, 1993b).

9   Analysis of variance enables us to determine whether observed difference in the mean (average) values of a variable between two or more groups might have arisen by chance. The results showed statistically significant differences in the mean scores for the values of boys and girls. This means that the odds against the differences having arisen by chance was more than one in 20.

10   Compare this thinking with a notion that goes back to nineteenth-century romanticism and which has been elaborated in twentieth-century anthropology, in particular cultural relativism with a notion of cultures as a whole (Pieterse, 1995, p. 61).

References

Appiah, K. A. (1994), 'Identity, Authenticity, Survival: Multicultural Societies and Social Reproduction', in A. Gutmann (ed.), *Multiculturalism. Examining the Politics of Recognition*, Princeton University Press, Princeton, pp. 149-163.

Beck, U. (1992), *Risk Society. Towards a New Modernity*, Sage Publications, London.

Biorcio, R., Cavalli, A. and Segatti, P. (1995), 'Cultural Change and Political Orientation among European Youth', in S. Huebner-Funk, L. Chisholm, M. du Bois-Reymond and B. Sellin (eds), *The puzzle of integration. European Yearbook on Youth Policy and Research*, Walter de Gruyter, Berlin/New York, pp. 33-47.

Bourdieu, P. (1987), *Outline of a Theory of Practice*, Cambridge University Press, Cambridge.

Brown, P. (1996), 'Cultural Capital and Social Exclusion: Some Observations on Recent Trends in Education, Employment and the Labour Market', in H. Helve and J. Bynner (eds), *Youth and Life Management: Research Perspectives*, University Press, Helsinki, pp. 17-43.

Bryman, A. and Cramer, D. (1990), *Quantitative Data Analysis for Social Scientists*, Routledge, London/New York.

Campbell, A. (1993), *Out of Control: Men, Women and Aggression*, Pandora, London.

Commission of the European Communities (1991), *Young People in the European Communities*, Commission of the European Communities, Luxemburg.

Commission of the European Communities (1993), *Young Europeans in 1990*, Commission of the European Communities, Luxemburg.

Côté, J. (2000), *Arrested Adulthood. The Changing Nature of Maturity and Identity*, New York University Press, New York/London.

Dahlgren, A. (1977), *Två världar. Om skillnader mellan unga kvinnors och unga mäns verklighetssyn (Two Worlds. Differences in a Picture of Real Life among Young Women and Men)*, GWC Gleerup, Lund.

EVA (1991), *Suomi etsii itseään. Raportti suomalaisten asenteista 1991* (Finland Searching for Itself. Report about the Attitudes of Finnish People 1991), Elinkeinoelämän valtuuskunta (Centre for Finnish Business and Policy Studies), Helsinki.

Fornäs, J. (1995), *Cultural Theory and Late Modernity*, Sage Publications, London.

Fraser, N. and Nicholson, L. (1991), 'Social Criticism Without Philosophy', *Theory, Culture & Society*, Vol. 5(2-3), pp. 373-394.

Friesl, C., Richter, M. and Zulehner, P. M. (1993), *Values and Lifestyles of Young People in Europe*, Report, Vienna.

Giddens, A. (1994), 'Living in a Post-Traditional Society', in U. Beck, A. Giddens and S. Lash, *Reflexive Modernization: Politics, Tradition and Aesthetics in the Modern Social Order,* Polity Press, Cambridge.

Gutmann, A. (1994), *Multiculturalism. Examining the Politics of Recognition*, Princeton University Press, Princeton, New Jersey.

Helve, H. (1993a), *The World View of Young People*, Academia Scientiarum Fennica, Gummerus, Jyväskylä.

Helve, H. (1993b), *Nuoret humanistit, individualistit ja traditionalistit. Helsinkiläisten ja pohjalaisten nuorten arvomaailmat vertailussa* (Young Humanists, Individualists and Traditionalists. The Values of Young People Living in Helsinki and Ostrobothnia), Suomen Nuorisoyhteistyö Allianssi ry, Nuorisotutkimusseura, Helsinki.

Helve, H. (1996), 'Values, World Views and Gender Differences among Young People', in H. Helve and J. Bynner (eds), *Youth and Life Management. Research Perspectives*, Helsinki University Press, Helsinki, pp. 171-187.

Helve, H. (1997a), *Arvot, maailmankuvat, sukupuoli* (Values, World Views, Gender) Helsinki University Press, Helsinki.

Helve, H. (1997b), 'Perspectives on Social Exclusion, Citizenship and Youth', in J. Bynner, L. Chisholm and A. Furlong (eds), *Youth, Citizenship and Social Change in a European Context*, Ashgate, Aldershot, pp. 228-233.

Helve, H. (1998), 'Unification and Marginalisation of Young People', in H. Helve (ed.), *Unification and Marginalisation of Young People,* Hakapaino Oy, Helsinki, pp. 211-221.

Helve, H. (2001), 'Reflexivity and Changes in Attitudes and Value Structures', in H. Helve and C. Wallace (eds), *Youth, Citizenship and Empowerment*, Ashgate, Aldershot/Burlington, USA/ Singapore/Sydney, pp. 201-218.

Helve, H (2002), *Arvot, muutos ja nuoret* (Values, Change and Young People), Helsinki University Press, Helsinki.

Helve, H (2004), 'The Situation of Girls and Young Women', in *World Youth Report 2003: The Global Situation of Young People,* UN Publications, DESA, New York, pp. 248-269.

Inglehart, R. (1977), *The Silent Revolution: Changing Values and Political Styles among Western Publics*, Princeton University Press, Princeton, New Jersey.

Inglehart, R. (1990), *Culture Shift in Advanced Industrial Society*, Princeton University Press, Princeton, New Jersey.

Inglehart, R. (1997), *Modernization and Postmodernization. Cultural, Economic and Political Change in 43 Societies,* Princeton University Press, Princeton, New Jersey.

Lyotard, J-F. (1984), *The Postmodern Condition. A Report on Knowledge,* Manchester University Press, Manchester.

Lyotard, J-F. (1985), *Tieto postmodernissa yhteiskunnassa (The Postmodern Condition. A Report on Knowledge),* Vastapaino, Tampere.

Pieterse, J. N. (1995), 'Globalization as Hybridization', in M. Featherstone, S. Lash and R. Robertson (eds), *Global Modernities,* Sage Publications, London, pp. 45-68.

Pieterse, J. N. (2002), *Many Doors to Multiculturalism,* in B. Saunders and D. Haljan (eds) *Whither Multiculturalism?,* Rodopi, Amsterdam.

Rauste-von Wright, M., Kauri, L. and Niemi, P. (1975), *Nuorison ihmis- ja maailmankuva. Osa 3: Nuorten käsityksiä maailmasta (The World View of Youth. Part 3: Young People's Ideas about the World),* Turun yliopisto, psykologian laitos, Turku.

Statistics of Finland, (2000), *Suomen tilastollinen vuosikirja (Finnish Statistical Yerbook),* Tilastokeskus, Helsinki.

Suurpää, L. (ed.), (1998), *Black, Light, White Shadows. Young People in the Nordic Countries Write about Racism,* TemaNord Series, Vol. 538, Nordic Council of Ministers, Copenhagen.

Tipton, S. (1984), *Getting Saved from the Sixties: Moral Meaning in Conversion and Cultural Change,* University of California Press, Berkeley.

Vainikainen, T (2003), 'Day Care in the Front Line of Multiculturalism', *Monitori,* Vol. 3.

Van Dijk, T. A. (1998), *Ideology. A Multidisciplinary Approach,* Sage Publications, London.

Vinken, H. and Ester, P. (1992), 'Modernisation and Value Shifts: A Cross Cultural and Longitudinal Analysis of Adolescents' Basic Values', in W. Meeus, M. De Goede, W. Kox and K. Hurrelman (eds), *Adolescence, Careers and Cultures,* Walter de Gruyter, Berlin/New York, pp. 409-428.

Vinken, H., Soeters, J. and Ester, P. (eds), (2004), *Comparing Cultures. Dimensions of Culture in a Comparative Perspective,* Brill, Leiden/Boston.

Watson, R. (1997), 'Do it, Be it, Live it', *Newsweek,* October 6, pp. 28-35.

PART II:
YOUNG PEOPLE AND RELATIONS BETWEEN GENERATIONS

Chapter 6

Solidarity in New Zealand. Parental Support for Children in a Three-Generational Context

Sarah Hillcoat-Nallétamby and Arunachalam Dharmalingam

Introduction

This chapter examines whether young people continue to benefit from their parents' support once they have made the transition away from home, and if so, whether the likelihood of receiving support will in any way be influenced by the presence of a third generation, their own grandparents. Our focus is on a particular group of young people who make up the last of a successive line of generations of grandparent, parent and child, and whose parents are aged in their forties and fifties.

There has recently been a growing awareness in New Zealand that the transitions leading from youth to young adulthood are becoming increasingly complex (Statistics New Zealand, 1998; Bird and Drewery, 2000). Recent education sector and labour market changes suggest that as they move into early and even mature adulthood, young people will increasingly need to rely upon their families for support during these transitional periods. Although they continue to improve their educational achievements, spending longer at school, and obtaining higher education qualifications, the recent introduction of a tertiary and higher education student loan scheme has sparked awareness that young people's future life-course decisions such as family formation, savings behaviour or investments in the property market may be adversely affected (Ministry of Youth Affairs, 2002; Ministry of Education, 2003).

On the labour market front, particularly since the mid 1980s, unemployment rates for those in their twenties have increased, the proportions working full-time have dropped, median incomes have shown a downward trend, and there is some indication of an increasing reliance upon state funded-benefits (Baxendine, 2003). The drop in full-time employment rates amongst youth in their late teens and early twenties, of course partly reflects their increasing involvement in education, and this has recently been mirrored in rising proportions taking on part-time work, partially as a means of combining income needs with study

(Statistics New Zealand, 2003a). However, youth unemployment, higher amongst the 15-19 than 20-24 year olds, is both disproportionately and consistently higher than the national average; for the youngest of these groups for example, unemployment stood at about 15 per cent in 1997, a figure which more than doubled the national rate of unemployment at that time (Statistics New Zealand, 2003b).

Several factors compound the difficulties of linking the financial costs of tertiary education and finding employment, to the propensity for young people to carry on living with their parents. Even when youth are not in the labour force for example, the likelihood that they will be living with parents seems to be influenced by their proximity to tertiary education or employment infrastructures and opportunities (Statistics New Zealand, 1998). Suffice to say that in the mid 1990s, about two out of three young people aged between 12 and 25 were living with their parents, these proportions decreasing rapidly with increasing age, with variation by gender, ethnicity, education and labour force status. As they approach their twenties for example, young New Zealanders, particularly females and those of Maori ethnic origin, are increasingly more likely to be living away from their parents' home.

In New Zealand, partly as a reflection of quite radical reforms to the principles and mechanisms underpinning social policy and social assistance measures (Cheyne et al., 2000), there has been an increasing, albeit at times implicit, assumption that the direct and indirect costs of the changes encountered by youth will be absorbed at the micro-level of family relations and transactions (McPherson, 2000). Policy reforms for example, have tightened eligibility to income support measures for young people based on age, and the calculation of student allowances is now means-tested based on parental income (Higgins, 2002).

Yet little time has been taken to see whether parents, particularly for those reaching mid-life and who are the most likely to have children leaving home, will actually be in a position to offer this help, regardless of other obligations and commitments they may have towards the workplace, the community or other family members, in particular, ageing parents (Koopman-Boyden, et al., 2000; Pool 1992; Hamill and Goldberg, 1997; Brody, 1990). In this chapter, we are particularly interested in establishing whether a parent's ability to continue providing support to their children will be influenced by the presence of a third generation, the child's grandparent. Underlying this interest is a postulate that the transactions between parent and child do not occur in a vacuum, in isolation from the broader network of generational structures and intergenerational transactions of which they form part (Hagestad, 2000; Bengtson, 2001).

The structure of the chapter is as follows: we first outline how the concept of solidarity is taken as the basis for the empirical analysis of the factors influencing the transactions observed between parent and child generations, briefly reviewing previous research in this area. This is followed by an outline of the data sources, methodology and statistical models used for our empirical analysis. A subsequent section provides descriptive and multivariate results, focusing on the influence that grandparent characteristics have upon the likelihood that the child generation will continue to receive support from their parent even when they have left home. We then discuss these results prior to concluding.

Solidarity at the Micro-Social Level

Our empirical analysis draws on work that has examined at the micro-social level, the nature of relations between generations of grandparent, parent and child (Bengtson and Harootyan, 1994; Silverstein and Bengtson, 1997; Coenen-Huther et al. 1994). These relations, generally conceptualized and measured in terms of interdependent or isolate elements, represent the solidarity or cohesion of intergenerational bonds, and include the following dimensions: *structure* (shared living arrangements or geographic distance separating individuals); *association* (contact or communication between individuals); *affection* (feelings of emotional closeness); *consensus* (shared opinions); *function* (exchanges of support and assistance); *norms* (values pertaining to obligations across generations) (Mangen et al, 1988).

Our focus in this chapter is on functional solidarity – the types of support that the child generation continues to receive from their parent once they have left home. Figure 6.1 represents the premise that the parent's ability to provide this support could be influenced by the attributes of the three co-surviving generations (Ri – parent; Ci – child; Pi – grandparent), particularly those of the grandparent generation whose needs for support may conflict with those of the child generation, rendering it difficult for the parent to maintain intergenerational solidarity by providing help to both groups.

Factors influencing provision of support

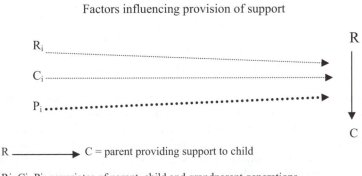

R ⟶ C = parent providing support to child

Ri, Ci, Pi: covariates of parent, child and grandparent generations

Figure 6.1 Conceptual framework

Previous Findings

The work we have thus far developed to examine relationships of solidarity across only two generations, parent and child, has focused on the transitional and post-transitional phases of leaving home (Hillcoat-Nallétamby and Dharmalingam, 2001, 2003; Hillcoat-Nallétamby et al., 1998). For young adult children aged between fifteen and twenty four, we have examined factors which make some more likely than others to be living at home with their parents (*structural solidarity*). Amongst those aged fifteen or more who have *already* completed the transition to independent living, we have established the factors influencing whether their parents will keep up regular contact with them (*associational solidarity*), as well as the factors influencing the different types of support they continue to receive (*functional solidarity*).

Bearing in mind that these studies have focused on a particular group of young adults whose parents are aged between 40 and 54, some clear patterns have nonetheless emerged, that reflect other findings on the determinants of exchanges of support between parents and adult children, and on the factors influencing young people's transitions of leaving home (Attias-Donfut, 1993; Dharmalingam et al., 2004; Cooney and Uhlenberg, 1992; Eggebeen and Hogan, 1990; McPherson, 2000; White, 1994; White and Rogers, 1997; Mortimer and Larson, 2002; De Vaus and Qu, 1998).

First, we have found that the chances of young adult children still living with their parents, still having contact with them once they have left home and still benefiting from different sorts of help vary markedly depending upon the child's age and gender. Not surprisingly, the age period of 15 to 24 is a transitional stage towards residential autonomy, and is patterned according to gender, with daughters more likely than sons to have made the transition away from home during these years. For young adults who have left home, weekly contact is greater between daughter and parent and for the ages 20-24. When it comes to providing help, parents appear more disposed to offer financial support to sons. The influence of gender and age are to some extent mirrored through the parents: the older a mid-life parent, the more disposed they appear to offer in-kind help like gardening or babysitting, perhaps as a response to the changing needs of their children who focus upon easing themselves into independence as they assume family formation or career commitments.

It appears that young adult children whose relationship to their parent is not based on a direct link of birth (that is they are either adopted, fostered or step-children), are less likely to be living with their parent or to have frequent contact with them, but are nonetheless clearly the most likely to benefit from emotional support once away from home. This is reflected in parental union history, as children whose parents have been divorced or separated are both less likely to be co-residing with them or to have weekly contact once they have left home. Finally, young adult children whose parents are from rural or town areas are less likely than city dwellers to be living at home between the ages of 15 and 24.

In this chapter, we now extend this work a stage further by examining whether being part of a *three generational group* of grandparent, parent and child affects the likelihood that children will still benefit from their parents' support once they have left home. Four new factors are considered – the total number of surviving grandparents, grandparent gender and whether they receive emotional or in-kind support from their own mature adult child, the parent generation.[1]

Data and Methodology

The data we draw on are from the 1997 New Zealand survey 'Transactions in the Mid-Life Family' (Koopman-Boyden et al., 2000), which provides a sample of 750 males and females aged between 40 and 54, including information on certain characteristics of all their surviving children and parents (the grandparent generation). The sample was selected on a nationwide basis and identified by area stratification according to population size. Of all eligible respondents randomly selected for interview, the final success rate for contacts throughout New Zealand was 54 per cent. The survey is the only nationally representative source of unit-record data providing some information on family transactions, but the data do suffer from certain shortcomings. Only three dimensions of solidarity can be measured, those of association, structure and function, there is no information on the occupational, economic or educational statuses and family circumstances of children who no longer live with a parent, and information on the child and grandparent generations is based on reporting from the mid-life respondents only.

Analysis in this chapter is restricted to a sample of 310 triads of grandparent, parent and a child aged 15 or more, none of whom live together. The types of help the parent reports giving to their child are regrouped into four categories as indicators of functional solidarity, each category representing a dichotomous, dependant variable in our statistical analysis (Table 6.1).

Model Specifications

We use logistic regression techniques for statistical analysis because each of the dependant variables we are interested in have only two possible response categories, *yes* or *no* (Table 6.1). The statistical models obtained show the probability that survey respondents will be in a particular category of the dependant variable, for example, the probability that mid-life New Zealanders will give emotional support to their child (as opposed to not giving it), depending on the influence of other explanatory variables (Tabachnick and Fidell, 1996). The model coefficients for the explanatory variables are shown as odds ratios. As individuals can receive more than one type of support, analysis is limited to whether giving at least one type of help was reported.

Table 6.1   Typology of support provided by parent to child

Dependant variables
(Responses: *yes/no*)

Any support given	Care or support provided by parent to child at least once a year
Financial support	Direct financial help
In-kind support	Gardening, house maintenance/work, meal preparation, personal health, shopping, transport, childcare, other
Emotional support	Emotional support, financial advice, sport, leisure. Of the 56.7%, 50.2% received emotional support

Results

The majority of the child generation, about two out of three, are below twenty five, most are of non-Maori ethnicity, and about half are related to their parent through direct biological descent. Once having left home, only a small proportion remain within very close geographic proximity to their parents, and close to half live over 100 kilometres away (Table 6.2).

Over half of the parent generation are female, about one quarter are forty five or younger, the majority of non-Maori ethnicity, with almost three quarters declaring some form of religious affiliation, and a significant proportion (over one third) suffering from a long-term health condition which limits their activities. One fifth is currently single, approximately the same proportion living in rural locations, and a third has four or more children. The majority have some form of paid employment, and about four out of ten earn a personal annual income of between $NZ 15,000 and $NZ 41,000 (Table 6.3).

The oldest generation of grandparents is predominantly female. Two thirds of the parent generation have one or two surviving parents of a potential of four (and likewise for the child generation, in terms of the number of surviving grandparents). About one out of every three of the oldest generation benefit from emotional or financial support offered by their mature adult child, the parent generation (Table 6.4).

Table 6.2 **Percentage distribution of study population of child by individual characteristics (N = 310; weighted data)**

Child generation	%
Gender:	
Male	46.2
Female	53.8
Age	
<25	64.2
>25	35.8
Ethnicity	
Non-Maori	85.7
Maori	14.3
From current/past parental union?	
Born of current union	47.2
Other (step, foster)	14.1
Born of previous union	38.7
Child has health problem?	
Yes	15.7
No	84.3
Distance from parental home	
<3km	13.4
3-100	41.3
100+	45.3

**Table 6.3a   Percentage distribution of study population of parent by
individual characteristics (N = 310; weighted data)**

Parent generation	%	Description of variable categories
Gender		
Male	42.7	
Female	57.3	
Current age		
40-44	26.2	
45-49	38.4	
50-54	35.4	
Ethnicity		
Non-Maori	89.7	
Maori	10.3	
Residence		
City + Town	77.7	
Rural	22.3	
Religion		
None	29.2	
Some	70.8	
Union status		
Not currently in union	20.0	(Single, widowed, divorced, separated)
In union	80.0	(Legal and de facto)
Highest educational qualification		
None	22.7	
Secondary	49.3	
Tertiary other	18.9	
University	9.1	

Table 6.3b Percentage distribution of study population of parent by individual characteristics (N = 310; weighted data)

Parent generation	%	Description of variable categories
Employment status		
Self-employed	29.4	
Homemaker	11.0	
Full and part time	54.4	
Unemployed and other	5.2	(Retired, student, voluntary worker)
Partner employment status		
No partner	16.1	
Self and family	21.8	
Homemaker + other	10.5	
Full and part time	51.6	
Has health problem? (yes)	34.4	Any long term health problem/condition lasting six months or more and which limits activity
Total annual income (New Zealand dollars)		
0-14,999	18.1	
15-40,999	40.9	
41,000+	26.5	
Other	14.5	(Don't know and missing)
Total number of children		
1-2	34.9	
3	28.3	
4+	36.8	
Total in household		
1-2	43.8	Total number of individuals living in parent generation's household
3	25.4	
4+	30.7	

Table 6.4   Percentage distribution of study population of grandparent by individual characteristics (N = 310; weighted data)

Grandparent generation	%	Descrip. of variable categories
Gender		
Male	22.8	
Female	77.2	
Total surviving grandparents		
1-2	66.1	
3+	33.9	
In-kind support from parent generation?		(Includes financial)
Yes	37.5	
Emotional support from parent generation?	35.8	
Yes		

Looking at the associations between the characteristics of the grandparent generation and the dependant variables representing functional solidarity (Table 6.5), we find that children with grandmothers appear less likely than those with a grandfather to be receiving financial help from their parents.

Table 6.5   Bivariate percentage distribution by dependant variables and grandparent generation characteristics (% = 'yes'; N = 310; weighted data)

Grandparent characteristics	Parent provides support to child?			
	Support	Financial	In-kind	Emotional
Gender				
Male	81.7 (d)	73.2 (c)	21.4 (d)	60.6 (d)
Female	80.3	47.5	29.2	55.6
Tot. surviving grandparents				
1-2	80.0 (d)	48.3 (c)	29.3 (d)	52.7 (b)
3+	81.9	63.2	23.8	64.8
In-kind support				
Yes	84.2 (d)	52.5 (d)	39.2 (c)	55.8 (d)
Emotional support				
Yes	92.8 (c)	71.2 (c)	34.2 (b)	81.1 (c)

(a) p<10% ; (b) p<5% ; (c) p<1% ; (d) not statistically significant.

They are also less likely to receive financial and emotional support if their grandparent is one of only two surviving members of that generation, but appear more likely to receive all types of support if their grandparent also benefits from emotional help, exception perhaps being in-kind help where the association is weaker.

Our results in Table 6.6 show that parents certainly continue to provide support to their child once they have left home, whilst at the same time also providing help to the child's grandparent (less than 40 per cent and 20 per cent of either group respectively receive no assistance).

Table 6.6   Types of support provided by the parent generation to the child and grandparent generations (percentages and odds ratios; N = 310)

Type of support	Grandparent N = 310	Child N = 310	Odds ratios c/p
Emotional	35.8	56.7	2.35 (c)
Financial	3.7	53.4	31.22 (c)
In-kind	36.0	27.4	0.66 (b)
Gardening	5.2	1.2	0.24 (c)
House maintenance/work	14.7	4.5	0.31 (c)
Meal preparation	5.8	6.1	1.05 (d)
Personal health	5.5	1.8	0.28 (c)
Shopping	7.0	2.0	0.25 (c)
Transport	10.0	5.5	0.52 (b)
Childcare	-	6.9	-
Other[2]	11.4	14.5	1.33 (d)
None	39.5	19.3	0.49 (c)

(a) p<10% ; (b) p<5% ; (c) p<1% ; (d) not statistically significant; percentages do not add up to 100% due to multiple responses.

When examined separately however, the types of help received by each generation vary considerably. Over half of all the child group continue to receive emotional and financial help (56.7 per cent and 53.4 respectively), but only a minority of grandparents receive financial assistance (3.7 per cent), and just over one third, emotional support. The types of in-kind support received also vary quite markedly. Compared to their grandparents, the youngest generation are clearly less likely to receive any form of in-kind help (with the exception of meal preparation and childcare), but are over thirty times more likely to benefit from financial help, and nearly two and a half times more likely to receive emotional support.

There is therefore a clear generational difference at play in the likelihood of a parent providing a given type of support to their child and own parent. The flow of help certainly appears to favour the youngest over the oldest generation, but both child and grandparent share the need for emotional support, although it is the youngest generation who need continued financial help, whilst their grandparent will benefit from in-kind help with daily living tasks.

Multivariate Results

As Figure 6.1 has shown, the aim of the multivariate analysis is to establish the net effect that grandparent characteristics have on the likelihood that the parent will continue to provide help to their own child who has left home. To achieve this, we ran the statistical models in several stages, progressively adding in the explanatory variables so as to control for their effects on the dependant variables of functional solidarity. For each dependent variable, we ran three separate models. The first included only the characteristics for the grandparent generation (Model 1), the second including child characteristics in addition (Model 2) and finally, a model including the characteristics of all three generations (Model 3). By limiting the presentation of results in Tables 6.7, 6.8, 6.9 and 6.10 to the effects of the grandparent characteristics only, we are able to see the net effect of this generation's characteristics on the odds or likelihood that the child will benefit from emotional, financial and in-kind support from their parent.

Once all multivariate models have been run, we find that across all models and all indicators of functional solidarity, the child is more likely to have help if the grandparent also benefits from emotional support, an effect which is the most pronounced when the child also receives emotional support (Table 6.10, odds ratios for emotional support are all close to 6). If the grandparent benefits from in-kind help, the likelihood of the child receiving this support also increases almost three-fold (Table 6.9). This result is somewhat surprising,[3] if we consider this intergenerational transaction as one involving a significant investment in time on the part of the parent generation, who provides unpaid services or assistance to two generations at the same time. Table 6.6 provides some explanation, because the types of in-kind support each generation receives are quite different, the grandparent on average, being more likely than the child to receive each type of in-kind help. On balance therefore, the variation in the types of in-kind support given to the child and grandparent probably accounts for the strong and positive correlation of the odds ratios obtained.

All models in Table 6.8 indicate that a parent is much less likely to give financial support to their child when the grandparent is female. This is initially plausible, as older women are perhaps more in need of financial assistance than their male counterparts, partly because of economic dependence on male earnings, but also due to life expectancy differences which would render the likelihood of living alone more probable for women. The parent generation may therefore find that they have to forego providing financial help to their children in favour of offering it to their own parents. However, our data do not support this initial explanation, because as noted earlier (see Table 6.6) only a very small number of the grandparent generation actually receive financial support. A second possible explanation might be then, that the gender of the grandparent is a proxy for some characteristics of the child or parent, but this explanation can be ruled out because with each successive model, we have introduced child and parent characteristics, with no effect on the direction, magnitude and significance of the odds ratios (Table 6.8, odds ratios for the variable 'gender'). Alternatively, the relationship between child receipt of financial assistance and grandparent gender may be spurious, the observed relationship perhaps being due to the interaction between the grandparent's gender and the child and parent characteristics. In our multivariate analysis we found that child age was very strongly associated with receiving financial support. The older the child, the less likely they are to receive parental help. When incorporating an interaction term for the two variables in the full model (grandparent gender and child age, not shown here), we found that grandparent gender lost its independent effect on the likelihood of the child receiving monetary support, but the interaction effect and the effect of child age were significant.

How do we make sense of these findings? From exploratory analysis we know that most female grandparents are single or widowed, and that older children are less likely than younger offspring to receive financial support from their parent. As widowed women are likely to be older than non-widowed, it is possible that their grandchildren are on average, older as well. The relationship between grandparent gender and child receipt of financial support (models in Table 6.8) would therefore be spurious as it would be attributable to grandparent and child age. We are unable to explore this further because we do not have data on the age of the grandparent, but using secondary sources, the New Zealand Census data for 1996 indicate the average age of widowed women amongst all those aged 60+ to be 76.3 years, but for all those who are not widowed, to be 67.5 years.

Table 6.7 Estimated Odds Ratios for Models of Functional Solidarity (N = 310; Odds ratios: yes = 1, no = 0). Set I: Any support given

Grandparent gen. characteristics		Set I: Any support given (yes/no)		
		Model 1	Model 2	Model 3
In-kind support	No	1.00	1.00	1.00
	Yes	1.28 (d)	0.98 (d)	0.93 (d)
Emotional support	No	1.00	1.00	1.00
	Yes	4.19 (c)	3.83 (c)	2.99 (b)
Gender	Male	1.00	1.00	1.00
	Female	0.89 (d)	0.85 (d)	0.56 (d)
Tot. surviving grandparents	1-2	1.00	1.00	1.00
	3+	1.08 (d)	1.17 (d)	1.61 (d)

(a) p<10% ; (b) p<5% ; (c) p<1% ; (d) not statistically significant.
Model 1: includes characteristics of grandparent only.
Model 2: includes characteristics of grandparent controlling for child characteristics.
Model 3: includes characteristics of grandparent controlling for child and parent characteristics.

Table 6.8 Estimated Odds Ratios for Models of Functional Solidarity (N = 310; Odds ratios: yes = 1, no = 0). Set II: Financial support

Grandparent gen. characteristics		Set II: Financial support (yes/no)		
		Model 1	Model 2	Model 3
In-kind support	No	1.00	1.00	1.00
	Yes	1.00 (d)	0.89 (d)	0.95 (d)
Emotional support	No	1.00	1.00	1.00
	Yes	3.31 (c)	3.03 (c)	2.39 (c)
Gender	Male	1.00	1.00	1.00
	Female	0.32 (c)	0.35 (c)	0.35 (c)
Tot. surviving grandparents	1-2	1.00	1.00	1.00
	3+	1.68 (a)	1.46 (d)	1.36 (d)

(a) p<10% ; (b) p<5% ; (c) p<1% ; (d) not statistically significant.
Model 1: includes characteristics of grandparent only.
Model 2: includes characteristics of grandparent controlling for child characteristics.
Model 3: includes characteristics of grandparent controlling for child and parent characteristics.

Table 6.9   Estimated Odds Ratios for Models of Functional Solidarity (N = 310; Odds ratios: yes = 1, no = 0). Set III: In-kind support

Grandparent gen. characteristics		Set III: In-kind support (yes/no)		
		Model 1	Model 2	Model 3
In-kind support	No	1.00	1.00	1.00
	Yes	2.98 (c)	2.51 (c)	2.98 (c)
Emotional support	No	1.00	1.00	1.00
	Yes	1.73 (a)	1.71 (a)	1.81 (a)
Gender	Male	1.00	1.00	1.00
	Female	1.34 (d)	1.14 (d)	1.18 (d)
Tot. surviving grandparents	1-2	1.00	1.00	1.00
	3+	0.89 (d)	0.88 (d)	1.15 (d)

(a) $p<10\%$; (b) $p<5\%$; (c) $p<1\%$; (d) not statistically significant.
Model 1: includes characteristics of grandparent only.
Model 2: includes characteristics of grandparent controlling for child characteristics.
Model 3: includes characteristics of grandparent controlling for child and parent characteristics.

Table 6.10   Estimated Odds Ratios for Models of Functional Solidarity (N = 310; Odds ratios: yes = 1, no = 0). Set IV: Emotional support

Grandparent gen. characteristics		Set IV: Emotional support (yes/no)		
		Model 1	Model 2	Model 3
In-kind support	No	1.00	1.00	1.00
	Yes	0.95 (d)	0.97 (d)	0.85 (d)
Emotional support	No	1.00	1.00	1.00
	Yes	5.92 (c)	5.91 (c)	5.83 (c)
Gender	Male	1.00	1.00	1.00
	Female	0.89 (d)	0.88 (d)	0.97 (d)
Tot. surviving grandparents	1-2	1.00	1.00	1.00
	3+	1.66 (d)	1.65 (d)	1.93 (a)

(a) $p<10\%$; (b) $p<5\%$; (c) $p<1\%$; (d) not statistically significant.
Model 1: includes characteristics of grandparent only.
Model 2: includes characteristics of grandparent controlling for child characteristics.
Model 3: includes characteristics of grandparent controlling for child and parent characteristics.

Variation Between Models – Controlling for Child and Parent Characteristics

Of the four grandparent generation variables included in the multivariate analysis, some have captured the effects of child and parent characteristics. Although children whose grandparents receive emotional support are more likely to receive financial and emotional assistance (Table 6.8 and Table 6.10), this likelihood is progressively reduced as child and parent characteristics are introduced into the models (Models 2 and 3). This notwithstanding, the odds for emotional support remain positive and significant in the final model, indicating that it clearly does have an independent effect upon the likelihood of the child generation benefiting from parental support. In the case of children receiving in-kind help (Table 6.9) the introduction of child characteristics (Model 2) has the effect of slightly reducing the odds ratios for both solidarity variables, but they are then strengthened once the characteristics of the parent generation are introduced.

We find that when considering the total number of grandparents, the likelihood of the child generation receiving financial support progressively diminishes as the child (Model 2) and parent (Model 3) characteristics are introduced, with odds losing their statistical significance. Conversely, in the case of children benefiting from emotional support, this explanatory factor gains statistical significance and increased magnitude once both child and parent characteristics have been added. Hence, the greater the number of surviving grandparents, the greater the likelihood of the child receiving emotional support (Model 3, odds ratio of 1.93).

Interpreting the Findings

In a climate of social, economic and political change in which New Zealand's youth are facing increasingly complex and prolonged transitions to full adulthood, the aim of this chapter has been to examine whether young people continue to benefit from their parents' support once they have made the transition away from home. If so, we have questioned whether the likelihood that the support they receive will be influenced by the presence of a third generation, their own grandparents. In conceptualizing these exchanges of support in terms of a bond of functional solidarity between a parent and their young adult child, we have set out to see whether there is any indication that parents aged in their forties and early fifties will find themselves compromised in the extent to which they are able to maintain this bond with the younger generation, because of the competing needs they may encounter as they also offer help to their own ageing parent, the child's grandparent.

Our findings suggest that if the grandparent's relationship with their own offspring is characterized by a strong element of emotional support, then this in turn, will enhance the chances that the youngest generation will continue to benefit from all of the types of help we have observed. The fact that children are more likely to benefit from help with daily activities like meal preparation, gardening or housework if their own grandparents also receive in-kind help suggests that both generations have quite age-specific needs. In the long run, they do not appear to place the parent generation in a position in which they have to choose between helping one generation to the detriment of the other. In the same vein, it seems that a parent will not have to compromise the financial help they offer their child as a consequence of having had to channel such resources towards the child's grandmother. Rather, it is the interplay of both demographic-driven and life course factors – longer life expectancies for grandmothers than grandfathers, coupled with increasing financial autonomy of children as they mature to young adults – which explain the effect that the grandparent generation's gender has in reducing the likelihood of children receiving money from their own parents. Finally, whether the child generation has one or more surviving grandparents seems to have little effect upon the likelihood that their parents will still be able to provide them with help, again suggesting that these parents are not necessarily having to prioritize the needs of one generational group over the other.

We also suggest that the ways in which these parents continue to support the youngest generation is very much in response to what would be the needs of young adults making the transition to full adulthood – despite having flown the nest, they still turn to parents for emotional support and help with finances. These findings in fact reinforce what we have already observed when considering intergenerational transactions across only two generations of mid-life parent and adult child – with increasing age, both the need for emotional and financial support decreases (Hillcoat-Nallétamby and Dharmalingam, 2001, 2003). At the other end of the life course spectrum, the help provided to the grandparent generation also suggests a response to age-based needs – perhaps due to progressively limited physically mobility (lack of transport or physical disability), the older generation require more help with daily tasks. To our knowledge, there is no other New Zealand empirical research on intergenerational transactions observed across a three-generational structure which enables a comparative focus for our findings, although other small-scale studies have tended to confirm the inverse relationships between young adult age and amount of help received by parents, particularly financial support (McPherson, 2000).

We must however add to these interpretations, a few notes of caution. We have used data which reflect only the perspectives of the parent generation regarding the help they provide. Perhaps more importantly, given the rich and complex ethnic diversity of New Zealand's population, our data provide no qualitative insights into the norms, values or expectations underpinning the transactions we have observed, and in particular, those held by parents regarding their obligations or responsibilities to assist their children. Of the little qualitative research we have in New Zealand addressing such questions, it appears that parents expect to keep providing support to their children who have left home (particularly financial aid), even when their own circumstances make this difficult. Some explanation for this resides in the different cultural expectations underpinning the value placed by parents on educational training and qualification, on the cultural expectation of reciprocity of aid across generations and on the value placed by some on assisting children to move towards financial independence in adulthood (Fleming and Kell-Easting, 1994; Kell-Easting and Fleming, 1994; Fleming, 1997; Taiapa, 1994).

Conclusion

Bearing these comments in mind, we conclude that our findings do not provide any clear indication that as part of a three-generational structure, the youngest members of adult children will find themselves lacking in parental help because of the presence of an older generation, their own grandparent. What in fact appears to characterize these bonds of solidarity across three generations is that the help received by the eldest group seems to complement, and even enhance the chances that the young adults will be able to count on continued support from their own parents, even once they have made the transition away from home. On balance, this suggests that as the pivotal generational group, parents find themselves at the nexus of complementary rather than competing multi-generational demands. As a result, they continue to help both generations, albeit in quite different ways.

Notes

1 As the mid-life respondent may have more than one child and ageing parent, a focal individual in each generation group was selected. Of all children not living with their parents, a focal child was identified as follows: child receiving the greatest number of types of assistance from their parent selected; amongst those receiving no support, those maintaining the most frequent contact with the respondent selected. This gave an initial study population of 380 dyads. Based on this set, a focal member of the generation of parents of the respondent was selected for all those with a surviving parent or parent-in-law. When more than one parent or in-law was alive, we selected them based on the same criteria as those used for identification of the focal child. In this way, we have maximized the potential for the mid-life respondent to be exposed to the giving of help to two other generations.
2 Frequencies less than <5 per cent of total reportings. Parents: care/disability, childcare, advice, education, sports, leisure, general care, clothing, gift, accommodation, car repair, social assistance, help business, all sorts, other. Child: care/disability, advice, education, leisure, general care, clothing, sport, gifts, accommodation, car repairs, social assistance, help with business, all types, other. Also includes mobility.
3 Statistically speaking, we might have expected a negative relationship between child and grandparent receiving in-kind support.

References

Attias-Donfut, C. (1993), 'Solidarités familiales, solidarités entre générations', *Solidarité Santé, Etudes statistiques*, Vol. 4, pp. 99-104.

Baxendine, S. (2003), 'Regional Population Dynamics: Young Adults in New Zealand, 1986-2001', *New Zealand Population Review*, Vol. 29(1), pp. 71-98.

Bengtson, V.L. (2001), 'Beyond the Nuclear Family: The Increasing Importance of Multigenerational Bonds', *Journal of Marriage and the Family*, Vol. 63(1), pp. 1-17.

Bengtson, V.L. and Harootyan, R.A. (1994), *Intergenerational Linkages. Hidden Connections in American Society*, Springer Publishing Company, New York.

Bird, L. and Drewery, W. (2000), *Human Development in Aotearoa: A Journey through Life*, McGraw-Hill, Auckland.

Brody, E.M. (1990), *Women in the Middle: Their Parent-care Years*, Springer, New York.

Cheyne, C., O'Brien, M. and Belgrave, M. (2000), *Social Policy in Aotearoa New Zealand. A Critical Introduction*, Oxford University Press, Auckland.

Coenen-Huther, J., Kellerhals, J., Allmen von, M., Hagmann, H.M., Jeannerat, F. and Widmer, E. (1994), *Les réseaux de solidarité dans la famille*, Réalités socialés, Lausanne.

Cooney, T.M. and Uhlenberg, P. (1992), 'Support from Parents Over the Life Course. The Adult Child's Perspective', *Social Forces*, Vol. 71, pp. 63-84.

De Vaus, D. and Qu, L. (1998), 'Intergenerational Transfers Across the Life Course', *Family Matters*, Vol. 50, pp. 27-30.

Dharmalingam, A., Pool, I., Sceats, J. and Mackay, R. (2004), *Patterns of Family Formation and Change in New Zealand*, Wellington, New Zealand: Centre for Social Research and Evaluation, Ministry of Social Development.

Eggebeen, D.J. and Hogan, H.P. (1990), 'Giving between Generations in American Families', *Human Nature*, Vol. 1, pp. 211-232.

Fleming, R. (1997), *The Common Purse: Income Sharing in New Zealand Families*, Auckland University Press, Auckland.

Fleming, R. and Kell-Easting, S. (1994), *Couples, Households and Money. Report of the Pakeha Component of the Intra Family Income Study*, published by the Intra Family Income Project, Wellington, in association with the Social Policy Research Centre, Massey University, Palmerston North.

Hagestad, G.O. (2000), 'Intergenerational Relationships', paper presented for the 'Gender and Generations Programme', United Nations, Economic Commision for Europe, Population Activities Unit, August.

Hamill, S.B. and Goldberg, W.A. (1997), 'Between Adolescents and Ageing Grandparents: Midlife Concerns of Adults in the "Sandwich Generation"', *Journal of Adult Development*, Vol. 4(3), pp. 135-147.

Higgins, J. (2002), 'Young People and Transitions Policies in New Zealand'. *Social Policy Journal of New Zealand*, Vol. 18, pp. 44-61.

Hillcoat-Nallétamby, S., Dharmalingam, A., Koopman-Boyden, P. and Pool, I. (1998), 'Family Solidarity and the "Sandwich Generations" in New Zealand', paper presented at la Chaire Quetelet – Ménages et familles face à la crise', Louvain-la-Neuve, Belgium.

Hillcoat-Nallétamby, S. and Dharmalingam, A. (2001), 'La solidarité familiale en Nouvelle Zélande: Esquisse d'un modèle des échanges entre générations', in Association Internationale des Démographes de Langue Française (éds), *Vivre Plus Longtemps, avoir moins d'enfants, quelles implications?*, Presses Universitaires de France, Paris, pp. 373-382.

Hillcoat-Nallétamby, S. and Dharmalingam, A. (2003),'Mid-Life Parental Support for Adult Children in New Zealand', *Journal of Sociology*, Vol. 39(3), September, pp. 271-290.

Kell-Easting, S. and Fleming, R. (1994), *Families, Money and Policy. Summary of the Intra Family Income Study, and discussion of policy issues*, Published by the Intra Family Income Project, Wellington in association with the Social Policy Research Centre, Massey University, Palmerston North.

Koopman-Boyden, P., Dharmalingam, A., Grant, B. et al. (2000), *Transactions in the Mid-life Family*, Monograph Series No. 1, Population Association of New Zealand, University of Waikato, Hamilton.

Mangen, D.J., Bengtson, V.L. and Landry, P.H. (1988), *Measurement of Intergenerational Relations*, Sage Publications, London.

McPherson, M. (2000), 'The Extended Family in New Zealand: Demographic Description and Policy Implications', *New Zealand Population Review*, Vol. 26(1), pp. 67-91.

Ministry of Education (2003), 'Student Support in New Zealand. Discussion document', http://www.minedu.govt.nz/web/downloadable/dl8732_v1/student-support-in-nz---final-pdf.pdf., accessed 10 October 2003.

Ministry of Youth Affairs (2002), 'Key Stages of Young Peoples Development', in *Youth Development Strategy Aotearoa: Action for Child and Youth Development*, http://www.youthaffairs.govt.nz/media/pdf/YD_LitRev_key_stages.pdf, accessed 8 May 2003.

Mortimer, J.T and Larson, R.W (eds), (2002), *The changing Adolescent Experience: Societal Trends and the Transition to Adulthood*, Cambridge University Press, Cambridge.

Pool, I. (1992), *The Generation Game: Intra-Family Competition for Resources*, paper presented at the Sociological Association of Aotearao, Wellington, December.

Silverstein, M. and Bengtson, V.L. (1997), 'Intergenerational Solidarity and the Structure of Adult Child-Parent Relationships in American Families', *American Journal of Sociology*, Vol. 103(2), pp. 429-460.

Statistics New Zealand (1998), *New Zealand Now – Young New Zealanders. Supporting the Development of Young People in New Zealand*.

Statistics New Zealand (2003a), *More young people work part-time*, retrieved from http://www.stats.govt.nz/domino/external/web/nzstories.nsf/Response/More+young+people+work+part-time, accessed 4 September 2003.

Statistics New Zealand (2003b), *Unemployment Trends for Young People, 1991-2000*, retrieved from http://www.stats.govt.nz/domino/external/web/nzstories.nsf/092edeb76ed5aa6bcc256afe0081d84e/954f9f7b7fc367b3cc256b18006cd6d6?OpenDocument, accessed 4 September 2003.

Tabachnick, B.G. and Fidell, S. (1996), *Using Multivariate Statistics*, Harper Collins College Publishers, New York.

Taiapa, J. (1994), *The Economics of the Whanaua: the Maori Component*, Department of Maori Studies, Massey University, Palmerston North.

White, L. (1994), 'Co-Residence and Leaving Home: Young Adults and their Parents', *Annual Review of Sociology*, Vol. 20, pp. 81-147.

White, L. and Rogers, S.J. (1997), 'Strong Support but Uneasy Relationships: Coresidence and Adult Children's Relationships with their Parents', *Journal of Marriage and the Family*, Vol. 59, pp. 62-76.

Chapter 7

Living with Parents.
A Research Study on Italian
Young People and their Mothers

Monica Santoro

The Background: Changes in Transition to Adulthood

This chapter aims at investigating the phenomenon of the extended stay of young people in the parental home through the results of a qualitative research conducted in Italy, where the percentage of young people living with their family is progressively increasing.

The institutional and social changes produced in Western countries in the last two decades have profoundly modified the patterns of transition to adulthood. The extension of education, the labour market crisis and the establishment of informal and temporary work have strongly contributed to lengthening the youth phase, making it uncertain and unpredictable (Cavalli, 1980; Cavalli and Galland, 1996; Leccardi, 1991).

Patterns of transition to adulthood which were traditionally characterized by socially foreseeable events (leaving full-time education, access to the labour market, family formation) now show signs of non-linear transition, characterized by the postponement of some steps (for example postponing marriage and parenthood) or by their extension over time (extended education, late access to the labour market). In particular the attainment of independence from the family of origin is now postponed partly because of extended education, partly due to greater difficulties experienced in the labour market. Although prolonged youth is a widespread phenomenon among upper-middle class young men, who invest more in their education and vocational training, it now tends to be also typical of young women and working-class youth. The extension of vocational training and the crisis of manufacturing industry with the consequent development of the service sector has contributed to postponing the access to the labour market of working class youth who, until the seventies, had experienced a rather smooth, rapid transition (Cavalli and Galland, 1996). Moreover, although young women achieve independent homes earlier than young men because they start a stable life with a partner at an earlier age, this trend has progressively shifted in the last decades due to the extended education of women (for example, see Cherlin et al., 1997; Schizzerotto, 2002).

A protracted dependency on the family of origin has been found in all Western countries, although there are some differences in Southern European countries. In the nineties, for instance, Italy, Spain and Greece had the highest percentage of young people aged 25-29 living in the parental home (Cherlin et al., 1997; Cordón, 1997). Indeed, in these countries (especially in Italy), unlike Central and Northern European countries, alternative family patterns (cohabitation, singleness[1]) are rarely found among young people and marriage is still the event marking household independence.

According to the last Multiscopo survey[2] of Italian families, conducted by ISTAT (Central Statistics Institute) (2001) in 2000, 60.2 per cent of young people aged 18-34 live with their parents, compared with 51.8 per cent in 1990 and with 59.1 per cent in 1998. The most interesting datum is that the propensity of young people to stay in the parental home does not only seem to be motivated by particularly unfavourable working conditions. The evidence is that more than 50 per cent of young workers resident in Northern Italy – the geographical area with highest employment – live with their parents, and this percentage drops to 14 per cent in Southern Italy. Extended stay in the parental home therefore seems to be more the outcome of a voluntary choice than the consequence of lack of working opportunities. However this is a problematic choice from several standpoints in the light of recent changes in the Italian labour market. Italy is characterized by a marked inequality between generations, which disadvantages young people and favours adults. For instance, from the nineties on the progressive enforcement of labour laws has increased flexibility in the labour market. Nevertheless these measures have not led to dismissals but have given young people a greater supply of atypical or temporary jobs characterized by low salaries. In this way, in the last few years Italian young people have witnessed a progressive weakening of their position on the market while adult generations have kept their regular, secure jobs (Isfol, 2000; ISTAT, 2003).

Moreover, the absence of social policies for youth makes family support an essential resource for young people in transition to adulthood. This implies two consequences: from an individual point of view, protracting the economic and social dependence on parents contributes to strengthening family bonds and can make emotional and practical independence from the family of origin more difficult; from a social point of view, postponing housing independence is not a stigmatized behaviour because in the absence of government aid, families support their children as much as possible.

On the basis of such considerations, in this chapter we will try to highlight the reasons which make Italian young people stay in their family of origin and lead parents to consider prolonged cohabitation with their adult children a desirable condition. By analysing the results of a qualitative research study carried out in Milan in the year 2000 we will investigate the relationship dynamics emerging in parents-children cohabitation that can favour a prolonged stay of young people in the parental home.

The Methodology

The research was conducted in Milan for my Ph.D. degree in Sociology in spring 2000 (Santoro, 2002). In-depth interviews were carried out on twenty young adults (ten young women and ten young men) aged 24-35 who live with their family, and on their mothers.[3] The objective of this research was to reconstruct the representations of the transition to adulthood from the mothers' and children's viewpoint, to compare them and to verify the existence of common outlooks. Then we tried to explore the whole set of reasons determining the decision of young people to extend their stay in the parental home and how the presence of their children in the household is perceived by mothers. In particular, in the interviews conducted on young people, specific attention was devoted to the whole set of justifications advanced by respondents to explain their choice to stay with their family, in order to reconstruct the set of meanings they give to this life choice.

At the family level, we tried to reconstruct the family atmosphere and the organization of roles and relationships within the family of origin in order to highlight how parents can help or hinder their sons/daughters in the attainment of an adult status.

As already mentioned, respondents were aged 24-35,[4] an age bracket which includes young people who have finished or are finishing their educational career and have already undertaken some steps in the transition to adulthood. The decision to also include young people over thirty enables us to understand the various positions in the life course as well as the different representations of the transition to adulthood. Between the age of twenty-four and thirty-five, subjects have in fact to make very important biographical choices (for example: reaching a stable job, housing autonomy, family formation) to achieve full independence from their family.

The decision to limit this analysis to young people from Milan allowed us to understand the reasons for and possible causes of extended stay in the parental home in a context characterized by specific structural conditions. Milan is indeed the industrial and economic capital of Italy and is differentiated by a low unemployment rate and a dynamic labour market. Moreover, Milan is one of the biggest cities in Northern Italy, a geographical area with good employment opportunities and the highest percentage of young people in employment.[5] Based on this figure, concentrating on young Milanese people made it possible to thoroughly investigate the nature of a longer cohabitation with parents, without limiting it to merely economic reasons. This objective led to the decision to interview working young adults and students with a temporary or a regular job and an average or high educational background, from the middle and upper-middle class, in order to assess the economic variable. To be more precise, with this methodological choice we wanted to limit resort to economical or professional reasons (lack of financial resources, unemployment) in the set of justifications that young people could put forward during the interview to explain the postponement of their housing autonomy. As for the survey on mothers, the choice to exclude fathers depends on the key role played by mothers in Italy in the organization of family life and in the socialization process of their children. Considering the functions traditionally attached to genders, mothers are given more protective tasks, around which develops the so-called 'mammismo'[6] of Italian young people.

The analysis of interviews with mothers, aged 49-69, was also useful to focus the role of women in the family support network. Indeed, the mothers interviewed belong to a generation of women who often, apart from having a regular job, take care of their parents or parents-in-law as well as their adult children who delay home-leaving. A complex family picture emerges, made up of a network of relations between generations, where women between fifty and sixty years of age are the main reference.

The Research on Young Adults

Reasons for Staying in the Family

Young respondents give two types of reasons to explain and justify their extended stay in the parental home. First of all, they refer to general reasons linked to cultural and social factors which differentiate Italy from Central and Northern European countries, slowing down the process of emancipation from the family: family upbringing patterns, the school system organization, the lack of a housing market for young people and the absence of suitable social policies, the lengthening of the educational period, especially university education.

Other types of reasons are also put forward. Apart from students, who postpone any project for an autonomous life to the end of their education, most young people mention a lack of sufficient financial resources preventing them from leaving home without depending on their parents. Therefore the most rational solution is to remain living with the family in order to save enough money to buy a home, rather than living on their own and paying rent, which would dip into a significant part of their salary.

However, an in-depth analysis of the interviews shows that young people are not really interested in achieving independence from their parents. Leaving the parental home is neither perceived as a need nor as an unavoidable step in the process of complete autonomy from the family of origin. Evidence is that no respondent seems to have thought of how to overcome obstacles preventing him/her from leaving home or from exploiting available opportunities to achieve successful emancipation from the family. Some respondents, for instance, own a flat but do not consider it a sufficient reason for achieving autonomy. They did not mention[7] it during the interview; instead they are worried about the housing problem. This is the case of Massimo, a young man interviewed:

I am convinced that until I get a good monthly salary which allows me to pay the housing rent, all the expenses typical of a person who lives on his own: food, petrol, road tax, car insurance, etc. and to save some money for the future, it's difficult to leave home (Massimo, male, 29, freelance professional).

What strikes us is that the financial issue is part of the most obvious, and above all most legitimate, set of justifications and that postponing the process of independence from the family could be ascribed to unexpressed motivations. In trying to shed light on the hidden motivations, there are first of all cultural reasons emerging in the normative representation of transition: the decision to leave home must be made at the right time, after completing education, finding a regular, financially rewarding job and, if possible, after finding a partner. Therefore leaving the parental home is the last step in the transition which must be made for socially legitimated reasons, like getting married or moving away for job reasons.

In the Italian social and economic context, which is more focused on protecting the family rather than the individual and at guaranteeing the well-being of older adult generations, the choice to remain living with parents is not subject to social criticism but is part of a common logic. It proves to be the optimum strategy to achieve tangible working results in a limited time span, concentrating on a professional career or on the completion of education in order to obtain more credentials in the labour market. Following this rationale,[8] the achievement of an independent household loses attraction and becomes an irrational, expensive option. Indeed, living with parents entails both financial advantages (possibility of saving money for oneself, possibility of accepting temporary jobs) and practical advantages linked to the management of a house and a family:

> I must admit that if in the last few years I hadn't lived with my mother it would have been very hard for me, because between my job and the public examinations I didn't even have the time to breathe. If I had lived on my own and I had to cook, clean the house and do the washing it would have been really a hard time (Enrica, female, 35, hospital doctor).

> At a certain age you enjoy some freedom, and living in the parental home has all the advantages of this situation and few disadvantages. It's not only being totally free in terms of what time you can come home, but also having the opportunity to build a professional career, which would not be possible without, let's say, some help. (Tania, 30, lawyer).

The specificity of the relationship with parents further strengthens the advantage of staying in the parental home. The family appears as a protective place which offers support in difficult moments and provides an emotional and practical help. In accordance with other Italian research studies carried out on this topic (Scabini and Donati, 1988; Scabini and Rossi, 1997), young respondents are quite satisfied with the relationship with their parents and with the quality of the mutual relationship developed during cohabitation:

> They respect my ideas more or less, and therefore we get on well. Basically there has always been a good relationship because we have always talked a lot, we have always cleared up uncertainties, removed doubts that may have arisen during the last few years (Massimo, male, 29, freelance professional).

At present this situation is very convenient for me: there is someone who cooks the food and does all the rest, and cuddles me. This is OK for me now, also because my mother and I are like sisters. Therefore I don't find it hard living with her, I am at ease, we do a lot of things together (Roberta, female, 30, office worker).

However this intense family relationship also reveals a darker side: the difficulty for the young adult to distance himself/herself from the family and to face the inevitable separation, the conflicting opposition between an adolescent identity and the construction of an adult identity. A common element of respondents is their inability to think of themselves as 'alone'. Loneliness is not perceived as an inescapable element of the human condition, but as a burden to avoid and remove from one's life experience.

This fear can be better understood by considering the inexperience of these young people about some aspects of life. Thanks to their family's support they have been relieved of taking responsibility for ordinary daily tasks. In the lack of a direct and prolonged experience in managing daily problems, it is reasonable to doubt their ability to succeed in facing a totally new life condition they have never experienced before.

Fear of loneliness is overcome by planning a 'traditional' exit from the parental home, that is living with a partner. The alternative to family life is another life in a similar space, where the relations experienced in the family of origin are reshaped and re-proposed:

In general I think it's better not to live on one's own, far from the family, and anyway it would be better to form an independent family. Outside my family I imagine another family and not living on my own. I'd never live by myself, I would feel too lonely in a flat (Nicoletta, female, 25, student worker).

I am worried about the idea of being alone. It's not the fact that my parents give me a safety net, but the idea that I don't hear another voice, that there is nobody coming home before or after me, the fact that I close the door and I am the last one who goes out (Veronica, female, 29, hospital doctor).

I don't even think of living with a friend, although I have friends, but I can't think of myself leaving home without a partner or living on my own (Walter, male, 30, free-lance journalist).

This rejection of alternative housing solutions can be ascribed to the existence of socialization patterns leading young people to extend their co-habitation with their parents until they form their own family. Therefore, as already mentioned,[9] the prolonged stay in the parental home is a condition which is socially accepted and little stigmatized. Moreover, there is a lack of services in Italy that might encourage young people to live away from the parental home during their university education. For instance, the decentralization and spread of universities in all urban areas during the seventies and eighties discouraged student's migration to the main universities in Italian cities. Moreover, apart from a few exceptions, the university where they obtain a degree has little importance for their professional career. Therefore, unlike other countries, in Italy there is no push to obtain a degree from a prestigious university. This is a further reason for preferring to study in a university close to the place of residence.

Young Men and Young Women Facing Transition

Research on Italian young people's experience of time,[10] conducted since the eighties, has highlighted that young men and young women structure their life project in a different way, based on a different time experience (Cavalli, 1985; Leccardi, 1991, 1996). In particular, young women plan their biography around the reconciliation of two different worlds or two different time orders: the professional and the family one. Therefore they have to match these two time orders to make them compatible with a new unitarian time order. As Leccardi said (1991, p. 139):

> It does not matter if, in the present, there is an hegemony of only one temporality; their simultaneous presence in the future is part of the biographical horizon and forms the centre around which biography is structured and identity takes its shape.

The attempt at reconciling these two dimensions of the biographical project can also be reflected in the definition of the path towards adulthood.

In the accounts of young women interviewed, professional and family self-fulfilments have the same value for the definition of the self and the achievement of family autonomy. Most women interviewed wish to leave the parental home when they form a stable couple with a partner. However, for some of them, in particular women approaching thirty or over thirty, the family project is more and more uncertain due to the lack of practical opportunities (they do not have a partner) to carry it out. They feel they are approaching an age where setting up an independent home cannot be postponed for too long. Therefore if independence from the family cannot be obtained by starting a stable life with a partner, once they have achieved economic independence, this family autonomy must be obtained while single. Leaving the parental home has in fact a triple symbolic value for young women: the rejection of a historical and cultural role limited to family care (included the care of the elderly), emancipation from family control and the achievement of individual autonomy.

In the accounts of young women, the age of thirty seems to be a time limit by which they decide to achieve their autonomy. Surprisingly, the reference to the age of thirty is so recurrent among younger women that it can be considered as the age by which women feel they must make and implement the final decisions of their life. For young women over thirty, establishing independent housing is considered a fundamental and inescapable stage of life as well as an essential choice to define and build up an adult identity:

> At a certain point of your life you must leave, you must go your way alone... As I don't have a project with a partner, I can't live here for ever, I can't live with my parents until I'm forty. It's out of the question. I live with other two adults who have other rules and I don't like it any more (Veronica, female, 29, hospital doctor).

Even if I don't manage to form my own family, I consider it necessary for me to establish an autonomous life. Of course, there isn't a deadline by which I must leave, but sooner or later one must leave home, try and find one's own identity, free oneself in order to find one's own independence (Roberta, female, 30, office worker).

If for women, the age of thirty takes on the value of a symbolic passage to adulthood, in men's representation the idea of a symbolic age or of an event marking the border of a new status seems to be absent. The lack of perception of a time limit marking youth makes it difficult for young men to pass to adulthood. Moreover, while for young women family events (for example marriage, cohabitation, motherhood) are real status transitions by which they define their social identity and achieve their biographical projects, for young men this perception is less defined. Indeed, social expectations regarding family self-fulfilment are lower for men. Therefore the young men interviewed are less determined to achieve a final household autonomy. By adopting a strategy of waiting and a reversibility of decisions, the choice to leave the parental home can be considered as a temporary experience, it can always be changed and it is possible to go back and live in the family of origin:

If I had to leave home I would do it to spend a period abroad. I don't know, I could find a job there, I could try to live on my own for a while, but then I think I will come back, it will not be a final decision (Antonio, male, 34, with a temporary job).

The idea could be to leave away from home, I could start by renting a flat, to live outside the family context I have lived in so far, just to try... A person leaves home because he/she wants to try to live on his/her own for a period, and if it doesn't work out he/she leaves everything and comes back home (Massimo, male, 29, freelance professional).

The Survey on Mothers

Different Youths: Mothers, Children and Transition to Adulthood

A common element shared by mothers interviewed is the awareness of the social changes enacted in the last few decades. In the reconstruction of personal biographies a comparison with the period where these mothers were at their children's age is frequent. They stress the difficulties of the past but also the real possibilities to overcome them: despite the limited financial resources of their family of origin and the sacrifices they had to make, there was confidence in the future and above all the certainty they could improve their condition. On the contrary, their children have greater financial and cultural resources, but are faced with an uncontrollable lack of certainty which prevents them from planning and carrying out a clear life project. From this point of view, mothers perceive transition as a process full of risks.

Unlike the present situation of their children, in the sixties the (then) younger generations faced the transition to adulthood with clear objectives. This implied a different way of facing the various steps in their biography: they left the parental home because they had a clear life project, the paths to reach the objective were linear and visible and above all it was possible to adjust one's aspirations to initial available resources and foresee achievable goals with a degree of certainty. Instead, the path of their children appears tortuous because uncertainty often imposes a continuous adaptation of objectives and consequently a continuous adjustment of available resources to the changes of the biographical path.

Mothers are perfectly aware that the project insecurity is due to exogenous factors, linked to several dimensions, ranging from the increased cost of housing to the labour crisis, from the need for new professional training to the speed of social changes. While young respondents are personally the protagonists of these changes, their mothers are spectators who manage to grasp only fragments of a deeply diversified mosaic without a clear understanding of the elements. This creates an obscure view of transition where the logic of the connection between the stages escapes them. Consequently, the step related to an independent household does not find a specific place within the various stages of the biographical path and remains a stage strictly linked to contingent events, like marriage or leaving home in order to work:

> When my husband and I graduated we immediately started to build something together and our future prospects were to improve from the start. Now I have the impression that leaving home is a sort of regression to achieve something indefinite. A young person who decides to live on his/her own has to face certain difficulties that we didn't have because we left home to obtain something, to build and achieve... Leaving home does not only mean living in a one-room flat and going to the parental home to eat or to have shirts ironed, but trying to carry out a life project, so it doesn't have to be an end in itself, but subject to a marriage or a working project... If this didn't happen, I would worry a little bit about it (Massimo's mother, 60, teacher).

Living with parents is considered by the mothers interviewed as a winning strategy to reduce external risks. The widespread idea is that there are no alternative solutions to family support whose function is to 'check' uncertainty. Mothers are rarely worried because their children do not have an independent home project. In their opinion, it is right to postpone the decision to leave the parental home until full financial independence has been achieved.

This attitude is partly linked to the lack of suitable family policies which forces the family of origin to fully support their children from a financial point of view, until they enter the labour market and become financially independent. Very often this family support continues even after the children have achieved a working status and is also crucial in allowing them to establish an independent household (Sgritta, 2002).

Faced with these conditions, parents are ready to help their children in leaving home under certain circumstances, especially for normative significant events like marriage. They are unlikely to financially support their children's leaving the parental home in order to meet their need for independence – probably apart from very well-off families. The prevailing idea is that the desire for independence can be satisfied by their children when they can achieve full economic independence. However a different attitude can be found among mothers of children aged around twenty-six and over thirty. The former consider that their sons/daughters can still wait a few years before leaving the parental home because first they must reach important goals at the working or affective level. On the contrary, mothers of young people aged over thirty are more concerned about the 'young adult' condition of their sons/daughters. Although their children have already taken some of the most important steps in the transition, they still have doubts about a rapid achievement of the other steps (leaving the parental home, family formation, parenthood).

Mothers and Children in the Family: Mutual Advantages

Reasons given by mothers to explain the extended stay of their children in the family are not very different from the reasons mentioned by children. Financial difficulties, the cost of housing and the decision to continue in higher education are the main reasons which justify the postponement of transition stages. The comforts of family life are also frequently mentioned. In particular, in the light of the well-being provided by living with parents, it is more difficult to overcome economic, working or studying difficulties. According to mothers, 'feeling good' or 'being happy' at home summarizes the advantages enjoyed by young people who choose to live with their parents: first of all a high degree of freedom and a suitable emotional and practical support.

On the contrary, the mothers were brought up according to stricter models, subject to greater control by their parents. As a matter of fact, some of them (the oldest mothers, who are about sixty) belong to a generation where leaving home, usually for marriage, coincided with the end of the family control. The lack of independence within the family and the desire to escape restrictions imposed by parents drove children to accelerate their exit from the parental home. Nowadays these conditions no longer exist and living with parents proves particularly advantageous. Based on this logic, if children enjoy full freedom, full understanding, affection and support, the establishment of independent housing loses its value:

> One leaves home because one moves for one's work or because one gets married or for other reasons, but leaving home to have an independent life, to feel free, is a rather puzzling phenomenon for me because in my house there is total freedom. In the past children left home because they got married and if they did not marry they stayed in the parental home. I am happy with this situation (Ilaria's mother, 62, retired office worker).

Some opinions also shed light on the implications of social and family changes which, in their opinion, have modified the youth condition inside and outside the family. For several mothers, this young generation is weaker, has a smaller store of experiences to allow them to face difficulties. In a word they are more immature – an adjective frequently used by mothers to describe their children. There is also an inability to make 'sacrifices', especially financial ones, and this opinion is shared by most mothers:

> There is a world of difference between the time I was my daughters' age and the present day, life has completely changed and I don't consider myself an old woman. My parents had a totally different attitude from the one I have with my children, probably because at that time life was harder, based on different values and I didn't want my daughters to suffer what I did. That's the way my generation behaves and this has been bad for our children. I mean that when I was my daughter's age, 26, I was more mature, I was ready to face any situation, any sacrifice and not only from a financial point of view. Now my daughter is weaker than I was and I think this is because we have brought up our children in affluence. This means that they are so well-off that they are no longer used to making sacrifices... their parents must always be behind them (Manuela's mother, 46, office worker).

The mothers of young people over thirty are worried and critical about the choice of their children to delay leaving home. They realize that the excessive helpfulness and protection offered by parents may in the long run become an obstacle to young people's emancipation from parental authority. Basically there is, on the one hand, the inability to confront their children – who are now adults and free to make their decisions autonomously – with the need of becoming independent of their family and of the security it guarantees; on the other hand there is the idea that a mother or a father cannot impose her/his choices on the children because the parents' role is to 'protect' and 'assist' them:

> I think I have given them a lot and probably it's because I gave a lot that they are still in this situation, that they want to live with their parents at all costs. Perhaps if the family had given less they would have found a different solution. Problems are always solved, we help them to solve any kind of problem, and we make things smooth for them. This is the situation. I don't know, I wonder whether it is the same for others or whether it is only a financial problem which does not allow them to face life, to pay the rent for housing and all the rest... Maybe the family gives too much and creates this security (Dino's mother, 66, housewife).

In a nutshell, young people's emancipation from the family of origin requires a commitment by parents, who must promote this separation and adapt themselves to the new role as parents of adult children ready to establish their autonomy. Mothers are willing to give space for autonomy and expression to children who are no longer adolescents, to respect their needs, but seem reluctant to distance themselves from their children and to reduce at least this protection. The parents'[11] idea seems to be that children must leave home only when they feel ready to do so. The parents' task is not to help them in making this decision, but not to interfere. The ways and timing of home leaving are decisions that lie only with them, while their duties as parents are to create a family environment which is as harmonious and friendly as possible, so that their children's choice to become independent is justified only by personal needs and not by a fault in the family.

In short, the message that parents communicate to children is that leaving the parental home is neither an important step in the process of achieving individual autonomy nor a crucial choice in their biographical path. Consequently, access to independent housing is not perceived as a choice which is part of a life project and loses any constructive role in individual experiences and in the formation of identity, while marriage becomes the event which by definition guarantees a legitimated social status.

It is undeniable that mothers also benefit from living with their children. To a certain extent, the children's presence in the family is for mothers an extension of their youth and an opportunity to further enjoy their presence before the inevitable separation. In the opinion of several mothers interviewed, children are more a resource than a burden. Therefore the daily overwork due to their presence is not perceived as taking time away from themselves:[12]

I rather like having my children living at home, sometimes I'd like to have more freedom, but honestly I don't give up my freedom (Walter's mother, 54, retired primary school teacher).

Continuing to provide daily support is a further possibility to 'enjoy the presence of my son or my daughter'. This frequent expression in many interviews proves the symbolic irreversibility that the choice of leaving home has for mothers. The children's access to independent housing is a final solution, difficult to change, especially when it is determined by marriage. Therefore it is better to do one's best to take advantage of having their children near before they form their own family.

The wish most frequently mentioned by mothers is to see their children 'settle down'. 'To settle down' means basically to achieve a transition consistent with traditional schemes, therefore as linear as possible. Work, marriage and parenthood are the most important aspirations of mothers for the future of their children – considered as objectives which allow them to achieve stability and security. For most mothers and children the alternative to achieving this objective is to remain living in the parental home until the conditions for leaving home are created:

The children's leaving the parental home is important for parents because the parents' satisfaction is to see their children settled down. I am happy that my children live at home, if they don't settle down how can they leave home?... My daughter is studying, she has still to take her degree and cannot get married, and then she doesn't have a boyfriend. I'll be glad if she leaves home to marry (Nicoletta's mother, 59, retired office worker).

It should be pointed out that the mothers' accounts reflect worries and fears similar to those expressed by young people. The fear of loneliness, the loss of family support and the daily presence of the family members are for young people the main disadvantages affecting the decision of leaving home. The mothers' worry for their children being lonely is not only part of expectations stemming from a cultural process but of a greater perception of the physiological steps of life. Based on this awareness, they cast their minds to a future where procreation and family tasks will come to an end for their generation and their children will have to take on similar duties. The formation of an independent family by their children becomes a guarantee of continuity between generations, strengthens child-parent bonds and represents security for the future.

Conclusions

In the process leading to the establishment of adult status, achieving independent housing is a complex phase, which involves structural factors linked to the organization of the schooling and training system, the labour market conditions as well as social and housing policies. For this reason, an analysis of this stage, more than the other transition steps, requires an in-depth study of the relations between the different factors that can help to promote or hinder the transition process.

It is well known that an assessment of this phenomenon cannot disregard the strategies of social policies which in Italy have not focused on the youth issue. The lack of support to the younger generations, that should be aimed at promoting independence from the family of origin, is a well-established factor in the welfare model prevailing in Italy (Chisholm et al., 2003, Esping-Andersen, 1995). Unlike most European countries where young people leave home earlier, in Italy the family fully supports children after the age of eighteen. Furthermore there is a total lack of youth housing policies and a limited offer of small housing units because of the absence of a consolidated culture of independent living. Finally, the extension of education, in particular higher education, together with the labour market instability, offers a picture of cultural, social, economic and institutional obligations which favour the postponement of leaving the parental home.

Among the variety of factors at stake, the parent-child relationship models are also important differentials to explain the different transition patterns in various countries. Leaving the parental home is a decision involving both parents and children. Parents, in particular, play a fundamental role in promoting the independence of their children and their leaving the parental home. They socialize their children to specific social representations of transition and generate specific expectations about the sequence of biographic events. Moreover, they can help them to leave the parental home by offering some kinds of material support.[13] In this respect, a recent longitudinal research highlighted that Italian families tend to give their children property (a home) (Barbagli et al., 2003). The event that usually encourages parents to offer this kind of support is marriage. This tradition has become established in Italy since the seventies, where owning a home was a pre-requisite for marriage. This trend is still widespread nowadays and parents are more inclined to materially support their children in achieving living independence if they do it to form an autonomous family.

Social class is another determinant variable to structure transition patterns and timing. In Italy young people from the middle[14] and upper-middle classes are those who most extend their stay in the parental home (Buzzi et al., 1997). Conversely, in countries in Central and Northern Europe and in the United States, young people from the upper-middle class move earlier into independent living situations in order to go to university, which is usually located in a different area from their place of residence (Cherlin et al., 1997; Goldscheider and Goldscheider, 1993). The experience of early independence from the parental home allows these young people to take on responsibilities and tasks 'almost typical of adults'. Independently of the transitional nature of this solution, living away from home for a long time helps and makes the final achievement of independence from the parents more gradual. Young people who have gone through this experience earlier are more likely to think over the meaning of an independent home in the process of establishing an autonomous life and to value it as a step in the life path.

The lack of these experimental and preparatory steps before the final exit from the family of origin partly explains the difficulties experienced by Italian young people in achieving transition to adulthood. The fear of facing everyday problems on their own, of meeting urgent needs when relying only on themselves are worriedly reported by respondents. Although young women seem to be more ready to face the challenge of living independently than young men of the same age, because they depend less on the practical support given by their mothers, an extended stay in the parental home equally increases uncertainties about the ability of a young person to face life without the daily support of the family. Young respondents adapt to family life and appreciate its practical advantages, the guarantee of the continuous presence and support of their parents, but do not manage to think of themselves in a reality different from the family one. The parents' willingness to meet their children's needs, even without a specific demand, forces children to family dependency and denies them the acknowledgement of adult status. Access to adulthood imposes not only social recognition, by giving young people social roles and responsibilities, but also the same recognition at family level.

Interviews with young people and their mothers highlighted the existence of similar representations of the transition to adulthood. Both of them seem to have a rather linear vision of this transition, in which the attainment of an independent home is justified by family reasons (marriage, cohabitation with a partner, or a professional move). The difficulty of thinking of different reasons from the socially legitimated ones, such as the desire for autonomy or to experiment a life outside the family context, points to a lack of common reflections upon the meaning that the transition process steps have in young people's lives and on the importance they have for young people in accepting social responsibilities.

The lack of attention to the problematic issue of transition to adulthood is an indicator of the specific parent-child relationship, over-concentrated on the present and on daily life. The future generates too many uncertainties and may reveal the problematic nature of an extended cohabitation which must go on smoothly because it is impossible to foresee its end.

Especially for young people, the future is no longer an area of achievement of their biographical project from which present choices become meaningful, but a risky and often distressing dimension (for instance, the fear of loneliness found in many interviews to young people) (Leccardi, 1999). The family therefore becomes a place where they can seek refuge against uncertainty. For young people, extended stay in the parental home is a difficult condition to change because of the problems experienced in the labour market, but also because of the various practical advantages of this choice (they do not have to prepare meals and do the laundry) and the certainty of continuous family support at the financial and emotional level.

With regard to mothers, it should be pointed out that the process toward the establishment of an autonomous life from the family may be treated with opposition from the parents, for whom leaving home is a real 'stage' in life full of worries and uncertainties. For the mothers interviewed, especially for the older ones, who found their only self-fulfilment in the family, the prolonged presence of young adult children guarantees the continuity of their family tasks and of the organization of time around these responsibilities. In the light of the low birth rate and extended life expectancy, a high investment in children makes them more vulnerable to the experience of the early 'empty nest'.

Finally, another aspect must be taken into account when analyzing the convergence of the transition representation by mothers and children interviewed. Achieving a linear transition is desirable, although not always a realistically possible condition. Recent research on Italian youth shows that, together with traditional transition patterns, other less ordinary patterns are emerging, aimed at postponing certain steps of transition. To be more precise, it is not so much the sequence of the various steps that has altered, as the time to achieve these various stages (Buzzi et al., 2002). This trend stresses that, on the one hand, the climate of uncertainty and, on the other, the structural constraints (employment uncertainty, extended education, lack of social support) prevent young people from achieving normative transition paths and direct them at experimenting processes characterized by the postponement of professional and family choices.

Notes

1   According to ISTAT (Central Statistics Institute) data, in Italy 3.6 per cent of young people aged 18-34 live alone and only 2 per cent of them cohabit with a partner (see Santoro, 2002).

2   Multiscopo surveys conducted by ISTAT every three months, every year and every five years investigate specific topics like the health conditions of the Italian population, the use of leisure time and citizens' safety. Part of these yearly surveys is devoted to families, with particular attention to family structures and behaviours (solidarity networks, life as a couple, etc.). For further details, see the chapter written by Ruspini.

3   Interviews with mother and son or daughter were conducted separately on the same day, to avoid people having the opportunity to interact and exchange information between the two interviews that could compromise spontaneous answers to the interview.

4   Even ISTAT (Central Statistics Institute) – the leading research institute in Italy – and IARD – the leading research institute on youth condition in the country which every four years carries out a survey on Italian young people – have progressively extended the age bracket of young people in their research to underline the prolongation of youth and the difficulty in moving toward adulthood. For instance, in the first IARD research on Italian youth condition carried out in 1983, the age bracket considered was 15-24 (Cavalli et al., 1984), while in the last research study carried out in 2000 the age bracket considered was 15-34 (Buzzi et al., 2002).

5   According to the ISTAT Labour Force survey, conducted at regional level, in July 2001 the unemployment rate in Lombardy (Milan is its capital) was 3.7 per cent, slightly below the Northern Italian rate, which is 4 per cent. The total unemployment rate in Italy is 9.5 per cent but in Southern Italy it reaches 19.3 per cent.

6   By 'mammismo' we mean the tendency of Italian young people, mostly male, to remain linked to their mother and their consequent difficulty in becoming emotionally and practically independent from their mothers.

7   The mothers gave us this piece of information.

8   The rationale of young people prolonging their permanence in the family is, according to the Weberian meaning, a rationality vis-à-vis the objective, because the goal that must be achieved is very clear: investing as much time and resources as possible in their professional career and profiting as much as possible from family benefits. Extended stay in the family becomes a means to achieve these objectives.

9   See the first paragraph.

10 The first research study carried out on this subject in the early eighties and co-ordinated by Cavalli (1985) is still an essential reference in the frame of Italian and European studies on youth. It stressed the importance of the time dimension in the structuring of individual biographies and in the definition of identity. Researchers (Annarita Calabrò, Carmen Leccardi, Marita Rampazi, Simonetta Tabboni) who co-operated in this first survey have continued to conduct research in this field, concentrating also on gender differences. For an overview of this series of research, see Jedlowski and Leccardi (2003).

11 We refer to parents and not to mothers because during the interviews several mothers expressed their opinion on the extended stay of their children in the family not as a personal view, but including their husband's opinion, which stresses not only a concordance of opinion but also an agreement in the upbringing and in the way of relating to their sons or daughters.

12 A datum that cannot be disregarded in understanding the willingness of Italian mothers to support their children for a long time is the organization of the Italian pension system. The generation of women aged fifty to sixty enjoyed extremely favorable conditions and had the possibility of retiring after less than thirty years' contributions to the retirement pension. Some mothers interviewed retired at a young age and were able to take care of their family full time. But the possibility of family care as an alternative to working outside the home has now been definitively abandoned. As Facchini (2001) shows, one must also consider that family care could become a serious burden at an older age, especially if it is protracted and there is almost no reciprocity between son/daughter and mother.

13 According to research, the financial resources of the family are essential opportunities for young people to quickly establish independent housing (Goldscheider and De Vanzo, 1989; Goldscheider and Goldscheider, 1993).

14 It should be pointed out that, according to IARD figures (Buzzi et al., 1997), middle-class young people show a wider variety of behaviour in leaving the family of origin. The middle class includes young people whose parents are white-collar workers, artisans and traders (self-employed workers). The young people in the first category are more inclined to stay at home longer, even longer than upper-middle class youth, while the others achieve earlier housing independence.

References

Barbagli, M., Castiglioni, M. and Dalla Zuanna, G. (eds), (2003), *Fare famiglia in Italia. Un secolo di cambiamenti (Forming a Family in Italy. A Century of Changes)*, Il Mulino, Bologna.

Buzzi, C., Cavalli, A. and De Lillo, A. (eds), (1997), *Giovani verso il duemila. Quarto rapporto IARD sulla condizione giovanile in Italia (Young People towards 2000. IV IARD Report on Youth Condition in Italy)*, Il Mulino, Bologna.

Buzzi, C., Cavalli, A. and De Lillo, A. (eds), (2002), *Giovani del nuovo secolo. Quinto rapporto IARD sulla condizione giovanile in Italia (Young People of the New Century. V IARD Report on Youth Condition in Italy)*, Il Mulino, Bologna.

Cavalli, A. (1980), 'La gioventù: condizione o processo?' (Youth: A Condition or a Process?), *Rassegna Italiana di Sociologia*, Vol. 3, pp. 519-42.

Cavalli, A. (1985), *Il tempo dei giovani (Time of Youth)*, Il Mulino, Bologna.

Cavalli, A. (1997) 'The Delayed Entry into Adulthood: Is It Good or Bad for Society?', in M.J. Pais and L. Chisholm (eds), *Jovens em mudança. Actas do Congresso Internacional 'Growing Up between Centre and Periphery'*, Lisbon, 2-4 May 1996, Istituto de Ciências Sociais da Universidade de Lisboa, Lisbon, pp. 179-186.

Cavalli, A. et al. (1984), *Giovani oggi (Young People Today)*, Il Mulino, Bologna.

Cavalli, A. and Galland, O. (eds), (1996), Senza fretta di crescere. L'ingresso difficile nella vita adulta (Growing up with no Hurry: The Difficult Entry in Adulthood), Liguori, Napoli.

Cherlin, A.J., Scabini, E. and Rossi, G. (eds), (1997), *Delayed Home Leaving in Europe and the United States*, Special Issue of Journal of Family Issues, Vol. 18(6).

Chisholm, L., de Lillo, A., Leccardi, C. and Richter, R. (eds), (2003), *Family Forms and the Young Generations in Europe. Report on the Annual Seminar 2001. Milan (Italy), 20-22 September 2001*, Austrian Institute for Family Studies, Wien.

Cordón, J.A.F. (1997), 'Youth Residential Independence and Autonomy', in A.J. Cherlin, E. Scabini and G. Rossi (eds), *Delayed Home Leaving in Europe and the United States*, Special Issue of Journal of Family Issues, Vol. 18(6), pp. 576-607.

Erikson, E.H. (1968), *Identity, Youth and Crisis*, Norton, New York.

Esping-Andersen, G. (1995), 'Il welfare state senza lavoro. L'ascesa del familismo nelle politiche sociali dell'Europa continentale' ('Welfare State without Job. The Rise in Familism in the Social Policy of Continental Europe'), *Stato e Mercato*, Vol. 45, pp. 347-380.

Facchini, C. (ed.), (2001), *Anziani, pluralità e mutamenti: condizioni sociali e demografiche, pensioni, salute e servizi in Lombardia (Elderly People, Plurality and Change: Social and Demographic Conditions, Social Security and Services in Lombardy)*, Angeli, Milan.

Furlong, A. and Cartmel, F. (1997), *Young People and Social Change. Individualization and Risk in Late Modernity*, Open University Press, Buckingham.

Goldscheider, F.K and De Vanzo, J. (1989), 'Pathways to Independent Living in Early Adulthood: Marriage, Semiautonomy, and Premarital Residential Independence', *Demography*, Vol. 26(4), pp. 597-614.

Goldscheider, F.K and Goldscheider, C. (1993), *Leaving Home before Marriage. Ethnicity, Familism, and Generational Relationships*, The University of Wisconsin Press, Madison.

Isfol (2000), *Rapporto Isfol 2000. Formazione e occupazione in Italia e in Europa (Isfol Report 2000. Training and Job in Italy and in Europe)*, Angeli, Milan.

ISTAT (2001), *Famiglie, abitazioni e sicurezza dei cittadini. Indagine Multiscopo sulle famiglie 'Aspetti della vita quotidiana'. Anno 2000 (Households, Housing and Citizens' Security. Multipurpose Survey on 'Aspects of Everyday Life'. Year 2000)*, ISTAT, Rome.

ISTAT (2003), *Annuario statistico italiano (Italian Statistical Yearbook)*, ISTAT, Rome.

Jedlowski, P. and Leccardi, C. (2003), Sociologia della vita quotidiana (Sociology of Everyday Life), Il Mulino, Bologna.

Leccardi, C. (1991), *Orizzonti del tempo. Esperienza del tempo e mutamento sociale (Time Horizons. Experience of Time and Social Change)*, Angeli, Milan.

Leccardi, C. (1996), *Futuro breve. Le giovani donne e il futuro (Short-term Future. Young Women and the Future)*, Rosenberg & Sellier, Turin.

Leccardi, C. (1999), 'Time, Youth and the Future', *Young*, Vol. 7(1), pp. 3-18.

Rossi, G. (1997), 'The Nestlings: Why young Adults Stay at Home Longer: The Italian Case', in A.J. Cherlin, E. Scabini and G. Rossi (eds), *Delayed Home Leaving in Europe and the United States*, Special Issue of Journal of Family Issues, Vol. 18(6), pp. 627-645.

Sabbadini, L.L. (1999), 'Modelli di formazione e organizzazione della famiglia' ('Formation and Organization Patterns of Family'), paper presented at the Conference 'Le famiglie interrogano le politiche sociali'('Families Question Social Policies'), Bologna, 29-31 March.

Santoro, M. (2002), *A casa con mamma. Storie di eterni adolescenti (At Home with Mummy. History of Eternal Adolescents)*, Unicopli, Milan.

Scabini, E. and Donati P. (eds), (1988), *La famiglia 'lunga' del giovane adulto. Verso nuovi compiti evolutivi (The 'Long' Family of Young Adults. Towards New Evolutionary Tasks)*, Vita e Pensiero, Milan.

Scabini, E. and Rossi, G. (eds), (1997), *Giovani in famiglia tra autonomia e nuove dipendenze (Young People in the Family between Autonomy and New Dependencies)*, Vita e Pensiero, Milan.

Schizzerotto, A. (2002), *Vite ineguali. Disuguaglianze e corsi di vita nell'Italia contemporanea (Inequal Lifes. Inequalities and Life Paths in Contemporary Italy)*, Il Mulino, Bologna.

Sgritta, G.B (ed.). (2002), *Il gioco delle generazioni. Famiglie e scambi sociali nelle reti primarie (The Play of Generations. Families and Social Exchanges in Primary Networks)*, Angeli, Milan.

Chapter 8

Work and Care in the Life-Course of Young Adults in the Netherlands

Manuela du Bois-Reymond and Yolanda te Poel

Introduction

One of the greatest changes that has taken place in gender relations is concerned with the care of children. Since the second feminist movement of the 1970s women have put the issue of exclusion of 'one half of humankind' from participation in societal matters on the political agenda. One of the main issues concerned their exclusion from the labour market because of the ideology of a gendered normal biography demanding a far reaching division of tasks between men and women: he the breadwinner; she the mother and housewife.

As in most European countries, the participation of Dutch females in education and on the labour market has increased markedly over the last three decades. Until the beginning of the 1960s only 16 per cent of all Dutch women were on a payroll and at the beginning of the 1970s still only a quarter of the women belonged to that category (Kennedy, 1995). In 2001, 53 per cent of all women were working, and for the younger cohorts this has increased further to 75 per cent. However, it should be noted that 78 per cent of all women on a payroll work part-time: 16 per cent work less than 12 hours per week, 62 per cent work 12-34 hours per week. Only 22 per cent of all Dutch women on a payroll have a full-time job, that is 11.5 per cent of all women. Among the category of mothers with a child between 0-5 years of age and a partner, 56 per cent are working; among those without a partner only 37 per cent (Portegijs et al., 2002). If the division of employment between men and women is considered, it can be observed that among families with two wage-earners, one partner works full-time, the other part-time and it is usually the woman working on a half-day basis. In recent years that division has become even more unequal: the category of couples who work approximately the same amount of hours has decreased. On the other hand, there is no other European nation where so many men only work half a day, namely 17 per cent (Keuzenkamp and Hooghiemstra, 2000). However, 'the other half' of their working time is, in contrast to women, not dedicated to the household or children, but to their studies and hobbies. In addition to that, double wage-earners are significantly more often without children than other types of households.

These few statistics already show that the traditional division of work between the sexes, where the man is the main breadwinner and the women is mainly responsible for the house and children, is by no means as obvious as it used to be a few decades ago. Furthermore, several studies, both qualitative as well as quantitative, have shown that there is a gender specific view on the division between paid and unpaid (family-) work: in several European countries, like Germany and the Netherlands, males tend, in spite of societal changes that have taken place throughout the generations and sexes, to hold on to the 'old' division of work. Females, however, have a more ambivalent attitude toward the matter (Oechsle, 2000; Drew, 1998; Jansen and Liefbroer, 2001). Nevertheless, 'something is moving' even among young men. A more recent Dutch study shows that males give different reasons according to different social backgrounds for being willing or unwilling to care for the family. New patterns and balances of power are developing between the sexes which no longer allow straightforward statements on gender-differences or the time-frame wherein the changes develop to a more equal division of tasks between men and women (Hochschild, 1997; Grünell, 2001).

In our contribution we deal with negotiation processes between young women and men aged between 27 and 31 years who are either already parents or who are still postponing parenthood. Our data is derived from a longitudinal study on life and transition choices of young people from the time they left school into young adulthood (see the section on Research). From the beginning of the study we give information about the 'combination problem' and what young men and women thought about it. Here we will discuss the following problem: *Which changes in the area of division of work- and care-orientation evolve in the life-course of young-adult parents and postponers of parenthood, and which factors have an influence on the changes?*

In the following section we will discuss modernization paradoxes that evolve out of the discrepancies in expectations and actions of the different societal agents involved: children, women/mothers, men/fathers, and the governmental policy concerning care facilities. Furthermore, on the basis of our research we will present an 'orientation-typology' of the attitudes and solutions of young-adult parents and those who postpone parenthood. At the end we will examine the theoretical life-course implications of our findings.

Modernization-Paradoxes

In the Netherlands family life plays an extraordinarily important role. In comparison to other nations Dutch society is said to be particularly child-friendly and family-oriented (Rispens et al., 1996; du Bois-Reymond, 1998). According to public opinion, children have the right to caring love and the security of a family home provided by their parents. Many adults who are now parents have experienced this themselves. They speak of a protected childhood and of mothers who were always waiting 'with a cup of tea after school'. This has shaped their own as well as the public attitudes and views concerning parenthood and child-raising. In another report we have described this complex with the term 'domesticity-pedagogy' (du Bois-Reymond et al., 1999). At the same time the

Netherlands belong to those European nations where the gender-relation has radically changed and been modernized since the 1960s. This has led to a series of paradoxes, which, as we shall show, need to be dealt with by means of negotiation-processes.

For *children* the modernization of gender-relations manifests in an increasing autonomy as well as in an increasing institutionalization of their lives. By liberating themselves from the one-sided gender-role through work outside the home, at the same time women foster the independence of their children who no longer experience their mother only as a caretaker, but as a person with her own daily agenda to which the children need to adjust and learn to take care of themselves. Female employment, together with the overall longer school hours and years in education, in the long run foster earlier and longer periods of absenteeism from the family home. Children spend more hours in facilities outside the family, not only in crèches and in school, but also in leisure-facilities where they are confronted with people other than their own parental caretakers (Wittebrood et al., 2000; Zeijl, 2001).

Contemporary children are included in the negotiations between their parents on the distribution of family duties, as active and competent co-negotiators (on parental attention, family chores, leisure activities etc.). Babies and toddlers' reactions also influence the conflict management of their parents in the case of divergent needs, agendas, sickness or cancellation of nursery care. Thus, children experience the modernization paradox on the one hand in gaining more autonomy and independence within the family, on the other hand in having to release a part of the motherly overall care to other societal agents.

From the *women*'s view-point the modernization paradox presents itself as such that, on the one hand the shift of the gender-specific 'normal' biography has created space for self-realization and for the realization of a career; on the other hand women are put in a tight spot by that same career in terms of meeting all the expectations life puts on them: the existing expectations of the role of a mother, the increasing demands on the role as a partner, the new added duties related to their profession. Within that frame they experience a hardly endurable tension between *ideological continuity* in societal (and for a part also their own) expectations on the traditional mother role on the one hand and *inter-generational discontinuity* on the other hand: as women of today they live with different desires and options than previous generations.

Between the needs of the children, the expectations and the duties related to the occupation of their male partner, women have to negotiate the most. They need to create and maintain a *negotiating culture* within the family which prevents the divergent interests amounting to destructive conflicts and pain. In addition to that they also need to negotiate outside the family: with the principal of the day-care centre on pedagogical principles or with their employer on flexible work schedules for instance when the child is sick or the day-care centre is closed.

In comparison with women, the modernization paradox from the perspective of *men* consists of a greater continuity of the 'normal' biography in which they are the main wage-earners, while at the same time being increasingly confronted with partners who also want to build on a career and as a consequence put the main responsibility for childcare up for discussion. Thus men are forced by their partners into the negotiation process, whether they want to or not, and they experience at least a small part of the double burden women carry. For them the negotiations on childcare are stressful in that they are for the most part the main wage-earners and at the same time they want to (learn to) see themselves as modern partners as well as good, solid fathers who have a vital interest in the co-raising of their children. This is much more the case (and likelihood) nowadays than in the previous generation of fathers.

Finally, the modernization paradox arises for the *state and society* as a whole: on the one hand acceptance of the emancipation of the woman, for now even the labour market finds her indispensable; on the other hand the deeprootedness in motherhood ideologies and traditions. For a long time the government in the Netherlands had avoided creating and financially supporting childcare provisions outside the family. For several years now it has been forced to make provisions by the interests of the labour market and the pressure of women and mothers who insist on their (further) emancipation. In order to straighten out these divergent interests and ideologies, negotiations between the different governmental and social groups are necessary: ministry departments, labour unions, churches, employers etc.

The modernization paradoxes with the corresponding negotiation processes and cultures mentioned above are balanced out in the Netherlands with the *model of the one and a half family*. It consists of the man having a full-time job, and the woman (as mother) a part-time or half-day job. This is the Dutch solution to the afore mentioned modernization paradoxes. The *children* keep 'enough mother' and are content when they spend a part of the week in the nursery; if it is not too many days they are fairly happy with it. The *mothers* are also satisfied, because they can combine work with childcare. The double burden is manageable in that way. The fact that they are not able to follow their career with all their energy is compensated with the prospect of making up for this later when the children are 'out of the rough' phase. The *fathers* accept the model because it does not shake the foundations of their 'normal' biography as the main wage-earner. With the co-income of the women enough money is earned to achieve a lifestyle that corresponds to rising consumption standards (if possible an owner-occupied apartment or house, a car, and a holiday trip at least twice a year). Finally *society as a whole* is satisfied with the model: the part-time jobs are occupied by women, they are cheap and the state does not have to (at least not yet) provide a complete national covering of day-care centres.

However, this does not mean that the one-and-a-half model is static or stable. It is not. Increasingly more women want to work longer hours and thus demand more childcare facilities. Employers do too, because they need more female labour. The general pressure on the state to respond to these needs is increasing. At the same time a counter tendency is noticeable: well educated women who clearly choose against accepting paid work in the period when their children are small. They resist the pressure they sense from the outside that expects them to let the community profit from their education and professional competences; they are (for the time being) satisfied with a lower family income and a lower living standard because without a job they have more time for their children (Orriëns, 2002).

Historically, this development can be illustrated in the following conspectus:

Table 8.1   Changes over time in normal biography and ideology

	Gender and biography	Ideology and institutions
1950/60	Complementary gender roles; mother responsible for child care	(Christian) ideology of motherhood; no child-care facilities
1960/70	Breach with gender-based 'normal' biography; mothers in need of child-care facilities	2nd feminist movement fight for child-care facilities; motherhood ideology under siege
1970/today	Growing family pluralization; growing need for child-care facilities; increasing numbers living the one-and-a-half model	Pluralization of family ideologies; creation of child-care facilities; propagation of the one-and-a-half model

The Research

The results of a longitudinal study on orientations and choices concerning education, work and care within (sexual) relationships among youth and young adults, which was carried out in the period 1988-2002, show the different ways young parents as well as young adults without children, but who are living with a partner, participate in and organize the one-and-a-half model. The research was partly supported by the Ministry of Social Affairs who wanted to get information and insight into the problems of young mothers and fathers who have to combine work and childcare.

In 2001 we interviewed 68 young adults with whom we had already talked four times in depth over a period of 13 years after they left high school about important choices in their lives. They were part of a group of 120 adolescents, 54 young men and 56 girls who came from different social and economical backgrounds and whom we had interviewed in 1988 for the first time. They were divided in all the various forms of high school education in the Netherlands (vocational education, general education and preliminary scientific education).[1] During the first interview (in 1988) the then youths were between 16-19 years of age. By means of elaborate qualitative biographical interviews, changes in their view and choices in the areas of education, work, sexuality, relationships and care-work combination were documented in 1988, 1989, and 1990 with 120 respondents, in 1997 with 85 respondents. The general results of the study indicate that the initial orientation toward the traditional gender-based 'normal' biography almost totally disappeared from the orientation of most of the girls. Even though three years after completion of further education an increasing percentage of them still agreed to disrupt their working career at the arrival of a child, after the completion of tertiary education and/or after a couple of years of work and wage experience, most of them opted for a combination of work and care tasks (one and a half model). Even the greater part of the males, over the course of 10 years, showed more modern orientations. In 1988 not even 5 per cent of the boys planned to combine work with care tasks (part-time work) when they had children. It was difficult for them to imagine what life would be like in this combination. In 1997 however, approximately 40 per cent chose a combination of work and care tasks in the case of fatherhood, next to 35 per cent who aimed for a full-time job without care tasks, and a large group of remainders who were still in doubt about their choices (du Bois-Reymond et al., 2001).

In 2001 the youths were 27-31 years of age. The average age of parents at the arrival of the first child in the Netherlands is approximately 29 years (CBS, 1999). We expected that a large part of our sample would have had children in the meantime, and that even non-parents had made clear or tentative choices concerning (the combination of) care and work. We wanted to know how well young adults who had planned earlier on to combine work and care had succeeded, and what circumstances were supportive, or conversely, a hindrance. We wanted to study whether young adults who had intended to achieve a traditional trajectory earlier on, that is young men working full-time, young women caring full-time, either permanently or as long as the children are small, still made that choice. What conditions were the most important in the area of education, work, salary and secondary conditions of employment? We also wanted to know whether work-care choices were mainly a question of cultural orientation or whether clear structural influences such as high costs of day-care centres were determining these choices.

In all four interview rounds (1988, 1989, 1990 and 2001) we conducted biographical face-to-face interviews exploring the various life areas and life decisions in life-course perspective. The interviews were tape-recorded and protocolled, which clustered the material according to the relevant research questions. By analysing the material, the researchers found sensitizing concepts (Strauss and Corbin, 1998) which were then used to single out all the dimensions involved in a cluster (variables). We then coded the variables and analysed the material further with the help of SPSS to find broad trends as well as exceptional constellations. Our coding scheme allowed for analysis on an individual level (how certain attitudes changed or remained stable in the research period) as well as on an aggregated level (which changes can we discern between females as opposed to males, between different educational levels etc.). The essentially qualitative nature of the study was preserved by working extensively with case studies, paying attention to the interaction of specific life situations and life events and personal choices and coping strategies.

Although the themes under study remained the same over five rounds, after the first round the questions were adapted to fit specific respondents and his or her individual life course. In the fifth interview round, 68 of the 85 respondents of the 1997 sample remained. With regard to education and gender they give a good representation of earlier samples. They also form the basis for the longitudinal data presented here. The group consisted of 30 parents and 38 who had postponed parenthood, among which 38 were young women and 30 young men. Most of the parents have one child, born in the period between the previous and this interview round.

Orientation Typology of Young Adult Parents and Postponers

In the last study round we asked the young parents about the distribution of work and care tasks which they had achieved. This led to six work-care combinations:

1. Both partners work part-time and both care;
2. Both work full-time and leave the care of their child to a third party;
3. The man works full-time and the woman cares full-time;
4. The man works part-time, the woman works full-time and both care;
5. The woman works part-time and takes a lot of care-responsibilities, the man works full-time and takes few care-responsibilities;
6. The woman works part-time, the man works full-time and both care.

On the basis of their choices with regard to the distribution of work and care tasks between partners we differentiate between two groups of parents:

- 'normal' biographical and
- choice biographical oriented parents

   With 'normal' biographical we understand the new standard of one and a half wage earner families where the father works full-time and takes little or no time for care tasks and has few responsibilities. The mother is a full-time housewife or works part-time and next to this dedicates most of her time to caring for the home and the children. In this category there are also families where the mother stops working after the birth of her first child and lives a more traditional biography (from our sample only three).

   Within choice biographically oriented families, both partners spend a substantial part of their lives and time on care tasks and both take the responsibilities for the care of the children and the house chores on their shoulders next to their full-time or part-time work.

   Apart from these two groups of parents we discern a group of postponers of parenthood, young adults who have not yet taken the step to parenthood or who are not planning to do so (see Tables 8.2 and 8.3). Three respondents in this group were expecting a child at the time the interview took place.

Table 8.2   Number of 'normal' biographical parents, choice biographical parents and postponers, according to gender

	Women	Men	Total
Normal bio. parents	11	9	20
Choice bio. parents	7	3	10
Postponers	20	18	38
Total	38	20	68

Table 8.3   Number of 'normal' biographical parents, choice biographical parents and postponers, according to the level of education

	High	Average	Low	Total
Normal bio. parents	6	3	11	20
Choice bio. parents	5	3	2	10
Postponers	20	12	6	38
Total	31	18	19	68

Modern Parenthood and Negotiations: Expectations

For the past few decades the unequal work-care division has already been the subject of heated discussions. Since the 1970s, the feminist movement and several governmental publicity campaigns have broken through the natural course of the breadwinner family. In the combination scenario approved by the Dutch government, women and men have a part-time job during the period when they care for and invest in small children – both in equal division of care tasks. The aim is that both of them spend more time working in the period after the completion of their education until the beginning of parenthood, and after the period of raising their children begin to spend more time on work again, so that spread over their whole life-course they spend on average 30 to 32 hours a week working.

As shown by previous interview rounds the ideology of the equal work-care division puts all men, and in particular highly educated men, under pressure. As a result, a part of them are aware of the fact that they can't get away with withdrawing from a more equal division of work-care tasks with their partners. We therefore expected that mothers as well as women without children negotiated regularly with their partners on the involvement of their partner in care tasks, and that both talk with their employers in order to arrange the best possible working conditions. In particular *women* with a high education level would enter into discussion with their partners and search for solutions. We thought that highly educated *men* would voluntarily, or pressured by their wives, take on more care tasks and would also negotiate working conditions with their employers. We assumed that the negotiations in the families of more highly educated parents would turn out to be the most complicated ones: in all probability they would constantly have to negotiate compromises between career ambitions and the ambition to be a caring parent. Lower educated women would more easily accept the 'natural' course of gender differences and inequality in division which evolved out of the domination of the breadwinner model. Less highly educated men probably consider it a bestowed favour that their wife 'is allowed' to work and thus to a certain degree undermine their own position as supporters of the family.

The postponers of parenthood have in the main completed long education trajectories and invested a great deal in their career. Postponement of parenthood is a part of that. Following a career is probably more important for this group than for parents. In addition to that they do not consider the conditions under which they want to raise children yet.

How do these expectations match with the results of our study?

'Normal' Biographically Oriented Parents

H. is a 29 year old woman with vocational training. She works 20 hours per week on the administrative staff at a big brewery. H. is married and has a five-year-old son. When we first interviewed her in 1988 she wanted three or four children and to take care of them by herself as long as they were little. Even three years later when she had already had an adminstrative job for quite some time she considered the care for her children as the central activity in her life. 'There should always somebody be at home for the children', she said then. She thought it natural that this person would be herself. 'I have always made a choice for children. Even if I got the greatest job, I would want to be with my children.' She was 24 back then. Seven years later she bought a house with her partner and moved in with him. She wanted to postpone having children, but her plans to stay home with the children had not changed. The idea of having to work for her whole life was like a nightmare:

> Terrible. And if things work out I won't have to. And when we have established ourselves and gained a bit of financial stability with the house we have bought then I will stay at home the first couple of years until they go to school. And then I might look for a part-time job to work in the mornings or afternoons.

In the interview in 2001 she tells us that the birth of her son is the most important event in her life. She is in doubt whether or not to stop working. If it were possible financially she would probably do so. On the other hand she fears that she would get bored. If she were a full-time housewife she would miss the contact with her colleagues and the change, in particular since in her neighbourhood or environment there are hardly any other women full-time at home.

For two working days out of three her mother-in-law takes care of her son. Her own mother takes care of her son the third day. H. felt uncomfortable with the idea of leaving her son with strangers. Her husband's working less in order to take care of their son for one or two days has never even been considered as an option. He does not want to and he thinks it is not possible with his work. Since she earned less than he did it influenced the choice that she and not he would work less. But even if they had earned the same amount, the choice in care division would have been the same. She said she never talks with her husband about these things.

The result of her working part-time and him working full-time is that the care-load at home is unequally divided. Her husband helps her a little bit with housekeeping, but only if she asks him explicitly to do so. This goes against her feeling of 'justice' and sometimes she complains about him to her mother but justifies his behaviour at the same time. At the weekends her husband helps in taking care for his son, but also has to be pushed to do so. Nevertheless, H. is satisfied with her situation because the combination of work and care does not stress her out.

A 'normal' biographical work-care distribution had been arranged by 20 of the 30 parent couples of our sample. Characteristic of these one-and-a half wage-earners was that in those families, women used more options in the area of work while men did not carry more care responsibilities. Over half of this group is less educated (lower vocational education or early school leavers), and a fourth belongs to the highly educated group (higher professional education or university). Women from the 'normal' biographical families have part-time jobs that vary between 12 to 30 hours. Three quarters of them work fewer than 24 hours per week. Men work at least 36 hours or more.

Care and Work from a Biographical Perspective: The Power of 'Naturalness'

The work and care division of 'normal' biographical parents (n-parents) is firmly rooted in their background. Much of the time they were brought up in families where the mother stayed at home in order to care for the children. Full time work has never been an option for the n-mothers. Ten years ago a majority still intended to stop working temporarily or permanently after the arrival of children. From an early age they have already had a future in mind where they would have enough time for their child(ren) – a picture of the mother who stays at home until her children go to school and who wait at home with a cup of tea when they finally go to school. Only since they started working, have these women grown towards the decision to keep their part-time work due to positive experiences related to work such as their own income or an addition to the family finances. But perhaps even more important are the social contacts with colleagues on the work floor and the working climate in general. In her choices however the desire to enjoy her children predominates, at least until they go to school. This also implies that these women want more than one and maybe more than two children.

Most of the n-fathers had already chosen earlier on in their lives to have a full-time job without substantial care tasks, and were opting for a partner who would stay 'at home with the children'. Thus they belonged to the group of young men in earlier interview rounds who had made a traditional choice. Due to the influence of the public discussion on equal division of tasks and sometimes also due to financial needs, they accept that their wives are working. *My wife is free to work if she wants to.* For the fathers as well as for the mothers of n-families however it is still natural that their children are in better keeping in the hands of a loving and caring mother than anywhere else.

The structural inequality of prospects concerning the income of the n-fathers and n-mothers gives a rational basis for the biographical power of 'naturalness' (see Komter 1990). The better financial prospects of the n-fathers in our samples compared to their wives (even after compensation for part-time work) justify their gender specific choices. In addition, the unequal promotion prospects of n-mothers and n-fathers play a role. Both partners, men and women, experience and accept that men have more possibilities for promotion.

Negotiations on Unequal Work and Care Distribution

In n-families the division of work hardly seems to be a point of discussion between the partners. Only the amount of hours and days the woman is working seems to give rise to discussion or possible negotiation between the partners. Both partners in n-families experience that there is a more tolerant organization-culture for women concerning part-time work than for men. Employers and colleagues of n-mothers are always willing to change days and schedules or to change a meeting if there are problems at home. N-fathers, however, often experience a clearly intolerant culture with regard to part-time work, and they put little or no effort into trying to change this. The most important cause for the acceptance of the status quo and the lack of willingness to negotiate is rooted in the conviction of the mothers as well as the fathers that the employment of the mother must not be at the expense of family life. In comparison to the less highly educated males, several highly educated n-fathers feel the pressure of the predominant ideology much more to divide work and care more justly. However they justify their choice for full-time work with the claim that their partners are not as ambitious as they are:

> I think I need a job that is new and where there are possibilities to grow in my career. And if I now work for three days or so, well, in terms of possibilities that's not a good move (...) But S. (his wife) is far less ambitious. She thinks she needs a good job with an academic level, writing reports, she's not really expecting to get loaded with so much responsibility right now.

N-mothers, including the highly educated women with an extensive part-time job, do not look at work from a career perspective in the first place. Work must not burden their family life. They try to create a harmony between the care of their children, their work, and their social contacts.

This also implies that they do not have disputes with their partners on the unequal work-care division as well as the gradually evolving inequality in the division of household tasks. Even with exceptions, the fathers in these families only have a small part in household tasks; once a week helping with the dishes, putting children to bed, getting in some groceries. They feel they have contributed their share. The women consider their far larger part in the organization of the household to be a duty toward their husbands because they work less and receive less pay. This opinion is reinforced by their husbands who show them in many ways that as men they are not competent enough to complete household tasks. Requests and expectations to give a hand and help out is considered by n-fathers as complaining and nagging.

This does not mean that all n-mothers are satisfied. Several of them find the combination of care tasks and a (demanding) part-time job straining, and several mothers who do not have a job are nevertheless dissatisfied with the low care participation by their husbands. But they give up quite quickly on negotiations for a greater participation in the care of the children and household tasks and look for help from friends or their own mother. Working mothers reduce the stress of their double burden by postponing career perspectives to the future and strictly sticking to the working hours and times in the present.

Making Use of the Day Care

Most n-families do not make use of paid day-care centres. Only 3 in 20 n-families do that, the remainder relies on grandparents and other family members or friends. In their opinion a child should mainly be raised by the parents or close family members. They are not familiar with the organization of a day care centre and have the idea that their children would not get enough attention. They clearly criticize the 'career women' who 'get rid' of their children in the day-care centre:

> No, I wouldn't want another to be saddled with. Because if I want children so desperately, another has to pay the piper, no (...) if you choose for children, then you have to pay the piper. Having a child and then dumping him in the crèche – that wouldn't be it. If I see a career woman in pregnancy gymnastics that quickly wants to have a child, and then quickly gets rid of it in the crèche...

Next to the ideological rejection the high costs of a day care centre play an important in not using them.

The few n-mothers and n-fathers who do make use of a day nursery are all highly educated people. They find the continuity that a day-care centre offers is important and also mention pedagogical advantages. Because most of the mothers in their environment work all day, contrary to the low and averagely educated mothers, they see the day-care centre as an acceptable family-substitute where their child can also develop social skills on top.

In most 'normal' biographical oriented families, it is the woman who searches for an alternative to care-taking when, through sickness or other circumstances, the child cannot stay at a day-care centre. Grandmothers seem to be a most welcome support in all families. N-mothers are also more willing than their male partners to take a day off or to exchange a duty with a colleague. The man takes a day off or exchanges a duty only when there is no other option. In our interviews the women regularly mentioned that they would like their partners to search more actively for alternatives in case of need.

The small extent to which n-parents make use of day-care centres does not correspond to the provision their own employers make. In half of the n-families at least one of the two partners could make use of either a provision within the company or of financial re-compensation. Moreover, hardly any use is made of the provisions concerning maternity leave. N-parents and in particular men are not well informed about the matter and do not think it necessary to make use of them because they are content with the arrangements they have made: one part of the week they care themselves, and the other part they make use of the service of a grandmother.

Choice Biographically Oriented Parents

A. is a 31 year old married man,, and has a one and a half year old daughter. He has a degree in environmental physics and works as a physics teacher in a high school. Twelve years ago he was already dating his present wife, who back then studied political science. He was already very decisive in his plan to work part-time in order to take care of possible future children. Two years later he stated again that having children must not be at the expense of his wife's career:

> You see, giving birth is something women do, but mostly the woman is left paying the piper, too. That's why I think we need a sort of guarantee that my wife can go to work again after the pregnancy…you see many of them have a baby very early, and then the woman is stuck at home, with raising the children, I don't agree with that…. And of course it is really great having the opportunity to see your children growing up!

Now, in 2001, he works full-time (paid for 38 hours), but he divides his work over 4 days so that he can take care of his child, too. He has always wanted children, but waited with his wife until the timing felt right. Even though A. was a bit shivery when they made the decision, he thought it was a natural step in their relationship. A calls the birth of his daughter the most important change in his life, because it has determined what his life looks like now. When his wife got pregnant they decided to work four days each. He enjoys the amount of days he is working and at the same time he feels he is not missing out on his daughter, and he is taken serious at his work.

A. finds the way how he and his wife divide work and care tasks ideal. Each takes care of the child one day a week. Next to this they make use of a day-care centre. He thinks this is an ideal way of day care, because the staff is professional and because his daughter learns to interact with other children. They did not want to engage the family because he did not want to be dependant on them or get into discussions over differences in opinions on child raising.

Household tasks are divided equally between him and his wife, but most of it is taken care of by the cleaner. They have never actually talked about the division of household tasks or about the influence of income or amount of work on this task division. They consider their jobs equal, and the division of tasks in household is also equal. They 'rumble along'.

A third of the young parents from our research sample have made new choices with regard to work and care. In these choice biographically oriented families (c-families) it is not natural for the man to work full-time and only the woman be responsible for taking care of a child, and much less so in the combination with a part-time job. They organize work and care in different ways. In a large number of these families both parents work part-time because they want to share responsibilities. Or both of them work full-time and they release the care of their child(ren) mostly to a third party. In other c-families the father has a paid part-time job, the mother works full-time and they share the care tasks according to this pattern. Even in the families where the man works full-time and his wife works part-time, the care tasks are divided fairly equally, and most of this is, in the main, the desire of both partners. Half of the respondents of this group are highly educated, and only two respondents have a poor education. The part-time workers all have extensive part-time jobs, and the majority of them work more than 24 hours.

The young c-fathers choose throughout to care one day a week for their child. If their work situation does not allow them to work part-time,[2] they organize their workdays in such a way that they can save one care day by either working longer on other days or by taking some work home. A large part of the mothers combine care tasks with a full-time job.

Ideology and Participation in Care Tasks

Fathers from choice biographical families want to be involved in the care (tasks) of their children. They identify with the discourse on the equal work-care division and are willing to work part-time or to organize their working schedule in such a way that they can be involved in the upbringing of their children. Throughout the sample, these fathers stem from families where their own mother had had a paid job. Their willingness and desire to be involved in care tasks already dates back to the moment after completion of high school. They had already agreed on this with their girl-friend at that time, often long before the birth of a child. Moreover their girl-friends were not satisfied with a 'breadwinner' husband who did not offer them a chance for personal development and their own income. However, committed as the c-fathers may be, they are not as strongly care-task oriented as c-mothers. C-fathers show that they consider it a luxury to be able to stay home one day a week and care for their child. They argue from a work-orientation: care is desirable as long as it can be arranged within the frame of their work-organization, their ambitions and the need for financial security.

For young c-mothers work has several important functions – fulfilment of ambitions, financial independence and security, and social contacts. But their ambitions are, in the same way as with n-mothers, determined by their care orientation. Their biographies show that they have carefully anticipated motherhood, even though, contrary to the n-mothers, mainly within a combination scenario. Care for their child takes the first place in their lives, but not in the lives of the fathers. In addition to that, most of the c-mothers choose to care several days for their child(ren), whereas most of the fathers limit this to one day a week as already mentioned.

The care participation of fathers in c-families takes place in the frame of an acceptable income situation, where women generally do not earn less than their partners. In several families the women even earn more, either overall or after compensation for the part-time amount of hours, for instance in a family where the woman is a senior government civil servant and her husband is a high-school teacher. Parents in most of the c-families do not experience a great difference in their career perspectives. Fathers as well as mothers work in a tolerant organization culture (teaching, municipality services, welfare). Overall, there is greater understanding on the part of their employers and colleagues for their desire to work part-time.

Negotiations on Care Distribution

The young c-parents emphasize that the consideration of promotion prospects did not have an influence on their arrangements of work-care distribution. According to their explanation, the involvement of both partners in the care of their child(ren) has priority over a career. Nevertheless, the confrontation with pressures – big part-time or full-time jobs, the chores of family life, and maintaining contacts with friends and family of origin – gives rise to stressful situations and complicated discussions about arranging the weekly schedules (usually on Sunday evening), in particular with parents who both have a full-time job and who are constantly busy reducing the 'combination stress':

> Our lives seems to be one big work schedule. 'Did you think of that and can you take this along? We need to buy this and a present for so and so, because it's his/her birthday or we won't have time for that anymore'. I feel we are like two yuppies: both of us with a mobile stuck to our ears and making appointments and arrangements.

In the case of special circumstances such as the sickness of a partner or a change of job, the c-parents experience that the combination of work and care tasks is barely manageable. Several respondents postpone having a second child, because they think that the combination of two busy jobs and two children will be too difficult. Furthermore, all part-time workers indicate that they would like to have more time available for care and for social contacts. Several c-mothers show that they would like their partners to take more than one day to care for their child. This pertains in particular to mothers whose husbands have a full-time job spread over four days. However, they do not negotiate this clearly with their husbands and seem to condone the choice of their husbands which they base on their work situation and the financial situation of the family.

The experience of existing pressure forces these parents toward a pragmatic approach in keeping the household and making good arrangements. They seem to succeed in this without raising too many conflicts leading to nagging or serious disagreements. Often the partners take turns in the household tasks. One cooks, the other does the dishes, one does the laundry, and the other puts the child to bed. The next day the tasks are distributed the other way round. This does not mean that all this happens automatically. The combination of half care and half work demands that every day arrangements have to be settled anew, in particular when there is more than one small child. Especially the fathers who have a substantial part in the care for their child, show that they had to get used to having little time over for other things next to the child and household.

Making Use of a Day-Care Centre

Most of the c-families from our sample make use of paid day nurseries with or without the support of grandparents. The choice for paid day-care centre, however, does not always stem from a deep conviction. Only the highly educated women and men really make that clear choice. They make use of a day-care centre because of the professionalism of the staff, the continuity in care, the possibilities for social development for their child and their desire to be independent from their family. *You never have to raise your hand and beg 'oh, could you please look after our child?'* Average- and low-educated respondents make more or less use of a day-care centre out of necessity. Often they cannot rely on grandparents because sometimes they are still working themselves or they are sick. The choice biographical parents who make use of the day-care centre mainly belong to the highest and average income-bracket. They accept the high costs, in particular when they can make use of an arrangement for re-compensation for the expense. For c-parents with a low income the costs of a day-care centre seem to be far too high.

The big difference between n-parents and c-parents is that c-parents are far better informed about the financial provisions with regard to day care and as a consequence make use of it. Almost all n-families know that both or at least one partner can make use of a provision or re-compensation for day care through work. This reduces the costs immensely. The situation with regard to the option of taking maternity leave however is very different.[3] N-parents as well as c-parents hardly choose this option. They do not think the financial provisions are good enough, and they do not think it necessary because both or one of the partners has a part-time job, or because they are not sufficiently informed about the provisions and regulations.

Postponers of Parenthood

M. is a thirty year old woman. The last education she completed is high school. Since that she has started several different educations, but she never completed any. In about three weeks she is going to marry her boyfriend. They have known each other for four years.

The most important change in her life is her present job. Two and a half years ago she started her own business. She organizes music events and performances for big companies. M. enjoys her present work very much and it determines a great part of her life. She realizes more and more that she is focusing on a career. She really wants to be good at what she does. She cannot imagine stopping working. Her leisure time and work are intertwined. She works a lot of overtime. At the weekends she goes every now and then to a band for her work, to an exhibition or to the movies.

Her boyfriend is an X-ray assistant. He works full-time with irregular working hours. Working part-time is possible. He is planning for the future to work in periods of three months abroad. M. and her boyfriend talk a lot about work, but not about their income or about working less. They mainly talk about differences in work motives. He works because he likes it; M. works because she wants to make a career.

In her last interview M. stated that she wanted children, but not at the cost of her own development and her work. 'The most important thing in life is me and my development. Having children is of course a development in itself, but it is not something I'm sure I really want.' Even much earlier, in the first years after her high school, M. had this opinion. When she was twenty and just started studying political science she said:

> I'm sure sometime I will have these mother feelings, oh the little ones and cute babies etc., but I don't think I can really cope with it. I want too much for myself, and I can't do that to a child.

Even though the option for children comes closer to an end because of the biological clock, M. still considers her work more important. She assumes already in advance that the combination of her work with a family will only amount to stress. She considers having children mainly as 'giving in', because she will be more bound to the house. Her boyfriend would like to have children. But this has not been a point of discussion yet.

Her boyfriend would be the one that would work less and organize the care of the child if they chose to have one. In that case her career would not suffer. At the moment she and her boyfriend divide the household tasks and they are both satisfied with it. They take over if one of them is busier at work and cannot cope with doing the dishes anymore in the evenings, or doing other things. Then the other does more at another time. They do not want to think about how the work-care and household tasks are going to be divided later. M. is satisfied with her present situation in life. She realizes she needs to work less hard at times and spend more time with her friends or take time for herself. At present she is mainly busy with finding a balance between work and private life.

More than half of our research group, 38 young adults, did not have any children yet at the time of our interviews. This group mainly consists of highly educated respondents. Approximately half of this group has completed a college or university education, and almost one third has a grammar or high school diploma. Not even one sixth is poorly educated. Almost three quarters of the group of those who postpone parenthood live with a partner or are married. The rest live by themselves. Among the group of postponers the difference between 'normal' biographically and choice biographically oriented couples fades. They are actively engaged in their career, but at the same time they are still attached to their phase of youth, and follow life patterns where freedom, travelling and consumption make up the basic values of their lives. Many of them, men as well as women, are still busy with exploring the different options of a career, and exploring their own abilities. They enjoy their economic independence and their luxury lifestyle. Most of them want children, but not within the next 4 or 5 years, and they do not have any specific ideas on child planning. As a result, they still have very vague ideas on the work-care scenario.

Negotiations on Care and Work

Nevertheless there are a number of postponers who are starting to think more concretely about the combination of care and work. Their ideas on this indicate that they would fit more into the category of choice biographical than to the category of 'normal' biographical parents. Most of the young women have already since high school had the conviction that having children must not be at the expense of their work. This conviction is reinforced by the positive experiences they have had in their education and jobs. It became obvious from the interviews that many of these young women expect their partner to give them enough space for that, and to be involved in taking care of the children.

Even half of the male postponers anticipate a combination of work and care tasks. This choice has mostly been formulated during recent years under the influence of the desires of their girl-friends. A young man who had completed business studies used to hold the opinion that the most successful partner should continue to work full-time after the birth of a child. However, he adjusted his views when his girl-friend confronted him with the questions as to what being 'successful' actually entails:

> Successful of course is a strange term. Is it the one who earns the most...? Or the one who has the nicest job? Or am I successful only when I take good care of my child...? Slowly but surely the points of view shift.

Couples who postpone parenthood, much more than the group of young parents, are active negotiators with regard to the household they share. Most of the time, both of them have full-time or extensive part-time jobs and consider each other as equal in that area. On the basis of the feeling of equality, they come to an equal division of the household tasks. However this does not eliminate the fact that even in this group, too, women feel more responsible for keeping the house, or they are the ones who are upset the soonest when tasks are not being fulfilled according to their standard of perfection. The male partners are much more lax about it and do not care one way or the other. They consider themselves more as a counter pole and leave the initiative up to their wives. But we also see a number of 'new', caring men who give space to their girl-friends for development and self-realization in their career.

Contrary to the 'normal' biographical parents almost all of those who postpone parenthood want to make use of a day-care facility and appear to have few pedagogical scruples (that is, against 'dumping' your child at the day-care centre). This too is a sign of the likelihood that they will turn into choice biographical parents later on. But the danger for the development of an unequal distribution of tasks later on, lies with the women who at present take on most of the household tasks and do not 'educate' their partners in this respect. The same can be said about women who, after having had a busy job for years, work less in order to have more time for hobbies, but realize after a period of time that they actually fill most of the extra time with household chores. Men who follow their desire to keep on working full-time will probably later put more pressure on their partners to take the care and responsibility for the children on their shoulders, and in particular if this goes together with stepping back from making use of a day-care centre due to the high costs involved.

Simultaneity of Modernization in the Biography of Young Adults

In this last part of our explorations we will again have a closer look at the modernization paradoxes that we discussed in the beginning and summarized in a conspectus. The conspectus presented in Table 8.1, pictured the modernization of the gender relations in a chronological timetable, beginning in the 1960s until today. Now, after our empirical research, we notice that old and new biographical solutions for the 'child-work problem' in (post-)modern societies exist *at the same time.* Furthermore – as we will show – we notice that the *women* produce more variations between old and new solutions than the men. In as much as modernization is being enhanced by differentiation, the gender relations are modernized more by the changes within the female than the male biography, as we can show by pointing to gender-specific variants within old and new biographical options. Among the *'normal' biographically oriented women* we discern three variants:

- the 'tea mother';
- the traditional co-wage earner;
- the social-contact-employee.

The 'tea-mother' is familiar to all older and also to a lot of young Dutch people. When they came out of school, she would be waiting with a cup of tea at the kitchen table and listen to what her children had experienced and what they had been busy doing over the last couple of hours. Amongst young women, this 'housewife-only' mother still exists today. Nowadays however they do not have to take on this role because of tradition, but rather because they have clearly chosen it for themselves. According to our sample, in general these women have limited educational assets and career prospects.

At least for the period of several years, they consider it attractive to exchange the work outside their house for the work inside the home after the birth of the first child.

A second variant is formed by women who, out of financial needs, continue to work after the birth of a child. Many families make that decision under the pressure of increasing consumption costs. These, too, have rather limited educational assets, even though this is not as obvious as with the tea-mother variant; this applies for instance to helping in their husband's company, which in the Netherlands could be large horticultural and agricultural enterprises.

The third variant is represented by women who in the first instance continue to work not because of financial reasons, but because they do not want to lose the social contacts at work after the birth of a child; this can be a job without education as well as a professional job.

Among the *'normal' biographically oriented men* we only discern two variants:

- the classical traditional main wage-earner with the corresponding opinion on gender relations;
- the man who slightly modifies this classical position due to the pressure of general societal modernization: his wife 'is allowed to' work, or has to do this due to financial reasons, but this, in his opinion, does not really change anything pertaining to the gender-specific work distribution.

As we have seen, in all 'normal' biographical constellations women feel more responsible for house and child care than their male partners, and neither of them has high expectations on a significant shift of the power-balance between the sexes. Because of that these families have no serious debates or disputes about a (more) equal work distribution. Depending on the financial and family situation, the one-and-a-half model is varied between housewife-only and mother, or an increasing periodical work load (extensive part-time jobs of the women).

However, it is different with the *choice biographically oriented women*. Here too we discern three variants:

- the 'stress woman';
- the career woman;
- the neo-traditional woman.

The 'stress woman' wants to combine four life-tasks and areas in her present way of life: work and career, children and family, the relationship with her partner, and social contacts and leisure-time engagements. She is highly educated, starts having children at a later age, and by no means wants to quit her job and thus lose her independence and self-assurance. She has high expectations of herself and her partner and together with him she does not only want to enjoy life within their family, but also outside: with friends, travelling, and in many cultural activities. The one-and-a-half model is a satisfactory solution to the child-work problem if the half-day job is interesting and the partner earns enough money to satisfy the desires for consumption on a high level and to keep the social position. It is possible that the stress woman used to be a stressed career woman. And it is possible that she may turn into a neo-traditional woman.

The second variant consists of women who do not want to give up their career, not even when children come and therefore 'put up' with the double burden. There is nothing fundamentally separating them from stress women, because they also want to combine as many areas of life as possible, however they cut back in areas that would endanger their career. In the Netherlands women with a full-time job are few in number in comparison to other nations. When career women change to the one and a half model it is because they cannot cope with the work-child combination anymore; maybe because a second or third child is on its way, or maybe because they cannot defend their professional position against male competitors any longer.

The third variant is formed by the 'neo-traditional women'. They confront the dominating ideology on the emancipation of women by fighting for equality in all areas of societal life with the ideology of the women who deliberately choose for motherhood. They are higher educated sisters of the tea-mother and may have been a 'stress woman' before their ideological shift, and are searching for happiness in the opposite role.

How is the situation with *choice biographical men*? Here are also only two variants. We differentiate between:

• the outside-emancipated man
• the inside-emancipated man

The outside-emancipated man has not released his position out of personal endeavour, but mainly because his wife has exhorted him again and again, and has confronted him with her own desires that can only be fulfilled if he has more time and energy to invest in the children and household.

In contrast, as our interviews show, the self-emancipated man has separated himself from the traditional role through various personal and social experiences and adheres to a fairly egalitarian model of division of work. Even though he works more hours per week than she does, he makes an effort to actively contribute to the work in the house, in particular in taking care of the children. He does not do this out of a sense of duty, but because he wants to do it. With that he separates himself from the male role which became so familiar to him in his own upbringing – his father was almost always the husband of a 'tea-mother'.

Conclusion

Our results show that young adults in Dutch families mainly negotiate on a pragmatic level: for women it is important that their partners participate in the house duties and help with taking care of small children during the times of the day when it is busiest. But in terms of more fundamental questions such as the division of paid work-hours and care-hours between partners, or the use of leave regulations, the needs, wishes and desires of both partners are hardly put on the scales. Negotiation processes in every day family-life are more frequent among choice biographically oriented couples than among 'normal' biographical families. They are most common among constellations where both partners are strongly involved in their jobs, where the children are not yet in the 'rough phase' (in Dutch *de tropenjaren*), and when the child-care outside the family is not sufficient.

However, negotiation processes can also be expected among families with stress-women, for even though they 'only' work part-time, they are still making demands that are too hard on themselves and on their partners.

'Negotiation' has negative and positive connotations, both coming to the surface within every day family-situations when partners dispute on the division of work and the new definition of gender-relations. The fact is that nowadays family members – women/mothers, men/fathers and children – communicate more verbally than the generations in the past where so many things were 'normal' and determined in advance by a 'normal' biographical arrangements of life. This change within the family is the most tangible sign of its modernization.

The exploration of our typology in this chapter is only based in part on our empirical data; we have also included systematic everyday and media knowledge. Thus we come to the research-desideratum. Women, youth and family studies have repeatedly shown that the 'child-work dilemma' significantly influences the life-plans and chances of young girls and women. This invites further study of this complex subject in life-course research. This could entail in detail testing the presented typology on its applicability and usefulness within a nation, but even more within a quantitative-qualitative inter-country comparison.[4] The creation of typology, however, serves heuristic, not essential aims. Whether a woman is 'stress-woman' or a 'tea-mother' and more so if and under which circumstances she remains that, or seeks another social or personal identity, are questions that can only be answered within a life-biographical longitudinal approach.

Notes

1   Nowadays in the Netherlands there are ca. 15 per cent of young people (15-25 years of age) whose parents have emigrated from Morocco, Turkey, Suriname, Aruba and the Dutch Antilles (a small group from South-East Asia, China and several African countries); 50-60 per cent of the total amount of high school students in the four major cities (Amsterdam, Rotterdam, Den Haag en Utrecht) belong to that category. In our sample these minority groups were not systematically included.

2   In the Netherlands a full-time week of work is defined between 32-36 hours.

3   Every employee in the Netherlands who has worked at least for one year for his or her employer has the right to (unpaid) parental leave with retention of pension rights and financial years. The length of leave is determined by the amount of hours the employee works per week. The leave has to be completed before the eighth birthday of the child in an uninterrupted period of maximum half a year.

4   The European Group for Integrated Social Research (EGRIS) at present carries out a 10 country project called FATE (Families and Transitions in Europe) where, among other things, different family styles are compared (www.socsci.ulster/policy/ fate/fatepublications.html).

References

du Bois-Reymond, M. (1998), 'Der Verhandlungshaushalt im Modernisierungsprozess', in P. Büchner, M. du Bois-Reymond, J. Ecarius, B. Fuhs and H.H. Krüger (eds), *Teenie-Welten. Aufwachsen in drei europäischen Regionen*, Leske + Budrich, Opladen, pp. 83-112.

du Bois-Reymond, M., Poel, Y. Te and Ravesloot, J. (1999), 'Moderne Kindheit zwischen familialer und außerfamilialer Häuslichkeitspädagogik: Diskurs und Praxis in den Niederlanden', *Zeitschrift für Soziologie der Erziehung und Sozialisation*, Vol. 19, pp. 243-258.

du Bois-Reymond, M., Plug, W., te Poel, Y. and Ravesloot, J. (2001), 'And then Decide What To Do Next. Young People's Educational and Labour Trajectories', *Young*, Vol. 9(2), pp. 33-52.

Centraal Bureau Statistiek (1999), 'Later en minder kinderen' ('Later Children – Fewer Children'), *Index. Special bevolking*, CBS, Den Haag.

Drew, E., Emerek, R. and Mahon, E. (1998), *Women, Work and the Family in Europe*, Routledge, London.

Grünell, M. (2001), *Mannen zorgen. Verandering en continuïteit in zorgpatronen (Men Are Caring. Change and Continuity in Patterns of Care)*, Aksant, Amsterdam.

Hochschild, A.R. (1997), *The Time Bind. When Work Becomes Home and Home Becomes Work*, Metropolitan Books, New-York.

Jansen, M. and Liefbroer, A.C. (2001), 'Transition to Adulthood in the Netherlands', in M. Corijn and E. Klijzing (eds), *Transition to Adulthood in Europe*, Kluwer Academic Publications, Dordrecht/Bosten/London, pp. 209-232.

Kennedy J.C. (1995), *Nieuw Babylon in actie. Nederland in de jaren zestig (New Babylon in Action. The Netherlands in the Sixties)*, Boom, Amsterdam/Meppel.

Keuzenkamp, S., Hooghiemstra, E. (2000), *De kunst van het combineren. Taakverdeling tussen partners (The Art of Combining Tasks)*, SCP, Den Haag.

Komter, A. (1990), *Omstreden gelijkheid, de macht van de vanzelfsprekendheid in huwelijksrelaties (Contested Equality, the Power of Self-evidency in Marital Relationships)*, SUA, Amsterdam.

Oechsle, M. (2000), *Gleichheit mit Hindernissen*, Stiftung SPI, Berlin.

Orriëns, N. (2002), *Nieuwetijds moederen (New Manners of Mothering)*, SWP Publishers, Den Haag.

Portegijs, W., Boeiens, A., Keuzenkamp, S. and Hooghiemstra, M. (2002), *Emancipatiemonitor 2002 (Emancipation Monitor 2002)*, SCP/CBS, Den Haag.

Rispens, J., Hermanns, J.M.A. and Meeus, W.H.J. (1996), *Opvoeden in Nederland. (Education in the Netherlands)*, Van Gorcum, Assen.

Strauss, A. and Corbin, J. (1998), *Basics of Qualitative Research*, Sage Publications, Thousand Oaks/London/New Delhi.

Wittebrood, K. and Keuzekamp, S. (2000), *Rapportage jeugd 2000. Trajecten van jongeren naar zelfstandigheid (Youth Report 2000. Trajectories of Young People on Their Way to Independence)*, SCP, Den Haag.

Zeijl, E. (2001), *Young Adolescents' Leisure: A Cross-cultural and Cross-sectional Study of Dutch and German 10-15 Year-Olds*, Leske + Budrich, Opladen.

Chapter 9

Daughters of the Women's Movement. Generation Conflicts and Social Change

Ute Gerhard

Introduction

The social relationship of generations may always be characterized by a whole bundle of expectations as well as disappointments, by prejudices or simply by not-understanding on both sides. This is even more the case, if one has to discern so profound social, political and cultural changes as happened during the last decades, particularly with regard to women's conduct of life, younger women's degree of education, their extended participation in the labour market as well as in public life. In order to understand the 'new youth' from a sociological point of view it is advisable to analyse the reasons for generational differences or even conflicts especially with regard to changed social conditions and life plans of the younger generation. Here Karl Mannheim's concept of generations offers a theoretical framework, which detaches the term generation from biological rhythms or demographical aspects and considers the context of each generation as a social phenomenon, constituted by particular social conditions and cultural influences on an age-group that is similarly situated in a socio-historical realm (Mannheim, 1964). In this concept also social movements play an eminent role, because they are both a product of as well as a motor for social change, and their continuity, failure or success depends on how the next generation is ready to accept, to take over or to distance from their respective achievements or goals.

In the following chapter I will take into consideration young women and their attitudes toward feminism as a main issue and as an example for the significance of cultural change in gender relations. The focus will be the German situation, since the debates and discourses around feminism and gender roles are specific, are to be discussed in a concrete social and historical context, although the reactions to and the impact of feminism as an international social and political movement might be at least similar in diverse Western countries. To introduce into this context my starting point will be some striking results of opinion polls about political orientations and attitudes of young women. The first section then will shortly present obvious social changes and especially the distinct aspirations and a new self-confidence of younger women in comparison to their mothers, whereas the second part discusses the problems of generational transfer or of distancing from feminism as a social, cultural and political movement.

Young Women and Politics

The 14th Shell study of youth, 2002, a representative questionnaire and survey of attitudes, values, and plans of German youngsters, again captured a decreasing interest in politics on the part of young people. A mere 30 per cent of those between 12 and 25 claimed to be interested in politics. However, a closer look reveals a marked difference according to educational level and sex. In general, the higher the educational level, the greater the interest in politics. Yet girls, whose interest in politics, despite a higher educational level and better grades than boys, seems lower than theirs, define their engagement and what they consider the common good in a different manner: 'Girls become politically engaged in instances where they can shape their local environments' (Shell, 2002, p. 41). Interestingly, the girls tend also to be more left wing and assign to the Green Party a higher competence in solving existing problems (Shell, 2002, p. 217).

These results second earlier findings according to which girls and women in particular, standing apart from established political forms, parties and associations, prefer participation in informal groups, citizen's initiatives and social movements. At the acme of the feminist movement, women's and gender researchers saw in this alternative political participation evidence of an 'other' feminine understanding of politics (Meyer, 1992) and, on the basis of these findings, called for a change in perspective. It was not merely a question of exclusion or discrimination against women; rather, at stake was a new political concept capable of capturing the specific experiences and moral orientation of women, taking stock of and rehabilitating that 'other voice' (Gilligan, 1984). Indeed, a new segment or counter public evolved in the form of the women's movement, its networks, media and projects, promising a new capacity to act and influence. Yet, as women's movements became muted and feminist theorists clearly rejected the 'we' of an identity politics for women, explanations as well as political strategies grew more complex. And the question remains: why has 1970s feminism been able to achieve so little, or, turned around, why – given that equal participation of women in the public sphere is far from being achieved – is the younger generation of women clearly unwilling to step into the shoes of the feminist pioneers, thereby ensuring victory for gender democracy?

There are very different, seemingly contradictory explanations. Based on empirical studies I would ask, does the minimal or diminishing interest in politics evinced by the younger generation of women have something to do with the doldrums, the ebbing, the reverses of the women's movement, or instead with the movement's successes? Have achievements led to a new insouciance, an individual indifference to greater societal questions? This question touches at least two levels of analysis. On the one hand, we'd have to clarify if or to what extent the women's movement initiated changes in gender relations and, since the 1970s, what it was in young women's self-awareness, professional orientation and approach to the world that had changed. This in turn touches on the question of structural barriers that nonetheless remain. That is, it's a matter of the relationship between the women's movement and social change (1). On the other hand we should consider that social movements cannot last forever; they are characterized by instability, 'movement' as it were, and changes in aims, action, and actors. Could it not be that the women's movement has become obsolete, has outlived itself, or at least, in a wholly different form or unnoticed by us, underground, continues its influence? Because this question will be answered differently depending on age and experience, various opinions on this matter will tend to be handled in terms of generational conflict, with metaphors and images of movements as mothers and daughters. With the help of Karl Mannheim's 'generational situation' (*Generationenlagen*) I will try to provide an answer (2) not least out of interest in the question of where, today, the women's movement for feminism stands.

The Women's Movement and Social Change

Empirical studies of attitudes and 'lifetime planning of younger women' in the Federal Republic of Germany (Geissler and Oechsle, 1996; Seidenspinner et al., 1996) produce a contradictory picture, characterized by a tense proximity of conflicting orientations, incompatibilities and ambivalence that can be subsumed under the idea of 'unequal equality' (Oechsle and Geißler, 1998). Nonetheless, we can make out trends and clear alterations in comparison to the mothers' generation. Today's young women find it self-evident to prepare for a profession and be gainfully employed, regardless of differences in class origin, academic or professional degree and independent of the manner in which they envision their lives unfolding. In other words, in the last thirty years, regardless of educational level, diploma or other career preparation, girls and young women in Germany have, to an astounding degree, not only caught up with but even in some domains overtaken their male peers. And as the latest Shell Study of Youth underscores, girls and women, not unlike young men, exhibit a strong career orientation (Shell 2002). In higher education females also generally have better grades; they are more than half of degree candidates (54.9 per cent) and since 1997 more than half of those who start university study (52.4 per cent) (Klammer et al., 2000). Yet, at the same time, in all later career development, ranging from graduation through doctoral degree candidates to managerial levels in academia, business and politics, the proportion of women sinks dramatically (the nadir being a male quotient of 95 per cent at full professorial level). This can only be a result of continuing structural barriers that have been analysed so many times already and therefore will not be discussed here.

If we wish to evaluate social change, however, we really should distinguish between these stubborn social structures and the altered aspirations and life plans of younger women. Even though women's structural, gender-specific inequality is clearly visible in their worse positioning in business, in their lower incomes or, in comparison to men, in miserable social security payments in old age, younger women's projections for their lives can be viewed as nothing less than a 'cultural revolution'. Since today's young women have experienced little to no discrimination before they entered a profession or founded a family – or at worst in a subtle, almost imperceptible way easily interpreted as individual failure – the great majority take it for granted in evaluating their prospects that they are operating in a situation of gender equality. And up until early adulthood they have indeed experienced the relationship between the sexes as equal, in their conduct of life they even seem to be more independent than boys. For instance, more young women than men move out of their parents' and into their own apartments (Geissler and Ochsle, 1996; Geissler, 1998). If we look at these liberties in daily conduct of life and compare them to the options and orientation of the young women's mothers, we witness the extent of social transformation. Research on career paths and biography confirms this: the generation of women presently in their sixties highlights and praises their daughters' independence, and they also feel that something profound has changed, especially relations with parents, teachers and employers but also in (marriage) partnerships and the treatment of children. At least in their day you could take for granted either 'a rebellion against authority' or an anti-authoritarian upbringing. After all, in contrast to their experience, as a norm and a practical reality, the housewife model had lost its coercive character. And today, women's employment is no longer considered a transitory strategy ending with marriage or a second-best arrangement, but rather is 'a sign of freedom' and 'an aspect of fulfilment in a woman's life' (Born et al., 1996).

The extent of change becomes even clearer if we examine various normative models that guided the generation of women after 1945. Women in West Germany – and this is true for all Western societies including the USA (Friedan, 1963) after the Second World War – were prescribed a family-oriented option only (Pfeil, 1961). The premier destiny of women to be housewives and mothers together with the so-called re-masculinizing of society (Moeller, 1998) was considered a return to 'normalcy' following emancipation forced by contingencies of war and a gender order gone haywire. Yet, at least since the 70s, as an expanding market made increased demands on labour, and social reforms were compelled by, among other forces, the women's movement, people began to talk about a double role, a double orientation, and also a double burden on women, which was answered, in Europe, by very different socio-political programs aiming to increase the compatibility of family and waged work (Gerhard et al., 2003). In West Germany a conservative politics of the family espoused a three-phase model (Myrdal and Klein, 1962), which promised assistance to mothers who re-entered the workforce after raising children. This represented a conscious distancing from the so-called collective child-raising and forced integration of mothers into paid employment in the German Democratic Republic and was intended to retain and privilege, at least for pre-school-age children, the traditional mother role, although it could never really be practised or enjoyed by most women. Women's and gender studies uncovered the contradictions in this double binding, the so-called 'double social commitment' of women to both family and profession revealed as inherently contradictory because 'the one aspect was too little, but both together were too much' (Becker-Schmidt, 1984). The contradictions and ambivalence in the situation of employed mothers was especially evident in the conflicting demands made on women on the job and in their maternal roles. In crossing the boundaries of both, they had to contend with differing norms governing time-management,[1] satisfaction of needs or even what counts as work. In the meantime, what the early years of the new women's movement had elaborated theoretically and politically as an opposition between housework and waged work (Dalla Costa and James, 1972) has since given way to a more comprehensive understanding of care work which, whether paid or not, devolves mainly on women and cements their inequality in the family and professional worlds (see Lewis, 1998; Leira and Saraceno 2002; Tronto, 1996).

It is all the more remarkable that, despite the regime change and destruction of infrastructural preconditions, propagation in the GDR during the same post-war era of a model for employed mothers unfolded in as little as two generations with such strength that it is has continued to guide the aspirations and behaviour of former East German women. Job and family exist for them 'not next to each other, but are necessary *to* each other.' They cannot understand the problem as West German women experience it; for them it's 'not a big deal'; they simply want to 'live a full and complete life' (Keddi et al., 1999, p. 18).

Yet, however much the younger generation's aspirations differ from those of an older one, has not the problem simply remained?

All of the latest research emphasizes that the structural dilemma, finding a balance between employment and family, has not changed for younger women, such contradictions have not been resolved. What has changed, however, is the manner in which youth deals with these tensions. Numerous recent empirical studies prove that the lives of young women have indeed changed, in particular regarding aspirations, but also in terms of range and options in planning the future. That is, the picture is in no sense unequivocal and yet something typical emerges that permitted, for instance, Birgit Geissler and Mechthild Oechsle in *Aspirations of younger women* to identify five patterns in planning to coordinate family and work (Geissler and Oechsle, 1996).

First, the double life plan tries to balance family and profession in that the woman knows she must launch her career, and then interrupt it for family responsibilities followed by a return to employment, but preferably part-time, after the smallest children are out of the house. Such a scenario represents for these women 'the limits of a woman's biographical options' (ibid., p. 92) and, prevalent among West German women, suggests that modernization has been 'one-sided' in touching only the market dimension (Geissler, 1998, p. 109) not visions of family responsibility options that remain limited, as before. The independent woman model continues to appear incompatible with good mothering (Oechsle, 1998, p. 198).

The traditional biography, however, is disappearing. It once clearly ranked over career, which centres family based on a 'destiny of service to others' (Beck-Gernsheim, 1983). The new ingredient is education: the modern variant does not question the value of training for the job market although no intent to balance career and family is implied. This biography is, at least in West Germany, the most broadly preferred and is supported by ordinary ideas about gender difference.

Any young woman choosing to concentrate her energies on a 'masculine' career will encounter less tolerance, that is, if she aspires to economic independence, equality with her partner and above all success in the workplace. And these women are simply being realistic when they find it impossible to imagine having both a career and children. Finally, in their sample, the authors recognize a fourth minority among youthful women whose 'individualized biography' offers the clearest picture of social change. These young people emphasize the importance of profession for development of the personality and insist on independence and autonomy despite and in opposition to external economic coercion. Characteristic of this group is their insistence on defining the parameters of partnership and the search for new gender arrangements.

The last group we should mention are those who do not plan at all but simply accept the status quo or make do with short-term solutions.

In many ways, these findings support those in a long-term study of young women in East and West Germany undertaken since the end of the 1980s whose results have now been published. The newer work, however, pays greater attention to variation in the subjects' plans among those, the authors point out, for whom compatibility between work and family is by no means a major issue. Rather, new options have opened in the context of social processes of individualization: 'Young women enjoy more freedoms while at the same time – in contrast to their mothers – living under pressure to develop their own biographies' (Keddi et al., 1999, p. 9). Here vitae are described that contain neither profession nor family as structural fixed points, for instance, in the search for an independent life not oriented on preconceived norms or gender roles but rather a life understood as 'one's own path' in partnership outside the parameters of traditional family. Beyond career development – according to Angelika Diezinger and Maria S. Rerrich – the daily lives of younger women evolve around a number of axes representative of personal choices and different constellations. 'Marriage and family are not (any longer?) the only existing or meaningful "alternatives" to career and employment in young women's daily lives' (Diezinger and Rerrich, 1998, p. 165).

In general, then, empirical research confirms a variety of biographies among young women in which we might search in vain for a dominating pattern, but that reveal a multiplicity of life situations. Characteristic, however, is a juxtaposition of new and old models as well as experience of equality and inequality. In this regard, the increase in options appears to be an uncertain, unexplored terrain. The enormous expansion of opportunity, experienced from one generation of women to the next as a departure from things that had been self-evident, can be called an 'unfinished revolution' (Oechsle, 1998), because it fails to offer egalitarian models for the private realm to replace the inherited ideas about partnership, love or motherhood. In this regard, options are limited by extreme factors over which individuals have no power. These include structural conditions like social status or particular attitudes of parents or partners that either advance or impede a person's plans. All studies highlight partnership and the couple in which equality and equal rights are not merely negotiated with respect to division of labour but are fashioned with mutual consideration, yet still under conditions of social inequality.

Many young women conclude from the range of options, requirements and expectation that they can make decisions freely and take individual responsibility for the consequences. Theories of individualization thus appear to be correct when applied to the degree of differentiation and individualization in these women's lives, especially in terms of the need to 'catch up' in becoming individuals that is viewed in turn as 'risky' for society (Beck, 1986; Beck and Beck-Gernsheim, 1994) without, however, taking into account that 'individualization takes on a (perhaps) different meaning according to gender' (Rerrich, 1994, p. 202). Angelika Diezinger, in her study of individualization processes, concludes that the process for women – in contrast to the dominant form realized in the marketplace and associated with 'masculine professional humanity' – does not necessarily imply liberation *from* social bonds but instead is an effort to realize individuality *within* those bonds. Only if you subscribe uncritically to free market forces and accept the horror scenario of a 'totally mobile singles society' (Beck, 1986, p. 199) will you interpret maintenance of social bonds and acceptance of responsibility for social relationships as a barrier or deficit. Yet instead of integrating relationship into the concept of autonomy, private attachments continue to be erased from analyses. 'Only by changing perspective to accept the necessity of considering the formation and maintenance of social relationships,' Angelika Diezinger avers, 'will individualization cease to be a deficit model derived from individualization in the marketplace' (Diezinger, 1991, p. 26). Thus, due to their broader experience and praxis in juggling disparate tasks, I suspect it will be women, as late-comers to modernity, who pioneer new biographies in which waged labour and private life fit together smoothly.

Nonetheless, despite or perhaps because these considerations are inopportune, individualization theories seem to follow the Zeitgeist. In the over-simplified, popular version, individualization is understood in terms of each (male or female) being the author of his or her own happiness. The hegemony of neo-liberal discourse implies that individual experience of gender difference can no longer necessarily be understood as collective injustice or discrimination. Paula-Irene Villa cites in this context a typical statement by a student who opines, 'Whoever experiences discrimination today has only him or herself to blame' (Villa, 2003, p. 274).

Where does this conviction lead? In harmony with existing sociological theories of individualization, has the belief that problems can be solved by individuals surreptitiously led back to a privatization of the problem that the new women's movement worked so arduously to place on the public agenda? Trigger for the women's movement at the end of the sixties, a movement that has transformed far more than simply gender relations, was precisely this recognition that women's problems are not private but political and that they transcend existing limits of public institutions. But this still does not answer the question whether the women's movement is obsolete, nor explain if or why the new generation seems so little concerned.

Inheriting the Women's Movement or a Problem of Generations

In newspapers, TV talks shows and popular media in general, it has become customary to blame the women's movement for everything, its failures and omissions as well as any not-yet-achieved gender equality or emancipation. With a certain superciliousness, the movement's rise and fall are commented on, and yes, it is even somewhat 'classy' to distance oneself from the women's political movement or at least from *the* feminist: 'I'm not a feminist but...' Nonetheless, we hear from younger women, 'conditions will sometimes force you to take feminist positions or support feminist demands'. The pattern is of course familiar. First, feminists have always been a minority, even at the peak points of movement engagement. Second, opinion leaders and their media, from satirical magazines to scholarly literature, have always been more than eager to publish anti-feminist if not openly misogynistic points of view. That has everything to do with power and the fact that solutions to the woman question target the heart of the social order, making it uncomfortable for those in authority. As before, the characterization of opponents of feminism, as Hedwig Dohm saw it in the opening years of the twentieth century in her incisive analysis of 'Antifeminists,' still speaks to the core of the issue (Dohm, 1902). There's no getting away from the fact that at the latest since the 1990s, and not coincidentally in the wake of changes in the world order since 1989 and new political priorities, the question of the women's movement's status, even if it even continues to exist, has been posed with increasing frequency. At the start of the 1990s, diagnosis of a backlash (Faludi, 1991) elicited an angry reaction from women. (Susan Faludi in the original: 'Women never really surrendered', ibid., p. 454). Although some interpreted the reaction simply as the 'doldrums' or 'a recess' (Gerhard, p. 1999), a break needed by all politicians in order to react correctly to new challenges, the younger generation reacts to Feminism with a capital F by applying a new tone and a different quality of reaction. Those women who now engage in 'Feminism-bashing' are self-confident, polemical and liberal in their use of clichés when casting reproaches at 1970s feminists. As they perceive it, the women's movement was all too dogmatic, hostile to men and elitist, or at least – thus the apprehension – feminism is thought to have evolved into 'an increasingly closed club' (Weingarten and Wellershoff 1999, p. 29). They would contend, for instance: 'After so many movement decades, feminism has become once again a peripheral topic, monopolized in the hands of just a few women who devote themselves to the cause in such a way that most other people want nothing to do with them ... And more worrisome even than the intentional exclusion of men is that young women see no reason to think about feminism, women's politics or that ominous sounding concept of "gender". It's not any basic rejection of equality. But young women feel put off by the culture of "being concerned" associated with the '70s when victimization was the icon at the heart of a woman's vision of herself. And even if women really are multiple victims, young women today don't want to concern themselves with emotional belly-button gazing. They want to be subjects, not objects' (Bruns, 2000).

The long quote in O-tone is intended to convey the emotional distancing and the difficulty in presenting an objective assessment or interpretation. Yet it would be just as misleading to talk about THE feminist as to generalize 'the young woman'. Who is speaking here and for whom? The authors cited above, in this instance writing as journalists, not academics, belong to the generation that is now aged between thirty and forty, but by 'young women' could not they mean even younger ones, today in their twenties?

In fact, the critique of feminism or the women's movement on the part of a younger generation is a great deal more complex and multi-faceted. On the one hand, censure is aimed at feminist approaches and theories that start from the assumption that 'we' women or 'womanhood' represent the wellspring of feminist social analyses. This criticism was and is primarily expressed by younger academics who are at universities now treading in the footsteps of established women's studies scholars. They are about 40 years old and correct in insisting on difference between women as well as on the structural markers of class, race, sexual orientation, age etc. even if there is injustice in forgetting that feminist theorists had already pointed out early on how important relations were between class and gender or race and gender. On the other hand, young women, female students, and doctoral candidates today are raising critical voices in full knowledge of feminist successes but claiming nonetheless the right to articulate their own types of political intervention which may not at first glance be recognizable as 'politics'.

Here I will not be able to go into the global, theoretical, and intricate feminist debate about deconstruction of the category 'gender,' ignited in particular by Judith Butler's book *Gender Trouble* (Butler, 1990) which has led to a radicalization of feminist theory and a fundamental critique of identity logic or politics. The political consequences are, however, of interest here. Precisely this intricacy of post structural theory debated at a high intellectual level of self-critique and self-reflection, this so-called 'linguistic turn', has conquered for post modernism all of the social and cultural sciences and has actually contributed to political insecurity. With the 'end of the master narrative', the women's movement for emancipation also appears to lose its foundation in social theory. Even if post-structural theorists reassure us constantly that the entire debate is not intended to question women's political agency, feminist epistemology has had increasingly little to say about the daily lives and problems of the majority of women. Alice Pechriggl has therefore warned us not to confuse discussion of gender difference with feminism as protest or with any social movement (Pechriggl, 1992).

Interestingly, this epistemological disagreement and paradigm change are thematized in German feminist discussion as a generation conflict. Older feminists contend that apparently 'the background experience of younger academics and students is very different from that of the women's movement's early years, when the theory and practice of the anti-authoritarian student movement were recognized by many as a kind of revelation in whose light relations, including the personal, could be interpreted in new ways' (Feminische Studien, 1993; see also Modelmog and Gräßel, 1994). This represents an attempt to define various positions and mutual irritations as a generational problem as well.

Actually, the 'tense relationship between older and younger – feminist? – women' (Villa, 2003, p. 266), the subject of these discussions, can be defused in the light of Karl Mannheim's concept of generations and at the same time be taken seriously when analysing what feminism can be. Mannheim, who looked at generations and classes within the larger context of social change, thus illuminating the active role of social movements – in contrast to a demographic or biological understanding of generations at 30 year intervals – speaks of generations as 'a phenomenon of related age-group of people within a social context' (*dem Phänomen der verwandten Lagerung der Menschen im sozialen Raum*) (Mannheim, 1964, p. 526). He can therefore identify much shorter time spans and loci of experience which influence development of a similar consciousness in cohorts. In particular, if we are looking at social movements as dynamic motors of social change, we must consider on the one hand that the coming generation is born into altered conditions and successes resulting from, in this case, the women's movement. On the other hand, however, these accomplishments, the cultural inheritance of social change, cannot be simply taken over by youth but must, instead, become their own, and hence undergo additional change and transformation. In other words, distancing, totally different approaches and learning processes are necessary and productive, this being of benefit to both sides: older feminists will be compelled to accept that younger women today experience lifestyles and practice freedoms for which the older generation fought. Included here are alternative forms of partnership and life styles whose precondition is self-confidence and independence. Yet this independence does not mean that the 'heirs of their mothers' (Chodorow, 1985) accept their inheritance uncritically or administer it obediently. It is far more likely that feminist and political engagement appears today in other guises and cultural representations.

One example would be the 'Riot Grrrls Movement,' a group of young, feminist women in the independent rock scene characterized lately by the advent of numerous women's bands or individual artists (Gottlieb and Wald, 1995; Baldauf and Weingartner, 1998). These bands and the increasing visibility of women in the rock business – although far from all groups can be claimed for feminism –, nonetheless show that success is becoming self-evident to younger women who clear a path to rebellious sub-cultural possibilities. And although some may find it annoying or worthy of dismissal altogether to be marked as 'only women', because gender stereotypes in art and music have no place and should be unimportant both for production and reception, a 'positive attitude toward "girls"' emerges from the insubordinate performances and texts that negate gender but also ennoble it, "creating a girls" culture that speaks to "US", that shelters us and understands us' ('riot grrrl-Manifesto', quoted in Baldauf and Weingartner, 1998, p. 26). At www.grrrlzines.net/about you can read:

> Where in our adult-run media landscape can critically thinking girls and women, and lesbian, queer and transgender youth from around the globe express their voices without being censored or ridiculed? It is in self-made, independent zines (short for magazines) that we put together, publish and distribute ourselves where we freely unfold our own worlds. In zines such as Bendita (Brazil), Bitch (US), Clit Rock (Italy) ... we talk about our experiences and thoughts, as well as anger and resistance of growing up in patriarchal and homophobic society. While forming a global network of grrrl zinesters, we passionately discuss feminist theory, politics and activism and their impact on our lives...

With this short excursion into what is surely to many a little known world – thus Paula-Irene Villa – we become aware that 'then and now, a lively feminist application of the "personal is political" exists in a relatively new subculture' (Villa, 2003, p. 279; Gottlieb and Wald, 1995).

The need of younger women not to be marked primarily as women and thus be reduced to femininity appears characteristic of a new approach to problems of gender. It is often tied to an assurance of difference from the seventies feminist movement; the youth want to avoid perpetual struggle with men. For instance, in the female hacker scene, the so-called 'Haecksen' (German pun on witch = Hexe), explicitly refuse to define their aims as feminist and yet inspire younger women to train in computer technology and cultivate 'women's space' on the internet. (Advice of Anja Weckwert's dissertation project).

And yet, in the contradiction between not wanting to be identified as 'women' while realizing feminist political aims, the dilemma outlined above between a one-sided modernization and an unfinished social revolution appears again. On the one hand, young women today experience that gender has progressively lost its meaning, that women enjoy equal educational opportunities and must fulfil the same individualized professional obligations as men. On the other hand, they know how obstinacy in being a woman can limit their lives and continue to act as a marker of difference in a society that still functions as a gender hierarchy. It may be that precisely because they claim equal status, they vehemently reject being labelled 'women' or worse still 'feminist', and will avoid accepting the heritage of feminism in order to reduce the likelihood of being trapped in the discriminated category of 'women'.

Finally, in the myriad of lifestyles, another manoeuvre that both moves away from and approaches feminism should be mentioned. It is when younger academics insist that a person can be a feminist without having been part of a movement. Instead, it is sufficient to participate in the intellectual debate about insistent political and social structures governing gender relations. This 'intellectual and cognitive rather than emotional or identificatory socialization is not only possible today, but necessary', Paula-Irene Villa insists, herself a representative of this approach (Villa, 2003, p. 279). Here we see women's and gender studies at work politically and in terms of their influence on academic teaching and learning. The same awareness emerges from the European Union-sponsored comparative study of 'Employment and Women's Studies: The Impact of Women's Studies Training on Women's Employment' (see Griffin, 2002 and www.hull.ac.uk/ewsi/Comparative_Reports) covering nine countries. The study shows that women's and gender studies are in no sense limited to raising consciousness and increasing political savvy. They do indeed increase understanding of gender relations as socially constructed, encourage self-reflection and teach social criticism, but they also have a decisive influence on professional development by stimulating key qualifications, both personal and academic, that students unanimously see as opening doors to increased job opportunities. The training they enjoy in critical thinking and sociological analysis becomes an institutional resource that may form the groundwork of protest, possibly even of a renewed feminist movement.

Concluding Remarks

To sum up, we can see a clear transformation in consciousness, but above all a transformed lifestyle and increase in options for the younger generation of women.

This expresses itself in new images of women and men, egalitarian aspects of daily life that have come to be self-evident, but also in new forms of media and culture allowing for self-representation and participation. Nonetheless, the present situation is also marked by both equality and inequality in gender relations. Despite a stronger female presence in political life, the aim of 'another' politics, in the sense of more 'gender democracy', has not been achieved. Now, as before, working against equal participation in the labour market and dissolution of gender hierarchies are rigid structures and institutional measures in politics, the economy, and the family. Understanding these differences of opinion and misunderstandings only in terms of the mother versus daughter dynamic has been correctly identified as problematic (Thon, 2003, p. 113), because it has led to an oversimplification of the complex relationships and theoretical differences involved. And yet, the mother-daughter metaphor continues to creep into the picture, even into empirical studies.

However, it would be misleading to understand the mother-daughter dynamic as a family relationship or referring to theories of gender difference in the sense of the Italian 'Affidamento' approach (Diotima. Philosophinnengruppe aus Verona, 1989), in which older women in the women's movement function as 'symbolic mothers' to the younger ones. Whereas using this image in sociological terms means to crystallize out of it the relationship between the shaping of a generation, conflict between generations and social change. Finally, if a personal comment may be permitted here to a representative of the older generation, a risk does remain, with a concern about whether the next generation will succeed in transforming into power their new self-confidence and seemingly individual challenges and opportunities despite the remaining obstacles. For me, the question is whether younger women will develop the sufficient political energy to achieve a gender democracy in which feminism will really be superfluous.

Note

1   In this regard, contrast physical (measurable) with 'social time' in Elias, N. (1992), *Über die Zeit*, Suhrkamp, Frankfurt a.M.

References

Baldauf, A. and Weingartner, K. (1998), 'Lips, Tits, Hits, Power? Popkultur und Feminismus', folio, Wien/Bozen.

Beck, U. (1986), *Risikogesellschaft. Auf dem Weg in eine andere Moderne*, Suhrkamp, Frankfurt a.M.

Beck, U. and Beck-Gernsheim, E. (eds), (1994), *Riskante Freiheiten. Individualisierung in modernen Gesellschaften*, Suhrkamp, Frankfurt a.M.

Becker-Schmidt, R. (1984), *Eines ist zu wenig, beides ist zuviel*, Verlag neue Gesellschaft, Bonn.

Beck-Gernsheim, E. (1983), 'Vom "Dasein für andere" zum Anspruch auf ein Stück "eigenes Leben": Individualisierungsprozesse im weiblichen Lebenszusammenhang', *Soziale Welt*, Vol. 34, pp. 307-340.

Born, C., Krüger, H. and Lorenz-Meyer, D. (1996), *Der unentdeckte Wandel: Annäherung an das Verhältnis von Struktur und Norm im weiblichen Lebenslauf*, Edition Sigma, Berlin.

Bruns, G. (2000), 'Das verstaubte lila Gewand. Oder: Warum sich der Feminismus in Deutschland modernisieren muss', *Frankfurter Rundschau/ Dokumentation*, Vol. 6.

Butler, J. (1990), *Gender Trouble: Feminism and the Subversity of Identity*, Routledge, New York/London.

Chodorow, N. (1985), *Das Erbe der Mütter. Psychoanalyse und Soziologie der Geschlechter*, Frauenoffensive, München.

Dalla Costa, M. and James, S. (1972), *The Power of Women and the Subversion of the Community*, Falling Wall Press, Bristol.

Diezinger, A. (1991), *Frauen: Arbeit und Individualisierung: Chancen und Risiken; eine empirische Untersuchung anhand von Fallgeschichten*, Leske + Budrich, Opladen.

Diezinger, A. and Rerrich, M.S. (1998), 'Die Modernisierung der Fürsorglichkeit in der alltäglichen Lebensführung junger Frauen: Neuerfindung des Altbekannten', in B. Geissler and M. Oechsle (eds), *Die ungleiche Gleichheit. Junge Frauen und der Wandel im Geschlechterverhältnis*, Leske + Budrich, Opladen, pp. 165-183.

Diotima. Philosophinnengruppe aus Verona (1989), *Der Mensch ist zwei. Das Denken in der Geschlechterdifferenz*, Wiener Frauenverlag, Wien.

Dohm, H. (1902), *Die Antifeministen. Ein Buch der Verteidigung*, Verlag Andstrasse, Frankfurt a.M.

Elias, N. (1992), *Über die Zeit*, Suhrkamp, Frankfurt a.M.

Faludi, S. (1991), *Backlash. The Undeclared War Against American Women*, Anchor Books, New York.

Feministische Studien (1993), Kritik der Kategorie 'Geschlecht', Vol. 11.

Friedan, B. (1963), *The Feminine Mystique*, Dell, New York.

Geissler, B. (1998), 'Hierarchie und Differenz. Die (Un-)Vereinbarkeit von Familie und Beruf und die soziale Konstruktion der Geschlechterhierarchie im Beruf', in M. Oechsle and B. Geissler (eds), *Die ungleiche Gleichheit und der Wandel im Geschlechterverhältnis*, Leske + Budrich, Opladen, pp. 109-129.

Geissler, B. and Oechsle, M. (1996), *Lebensplanung junger Frauen*, Studien Verlag, Weinheim.

Gerhard, U. (1999), *Atempause. Feminismus als demokratisches Projekt*, Fischer, Frankfurt a.M.

Gerhard, U., Knijn, T., Weckwert, A. (2003), *Erwerbstätige Mütter. Ein europäischer Vergleich*, Beck, München.

Gilligan, C. (1984), *Die andere Stimme. Lebenskonflikte und Moral der Frau*, Piper, München.

Gottlieb, J. and Wald, G. (1995), Riot Grrls, Revolution und Frauen im Independent Rock', in C. Eichhorn and S. Grimm (eds), *Gender Killer. Texte zu Feminismus und Politik*, ID-Archiv, Berlin/Amsterdam, pp. 167-189.

Griffin, G. (ed.), (2002), *Women's Employment, Women's Studies, and Equal Opportunities 1945-2001. Reports from nine European Countries*, University of Hull, Hull.

Keddi, B., Pfeil, P., Strehmel, P. and Wittmann, S. (1999), *Lebensthemen junger Frauen – Die andere Vielfalt weiblicher Lebensentwürfe. Eine Längsschnittuntersuchung in Bayern und Sachsen*, Leske + Budrich, Opladen.

Klammer, U., Klenner, C., Ochs, C., Radke, P. and Ziegler, A. (2000), *WSI-FrauenDatenReport*, Hans-Böckler-Stiftung, Berlin.

Leira, A. and Saraceno, C. (2002), 'Care: Actors, Relationships and Contexts', in B. Hobson, J. Lewis and B. Siim (eds), *Contested Concepts in Gender and Social Politics*, Edward Elgar, Cheltenham, pp. 55-83.

Lewis, J. (ed.), (1998), *Gender, Social Care and Welfare State Restructuring in Europe*, Ashgate, Aldershot.

Mannheim, K. (1964), 'Das Problem der Generationen', in K. Mannheim, *Wissenssoziologie. Auswahl aus dem Werk. Eingeleitet und herausgegeben von Kurt H. Wolff*, Luchterhand, Berlin, pp. 509-565.

Meyer, B. (1992), 'Die "unpolitische" Frau. Politische Partizipation von Frauen oder: Haben Frauen ein anderes Verständnis von Politik?', in *Aus Politik und Zeitgeschichte. Beilage zur Wochenzeitung Das Parlament*, Vol. 42(25-26), pp. 3-13.

Modelmog, I. and Gräßel, U. (eds), (1994), *Konkurrenz und Kooperation*, Lit Verlag, Münster/Hamburg.

Moeller, R. G. (1998), 'Forum: The "Remasculinization" of Germany in the 1950s', *Signs. Journal of Women in Culture and Society*, Vol. 24(1), pp. 104-127.

Myrdal, A. R. and Klein, V. (1962), *Die Doppelrolle der Frau in Familie und Beruf*, Kiepenheuer & Witsch, Köln/Berlin.

Oechsle, M. (1998), 'Ungelöste Widersprüche Leitbilder für die Lebensführung junger Frauen', in M. Oechsle and B. Geissler (eds), *Die ungleiche Gleichheit. Junge Frauen und der Wandel im Geschlechterverhältnis*, Leske + Budrich, Opladen, pp. 185-200.

Oechsle, M. and Geissler, B. (eds), (1998), *Die ungleiche Gleichheit. Junge Frauen und der Wandel im Geschlechterverhältnis*, Leske + Budrich, Opladen.

Pechriggl, A. (1992), 'Die Philosophin und die Frauenbewegung', in M. E. Pellikaan-Engel (hg.), *Against Patriarchal Thinking. Proceedings of the VIth Symposium of the International Association of Women Philosophers*, VU University Press, Amsterdam.

Pfeil, E. (1961), *Die Berufstätigkeit von Müttern. Eine empirische Untersuchung von 900 Müttern aus vollständigen Familien*, Mohr, Tübingen.

Rerrich, M. S. (1994), 'Zusammenfügen, was auseinanderstrebt. Zur familialen Lebensführung von Berufstätigen', in U. Beck and E. Beck-Gernsheim (eds), *Riskante Freiheiten. Individualisierung in modernen Gesellschaften*, Suhrkamp, Frankfurt a.M., pp. 201-218.

Shell, Deutsche (ed.), (2002), *Jugend 2002. Zwischen pragmatischem Idealismus und robustem Materialismus*, Klaus Hurrelmann, Mathias Albert (Konzeption u. Koordination), Frankfurt a. M.

Thon, C. (2003), 'Frauenbewegung – Bewegungsgenerationen – Generationenbruch? Generationenkonzepte in Diskursen der Frauenbewegung', *Feministische Studien*, Vol. 21(1), pp. 111-122.

Tronto, J. (1996), 'Politics of Care. Fürsorge und Wohlfahrt', *Transit*, Vol. 12, pp. 142-153.

Villa, P. I. (2003), 'Woran erkennen wir eine Feministin? Polemische und programmatische Gedanken zur Politisierung von Erfahrungen', in G. A. Knapp and A. Wetterer (eds), *Achsen der Differenz. Gesellschaftstheorie und feministische Kritik II*, Westfälisches Dampfboot, Münster.

Weingarten, S. and Wellershoff, M. (1999), *Die widerspenstigen Töchter. Für eine neue Frauenbewegung*, Kiepenheuer und Witsch, Köln.

PART III:
TRANSITIONS TO ADULTHOOD, SOCIAL CHANGE AND SOCIAL EXCLUSION

Chapter 10

Young People and Family Life in Eastern Europe[1]

Ken Roberts

Introduction

Under communism young people's life-stage transitions were scripted by the system. It was possible for individuals to break out but far easier for them to comply. Most went to work (for life) in the industries, occupations and establishments for which their education had prepared them. There were no consumer markets as such. Self-organized free time could be spent at home, in streets or parks. Anything organized was under the auspices of the state and/or communist party. North American type 'dating' was never normalized let alone serial intimate relationships. Heterosexual intimacy developed as was normal in any parts of the Western world until the 1960s (see Leonard, 1980). Young people would normally experience just one serious relationship which, before long, all concerned including families, friends and the couple themselves assumed would lead to marriage. A young couple could wait to inherit the ownership or occupancy of a family dwelling. Or they could join a waiting list for a socially owned property. Either way, they would usually commence married life and parenthood while still residing in the home of one or another set of their parents or grandparents.

Much has now changed, but not everything, not yet at any rate. Some young people still make traditional school-to-work transitions from linked schools into state departments and services. As we shall see, even more are still making traditional family and housing life stage transitions. This chapter focuses on the latter. It asks exactly what has changed, for whom, and why?

Perhaps surprisingly, given that the changes began only in 1989, it is possible to give clear answers to these questions. Like all conclusions in social science, the answers delivered below are provisional. They will be exposed to new tests as new evidence becomes available, sometimes (no doubt) suggesting rather different answers, and sometimes leading to a rephrasing of the questions. That said, all the answers in this chapter are evidence based, and the evidence (see below) is from and about young people in many different regions of several ex-communist countries.

This evidence shows that young people in Eastern Europe have been in the front-line, the age group most affected by their countries' transformation into private enterprise market economies and multi-party political systems. One impact has been that most young people have been unable to obtain proper jobs, that is, full-time jobs that can be relied on to last, and which pay salaries that will support an adult lifestyle. Meanwhile, support for young people from state welfare has been withdrawn or seriously devalued. Youth political activity has declined steeply since the heady days of 1989-92. Nowadays few young people either receive or expect much from their governments. Few expect any politicians to solve their problems (see Aleshonok, 1998; Ruchkin, 1998; Ule and Rener, 1998). Whether we can speak of a slow-down in the pace of transitions to adult economic and political roles is still unclear. It seems likely that the experiences of many young people in the 1990s will prove to be foretastes of the new adulthood in their countries. Most young people have become more dependent on their families for material support, yet simultaneously families have become more dependent on any financial contributions that young people can make, and ageing parents, entering or facing retirement with devalued pensions, have been forced to look to their children for support. Of course, the detailed effects of the reforms have differed from person to person and family to family but, perhaps surprisingly, the main changes have been basically the same for all socio-demographic groups. Neither family backgrounds, education, gender, nor places of residence have offered reliable protection from the new risks. It seems that much has depended on that most quintessential of risks – pure luck.

This chapter proceeds by outlining its theoretical premises and its main sources of evidence. It then sketches the changes that have occurred during the 1990s in young people's economic and political contexts, and in gender roles and relationships in the former Soviet Union. The subsequent chapter section overviews the main trends in family formation and the discourses about these trends that are prevalent in the countries. Next, the chapter identifies young people's main pathways (some old, some new) in their life-stage family and household formation.

Theory and Evidence

Theory

This chapter rests on three theoretical premises (see Roberts, 2003, for an elaboration and a full justification), which should emerge consolidated when all the evidence has been presented.

First, youth is a life stage. Those involved are in transition between childhood and adulthood. Their circumstances and lives are forever changing. So cross-sectional snapshots inevitably distort. A biographical perspective is not just superior but absolutely essential.

Second, the key life stage transitions in youth are those from education into employment, and from families of childhood to child-rearing families, and (always closely related to relationship transitions) from living in dwellings headed by adult seniors to ones in which the young adults are the seniors. Young people in all modern societies experience changes in all areas of their lives: vis-à-vis politics, the justice system, the state welfare system, and as consumers. However, family/housing and school-to-work transitions are of fundamental importance. Everything affects everything else in some way or another in all social systems, but not to an equal extent. The pathways that young people follow during their school-to-work and family/housing transitions, and the points that they have reached at any moment in time, act as a sub-structure, an over-arching context, within which other youth transitions are experienced, situations encountered and problems addressed.

Third, the ways in which young people make their school-to-work and family/housing transitions are always inter-related, but neither determines the other. This chapter is not about dependent micro-level family life as opposed to the macro of politics and the economy. There are micro-levels within politics and the economy, and there are macro-patterns of family life and housing situations in any society. Neither the school-to-work nor the family/housing transition is bigger or stronger than the other. Thus part of the story in this chapter is about how young people's family and housing transitions have been made within, and have inevitably been affected by, the specific political and economic contexts that have arisen in the new East, but the story is equally about how 'life goes on'; how family and housing transitions have changed in some ways, and remained constant in others, as a result of processes which have their own momentum.

Evidence

Eastern Europe in this chapter means Europe to the East of the first and second wave of European Union accession states. All the more Eastward countries have shared broadly similar experiences during the late-twentieth century's great transformation. There have been similar interplays everywhere between youth biographies and history. Evidence is drawn from a wide range of sources, but principally from survey investigations coordinated by the author between 1997 and 2002 among 20-somethings in various cities and regions of Russia (Moscow and Vladikavkaz), Ukraine (Donetsk, Makeeva, Dneipropetrovsk, Lviv, and rural villages in the Lviv and Khmelnitsky regions of West Ukraine), Armenia (Yerevan and Vanadzor), and Georgia (Tbilisi and Telavi) (see Table 10.1). After the event, these studies can be described as a research programme, but it was not a programme that was planned in detail in advance. Successive projects became a *de facto* programme through successive bids for funding. Not every bid was successful. The locations where young people were studied were not selected according to a pre-conceived scheme. Rather, they were the locations that happened to be in the successful bids. However, in retrospect it seems fair to claim that the 'programme' covered a wide spread of locations: capital cities, other major cities and predominantly rural regions, in four different ex-Soviet countries.

Table 10.1   Sources of evidence

Dates	Ages of respon.	Places	Samples
1997	25-26	Tbilisi (600), Lviv (300) and Donetsk (300)	Home interviews with samples selected from registers of schools located in contrasting districts of each city
1997	20-22	Armenia (600)	Home interviews with respondents from registers of a selection of schools known to yield samples representative of the age group throughout Armenia
1999	25-26	Moscow (600), Vladikavkaz (600), Dneipropetrovsk (600)	Home interviews with samples selected from electoral registers in high status (city centre) and 'working class' (outlying) locations
2002	25-29	Yerevan, Vanadzor, Tbilisi, Telavi, Makeeva, 7 villages in West Ukraine	Home interviews with samples selected by household canvassing (supplemented by snowballing with the refugees and internally displaced persons) in districts chosen so as to yield socially homogeneous samples: from households in prosperous parts of Tbilisi (200) and Yerevan (200); from refugee families in Yerevan (200) and internally displaced households in Tbilisi (200); from economically depressed regional centres – Telavi (200) and Vanadzor (200); from coal mining communities in Makeeva (300) and from farm families in rural villages in West Ukraine (300)

All the projects used similar research methods. The interview schedule was passed from project to project with enhancements (so the current investigators believed) at every stage, but with considerable overlap throughout. The young people studied were always in their mid or late-20s. This age group was targeted because it was anticipated (correctly) that they would be at various stages towards completing their life-stage transitions, and the respondents would be able to provide biographical information about their family backgrounds, education and labour market histories, and so on. It was necessarily the case, given the ages of the respondents and the timing of the research (1997-2002), that the respondents' youth biographies were co-terminus with the post-communist transformations of their countries. The aim in all the studies was to explore how the macro-changes in the relevant locations had impacted on the youth transitions of the various socio-demographic groups. In most of the projects, and in most of the places, quasi-representative samples (always 200-600 per region) were selected, usually from districts where the local investigators knew that there would be adequate numbers from different social class family backgrounds and types of education. However, in some places the sampling was more focused. So, for example, in Tbilisi and Yerevan in 2002 (alongside samples from the general populations) the researchers also interviewed special samples of young people from refugee families. In all the locations, and with all the sub-groups, surveys using structured interviews were followed by open-ended qualitative interviews with smaller numbers and focus groups in some places. In addition to biographical data, a great deal of information was collected about the respondents' current or most recent jobs (if any), patterns and levels of income and spending, access to consumer goods, leisure activities, political and other forms of civic participation, and socio-political attitudes. Also, and of particular concern here, the samples were always questioned about their housing and household circumstances and plans.

The following passages present general conclusions from this programme of research. Generalizations are justified because there were so many similarities between the various locations. Needless to say, there were differences. In Vanadzor (Armenia) and Telavi (Georgia) in 2002 two-thirds of the samples of 25-29 year olds were unemployed. In Moscow in 1999 the level of unemployment was much lower, yet only just over a half of the 25-26 year old Muscovites had full-time jobs which paid at least $ 50 a month. Moscow had far more economically successful young people than any of the other cities or regions, but even in Moscow only a minority had full-time jobs and incomes in excess of $ 120 a month. It was basically the same in all the research locations: minorities (albeit varying in size) were doing well while much larger numbers were floundering. The pace and patterns of family and housing life-stage transitions were more similar than labour market conditions. This was because when incomes were relatively high, so was the price of housing, and economic conditions were having few short-term effects on the volume of the housing stock. So wherever they lived young people were facing similar problems when embarking on or contemplating their life-stage housing and family transitions.

Comparative cross-national research is always challenging, and conducting such research in the former Soviet Union has posed special challenges. These have not involved drafting questions capable of translation with identical meanings into different languages, or reaching agreement on questionnaire design, sampling methods and suchlike. All the partners in new East countries have shared a common (Soviet) social research heritage. They have also shared a common international language (Russian). And most of the new independent states had substantial histories of conducting (always quantitative) youth research (see Koklyagina Nurse, 2002). The special challenges have involved unreliable electricity and water supplies, shortages of basic commodities such as paper, and getting research material through customs without paying hefty bribes. In most places such problems had eased by the end of the 1990s but in others they had become normal problems with which local researchers had grown accustomed to coping.

Contexts

Economic

By the late-1990s privatization and marketization had been virtually completed in all the ex-communist countries, and everywhere the immediate effects of the reforms had included steep drops in output. Around a half, sometimes more, was ripped from people's standards of living. The impact of these reforms was akin to a major war. There have been no comparable peacetime economic disasters in any modern society. During these changes the countries were transformed from being among the world's most equal into some of its most unequal societies. Minorities have done exceptionally well. Very, very few young people have become multi (US$) millionaires but a significant minority have become 'new Russians' and their equivalents in other countries whose incomes will support a Western-type lifestyle. Meanwhile, in most places, most young people have been unable to find 'proper' jobs. Official unemployment figures have always been unreliable. Most of the young unemployed do not register. Moreover, many of those with jobs are under-employed – stood down temporarily or with only part-time hours and/or shrunken salaries. One way of measuring the proportions excluded from the core labour market is the proportion without 'proper' jobs, meaning with substantial if not full-time hours (20 or more a week) and with incomes in excess of an arbitrary (but not generous) threshold of $ 50 a month in the 1999 and 2002 surveys. On this definition, the proportions of 25-29 year olds in the 2002 surveys who were excluded ranged from a low of 39 per cent in Tbilisi to a high of 96 per cent in Vanadzor. By 2002 incomes were significantly higher in

Ukraine than in Georgia and Armenia. A 2002 survey of a nationally representative sample in Georgia found that 54.8 per cent of households were subsisting on less than 100 lari a month ($ 1 = approximately 2.5 lari) (Sumbadze and Trakhan-Mouravi, 2003). In 2002 one team of Western researchers judged relatively prosperous Ukraine to be still in the early stages of its transition (Konings et al., 2002). Khmelko (2002) was then arguing that the country had actually regressed to having more people working in agriculture than in manufacturing and extractive industries. 'Regression' is probably a more realistic description than the Donbass Development Agency's aspiration for its region to leap into post-industrial postmodernity (Zablotskiy et al., 2001). Economic conditions in Ukraine became bad in the early-1990s, they remained bad, and most people were still experiencing their economic situations as bad early in the new millennium (Gorbachyk, 2002). Similar harsh conditions have awaited young labour market entrants throughout most of Russia (Chuprov and Zubok, 1997; Zuev, 1997). While it is true that the ex-communist Central European countries have undergone economic recovery, in Poland (supposedly one of the clear success stories) in 2002 27 per cent of all 19-26 year olds were unemployed (neither working nor studying) (Jelonkeiwicz, 2002).

Dwellings are among the assets that have been turned into privately owned marketable commodities. Much of the housing (how much varying from place to place) was privately owned under communism, so owner-occupation itself has not been new. However, one of the ways in which young people could formerly qualify for their own places – by going on a waiting list for a socially owned property – has disappeared, whereas another customary way of gaining independent accommodation – 'inheriting' the right to occupy a family property – has remained extremely important. The new ability to sell dwellings (theoretical under communism because there was rarely any legal way in which anyone could accumulate the sum needed to purchase) is new, but just because dwellings have become commodities that can be bought and sold it does not automatically follow that this will actually happen. Markets do not always develop instantaneously. In some places there are empty dwellings. In many villages in West Ukraine there are empty properties that can be purchased for around $ 2000 but there are no buyers. Where there are buyers (in all major towns and cities) most young would-be purchasers are far too poor to join the markets. As yet there are no financial institutions offering long-term loans for house purchase in any of the ex-Soviet countries. And although some families are now able, if they wish, to transform their properties into cash (if there are buyers), they may continue to pass the dwellings down the generations. The feeling that dwellings are the inalienable property of families (extended families) has not yet been extinguished by market reforms. Older generations may realize that inheritance is their children's only hope of gaining their own accommodation. If so, they are unlikely to dash this hope. How easily and how rapidly young people have been moving into vacant family properties has depended largely on the size of the stocks of housing that families built-up under the old system. During the

1990s some families became the owners of surplus properties. So, for example, one might be sold to provide the capital to start a business. Other families (and their young people) have been less fortunate.

Another aspect of the economic reforms has been that consumer culture has flooded into the countries. Marketing has broadcast the culture but not the means to purchase. First of all the countries created capitalism without capitalists, and consumerism without consumers followed quickly. Few young people have been able to afford to make purchases from the upmarket shops, or to visit the smart restaurants, hotels and nightclubs, or to use the tour companies, that now have high profiles in all the major cities. These facilities are for foreigners and the local rich. Most young people have been affected more powerfully and more directly by the disappearance of the sports, holiday and cultural provisions formerly offered by the Pioneers, the Komsomol, trade unions, employers and government bodies. In most places young people's leisure opportunities have become extremely limited. They have been staying at home watching television, which they say has improved. If they go out this is most likely to just hang about. Sometimes they will have a drink in a bar or café. Many smoke. Some go to church. Very few belong to a leisure-based club or any other kind of voluntary association.

Tables 10.2 and 10.3 list the proportions of the 25-29 year olds in the various locations that were surveyed in 2002 who reported that they 'had the use of' various items of leisure-related equipment, and who took part at least once a month in a variety of leisure activities. The proportions vary from place to place but despite the likely impressions of tourists in Moscow most young people in most places in the new East do not have mobile phones. In most places most households do not have multi-channel television and most young people do not have access to the internet. Most young people spend money on tobacco and/or alcohol, and most visit bars/cafes fairly regularly, but the proportions who consume high culture have become tiny (even among those from intelligentsia families and who have been through higher education). Regular cinema attendance has become too expensive for most young people, and likewise visits to pop concerts.

Table 10.2 Leisure equipment (percentage values)

	Tbilisi born	Telavi	Tbilisi refugees	Yerevan born	Vanadz-or	Yerevan refugees	Makee-va	Khmel-nitsky	Lviv
Telephone	89	36	49	97	63	59	59	58	76
VCR	68	24	31	69	34	25	45	49	71
Car	42	24	12	38	21	15	27	43	28
Satellite dish/cable	71	2	27	7	3	5	36	5	16
PC	15	1	11	33	3	13	19	13	26
Mobile phone	65	24	39	27	-	11	27	25	50
Internet	16	1	5	28	1	12	10	9	5
N=	177	200	200	185	200	190	300	150	150

Table 10.3 Leisure activities: 'at least once a month' (percentage values)

	Tbilisi born	Telavi	Tbilisi refug.	Yerevan born	Vanad-zor	Yerevan refug.	Makeeva	Khmel-nitsky	Lviv
Pubs etc	47	27	26	64	44	27	47	30	23
Weak alcoholic drink	58	60	45	58	44	31	77	61	85
Strong alcoholic drink	41	40	29	34	27	20	51	45	56
Smoked	58	36	46	45	45	32	52	35	43
Played sport	21	24	28	31	25	22	42	19	45
Discos etc	23	2	12	15	1	7	15	22	5
Cinema	17	10	4	16	-	6	4	3	1
Theatre etc	14	2	4	16	1	7	2	1	9
Classical concerts	2	-	1	7	-	5	-	1	3
Museums, galleries etc	2	1	-	12	-	6	1	1	5
Watched sports	12	6	5	7	-	7	12	4	7
Pop/rock concerts	10	2	3	8	-	4	1	1	1
Church	32	43	26	21	3	25	9	25	79
Member of recreation club	3	5	7	2	-	5	4	1	3
Been on holiday during last year	73	36	38	43	12	19	40	32	39
N=	177	200	200	185	200	190	300	150	150

Politics

Single party government has been replaced by 'democratic' multi-party politics which have failed to engage all but a small minority of young people. The heady days of mass demonstrations and street marches were over by 1992. There are now fewer young political activists than there were under communism. Most young people are cynical, disillusioned, disgusted, and distance themselves from the new politics. Interest in politics is generally well-beneath the levels recorded in Western countries (see Table 10.4).

Table 10.4 Percentages who were 'very interested' or 'quite interested' in politics (percentage values)

1988-90

Liverpool	53
Swindon	38
Bremen	75
Paderborn	67

1993

Gdansk	18
Katowice	10
Suwalki	12

1997

Donetsk	38
Lviv	46
Tbilisi	18
Armenia	14

1999

Moscow	20
Vladikavkaz	30
Dneipropetrovsk	20

2002

Yerevan born	17
Yerevan refugees	15
Vanadzor	15
Tbilisi born	19
Tbilisi refugees	18
Telavi	33
Makeeva	22
Khmelnitsky	37
Lviv	45

In Armenia Shahnazian (2002) has found that 93 per cent of young people do not belong to any political party or, indeed, any other NGO. Civil society is developing slowly everywhere. People trust their families and friends (and sometimes God) but not their governments or private enterprises (Golovakha and Panina, 2002). Most young people have decided to rely on themselves. If they do not complain this is only because they have ceased to expect any support from their governments (Mussuri, 2003). Their governments still offer education but they no longer offer jobs, housing or welfare benefits that will keep the recipients out of poverty.

However, young people in the new East now live in and, indeed, have grown up in pluralist societies. Alternative views are disseminated through all the media. There is no longer a 'party line'. Everything is contested. Among other things, there is no longer just one proper way in which one is expected to live. Thus space has been created within which young people now regard it as normal that they should be able to make their own lifestyle choices. If their scope for choice is severely limited (by economic circumstances, for example) then young people may feel desperately frustrated.

Gender

From a Western perspective, women in the new East appear to have become more disadvantaged (vis-à-vis men) than they were under communism. On average they are now educated to higher levels than men (as is the case today in nearly all modern societies). And just as in most other countries (including Western countries), in upper secondary and tertiary education there are emphatically male and female subjects, and in the labour markets there are men's and women's jobs. On average single young women in the new East earn only around 70 per cent of male contemporaries' salaries. Unemployment has been higher among women than among men in most of the countries. Everywhere there are fewer women in politics. As under communism, housework and childcare are usually women's work. In many of the new independent states, young males (and even some females) do not agree even in principle with sex equality at home and in the labour market. In practice the division of labour is nearly always very unequal. However, it would be wrong to blame all this on the reforms. There were wide gender divisions under communism. Boys' and girls' experiences of their life-stage transitions used to be, and remain, rather different, but the main change since the 1980s has been the same for both sexes: it has become much more difficult for them to make satisfactory transitions into the labour market and to plan new family lives in their own places.

Very few young women have been celebrating their new freedom to 'live normally' as full-time housewives any more than young men have been celebrating their new opportunities to become sole family 'breadwinners'. Young women without paid jobs nearly always insist that they are unemployed and looking for work. Sex work has not really become a respectable occupation but it appears that many young women have welcomed their new freedom to use fashion to express their sexuality. Young women in Moscow appear (to an intermittent Western visitor) to have grown slimmer, and female Caucasian complexions appear to have become lighter. Western ideals of beauty have spread ahead of Western standards of living.

All the above is how things look from a Western perspective. Locals often see things differently. Very few young women in the new East feel any affinity with Western feminism. They continue to uphold the (past and current) official view that there is sex equality in their countries – that there are equal opportunities everywhere. They are extremely reluctant to open-up private life to any outside scrutiny. If they enter low paid jobs, and if they do most of the housework and childcare, young women usually insist that this is only because they choose to do so.

Gender has not protected either sex from the new risks. Nor have family backgrounds or education. It is true that some members of the former elites have been able to exchange old political capital for new economic capital and that some of their children have done rather well, but others have floundered. Children from intelligentsia families have remained by far the most likely to proceed through higher education but this has not guaranteed them good jobs (Roberts et al., 2000). The children of worker parents with experience of trading have been as likely to benefit from their family backgrounds. Worker families have been just as likely as most others to have 'inherited' surplus property from the old system. In the new labour markets much has depended on pure luck – being in the right place at the right time, having a friend who could 'put in a word' or provide crucial assistance in starting a business, joining a state firm that did not sink or a private business that happened to prosper (Roberts et al., 2002). As regards social stratification, the 1990s was a transition decade. Old strata disintegrated while new classes were still in formation. As yet here have been no true underclasses in Eastern Europe. Domanski (2002) has shown that unemployment and poverty have not been linked with the normal background predictors of disadvantage such as education or lifestyle correlates such as lack of household goods.

Family Formation: Trends and Discourses

Trends

The general trends are well known from government statistics (which are probably far more accurate on births, marriages and deaths than on personal incomes and rates of unemployment) (see Agadjanian, 2002; Roberts et al., 2003).

- There has been a net upward movement in the ages when young adults marry and first become parents. Whether exits from parental homes have been delayed is unknown, but probably not; under communism housing transitions were normally delayed for many years after couples married and had children of their own.

- Fertility has declined to well beneath replacement levels. Rising mortality rates in the 1990s (they are now declining in most of the countries), and net out-migration from some, have combined with the drop in fertility to reduce the total populations.
- There is more use of contraception by young adults.
- There are fewer abortions though these still exceed the number of live births in many ex-Soviet countries, and this method of birth control is still accepted by pubic opinion, more so for single than for married women (see Agadjanian, 2002).
- Divorce and separation have become more common.
- More parents are single (usually female) parents. Roughly a fifth of under 30 year old mothers are now living singly (see Roberts et al., 2000). They are mostly genuine lone parents rather than partnered but unmarried. Cohabitation remains far less common, and far less acceptable, than in North-West Europe.

The above trends are responsible for the public debates that have raged everywhere about the demographic crisis, and a crisis in family life.

Discourses

Within the ex-Soviet countries the most popular explanations of the above trends highlight the harsher economic conditions. This discourse is common (almost universal) among young people. They argue that they cannot afford to marry and have children; that these steps would be too hazardous especially for those who simply cannot envisage how they will ever gain independent housing, and that the prevailing conditions definitely make it too risky to have more than one child.

This discourse has a commonsensical ring. Economic conditions have definitely become harsher for most young people. Most young adults have miserable incomes. Meanwhile, some of the costs of parenthood have risen steeply. Maternity leave can no longer be relied on (no matter what the law says). Nurseries are no longer free or even heavily subsidized. These aspects of communism's 'social wage' have disappeared. Formerly they enabled women to pursue unbroken careers in full-time employment. Their special needs were catered for either by the welfare system or by 'indulgent' managers who 'understood' when, for example, women arrived late for work having spent hours queuing for household groceries. Housekeeping has become more demanding in places where electricity and water supplies have been, and remain, unreliable. The prices charged for energy and telephone calls have risen steeply everywhere.

However, there are several points to bear in mind before accepting the 'economic determinism' discourse at face value. First, there have been the same upward drifts in the ages when young adults typically marry and become parents, and the same downward lurches in fertility rates, in Central Europe and even in Western Europe where economic conditions cannot be described as harsh. Second, rates of marriage and fertility among young adults in the new East have declined, and rates of divorce and single parenthood have risen, *into* rather than beyond Western norms. Third, it is not the young people in Eastern Europe who experience the greatest labour market difficulties, or those with the lowest incomes, who are taking the longest to marry and become parents (Roberts et al., 2003). Fourth, as happened under communism, the majority are still living with one or the other set of their own parents at the time when they do marry and have children: young adults are not delaying until they have obtained their own accommodation (Roberts et al., 2003). Fifth, young people's most common aspiration is still lifelong marriage and two children (Agadjanian, 2002). Sixth, and finally, there is another parallel discourse, also common throughout the new East, which emphasizes how vital families are, and the ways in which they have become even more important since the end of communism.

Young people in the new East have not become self-centred materialists. They value their families, their partners, and sometimes their friends, above all else (Mussuri, 2003). These are the people (usually the only people) who they feel that they can really trust and rely on, and who, they believe, can trust them. Young people emphasize how personalized relationships have been more crucial than ever under the difficult post-communist conditions. Family members have needed to pool their resources in order to cope during adversity. Households have depended on maintaining several streams of income. The support of their own parents becomes even more crucial when young adults have their own children. The most common way in which people learn about jobs nowadays is from friends and families. Business start-ups often depend on pooled family resources. Friends and families are important sources of social and emotional support, and much more than this. For most young people, it is only through their families that they have any hope of gaining independent accommodation. House purchase typically depends on loans or gifts from within a family. Alternatively young people can wait until it is their turn to inherit the occupancy of a vacated family property. Parents and grandparents commonly realize that this is their children's only realistic hope. The young adults certainly know this. So they are not withdrawing from family life and obligations. They are determined that they will support their own ageing parents if and when circumstances require this. If they do sever family ties and/or if they fail to create new nuclear families of their own, they know that their own life chances will be seriously impoverished. So their aspiration remains to marry and to become parents, and in practice the vast majority are still making these life-stage transitions.

Paths to Family Formation

All young people in all countries (North and South, East and West) make their family and housing life-stage transitions in economic contexts that are not of their own making or choosing. These contexts, and individuals' own circumstances within them, place outer limits on their family formation and housing opportunities, but they do not force young people to behave in any particular ways as regards if and when to marry and bear children. Young adults in the twenty-first century new East have grown up in politically and culturally plural societies. They are far more aware than their parents were of Western 'models'. They know that they can make, or feel that they ought to be able to make, choices. Typically, as regards family and housing matters, the relevant choices are not made by solitary individuals but by couples, larger households, and sometimes by extended families (see Wallace, 2002). Four paths to adult family life in the new East are now evident (see Roberts et al., 2003).

The new middle class way Young adults with high incomes (by local standards) and/or whose families have surplus accommodation are able to move out of their parents' homes and into their own places, initially maybe to live singly, and then subsequently, or immediately, to marry. In the surveys described above these high earners were the only group of young adults among whom there was normally an interval of several years between couples living together (married or otherwise) and becoming parents. They were also the only young adults who could afford consumer-based lifestyles which, in many cases, just like young adults in the West, they wished to prolong prior to settling down. This lifestyle group is concentrated in capital cities such as Moscow (in fact Moscow is the only place surveyed where there were significant numbers in this group) where there are sufficient good jobs and prosperous families to create a critical mass of similarly-placed and like-minded young adults who can pioneer a young singles/couples lifestyle and make it acceptable. In Moscow 21 per cent of the 25-26 year old respondents who were surveyed were in couple-only situations (living together without children) whereas in Vladikavkaz only 9 per cent and in Dneipropetrovsk just 13 per cent were living in this way. In Moscow 38 per cent of the couples-only had their own places – a higher figure than in either of the other 1999 survey locations. However, it was not the Moscow culture so much as the wealth of those involved that was making this pattern of family formation possible. Across all the 1999 samples, over a half of the respondents with incomes in excess of $ 500 a month (most such respondents were in Moscow) were living as couples-only against less than 15 per cent in all the other (lower) income bands. Half of the highest income couples-only, and all of those with children, had their own places, and they were more likely to have bought their current dwellings outright, and were more likely to be planning to do this in any future moves, than any other respondents. These young adults were in fact adopting the North-West European pattern of making family and housing transitions.

First, they were moving out of the parental homes to live singly or as couples. Second, they were becoming home-owners. Third, and only after an interval of some years, they were embarking on parenthood.

The prudent These are usually on middle class trajectories, and males rather than females. They delay marriage and remain single, living with their own parents throughout their 20s, postponing family formation until they are able to obtain better jobs, or higher incomes, or until by one means or another they are able to move into their own places. In all the locations covered in this research programme it has been statistically normal for young adults aged 25-29 to be still living with their own (or the spouse's) parents. In 2002 two-thirds of the Georgia samples and over three-quarters in Armenia were living in their own parents' homes. Many had conjugal partners and nearly as many had their own children, but some were continuing to live as single. The singletons were usually middle class by origin and own occupation, and male. They were displaying the prudence that was typical among the pre-World War Two middle classes throughout Europe. Prudence was not necessarily going to be rewarded. Often, one suspects, it has to be sacrificed eventually. Or, who knows, many of those concerned in the ex-USSR may never marry and become parents. They may remain singletons who live with their ageing parents until they themselves face retirement.

Traditionals These are usually on working class trajectories, and the surveys found that this family formation behaviour is more characteristic among women than among men. They marry before their mid-20s and become parents shortly afterwards, all prior to moving into their own accommodation. They are labelled 'traditionals' here because theirs was the normal process of family formation in Soviet times. Most members of this group who were studied did not feel unwillingly trapped. They were not usually desperate to move into their own accommodation unless they were suffering severe overcrowding. They realized that households needed several streams of income, especially if none were reliable, and having grandparents in-house meant that assistance with child care was always at hand and housework could be shared. The young adults who were accomplishing family formation in this way usually knew that eventually they would inherit the properties in which they were living, or at least the right to become the principal occupants.

Couples who marry young in the ex-USSR are rarely abandoning consumption-based young singles lifestyles. Their incomes never permitted participation in these scenes. Courtship processes among this group still resemble what was normal in Western Europe in the 1950s. The young people typically experience only one serious relationship, which all concerned soon assume will become permanent. 'Dating' has not yet been normalized in most parts of the new East. Serial monogamy is still unusual (and frowned upon). Gays are not 'out'. Such alternative lifestyles are simply not an option.

Single parents   This group (virtually all women) usually marry and become mothers before their mid-20s but their partnerships prove fragile. If they had previously moved out, they usually return with their children to their parents' homes when their partnerships break-up. In all the ex-Soviet locations that were studied, around a quarter of all the young parents were single parents. Attitudes towards this status have varied from place-to-place. Pre-marital sex is still controversial in some. However, what the young adults were actually doing seemed far less variable than what other people were saying about it. According to the evidence from this research programme, young single mothers in the ex-USSR are not an especially deprived group (in economic terms). However, it is necessary to emphasize here that the single mothers who were identified in these investigations were in their mid or late-20s. They were not teenagers. Most were living with their own parents and were sharing the households' standards of living. Very few were living alone except for their children. In terms of participation in out-of-home social and leisure activities, they appeared no more disadvantaged than mothers who were living with husbands.

Discussion

Young people have been affected powerfully and profoundly by the post-communist transformations of their countries. The economies have been restructured. Labour markets have been created. There have been major changes in education. In most places technical/vocational secondary school enrolments have declined steeply, post-compulsory enrolments have risen, and business and law have replaced engineering as the prestige subjects. Housing has been privatized. Dwellings have become purchasable commodities. So young people are no longer confined to the state and its agencies and their families in efforts to obtain their own places. They are now entitled to earn, save and buy. Consumer culture accompanied by Western lifestyle models has swept across the countries. Nowadays the media propagate many different versions of truth. Young people are aware of alternative ways of living and are not just familiar with but enthusiastic about the idea of lifestyle choices.

Given all the above, in some ways it is surprising that so little has changed (so far) as regards young people's family and housing life-stage transitions. Most of the changes that have occurred are not confined to the new East and cannot be attributed entirely to post-communist conditions. These changes include delayed ages of marriage and parenthood, lower rates of fertility, and higher rates of divorce, separation and lone parenthood. Only two of the new East's distinguishable paths towards new family and household formation (see above) are new: single parenthood whose spread, as we have just observed, is not confined to the new East, and the new middle class way which still involves negligible proportions of young people in most places.

Thus we need to explain not just how and why there have been changes but also why, up to now, there has been so much continuity. There are three plausible reasons. First, young people's generally miserable incomes restrict their access to consumer markets and place severe limits on their ability to make lifestyle choices. Young singles scenes and the serial relationships that these permit (or encourage) cannot spread when few young people can afford to go out regularly for commercial leisure.

Second, young people's right to purchase a dwelling is nominal rather than real for the vast majority. Owners will not sell dwellings when the market price would be well beneath the costs of construction. Most young people cannot envisage how they will ever accumulate the sums necessary to purchase. The relevant sums look modest in a Western context – maybe $ 10,000 for a small city centre flat. However, the plain fact is that the only families (more often than individual young people) who can afford to become purchasers will either be selling a similarly priced property, or will have members in exceptionally well-paid jobs, or will have benefited from a windfall gained through spells working abroad, on a Western-funded project, or a project in the 'grey' economy.

Third, during the post-communist transformation the family has proved to be among the countries' strongest institutions. Explicit and implicit contracts between employers and workers, governments and their people, have been broken. State welfare entitlements and employers' customary obligations have been lost in the post-communist meltdown. In contrast, parents continue to honour their customary obligation, if they are able to do so, to house their grown-up children either in the former's own dwellings or by assisting the latter to obtain their own places. Young people with low personal incomes (the vast majority) know that they must rely on their families throughout their own family and housing life-stage transitions. Thus 'prudent' and 'traditional' paths to new family and household formation remain common – by far the most common – paths. Maybe this will change, but such changes are more likely to take decades or generations rather than just a few more years.

Note

1 The recent research cited extensively in this chapter was funded by INTAS (awards 93-2693, 20468 and 00-020).

References

Agadjanian, V. (2002), 'Adolescents' Views on Childbearing, Contraception and Abortion in Two Post-Communist Societies', *Journal of Youth Studies*, Vol. 5, pp. 391-406.

Aleshonok, S. (1998), 'Russian Youth: Searching for New Channels of Influence in Society', paper presented to the 'International Sociological Association Congress', Montreal.

Chuprov, V. and Zubok, J. (1997), 'Youth and Social Change', in C. Williams, V. Chuprov and V. Staroverov, *Russian Society in Transition*, Dartmouth, Aldershot, pp. 127-142.

Domanski, H (2002), 'Underclass and Social Stratification in Post-Communist Societies', *Sisyphus*, Vol. 16, pp. 109-121.

Golovakha, E. and Panina, N. (2002), 'Post-Soviet De-Institutionalization and the Formation of New Social Institutions', *Sisyphus*, Vol. 16, pp. 13-32.

Gorbachyk, A. (2002), 'Social Perception of Economic Changes and Strategies of Household Survival', *Sisyphus*, Vol. 16, pp. 85-100.

Jelonkeiwicz, J. (2002), 'Pounding the Pavement', *Warsaw Voice*, 18 May, p. 22.

Khmelko, V. (2002), 'Macrosocial Change in Ukraine: The Years of Independence', *Sisyphus*, Vol. 16, pp. 125-135.

Koklyagina Nurse, L. (2002), 'A Review of Russian Youth Research in the Late 1990s: A New Agenda and Identities', http: www.alli.fi/youth/;research/ibyr/articles/russian.html.

Konings, J., Kupets, O. and Lehmann, H. (2002), 'Gross Job Flows in Ukraine: Size, Ownership and Trade Effects', LICOS Discussion Paper 126/2002, Catholic University of Leuven, Leuven.

Leonard, D. (1980), *Sex and Generation*, Tavistock, London.

Mussuri, E. (2003), 'Poll Shows Youth Growing More Optimistic', *Kyiv Post*, Vol. 8(14), 3 April, p. 4.

Roberts, K. (2003), 'Problems and Priorities for the Sociology of Youth', in A. Bennett, M Cieslik and S. Miles (eds), *Researching Youth*, Palgrave, Basingstoke.

Roberts, K., Clark, S. C., Fagan, C. and Tholen, J. (2000), *Surviving Post-Communism: Young People in the Former Soviet Union*, Edward Elgar, Cheltenham.

Roberts, K., Osadchaya, G., Dsuzev, H. V., Gorodyanenko, V. G. and Tholen, J. (2002), 'Who Succeeds and Who Flounders? Young People in East Europe's New Market Economies', *Sociological Research Online*, Vol. 7(4).

Roberts, K., Osadchaya, G., Dsuzev, K. V., Gorodyanenko, V. G. and Tholen, J. (2003), 'Economic Conditions, and the Family and Housing Transitions of Young People in Russia and Ukraine', *Journal of Youth Studies*, Vol. 6, pp. 70-88.

Ruchkin, B. A. (1998), 'The Youth as a Strategic Resource for the Development of Russia in the XXI Century', paper presented at the 'International Sociological Association Congress', Montreal.

Shahnazarian, N. (2002), 'Aspects of Social and Political Integration of the Youth', *Armenian Social Trends*, June, pp. 41-42.

Sumbadze, N. and Trakhan-Mouravi, G. (2003), *Panel Survey of Georgia's Population: October 2002*, Institute for Policy Studies, Tbilisi.

Ule, M. and Rener, T. (1998), *Youth in Slovenia*, Ministry of Education and Sport, Ljubljana.

Wallace, C. (2002), 'Household Strategies: Their Conceptual Relevance and Analytical Scope in Social Research', *Sociology*, Vol. 36, pp. 275-292.

Zablotskiy, V. P., Koval, V. M., Koval, D. V., Liakh, O. V., Stassewicz, A. V. and Suprun, K. M. (2001), *Patho-Industralization, De-Industrialization, Post-Industrialization of Donbass Territories: Social Algorithms of Future Planning*, Regional Development Agency Donbass, Donetsk.

Zuev, A. E. (1997), 'Socio-Economic Situation of the Youth in a Labour Sphere in the Modern Russia', paper presented to conference on 'Youth Unemployment in East-Central Europe', Smolenice, Slovakia.

Chapter 11

Transition to Adulthood in Georgia. Dynamics of Generational and Gender Roles in Post-Totalitarian Society

Nana Sumbadze and George Tarkhan-Mouravi

Introduction

This chapter deals with the issues related to the changing role of generations and gender, and in particular the complex process of transition to adulthood, in the emerging reality of what has been wittily described as post-post-Soviet Georgia. Below are discussed the challenges posed by the economic/political transition in Georgia and its impact on transitions to adulthood. These issues are analysed both from theoretical and empirical points of view, by using survey data that allow the understanding of the changing values of young Georgians. After a general overview of the processes in the country related to the generational and gender-related factors, the data are presented in the sections that discuss the survey sample, power structure in families, social values, career and public participation.

Transition to adulthood is understood here along behavioural and social lines as developing psychological, economical and social independence of an individual gradually acquiring well-defined and full-fledged social status, responsibility and participation.[1] Our intention was to study the impact of the historical time, and such global trends as described by globalization, upon the process of transition to adulthood. Other factors such as new political and economic realities in which young people's personalities have been formed, in contrast to different realities characteristic of their parents' adolescence, were considered as potent factors shaping the value system and attitudes.

During the past decade Georgia has undergone drastic changes. The disintegration of the Soviet Union in 1991 and the subsequent establishment of independence in the South-Caucasian Republic of Georgia was strongly linked to the population's expectations of democratic development, prosperity and inclusion in global processes. However, it resulted in political instability leading to bloody ethno-territorial and civil wars, economic standstill, mass unemployment and impoverishment of the population. Weakness of the state, mismanagement and lack of strategic thinking resulted in the demolishing of the social security system and led to mass impoverishment. During these years the social stratification became more visible, partly due to an increasing income gap between the new poor (more than a half of the population is considered to live below the poverty line[2] and the thin layer of the new rich who either used available financial and social resources to accumulate capital mainly through privatization or trade, or acquired wealth through corruption. Another change is linked to the restructuring of political and economic system from the Soviet centralized type to an (embryonic) free market. Much of the new capital is concentrated in the cities, while most of rural areas experience full economic stagnation, increasing another gap – between rural and urban population – giving rise to growing migration to the capital city and other larger urban centres, but also to emigration to other countries.

These 'history-graded' changes and developments, along with the forces of globalization, had immense impact on the lives of people. They were reflected in the societal and personal transformation, in changing human values, social support systems and relationships, first of all within the family. There has been a strong impact on the relationships between the generations and on gender relations, but also increased differences between different groups of the population, particularly in the sphere of values and political preferences. Not only have ongoing social changes affected gender and family roles, but the process of transition within the life-cycle is itself undergoing drastic modification. In particular, transition to adulthood is very different now from what it used to be a decade or two ago. However, before describing these changes, it is important to specify which aspects of transition, and of adulthood itself, we are discussing, even if we take as a basis the so called 'Early Adult Transition' and 'Entering the Adult World' of Daniel Levinson (age 17-28) (Levinson, 1978). This means we are talking of those young people who were aged between 3 and 15 in 1990, when the political and social overhaul actually started with the disintegration of the Soviet Union. Naturally, this history-graded event was of the utmost importance for following social change, but it also naturally had different impacts on the young children and adults, men and women. It is no surprise that the cultural gap between these cohorts has widened, but it is more surprising to sometimes encounter an unexpected continuity and similarities between different cohorts, much more than continuity within cohorts themselves.[3]

As has repeatedly been stated, transition to adulthood is a multifaceted phenomenon, it has many different and strongly interrelated aspects, and hence an interdisciplinary perspective is needed to understand the complexities of the process.[4] We consider only factors that are not directly linked to physiological/biological transition and the legal status (close to 'Normative Age-Graded' influences of Baltes, Reese and Lipsitt, 1980), notwithstanding the great importance of these (actual determinants of adulthood in the strict sense), but primarily those related to changes in behaviour, worldview, value orientations,[5] social status/career and capitals/capacities, as well as temporal and social characteristics of transition.

While it is exciting to study all aspects of the very much under-explored transition to adulthood in Georgia, we have limited ourselves in our study both from the viewpoint of the methodology, the topics covered, and the social group that was researched. The main focus of the study was aimed at describing value profiles of young adults as compared to those of their parents, assessing the attitudes toward such issues as independence, traditions, equality, gender, tolerance towards minorities and similar. Thus, the topics that were covered in the questionnaire included the key aspect of transition to adulthood characteristic for Georgian society – that is independence in decision-making in private affairs, as well as some values that reflect both history-graded and age-graded developments. This means that a number of very important aspects of transition such as the role of peer groups and group behaviour in general, sexual behaviour, risk taking and delinquency, along with some others, were omitted from the study as requiring more refined and complex instruments. Of course, the observed difference in attitudes between adolescents/young adults and their parents can sometimes be attributed both to the general age-related changes and the generation/cohort-related changes, the latter more closely linked with globalization.

The study which we carried out did not allow us to differentiate between these two factors, which itself is not an easy task, but still was able to point to the important inter-generational differences and can allow for some assumptions in regard to their causes. Thus, in order to supplement general considerations discussed above, we carried out a small-scale survey, focusing on the generational and gender differences with regard to norms, values and practices concerning personal independence of young people, their obligations and responsibilities, personal ties, risks and attitudes. The format of a questionnaire which we used, while providing limited opportunity to understanding some of the listed aspects of transition, still offers, in our opinion, very valuable information about ongoing changes, or at times, about a surprising inertia, characterizing transition to adulthood in Georgia.

Georgian Society between Tradition and Change

When a society and a culture undergo a paradigm shift, the new paradigms do not immediately replace the old ones as the dominant patterns of thinking and behaviour. Some traditional elements lose their authority or relevance, while other elements retain their force.[6] Such reconfiguration is an intrinsic part of a more general process of social change, especially visible in a transitional setting such as in Georgia, and it affects in the first place the younger strata of society, more susceptible to change, – primarily family, gender and generational relations, as well as the general process of transition to adulthood in the general framework of the life cycle. The processes of change are not characterized by a straightforward replacement of existing behavioural stereotypes and value orientations, but rather they are gradual and non-homogenous, although there are examples of more rapid change. Such a 'mosaic-like' transition is taking place in Georgia, contributing further to its cultural diversity. Indeed, Georgia is a culturally and ethnically highly diversified country, so the traditions of family life, relations between generations and the gender role may differ strongly. Still, there are some overall patterns and stereotypes to be observed, rooted in the dominant centuries-long tradition of

Orthodox Christianity, the Mediterranean value system and the Soviet legacy, with the emerging role of Western influence.

Georgians thus ascribe great importance to kinship ties, and the kin are expected to share both happy events and grievances. Relatives meet regularly at important social events such as wedding parties or funerals, and neglecting the social duty to attend is disapproved of. The kinship system played a very important role in the period of extreme hardship (1992-1994), cushioning the implications of economic crisis, when social welfare appeared fully disrupted. Obligations towards family members and kin as well as friends are considered a priority and are placed before obligations to the state and society at large. The family structure in Georgia could, and to considerable degree still can, be described as traditional. The family even in urban settings often consists of three generations, and the eldest male is considered the head of the family, exercising high authority. Although basic households in cities commonly consist of a nuclear family – parents and children, quite frequently grandparents would still live with them, sharing responsibility for bringing up the children. Children are the focal point for any family, and much attention is paid to their education and development, especially in educated segments of the society.

The transition to new political, economic and social systems has to a considerable degree affected families, and in particular gender relations.[7] Although gender-neutral in design, current reforms are likely to affect men and women differently because of their different roles, responsibilities and capacities in society and the economy. Against this background of change there is increasing concern that some of the gender-related development gains of the pre-transition era may be deteriorating; the burden of the transition process may have differentially affected men and women, particularly in different regions; and, the gender dimension is not adequately reflected in governmental policies. The evidence suggests indeed that, while the consequences of market reform have not been gender-neutral, their magnitude and direction for men and women have varied considerably across the country. However, the gender implications of transition across the regions of Georgia remain a largely unexplored subject to date.

Gender equality was one of the major achievements of the Soviet Union. Women had equal access to schooling, health care, employment, and, to some extent, leadership. The consequences were evident across the region. Literacy rates were high among both women and men, levels of female employment were also often high, and benefits such as pensions were provided equally to men and women. Government policies, such as generous maternity leaves and extensive child care provision, encouraged women to work, while relatively high minimum wages, very centralized wage bargaining, and the highly regulated, almost exclusively public, labour market helped to keep wage differentials at a minimum. The difficulties of the transition process have, however, taken a toll on this legacy, as policies shifted, resources contracted, and market principles began to prevail. Poverty emerged as a new phenomenon, marked by declines in employment and household income and collapsing safety net systems.

In Georgian national culture women are supposed to fit into their predominantly subordinate roles, and concentrate on family-related duties. Their behaviour outside the family is traditionally more restricted by social norms than that of males, and marriage is considered to be a norm. In the first years after independence, however, deprived of work and their traditional role of breadwinners, men found themselves out of place in society and in the family. High male unemployment has indeed called into question the concept of the male as breadwinner and has contributed to the increase in the number of female-headed households. This has changed the power structure and bargaining power within the household and – in combination with more stable employment in the traditionally 'feminized' sectors – has introduced what was an unknown phenomenon in Soviet times – women as prime earners.

Unlike the more flexible and active women, in the first post-independence years men did not largely succeed in adjusting to new economic realities, and did not seek opportunities to open their own business or find jobs outside their professional field. The base of their authority became eroded to a certain degree, and frequently even on re-establishing their economic role in the family in the subsequent period, they would not fully return their habitual dominance in family-related decisions. Indeed, confronted with the urgency of finding the means for feeding the family, women proved to be more flexible than their spouses, and showed more readiness to 'downgrade'. Thus many women with an academic degree gladly took the jobs of housekeepers or other caring work. Petty trade was the most vibrant business, especially in the nineties, and almost exclusively carried out by women. Making shuttle journeys to Turkey and Russia, bringing food and commodities for resale in Georgia, trading in small kiosks or market places – still remains the domain of females. Women are also active in the rapidly developing hotel and bed-and-breakfast business. They, more than men, are employed by international organizations. While at the beginning of transition men comprised the majority of economic migrants, now the pattern is apparently changing. Women seem to find jobs abroad more easily than men. However, if the male migration target is Russia, where men are mostly occupied in the construction business or trade, women more often go to Greece, Israel and the US, where they work in families as housekeepers, *au pair*, or care for the elderly.[8]

In addition, the last decade has brought about substantial changes in the pattern of family formation, with a sharp decline in marriage rates and an increase in divorce. These trends have also contributed to the increase in female-headed households. It is not yet clear to what extent these new identities of women as household heads and/or sole earners will overcome the labour market disadvantage associated with the perception of women as secondary earners. Finally, the economic recession and increasing inequality in incomes have made women's earnings increasingly essential for raising, and keeping, households out of poverty – again eroding the male breadwinner model. On the other hand, the transition has enabled some women to opt out of the labour market. The dismantling of the family support system has increased demands for women's time in caring activities. But the transition process has also led to shrinking government budgets and a sharp reduction in the share of public expenditure going to the social sectors and to support for family formation. The retreat of the state from this arena has shifted parental duties back to the household. One obvious example is the reduction in availability of public childcare facilities. In a society that had remained for the most patriarchal, the resulting increase in caring responsibilities has fallen to women. In addition, pension and benefit system reforms increasingly reward productive activities at the expenses of caring and nurturing.

At the same time the transition has imposed heavy costs on men also. Economic restructuring appears to have resulted in a decline in men's advantages in some key welfare indicators and has led to inequalities favouring women in some cases. For example, as life expectancy fell during the 1990s, men experienced a greater, and unprecedented, decline in life expectancy than women. In the families where women became prime breadwinners, male heads of families lost much of their power and authority. Husbands known for their authoritarianism and adherence to traditional role division can now easily be found doing all kinds of house chores and looking after the children. The possibility of generating income has increased the self-esteem and independence among previously dependent women. It has also contributed to the increase of responsibility and self-reliance. This tendency is apparent not only in urban families with high levels of education, but now also in rural areas, although it should be noted that male authority is seldom challenged openly and in public either by women or the younger generation.

The economic changes have among other things influenced the power structure of the family previously fully dominated by elder members who were also the main breadwinners, while the younger members remained economically dependent upon their parents until quite late in their lives. Now families deploy young adults for work as part of a larger household survival strategy, or young adults enter the labour market out of economic need to help reduce the vulnerability of their households as well as to pursue their own career. This way they are nonetheless provided with opportunities to sustain their families, but also to learn, to grow as individuals, and prepare for the future career, as how and when a young person enters the labour force can set the stage for future status and work opportunities. Economic globalization is providing unprecedented opportunities for young adults, especially girls, to earn incomes that can increase their social and economic standing, self-esteem, and skills. Simultaneously, this changes their status within their respective families. The young, who in many cases appear to be more flexible and active in the labour market than their less dynamic parents, start to contribute more and more significantly to the family budget, which radically increases their say in family matters. At the same time, there is higher unemployment among young adults than other age groups. Youth unemployment has many implications: the inability to find work exacerbates economic exclusion, poverty and the probability of future joblessness. As working is an important means for young people to develop adult roles and responsibilities, unemployment obstructs the movement of young people towards adulthood. These two factors create increased diversity in the power structure within a family, but in any case lead to earlier maturing of youth.

Under the Soviets until 1991, young people enjoyed a hundred per cent literacy rate, easy access to education, full employment, and a reliable and free medical system. Today, most of this has been lost: young people are increasingly poorly educated, and find it difficult to get work. Their health is seriously threatened by drug abuse, unhealthy life styles and other health risks. Other dramatic changes took place in the education system. After having gained independence in 1991, the new Georgian state immediately faced huge problems in financing the state system of universal education. This has been an enormous challenge, but the government has not addressed the main problems causing today's failure: rampant corruption, growing inequality, and the inability of the new system to offer employment prospects. While many analysts of the post-Soviet transition have suggested that positive changes would appear both with consolidation of the country and as more young people came through the system, the reality has appeared to be quite different, at least until now. Instead of a new generation with new ideas coming to power, the best and the brightest are leaving for other countries, while those left behind are worse educated and less equipped to handle a complex world and live a decent life. As noted recently by Henrik Urdal (2001, p. 9), referring to Paul Collier:[9] 'if young people are left with no alternative but unemployment and poverty, they are likely to join a rebellion as an alternative way of generating an income'.

Still, the numbers of young people who actually get involved in politics, or even more so in various radical or other potentially destabilizing groups is very small, while young people are absent from many areas of social and political life. But behind those who actually join is a much larger disaffected group that sees little hope in the future, except through migration. In Georgia, the potential for radicalization of youth is already visible, as demonstrated by recent political events after and before the parliamentary elections of November 2003. The attitudes and abilities of young people remain a critical political issue in Georgia.

Finally drug-consumption, prostitution and crime must be addressed as top priorities due to the way they are rapidly threatening youth and future generations. This is especially important in the context of the growing influence of peer-groups, and the growth of numbers of impoverished youth without a sustainable livelihood or family care. Young adults, when forming their own values and perceptions, are very vulnerable to peer pressure. Friendships and peer groups are very important during early adulthood – young persons rely on friends for support and advice, mutual openness and personal disclosure, and groups provide them with a support base outside the family to explore and develop different identity roles. Conformity to peer pressure may also arise at this time, leading to alcohol, drugs, and criminal activity. At the same time, early adulthood is a period of 'floundering' for many young people, particularly for the youth not bound by the educational system or family authority in the situation when the society fails to help them organize their time and facilitate their development. The more so that youth and early adulthood are the prime period for thrill-seeking risks[10] that involve socially unacceptable behaviours challenging social norms, such as involvement in violent gangs or criminal networks, currently flourishing in Georgia. Sexually transmitted diseases are also becoming most common in the 15-24 age group, with more sexual permissiveness on the scene while awareness about prevention measures is low, and promiscuous young people are becoming the most susceptible to various diseases. Rapid urbanization and impoverishment, resulting in large numbers of unskilled boys and girls on the economic margin and only tenuously connected to their families, along with a ready market for sex, has led to large numbers of young people entering prostitution. The risk of infection has particularly increased for young women of low social status who may be forced into sex or have little power to negotiate condom-use with sexual partners, as sexually transmitted infections can lead to infertility and have a devastating impact on their life courses.

In previous times, notwithstanding the relatively early physiological maturing of young adults typical of the Caucasus, and an equally early acquisition of civil rights at 18 (marriage was allowed from 16; the same age – 16-18 – was an average norm for graduating from school), the transition to adulthood from the above-mentioned perspective was somewhat delayed if compared to Western analogues, or even to Northern parts of the Soviet Union. This had partly to do with traditionally close family relations and prolonged intimacy between parents and children characteristic of Caucasian societies, but also with economic dependencies and the way society was organized – in the situation of: restricted geographic mobility of the young in a small country with limited employment and educational opportunities; the virtual impossibility for a young person to acquire independent housing due to a lack of accommodation; low salaries and restricted career opportunities – the latter as a rule lived with their parents even after marriage, relying on their financial assistance for livelihood, and had a limited say in family matters. At the same time, careers were strongly dependent on age and, with minor exceptions, the young could rarely achieve a high managerial or political position/role.

Currently, there are many new opportunities opening for young women and men that have an impact on the role of the young and hence on their social standing. Firstly, jobs and well-paid employment are more easily available for those with dynamism, skills and knowledge that are more easily acquired at the young age, whether they be new technologies, foreign languages or computer-related competences. Especially in urban areas, the westernization of lifestyles has brought more equality in the social status of different cohorts. The changes concerned primarily the younger generation, and the distribution of roles among generations. Relative freedom from the Soviet mentality, knowledge of the English language and computer skills have enabled a young generation of urbanites to find employment more easily. There are many cases when men and women in their early twenties are the sole providers of their parents who are still at a productive age. Young people also more easily go abroad, whether to study or to work, or frequently to combine work with studies, while money remittances from them are often an important contribution to the family livelihood. The young can easily pursue a successful career in business, politics or in the public services. In education, the multitude of newly emerged private and state-owned commercial educational institutions provide easy access to higher education in almost every small town, even if the quality of studies is rather low. Still, there is increased migration of young people to larger urban centres were there are more opportunities for careers and employment, drastically changing the age structure of many rural and especially mountain settlements. While in Soviet times the young were obliged to live with their parents because there was little opportunity to have separate housing, the emergence of the real estate market has totally changed the situation, and if the young still live with their parents, it is often not due to lack of alternative opportunities, but rather to support aging parents or because it is easier to raise children together under conditions of poor pre-school care provision.

Now, while the juvenile phase is expanding in the West, the opposite trend is observed in Georgia, as the young acquire independent social identity at an earlier age. Many factors lead to earlier transition to adulthood, in addition to economic independence, and the cultural differences between different generations are especially important. While the elderly were brought up under the Soviet regime, and the legacy of the Communist ideology and Socialist life experience have formed their value orientations and habits, the young generation knows little about that time, and cares even less. This gap between life experiences makes the transition to adulthood somewhat different from what it was in the past, with a more inertial and conservative society, where transition meant simply ageing and acquiring the culture of the adults, their rules of the game and their values. Now the new cohorts are bringing a totally new culture along with them to early adulthood, squeezing out the old culture and the older people from their dominant position. Even the language skills of the new adults are different, and a knowledge of Russian is no longer a social indicator, with English gradually taking its place.

New generations are much more westernized, business oriented, sexually liberated and politically indifferent than the previous one. One may expect the young to be increasingly intent on pursuing non-material and emancipatory goals, as happens in societies with a longer democratic tradition. However, not only is the cultural gap between cohorts increasing, but there is even stronger divergence among young adults themselves as we find a mixture of opposing orientations which might be classed as individualism, self-realization, independence or emancipation, on one hand, among the majority of more educated and well-to-do social layers, but also more common emphasis on material well-being, respect for authority, narrow pragmatism, careerism, religious traditionalism and intolerance mixed with habits of political obedience, and moral egocentrism, among others. In general, secularized orientations, post-materialism, sexual permissiveness, environmentalism, feminism, postmodernism, and libertarianism are more evident among highly educated young urbanites, who are exposed most intensively to new social arrangements and Western ideological influences, show greater willingness to accept new ideas, and who bring these to adulthood. Their ideals are linked to personal wealth and life in the West, rather than material well-being in the sense of a comfortable life and having an apartment or a car, also family responsibility or nationalism. However, unlike Western European societies – left-wing materialism, idealism, as well as political activism rarely occur among every social stratum of the young adults, due to the negative legacy of the past. Still, in general, young adults are more optimistic, more self-confident, more satisfied with their lives, show less interpersonal trust, and, surprisingly, in spite of evident political passivity and mistrust of political elites, believe in the effectiveness of civil participation, compared to the older generations.

Transition to Adulthood: The Survey

Young adulthood – a formative time in the life course between sexual maturity and the assumption of adult roles and responsibilities – has changed dramatically in recent times, and especially over the past decades. In fact, earlier sexual maturity, later marriage and prolonged education have contributed to the acceptance of young adulthood as a distinct and important phase of life. The early years of adulthood – from about age 16 to 24 – mark the coming together of a number of developmental challenges and tasks considered essential for the assumption of adult responsibilities. This is the time when most young people face new challenges of adulthood, take on new roles, develop new behaviours and new ways of interacting; they explore the possibilities for adult life, test some initial choices, acquire the skills they need for jobs and careers; establish positive interpersonal relationships and begin to prepare for parenthood. This is the period when young adults make a commitment to a particular life course and become able to contribute in a positive way to their community. There are multiple transitions of young adulthood taking place – leaving home, entering or leaving educational institutions, finding employment, marriage, cohabitation, childbearing – and the variety of combinations and sequences in which these occur.

In order to understand these processes better, we carried out a small-scale empirical study. The survey was actually conducted by the Institute for Policy Studies in Tbilisi, the capital of Georgia, among young unmarried adults between the ages of 18 and 22 and their respective parents, with both parents living together in the same household. Two especially designed questionnaires were used in each case of parents and their children, and in each family three persons were interviewed. The resulting data were analysed by the standard SPSS software. The interviewers visited respondents at home and conducted interviews individually, covering 176 families. Young adults (45 per cent male and 55 per cent female), as well as their parents were interviewed separately at their homes in the city of Tbilisi. Summarily, 528 respondents, that is three members from each of 176 families (that is twice as many parents as young adults) were interviewed. The majority of questions in the two questionnaires designed for the study were identical, containing both specific questions and some standard instruments (measuring satisfaction with life, general trust and optimism). The young adults' questionnaire consisted of 119 questions; the one addressed to their parents, of 111 questions.

The sample represented a relatively educated and urbanized layer of society, with parents able to afford their children studying full time. This sample, small as it was, was chosen not only from the viewpoint of operational and logistical simplicity, but because such families[11] were considered to represent a better informed, flexible and more dynamic social group, in which the new trends in intra-family relationships are more evident, as their value system and practices adapt more easily to ongoing political and societal changes. Of course, despite the individualization of the life course across social classes, there are significant differences in the experience of transition to adulthood in the population groups distinguished by social status, rural/urban divide and geographic location, including precocious family transitions, and more problematic transition to adulthood for those of lower socio-economic status. We were not able to fully tackle these differences in our study due to the limited size of our sample, and therefore chose to concentrate on the selected social group.

The families of respondents consisted of three to eight members.[12] Among young adults the majority – 71 per cent – were university or college students; 18 per cent already had a university degree and 11 per cent were high school graduates. Among their parents the overwhelming majority – 92 per cent – had a university education. Most of our respondents (78 per cent) estimated their families as neither poor nor rich, while 11 per cent considered themselves as poor and 11 per cent as affluent. 99 per cent belonged to the Georgian Orthodox Church. Gender differences were quite noticeable in observing religious practices, measured through the frequency of attendance at church worship. Women of both generations[13] attended services more often than men. 40 per cent of young men compared to 58 per cent of young women visited church on festivities or regularly attended a service. Corresponding numbers for the generation of parents were 35 per cent and 48 per cent for men and women, respectively.

Family: Personal Independence and Power Relations

As family plays an extremely important role in Georgian society, it is meaningful to start our discussion with intra-family relations. Indeed, one of the major indicators of transition to adulthood is the shift from personal dependence to independence, marked by undertaking obligations and responsibilities, but also by radically more freedom of choice and decision. A number of questions tapped the perception of the actual situation in regard to independence, as well as the age-norms concerning it. Respectively, respondents were initially asked to assess their general state of independence within the family, before going into different concrete aspects of personal independence. 61 per cent of young respondents (supported by the opinion of 73 per cent of their mothers and 74 per cent of fathers) stated that they feel rather independent. Respondents also estimated different aspects of independence as revealed through possessing various behavioural options and choices, but the overall pattern was the same.

The distribution of power in families, in the majority of cases, continues to follow a well-established traditional pattern of male dominance. Fathers are perceived to be the most influential members of a family, while mothers occupy the second place. Almost half of all groups of respondents considered young adults to occupy the third position in a family power structure.

Transition to adulthood and acquiring independence may be a painful process. Family functioning involves effective communication and sporadic conflict. Slightly more girls (84 per cent) than boys (81 per cent) experience conflict at home – 33 per cent of girls and 24 per cent of boys reported that they had conflicts at home at least once or twice a month. Parents in their turn provided lower estimates for family conflicts with the involvement of their children, especially of their daughters. 78 per cent of boys' parents and 73 per cent of girls' parents admitted experiencing conflicts with their children. The way adolescents and parents view their communication with each other affects the way they view their relationship and themselves. The male-dominated power structure leads to the fact that the majority of boys have more frequent conflict with fathers (42 per cent), than with mothers (28 per cent), brothers (10 per cent) or sisters (10 per cent), while the girls conflict with almost equal frequency with mothers (27 per cent) and fathers (26 per cent), but also quite often with brothers (20 per cent), and with sisters (13 per cent).[14] In the opinion of the majority of boys (36 per cent), the most frequent conflict concerns financial issues, while 16 per cent think that the reason for conflict is dissatisfaction of parents with their educational performance. Most of their parents agree that money and studies are the strongest reasons for conflicts with their sons. However, for girls, going out is the number one problem (17 per cent), next is the incompatibility of character or bad moods (16 per cent), and then division of household chores (12 per cent). Their parents add to that list differences in opinions, and money.

Possession or lack of independent income is an important factor with a strong impact on family relations. The majority of young adults are economically dependent on their parents.[15] 65 per cent of boys and 74 per cent of girls admit having no income except money given to them by their parents.[16] Of the latter, 47 per cent of boys and 74 per cent of girls admit to spending their independent income mostly on themselves. It is interesting to note that parents overestimate such spending of their sons and underestimate the spending of daughters. Being economically strongly dependent upon their parents, the family role of young adults is quite secondary – 72 per cent of boys and 68 per cent of girls state that they do not have clear-cut responsibilities at home, while most parents (74 per cent of boys' and 68 per cent of girls' parents) agree. A slightly bigger share of girls than boys admit having responsibilities at home. Most often these include domestic chores and looking after the younger children. The above-mentioned dependency did not seem, however, to cause much distress among the majority of young adults: 65 per cent of young males and 50 per cent of young females were satisfied with the degree of freedom they enjoyed at home. Overall, 72 per cent of boys and 53 per cent of girls feel themselves to be fairly independent. Gender difference was found in this respect[17] not only in the perception of young adults themselves, but also that of their parents – 79 per cent of boys' parents and 69 per cent of girls' parents admit that their offspring are quite independent. Here again we see that a higher proportion of boys perceive themselves to be more independent than girls, and so do their parents. At the same time, parents tend to overestimate the independence of their children, particularly of their daughters. Even more surprising under such conditions is satisfaction with their own independence – boys 14 per cent more frequently than girls are satisfied with the degree of independence they enjoy, while the difference in perceived independence is significantly higher and amounts to 20 per cent.

Life in the Family: Practices and Norms

Freedom is a complex phenomenon, related not only to the objective existence of options and choices, but also to their interpretation by an individual. Therefore it is natural that the indicators of the state of individual freedom include both its perception and actual practices through which it is achieved. Also, there are differences in various aspects of family practices. Young adults do not feel their families to strongly restrict their freedom of opinion or of choice. 84 per cent (confirmed by 91 per cent of their mothers and 88 per cent of fathers) stated that they are able to freely express their opinion to other family members even when it contradicted the opinion of their parents. The majority in all respondent groups stated that parents did not interfere in such issues as the choice of a friend by young adults.

However, while opinions may be freely expressed, or choices made, it is acknowledged that this is much less the case regarding freedom of action. Respondents pointed to more restrictions in such issues as living apart from the family. About 40 per cent think that their families would not allow them to live alone. This reflects the real and universally shared attitude, as on this issue again the opinions of young respondents and their parents do not differ much. The young adults are even more restricted in their ability to live apart from the family together with an intimate person (a boyfriend or a girlfriend). At the same time, only 20 per cent (and the same proportion of parents) consider this possible, even though only 16 per cent (20 per cent of their mothers and 14 per cent of fathers) think that their family restricts them in the choice of their love object.

Gender differences become increasingly important from the viewpoint of actual practices. Everywhere society continues to have different expectations and norms about boys' and girls' sexual roles and relationships, and different social mechanisms for maintaining these. Gender-related double standards are commonplace. With the only exception regarding freedom in the choice of friends, in almost all practices that were tackled by the questionnaire, girls perceive themselves, and are granted by parents as reported by the latter, much less freedom of action than boys. Especially significant are differences related to living separately, going for a vacation or bringing a boyfriend or a girlfriend home without preliminary agreement. A much smaller proportion of girls, compared to boys, think that they have freedom to live alone. In all aspects, except freedom in the choice of friends, parents assume that their daughters have more freedom than is experienced by the daughters themselves. However, in the case of young males this difference is much smaller – both they and their parents have the same perception of freedom as the former to express opinions, to choose a girlfriend, to bring her home and freedom to live alone. A high percentage of young male adults indicate the freedom to choose love object (90 per cent), to express opinions contradicting parents' views (89 per cent) and to bring their girlfriend home without preliminary agreement with parents (81 per cent). In all these cases young males perceive having more freedom than admitted by their parents (Table 11.1).

Table 11.1   Actual freedom as perceived by young adults and their parents (percentage values)

	Young adults		Parents	
Issue	Male	Female	Male	Female
Freedom to express opinions contradicting those expressed by parents	88.6	79.4	89.2	89.2
Freedom in the choice of love object	89.9	79.4	89.8	77.7
Freedom to bring girl/boy friend home without preliminary agreement with parents	80.8	48.4	83.3	56.7
Freedom to go for a vacation with girl/boy friend	71.8	13.4	61.4	27.8
Freedom to live alone with girl/boy friend	41.0	3.1	36.0	5.7
Freedom in choice of friends	60.8	61.5	51.6	40.4
Freedom to live alone	53.2	27.8	52.2	32.5

Source: Authors' calculations based on survey data

The Univariate Analysis of Variance[18] reveals significant differences between generations in the perception of the age of young male and female adults when it is possible to go on a vacation trip without parents, and to live apart from the family alone or with a boy/girl friend. In all these cases parents' estimation of the respective age is higher than that expressed by the young adults. The age at which girls should be free to decide to go for a vacation or live alone, is perceived both by young adults and their parents (of either gender) as higher for young females than for males (Table 11.2).

As is evident from Table 11.3, the generation-related difference is quite strong. It is found regarding the age norms concerning freedom to return home any time without preliminary discussion with parents, freedom of choice of friends, freedom of sexual life, possibility to bring a girl/boy friend home and living with a girl/boy friend. Gender difference was found only regarding freedom of sexual life, males setting a higher age for females than females themselves and females setting a higher age for males than males for themselves. Again, as in existing practices, the older generation sets a higher age than the younger generation. Age norms for girls are higher in all respects than for the boys.

As young people in Western societies today are delaying marriage, they are more likely to be cohabiting. However, in Georgia this is rarely the case, and although there is an increasing freedom of sexual relations compared to the tradition of highly valued virginity (for girls), a couple would very seldom live together in cohabitation, and in most cases families would not approve of this.

In most cases there are expectations from the surrounding culture which determine age-appropriate norms and a respective timetable ('social clock'). This would include developing a career, getting married, or separating from a family. Comparison of the perception of the age at which young people can live apart from the family with their boy/girl friends with the admitted norms demonstrates a dissatisfaction with the existing practice. The age at which a young adult may live separately with a girlfriend is estimated by young adults as 24 and by parents as 25, the norm these generations set is correspondingly 23 by young and 24 by older adults. For the girls, however, the existing separation practice is estimated at the age of 26 by the young and as 28 by the older adults, while the norm is set at respectively 23 and 25 by the young and older adults. Both the existing practice and the norms point to the late acquisition of this aspect of freedom by young adults, as compared with Western practices.

Table 11.2 Generational differences in the age at which young people become independent (percentage values)

		Young adults			Parents			Difference
		M	F	Tot.	M	F	Tot.	
Freedom to go on a vacation with peers for young males	M	17.2	17.9	17.6	18.6	18.7	18.7	Generation F=32.6 p<.001
	SD	1.7	1.7	1.9	2.4	2.1	2.2	
Freedom to go on a vacation with peers for young females	M	18.9	18.2	18.5	20.2	19.5	19.9	Generation F=29.4 p<.001
	SD	2.7	2.1	2.4	2.8	2.5	2.7	
Possibility to live alone for young males	M	21.2	21.2	21.2	22.9	23.1	23.0	Generation F=32.6 p<.001
	SD	3.1	3.3	3.2	3.3	3.6	3.5	
Possibility to live alone for young females	M	23.1	22.1	22.5	25.1	24.6	24.8	Generation F=34.9 p<.001
	SD	3.9	3.6	3.7	4.2	4.1	4.1	
Possibility to live with a girl-friend for young males	M	23.6	24.9	24.3	26.0	25.6	25.8	Generation F=8.7 p<.005
	SD	3.4	4.1	3.8	4.4	3.8	4.1	
Possibility to live with a boy-friend for young females	M	25.5	26.6	26.1	28.6	27.4	28.1	Generation F=7.7 p<.05
	SD	4.1	5.2	4.7	4.3	4.8	4.5	

Source: Authors' calculations based on survey data

Table 11.3 Generational differences in the age setting of the norm for independence of young adults (percentage values)

		Young adults			Parents			Difference
		M	F	Tot.	M	F	Tot.	
Freedom to return home any time for young males	M	20.2	21.5	20.9	23.1	23.5	23.3	Generation $F=41.5$ $p<.001$
	SD	3.6	3.6	3.7	4.2	4.1	4.2	Gender $F=5.1$ $p<.05$
Freedom to return home any time for young females	M	23.1	22.7	22.9	25.9	25.6	25.7	Generation $F=36.2$ $p<.001$
	SD	5.5	4.2	4.8	4.8	4.8	4.8	
Freedom in choice of friends for young males	M	15.6	16.6	16.1	17.1	17.8	17.5	Generation $F=11.2$ $p<.005$
	SD	4.5	4.4	4.4	4.3	3.8	4.1	
Freedom in choice of friends for young females	M	16.3	16.5	16.4	17.5	17.9	17.7	Generation $F=8.9$ $p<.005$
	SD	4.3	4.6	4.5	4.4	4.4	4.4	
Freedom of sexual life for young males	M	16.1	16.7	16.4	16.9	17.4	17.1	Generation $F=9.5$ $p<.005$
	SD	2.3	2.4	2.4	2.4	2.7	2.6	Gender $F=5.6$ $p<.05$
Freedom of sexual life for young females	M	22.3	21.3	21.8	24.9	23.9	24.4	Generation $F=30.2$ $p<.001$
	SD	5.6	4.9	5.2	4.3	4.3	4.3	Gender $F=4.3$; $p<.05$
Possibility to bring girl/boyfriend home	M	18.2	18.6	18.4	19.1	19.0	19.0	Generation $F=6.9$ $p<.05$
	SD	2.9	2.1	2.5	2.6	2.4	2.5	
Possibility to bring girl/boyfriend home	M	19.2	18.8	19.0	20.1	19.5	19.8	Generation $F=32.6$ $p<.001$
	SD	2.9	2.7	2.8	3.1	2.5	2.8	
Living with a girlfriend for young males	M	22.8	23.0	22.9	24.1	24.5	24.3	Generation $F=10.7$ $p<.005$
	SD	3.2	3.4	3.3	3.4	3.5	3.5	
Living with a boyfriend for young females	M	23.2	22.9	23.0	25.7	25.0	25.3	Generation $F=15.2$ $p<.001$
	SD	3.6	3.5	3.5	3.6	4.9	4.3	

Source: Authors' calculations based on survey data

Social Values

Values are defined as measures of the relative importance of various ideas, events, actions or material things, and they clearly influence and define almost every facet of our lives and action. Although cohorts may differ in many aspects, in Georgia in some cases there is also a continuity which is strong and surprising, taking into consideration ongoing dramatic changes in all aspects of social life.

In our survey, we used the instrument measuring 'Materialist' and 'Post-materialist' value orientations (Inglehart, 1977). Respondents were requested to indicate their first and second priorities from a scale comprising four items of materialist/post-materialist values. Two items in the scale correspond to materialist ('maintain order in the nation' and 'fight rising prices'), and the other two to post-materialist orientations ('give people more say in government decisions' and 'protect freedom of speech'). Accordingly, on the basis of their choice, respondents can be grouped in having materialist, post-materialist or mixed orientations, that is choosing one materialist and one post-materialist item. Remarkably, the largest share of the respondents, youth as well as their parents, chose order (43.8 per cent of adolescents, 43.2 per cent of mothers and 44.6 per cent of fathers). But the generations differ in their second choice. The largest proportion of them – 23.6 per cent chose 'freedom', while the parents' most frequent second choice was the 'say' – 21.6 per cent among mothers and 25.0 per cent among fathers. In fact mixed values were the predominant choice (68.2 per cent), that is, respondents most frequently chose one materialist (most often order in the country) and one post-materialist value (most often people have a say in decisions), and the actual difference was in the choice of a post-materialistic value; 25.4 per cent adhered to both materialist and only 6.4 per cent to both post-materialist values. Interestingly, neither gender nor generation related differences were found to be significant.

It was equally interesting to observe this continuity regarding such issues as economic equality. The majority of all groups of respondents supported the egalitarian principle in economy – 54 per cent of young respondents, 64 per cent of their mothers and 61 per cent of fathers stated that all people should be economically more or less equal. In the concrete case of access to education this showed even more strongly – so, only 13 per cent of adolescents, 7.4 per cent of mothers and 8 per cent of fathers supported the existence of private universities.

Further, respondents were asked to choose three most important issues from the listed seven. As can be seen from Figure 11.1, family, friends and income were chosen the most often. While the difference between generations is not substantial regarding 'family', 'income' constitutes much a higher value for the parents' generation, while 'friends' is relatively more important for the young adults.

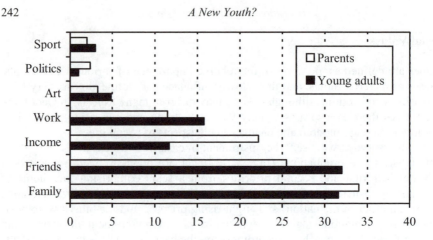

Figure 11.1   The most important aspects of life (percentage values)

Source: Authors' calculations based on survey data

The importance of the three traditional areas of social interaction, that is those of family life, friendship and personal relationships, and feasting, were measured along with the risk of losing respective traditions within next ten years. The existing pattern of personal relationships/friendship was taken as the most valued tradition and, at the same time respondents estimated the risk of its loss as the lowest. Males of the different generations differed in the evaluation of significance of personal relationships,[19] a higher proportion of fathers than of sons evaluated this tradition as very important, although no significant gender differences have been observed.

The two generations, both males[20] and females,[21] differed significantly in their assessment of the importance of family life – more parents than their children estimated family as of prime importance. It is interesting to note that males ascribe more importance to family, even if strictly speaking the gender-related difference is not statistically significant in this case.

A significant generational difference was found however among men in the evaluation of the importance of feasting.[22] A much higher proportion of fathers than their offspring considered it as very important. Of course, as traditional feasting is as a rule male-dominated; women are much less enthusiastic in assessing it highly.

Adolescence and early adulthood comprise the period used for exploration and self-determination, especially in sex and sexual identity. Gender relations, marriage and sex are the issues where, in all societies, there is a large gap between the attitudes of different generations, both due to age and to cohort-related factors. As a rule, the younger generation is expected to be more liberal, or even more libertarian, in its attitudes.

However, our findings are still very far from either libertarian or liberal attitudes, particularly in restricting sexual freedom for young women. 55 per cent of the young adults and 84 per cent of the older respondents expressed their rejection of premarital sex for women, while significant generational differences regarding this issue were found between both genders.[23] According to 60 per cent of young men, and 88 per cent of male parents, young women should retain their virginity until marriage. Fewer young women opt for this norm, but still 53 per cent of young women and 81 per cent of their mothers support it. At the same time, only 2 per cent of young adults and 3 per cent of older respondents supported the norm prohibiting premarital sex for men.[24]

Divorce and adultery are other important issues. While in the case of women the norm prohibiting adultery is much stronger, once again the attitude is more liberal in the case of males. More young people than parents admit that divorce is an appropriate action in the case of a husband's adultery. The generational difference in this case was found among females.[25] Gender difference on this issue was also quite significant among the young adults.[26] However, a much higher proportion of respondents would opt for divorce in the case of a wife's adultery. Gender difference was again found among the young adults.[27] It is interesting to note that this is the only norm we observed, where younger generation is more categorical and stricter than the older one. This is probably related to less life experience and more idealism when thinking of their own marriage.

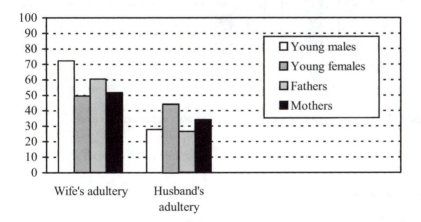

Figure 11.2   Divorce due to adultery (percentage values)

Source: Authors' calculations based on survey data

Another important dimension is the attitude toward sexual minorities – gays and lesbians, traditionally strongly marginalized by society. Twice as many young people as their parents demonstrated a tolerant attitude toward homosexuals, male or female. A generation difference was found regarding male homosexuality among women – a much higher proportion of young women than their mothers expressed tolerance in this case, while gender difference in tolerance toward male homosexuality was found among both generations,[28] females being in general more tolerant than males. The attitude towards lesbian relations also differed between generations,[29] both among male and female respondents.[30]

While tolerance toward sexual minorities show a gradual increase in tolerance by younger generations, religious tolerance demonstrates a different pattern. For example, a tolerant attitude toward the most controversial religious group – 'Jehovah's witnesses' – was expressed by the same 14-15 per cent of both young and older respondents.

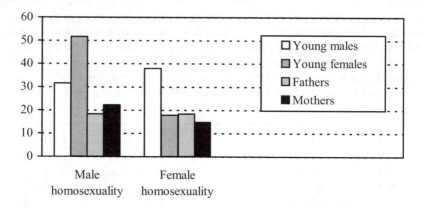

Figure 11.3   Tolerance towards homosexuals (percentage values)

Source: Authors' calculations based on survey data

Career and Participation

The transition to adulthood, among other things, implies stronger integration into society, while family links are gradually weakened. One of the most important aspects of such integration is employment. In Georgia, higher education is a popular choice for the majority of young persons, particularly in urban environments. This causes a certain delay in employment, although there is also a general difficulty for a young person to find a job. Indeed, among the young generation only 20 per cent were employed, while among the older respondents the rate was 77 per cent. The structure of employment is also different. Among those young adults who work, the majority (39 per cent) work as state employees; 32 per cent work in a private organization/business, while 13 per cent found their job with an international organization. At the same time 57 per cent of the parents' generation are state employees, 28 per cent work in a private organization, 6 per cent have their own business, and none of them worked for a foreign organization. This employment structure is reflected in plans and intentions. Respectively, the relative majority of young respondents – 42 per cent – would like to work for a foreign organization (where salaries are as a rule much higher), 23 per cent want to start their own business, 15 per cent intend to work as state employees and 12 per cent for a private organization/business. Regarding the older adults, 40 per cent of them would like to have their own business, 26 per cent to work for the state, 16 per cent for a private company and only 14 per cent for a foreign organization.

Gender is an important factor in employment, although again it is not the numbers but the types of jobs that matter. However, asked about the usual practice in Georgia regarding gender preferences, only about a quarter of both young adults and of parents supposed that women would be preferred as state employees. But when asked about their personal preference to select male or female candidates as employees, the expressed preference for women was much higher. The difference between generations was found among men. Gender difference was also obvious among parents in their preference for women employees.

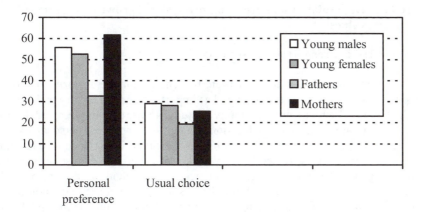

Figure 11.4 Personal preference and perceived common practice of choosing females as employees (percentage values)

Source: Authors' calculations based on survey data

The young adults seem to be more idealistic, or maybe less burdened by responsibilities, when choosing a job. When asked to express a preference between remuneration and interest in their job, far fewer young adults than parents expressed a preference for money. Men are traditionally perceived as the breadwinners. Respectively, young females are less motivated by income, and tend to be less materialistic in general – many more of them than young men choose an interesting job. A generation difference was found among women, as the preference for an interesting job over high salary was expressed by many more young women than older ones. As for the choice of high salary over professional growth, more older adults than young ones preferred a higher income. There was also a significant gender difference between the younger generation.

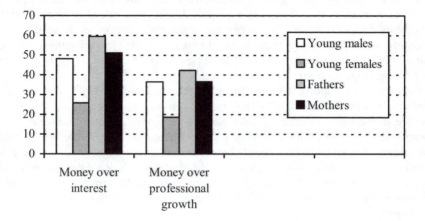

Figure 11.5   High salary vs. interest and professional growth (percentage values)

Source: Authors' calculations based on survey data

Higher education continues to be a preferred choice for the majority of young adults. In general, education is considered as important, and parents try their best to provide their children with an opportunity to study. 45 per cent of young adults and 47 per cent of parents think that education is a decisive factor for personal success in Georgia. Respondents assessed even higher the future importance of education in 10 years' time – as expressed by 70 per cent of all groups of respondents. No significant generational or gender differences were found in this respect. In general, optimism is widespread. While dissatisfied by the current situation in the country,[31] almost every second respondent (49 per cent of young adults and 47 per cent of parents) expressed a strong hope for the possibility to live decently in 10 years through honest work.

The absolute majority of young respondents (81 per cent) expressed their desire to study abroad, while fewer of them would want to work abroad for a period of about three years, or to emigrate. Men appeared to be more willing to work abroad and to emigrate. The gender difference was significant both among the young (as well as the older respondents[32] – 64 per cent of young men and 54 per cent of young women, against 50 per cent of fathers and 32 per cent of mothers, expressed a desire to work abroad. The attitude towards permanent emigration is negative in general, only 10 per cent of respondents expressed willingness to go abroad for good. Gender difference is significant among the young generation[33] – 25.3 per cent of young men compared to 9.3 per cent of young women would like to live abroad on a permanent basis. A generational difference was also found among males regarding working abroad and emigration.[34] Young males are more willing to work abroad than their fathers (64 per cent vs. 50 per cent). The corresponding figures for emigration were 25 per cent for young respondents as compared to 8 per cent of parents. A generational difference among women was found only in the case of readiness to work abroad;[35] again it is the younger women who were more eager to work abroad (54 per cent) than the older ones (32 per cent).

Georgians tend to strongly identify with their national culture, or their perception of it. When respondents were asked to choose two (out of four) cultural traditions that they felt to be closest to them, the first choice for the overwhelming majority – 89 per cent of young adults of both sexes, 96 per cent of mothers and 97 per cent of fathers – was the Georgian cultural tradition. About 60 per cent of all respondents equally named European culture as their second choice, while 16 per cent of youth (8 per cent of their parents) named American culture. About 12 per cent named Oriental culture as their choice. In fact, generations differed mainly with regard to American culture, adolescents showing a higher preference for it than their parents.[36] At the same time, there is clear preference for the USA as expressed by the youth, who do not show any interest in going to Russia, while there is a weaker preference for Russia expressed by parents. Such preference is clearly reflected in the fact that the generations differ in linguistic skills.

While the foreign language known by the majority of respondents is Russian, a slightly higher proportion of parents than youth knows it, although it is not so much the headcount itself but rather the level of knowledge of Russian that is also falling, according to other sources. At the same time, English is increasingly known among the youth.

The young people were less interested in politics.[37] A generational difference among males was found regarding readiness to take part in parliamentary elections,[38] almost twice as many fathers (58 per cent) as sons (31 per cent) intended to vote. Respectively, the young showed less interest in following political news – a significant generational difference was found regarding watching TV news both among male and female respondents.[39] A higher proportion of parents (74 per cent of fathers and 60 per cent of mothers) than young adults (32 per cent and 31 per cent) regularly watched TV news programmes. Equally, a higher proportion of fathers (61 per cent) than sons (34 per cent) would regularly read a newspaper.

The majority of respondents (62-63 per cent) were unanimous in thinking that the problems that their country faces can be solved only through active participation of the population. However, only a few respondents could envisage an opportunity for such participation. Only 4.6 per cent of young adults and 5.7 per cent of parents expressed their opinion that an ordinary person can have an influence on the actions and decisions of the government. Parents seem, however, to be more law-abiding than their offspring, as more young adults than their parents think that the laws can be broken. The generational difference was found both among men and among women[40] – 78 per cent of young men compared to 59 per cent of older male respondents admitted that laws could be broken, while corresponding numbers for women were respectively 74 per cent and 50 per cent.

Conclusions

Summing up, it can be said that the economic and social transition has caused dynamics of change in generational, gender and family patterns, gradually shifting them towards Western norms and lifestyles, and respectively influencing the process of transition to adulthood, among other factors through creating an increasing cultural gap between different cohorts of the population, but also dividing the generation of young adults themselves. What is surprising, however, is not the change but rather the inertia and continuity in values (apart from those related to sexual minorities) characterizing the sample which we have studied. In general, the resistance of traditional values is still very strong among the poorer, rural and small-town communities, where social institutions such as the kinship system have experienced little damage and continue to play an important role. Traditionalism is gaining force among the educated classes as well, as a reaction to the threats of globalization. Seemingly, what is emerging as a new pattern of social dynamic and texture is more closely related to that in South-Eastern Europe than observed in the North. However, paradoxically, transition to adulthood in Georgia has accelerated compared to previous circumstances, probably a temporary trend with the pendulum moving back in the case of new cohorts approaching the social scene. Within the limitations of our study described in the introduction, our results show that Georgian society shows somewhat different trends from those observed in Western countries. In some cases it is clear that there is certain time lag, and the forces of globalization along with economic development will bring change in the same direction, particularly with regard to more sexual freedom among young adults and more gender equality, or achieving economic independence at a younger age. Nevertheless, it seems that Georgian society will not become fully westernized in a foreseeable future, but preserve its cultural identity to a significant extent, and like other social phenomena here, the transition to adulthood will continue to show specific mixed characteristics of both East and West. It is clear that, in the short term at least, a strong continuity in values will take place, and the importance of kinship, parent-child interdependency, and a certain modesty in sexual relations will remain.

Our observations have demonstrated stronger generational differences among males than among females. Following tradition, females are achieving personal independence at an older age compared to young males, and in general their freedom is much more restricted. The younger generation is more liberal, and at the same time more radical in its opinions, and shows less respect for the law. Youth by far prefers loyalty to honesty, and prioritizes friendship and personal relationships. It is more oriented toward the West, having lost interest in Russia, accompanied by the loss of respective linguistic skills. But adolescents continue to keep a high respect for the national culture, and the tradition of close interpersonal relationships.

Notes

1   See also the chapter in this book by Kenneth Roberts: 'Young People and Family Life in Eastern Europe'.

2   United Nations Development Program (2004), *Millennium Development Goals in Georgia.*

3   'People do change as they get older. They learn more, fill new roles, and seek new means of coping with new circumstances in their lives. By and large, however, people remain basically the same in how they think, handle interpersonal relationships, and are perceived by others. For better or worse, adults tend to display many of the same general personality characteristics and the same relative level of adjustment that they did as adolescents' (Kimmel and Weiner, 1995).

4   See, among others, Kimmel, 1990; Kimmel and Weiner, 1995; Perlmutter and Hill, 1992; Ingersoll, 2003; Levinson, 1978.

5   'During adolescence, as teens develop increasingly complex knowledge systems, they also adopt an integrated set of values and morals. During the early stages of moral development, parents provide their children with a structured set of rules of what is right and wrong, what is acceptable and unacceptable. Eventually, the adolescent must assess the parent's values as they come into conflict with values expressed by peers and other segments of society. To reconcile differences, the adolescent restructures those beliefs into a personal ideology.' (The ideas of Robert Havighurst of the University of Chicago as quoted in: Ingersoll, 2003; the text accessed at http://www.michaelcarr-gregg.com.au/ParentsDevelopmentalTasks.htm.)

6   See, for example, Lucas, 1985; Woodhouse, 1996.

7   There are a few publications on the matter discussing gender dimension of reforms in Georgia, such as: ABA/CEELI, 2003; USAID, 2003; Sabedashvili, 2002; UNICEF, 2001; or a more general issue of gender in a transitional society (see, for example, Pierella, 2002).

8   See, for example, IOM, 2001.

9   Collier, P. (2000), 'Doing Well Out of War: An Economic Perspective', in M. Berdal and D.M. Malone (eds), *Greed and Grievance: Economic Agendas in Civil Wars*, Lynne Rienner, Boulder, CO/London, pp. 91–111.

10 Gullone and Moore (2000, p. 393) define that risk-taking 'Is the participation in behaviour which involves potential negative consequences (or loss) balanced in some way by perceived positive consequences (or gain)'. One can view risk-taking as either positive, or 'socially approved' behaviours and negative or 'deviant' behaviours.

11 We are aware of the importance of the issue of parental accord or economic status – so, for instance, many researchers have observed that there are higher levels of parent/adolescent conflict in families experiencing divorce, economic hardship and other stressors (for example Smetana, 1993).

12 M=4.6, SD=1.1.

13 Chi-square 8.3 p<.05 among young adults and Chi-square 22.5 p<.001 among their parents.

14 Mothers overestimate the frequency of conflict, while fathers tend to underestimate it, also a smaller proportion of fathers (37 per cent) than their sons (42 per cent as indicated above) admit to experiencing conflict.

15 87 per cent of boys and 94 per cent of girls regularly receive money from their parents.

16 19 per cent of boys and 16 per cent of girls claimed to have irregular income, and only 15 per cent of boys and 10 per cent of girls reported having a regular source of income.

17 Chi-square 8.4 $p<.05$ (Chi square is used most frequently as a non-parametric test of statistical significance for bivariate tabular analysis, which lets one know the degree of confidence possible in accepting or rejecting a hypothesis, that is, typically, whether or not two different samples are different enough in some characteristic or aspect).

18 Univariate Analysis of Variance is aimed at testing the null hypothesis that the means of groups of observations are identical. Rejection of this hypothesis is generally accompanied by the conclusion that the groups of observations are indeed different, or were generated by some different process, or come from different underlying populations. Analysis of variance compares the variation within the groups with the variation between the groups. Univariate techniques utilize only a single dependent variable. The statistical symbols below are used as follows: 'SD' is the standard deviation, while 'M' is the mean value. 'F' is the ratio of mean square between groups/mean square within groups. 'p' is respectively the probability, in this case – that random samples from different groups with equal mean sentences could yield certain F ratio.

19 Chi-square 12.3, $p<.005$.

20 Chi-square 29.6, $p<.001$.

21 Chi-square 38.3, $p<.001$.

22 Chi-square 12.3, $p<.005$.

23 Chi-square 27.3 $p<.001$ among men and Chi-square 29.2 $p<.001$ among women.

24 This norm should apply to men according to 1 per cent of young men and 4 per cent of their fathers, 2 per cent of young women and of their mothers.

25 Chi-square 11.9 $p<.005$.

26 Chi-square 19.0 $p<.001$.

27 Chi-square 11.4 $p<.005$.

28 Chi-square 16.3, $p<.001$ among young and Chi-square 6.4, $p<.05$ among older generation.

29 'Most adolescents view homosexuality as an acceptable sexual relationship among partners who consent and want such behavior, although most say they have no interest in homosexual behavior for themselves' (Soreneson, 1973).

30 Chi-square 13.8, $p<.005$ among men and Chi-square 23.6, $p<.001$ among women.

31 Only 26 per cent of young adults and 19 per cent of their parents assume that today one may lead a decent life by honest work.

32 Chi-square 7.4, $p<.005$, and Chi-square 13.2 , $p<.001$, respectively.

33 Chi-square 8.2; $p<.05$.

34 Chi-square 7.9, $p<.05$, and Chi-square 13.9, $p<.005$, respectively.

35 Chi-square 15.3; $p<.001$.

36 When respondents were asked to name the country they would like to live in, young adults most often chose the USA – 26 per cent, Italy – 12 per cent, the UK – 10 per cent, France – 6 per cent, and Spain – 4 per cent, while their parents chose the USA – 12 per cent, Russia – 5 per cent, France – 4 per cent, Germany – 3 per cent, and Italy 3 per cent. 33 per cent of youth and 68 per cent of their parents did not name as an option any other country than Georgia.

37 The situation evidently changed before and after the 'revolution of roses' of November 2004.

38 Chi-square 19.1 $p<.001$.

39 Chi-square 44.0 $p<.001$, and Chi-square 24.3, $p<.001$, respectively.

40 Chi-square 8.7, $p<.005$, among men and Chi-square 15.1, $p<.001$, among women.

References

ABA/CEELI (2003), *CEDAW Assessment Tool Report: Georgia,* October 2003, http://www.abanet.org/ceeli/publications/cedaw/cedaw_georgia.pdf.

Baltes, P.B., Reese, H.W. and Lipsitt, L.P. (1980), 'Life-Span Developmental Psychology', *Annual Review of Psychology*, Vol. 31, pp. 65-110.

Bernabè, S. (2002), *A Profile of the Labour Market in Georgia*, ILO, UNDP, Tbilisi.

Gotsadze, T., Chawla, M. and Chkatarashvili, K. (2004), *HIV/AIDS in Georgia: Addressing the Crisis*, World Bank Working Paper No. 23, January, Washington DC.

Gogishvili, T. (2002), *Trends of Child and Family Well-Being in Georgia*, UNICEF, Innocenti Research Center, Florence.

Gullone, E. and Moore, S.M. (2000), 'Adolescent Risk-Taking and the Five Factor Model of Personality', *Journal of Adolescence*, Vol. 23, pp. 393-407.

Inglehart, R. (1977), *The Silent Revolution: Changing Values and Political Styles among Western Publics*, Princeton University Press, Princeton.

Ingersoll, G.M. (2003), *Normal Adolescence*, Center for Adolescent Studies, Bloomington.

IOM (2001), *Hardship Abroad or Hunger at Home: A Study of Irregular Migration from Georgia*, IOM, Regional Office for the Caucasus and Mission to Georgia, Tbilisi, September.

Kimmel, D.C. (1990), *Adulthood and Aging: A Developmental Transition*, John Wiley & Sons, New York.

Kimmel, D.C. and Weiner, I.B. (1995), *Adolescence: A Developmental Transition*, John Wiley & Sons, New York.

Levinson, D. (1978), *The Seasons of Man's Life*, Knopf, New York.

Lucas, C. (1985), 'Out at the Edge: Notes on a Paradigm Shift', *Journal of Counseling and Development*, Vol. 64, pp. 165-172.

Perlmutter, M. and Hill, E. (1992), *Adult Development and Aging*, John Wiley & Sons, New York.

Pierella, P. (2002), *Gender in Transition. Human Development Unit, Eastern Europe and Central Asia Region*, World Bank, Washington DC, 21 May.

Sabedashvili, T. (2002), *Women in the Decade of Transition: The Case of Georgia*, Lega, Tbilisi.

Smetana, J.G. (1993), 'Conceptions of Parental Authority in Divorced and Married Mothers and their Adolescents', *Journal of Research on Adolescence*, Vol. 3(1), pp. 19-39.

Soreneson, R. (1973), *Adolescent sexuality in contemporary America*, World, New York.

Sumbadze, N. (1999), *Social Web: Friendships of Adult Men and Women*, DSWO Press Leiden University, Leiden.

Sumbadze, N. and Tarkhan-Mouravi, G. (2001), 'Democratic Value Orientations and Political Culture in Georgia', occasional paper in 'Public Administration and Public Policy of the Network of Institutes and Schools of Public Administration in Central and Eastern Europe' (NISPAcee), Bratislava, Vol. 2(3), pp. 3-43.

Sumbadze, N. and Tarkhan-Mouravi, G. (2003), *Panel Survey of the Georgia's Population: October 2002*, brief outline of results, IPS, Tbilisi.

Tarkhan-Mouravi, G. (forthcoming), *Human Development Report, Georgia 2003-2004*, UNDP, Tbilisi.

United Nations Development Program (2004), *Millennium Development Goals in Georgia*, UNDP, Tbilisi.

UNICEF (2001), *Women and Children in Georgia: A Situation Analysis*, UNICEF, Tbilisi.

USAID (2003), *Gender Assessment for USAID/Caucasus (2003)*, www.usaid.gov/our_work/cross-cutting_programs/wid/pubs/ga_caucasus_fu.

US Department of State (2003), *Trafficking in Persons Report – Georgia*, Washington, DC, 11 June.

Urdal, H. (2001), *The Devil in the Demographics: The Effect of Youth Bulges on Domestic Armed Conflict, 1950-2000*, International Peace Research Institute, Oslo.

Woodhouse, M (1996), *Paradigm Wars: Worldviews for a New Age*, Frog Ltd., Berkeley.

Chapter 12

Going Against the Tide.
Young Lone Mothers in Italy

Elisabetta Ruspini

Introduction

This chapter is about young lone mothers (between 13 and 24 years of age) in Italy, a Southern European country where traditional behaviours and family relationships still exist alongside dramatic changes. More specifically, my aim is to discuss the relationship between 'anomalies' in the transition process to adulthood and the development of factors of inequality: in this case, the link between poverty and social exclusion and the peculiarities that characterize young lone mothers' life courses.[1]

The theme of young lone mothers may perhaps appear alien in the context of this book. Reflection on this social group is, however, useful in casting light on a neglected dimension in youth issues and, at the same time, on the new forms that the transition to adulthood may assume.

Young lone mothers anticipate and accelerate and, at the same time, overlap the events which accompany the transition to adult life. They have considerably anticipated the reproductive function: motherhood precedes the conclusion of their education, their entry into the labour market, their leaving their family and a stable cohabitation with a partner. This sequence of events appears 'anomalous' if we think that the transition process towards adulthood is today – and not only in Italy – increasingly complex and contradictory and marked by delays: the lengthening of education; the search for a satisfactory, long-term job; the period preceding the setting up of a stable relationship; the time gap between establishing a relationship and the decision to have children. These delays are due to the influences brought about by trends in social change, which have contributed to the increase in risks linked to family and working life. Within a context of growing uncertainty, fragmentation, diversity and risk, the 'ideal' transition to adulthood seems to be the outcome of a sequence of events that ends with the decision to leave home 'at the right time', after having completed education, started a high quality and financially rewarding job and found a good partner and, possibly, legalized the union.

The biographies of young lone mothers are therefore of interest because they compress life events which one generally seeks to space out over a period of time: leaving home, forming a family and experiencing mother/fatherhood must take place when 'all the cards are right', without leaps in the dark and above all within the context of 'certainty and security' (see the chapter by Santoro in this volume). The latest generations of women are in particular well aware of the need for cultural training to achieve a satisfactory life. They achieve higher performances, their school careers proceed more smoothly, and they consider study more important; at the same time, they have high expectations regarding their entry in the labour market. Various research studies (see, for example, Schizzerotto, Bison and Zoppè, 1995; Bianco, 1997) show that, for girls, the lengthening of the training process brings much greater advantages compared with boys: it facilitates finding work and enables them to obtain qualified jobs.

In short, young lone mothers have lives which do not follow the 'right' sequence of events as it is considered today. Within transition processes to adulthood marked by growing complexity, fragmentariness and precariousness of experiences – with anticipations (of cohabitation as a couple and temporary job experiences) and postponements (of marriage, parenthood, regular work), starting and stopping (school, work, cohabitation: Cavalli and Galland, 1996; Rampazi, 2000) – young lone mothers shorten the paths and anticipate the stages, showing that the most varied growth patterns may be constructed within the forms of de-standardization.

In the light of these reflections, the chapter discusses the *relationship between early motherhood and social exclusion* in Italy through specific reflection on data from the Multi-Purpose Survey of Italian Families (*Indagine Multiscopo sulle famiglie italiane*). The idea is to understand what happens when, in Italy, a life 'goes against the tide', that is when the transition towards adulthood (or at least a part of it) takes place without 'the right cards', without respecting social expectations and shared patterns of behaviour. How is this linked to the development of factors of inequality? (the de-standardization of transitions includes a trend of individualization: young people have increased personal responsibility for their education and career decision: see the chapter by Biggart and Walther in this volume). And how do Italian social policies respond to the challenge laid down by the needs of young lone mothers?

Tradition and Change in the Italian Case

Lone mothers are certainly not a new phenomenon; but nevertheless the issue seems to have been 'discovered' by the Italian scientific community only in the mid eighties,[2] when their social visibility slowly started to grow. According to ISTAT – the Italian National Institute of Statistics (2000a), in Italy single-parent families account for 10.8 per cent of the total number of families. In 1988 they were 9.6 per cent. Their number has thus increased in time, though very slightly. Lone-parent families are particularly widespread in the Centre North, where there is greater marital instability.

The group of lone mothers still maintains traditional aspects in Italy. Firstly, the number of widowers and widows (accounting for much of previous single parenthood) is still considerable, though smaller than that of separated parents, unmarried mothers and above all of *divorcé/ées*, with the result that the average

age of mothers is higher than elsewhere. Despite this, the number of widowers and widows has gradually decreased, while the percentage of separated and divorced parents has risen. In Italy, therefore, the formation of one-parent families is also increasingly made up of persons who have experienced a family break-up.

A feature shared by Italian lone mothers and those in other European contexts is the prevalence of lone mothers over single fathers. Lone-parent families are in the majority of cases composed of women. According to the data from the Multi-Purpose Survey 'Families, social subjects, the condition of childhood' carried out by ISTAT in June 1998[3] (Sabbadini, 1999; ISTAT, 2000a), there are 103,000 lone fathers, 611,000 non-widowed lone mothers, 109,000 of which are unmarried, and 501,000 separated or divorced women (82 per cent of the total). Single-parent families also have fewer children than couples: 460,000 lone-parent families, 26.2 per cent, have at least one child under age. Just over two thirds of them have a single child (compared with 45.2 per cent of couples with children).

It is more difficult to describe and measure the sub-group of young unmarried mothers (especially if teenagers), due to the complication of conflicting demographic factors.

As far as the *size* of the phenomenon is concerned, we must take into account the fact that even if the fertility rate is one of the lowest in the world,[4] the family is still a crucial institution in Italy. Family solidarity is strong, the divorce rate is the lowest in the European Union, and the number of divorces and separations is rising slowly. Despite the progressive postponement of first marriages (also observable in the rest of Europe) and the decision to have children, traditional behaviour patterns and influences of a cultural nature are still very strong (seeing marriage as the prevalent form of union; leaving the parental home coinciding with the formation of a couple), placing the birth of children almost solely within marriage (De Sandre et al., 1997; Billari and Ongaro, 1998). This is all accompanied by a delayed entry into adult sexual life both compared with Europeans of the same age, and with groups immediately preceding them, and with birth control entrusted to relatively traditional methods (Bonarini, 1999). As a consequence, births out of wedlock are relatively few among all age groups. Children are mainly born within marriage, even when they are conceived before the wedding takes place. Natural fertility is one of the lowest in Western societies: 8.7 per cent of births take place outside wedlock, compared with 44 per cent in Denmark, 40.7 per cent in France, and 38.8 per cent in the United Kingdom (Saraceno and Naldini, 2001, p. 144). Cohabitation rarely occurs and when it does, it is very often for a limited period, prior to marriage and seldom involves the birth of children.

Another particular feature of the Italian model is the strength of the bonds between parents and children, with a strong central focus on children and intense support offered them (which continues even after their marriage). In Italy (and in Spain), young adults (both boys and girls) live with their parents until they get married, and are maintained by them as long as they stay in the family – even in families with a single breadwinner – whether they have a separate income or not. This trend is determined first of all by long study periods and employment difficulties. Housing problems are also underlined by some scholars, while the psychological and affective dependence on one's mother (momism) is less often cited but still operating to a certain extent. In other words we are witnessing a lengthening of the time span people spend in the family of origin. This phenomenon has come to be known as the 'famiglia lunga' ('long family)' (see the chapter by Leccardi for details). As will be recalled later, our definition of young lone mothers – while not underscoring the special needs of teenage mothers – has to be extended to include at least young women up to 24. Thus, in Italy (especially in the Southern part of the country) the network of social relationships between extended family, kin and neighbourhood – personal connections, affective links, networks of exchange and non-cash economy – still constitutes a safety net against poverty and social exclusion. We may think, for example, of aspects such as emotional support, living close by, and availability of time.

Due to the fact that pregnancy and maternity among teenagers are still quite uncommon events, the number of Italian young lone mothers is extremely low. Italy has indeed a very low teenage fertility rate compared to other national contexts (see for example Ditch, Barnes and Bradshaw, 1998; Singh and Darroch, 2000). Analysis of Tables 12.1 and 12.2 makes a further breakdown of the available data possible if one splits the 13-19 age group into two: 13-14 and 15-19, examining them separately. In the period considered (1989-1995), there were about 700,000 young women in this group but an average of only 9 births per year: this confirms the rarity of such an event in this age group.

Table 12.1   Women aged < 15 years

Year	Female population[a] 13-14 years	Conceptions	Terminations[b]	Deliveries
1989	799,193	155	137	18
1990	756,492	148	139	9
1991	718,041	158	152	6
1992	683,297	177	167	10
1993	649,255	176	161	15
1994	625,894	59	57	2
1995	614,070	264	259	5

(a)   Indicates the average annual population obtained as the simple arithmetic average of the sum of the population from 1 January to 31 December of the year the rate refers to. This average coincides with the overall years lived between the same dates by the subjects making up the population.

(b)   Including miscarriages and voluntary interruptions of pregnancy.

Source: Rimoldi, 1999 (processing ISTAT data – Rilevazione sulle nascite, 1989-1995; Annuario di Statistiche sanitarie, 1989-1995)

The overall picture changes very little if conception is considered (about 150 events per year) even though analysis of the relation between conception and birth highlights the fact that the former prevails (94 per cent of conceptions end in abortion at this age) and it should be stated that 74 per cent of these terminations of pregnancy are planned abortions. On examining the data relating to the 15-19 age group, a group made up of just under 2 million women, the birth rate rises considerably even though it still is relatively low: on average 15,000 events per year, a birth rate of about 7-8 per 1,000.

Table 12.2 Women aged 15-19

Year	Female population[a] 15-19 years	Conceptions	Terminations[b]	Deliveries
1989	2,155,637	33,816	14,016	19,800
1990	2,127,627	31,836	13,470	18,366
1991	2,082,136	30,187	13,126	17,061
1992	2,017,674	28,240	13,212	15,028
1993	1,945,477	28,056	12,910	15,146
1994	1,859,313	25,520	12,154	13,366
1995	1,765,984	25,342	11,983	13,359

(a) Indicates the average yearly annual population (see note (a), Table 12.1).
(b) Including miscarriages and voluntary interruptions of pregnancy.

Source: Rimoldi 1999 (processing of ISTAT data – Rilevazione sulle nascite, 1989-1995; Annuario di Statistiche sanitarie, 1989-1995)

Apart from the problem of the poor visibility of statistics, the phenomenon of young lone mothers is also difficult to describe and quantify because it is hard to define, which makes its *retrieval* difficult.

The 18-19 age limit does not constitute transition into adulthood in Italy and the problems linked to the coincidence of youth and motherhood also involve twenty-year-olds. It might therefore seem useful to take a broader group into consideration, without forgetting the specificity of the needs of the very young (May, 2000). As Trifiletti (2000) has highlighted:

Because of the 'long family', many young unmarried mothers still appear as daughters in censuses or sample surveys, and demographic reconstruction, based on births outside wedlock rather than on family structures, is also definitely more reliable for better comparisons.

Lastly, regarding *prediction*, opposing factors are at work. Some of them should lead to an increase in number. They include a more widespread sexual activity before marriage, and the increase of migration. From another point of view, however, the currently low numbers of young mothers living alone seem likely to decrease further. This is due to the sharp fall in levels of fertility which have affected the younger components of the population (Singh and Darroch, 2000). Apart from the growing importance of educational and training activities, a greater investment in education, young women's changing relationship with work (and hence the progressive abandoning of the traditional 'housewife-wife-mother' model), we should recall that the macroscopic drop in fertility in Italy is a direct consequence of the increase in periods of 'waiting' interposed between adolescence and adulthood, and this has probably also affected births outside wedlock for the very young (Trifiletti, 2000). We must also bear in mind that the 'young lone mother' social category is increasingly changing. This group – although very small in number – cannot be considered as homogeneous regarding its needs; on the contrary, we may hypothesize its polarization, in terms of the variable 'distance' from the family, into two segments with strongly differentiated needs: on the one hand, those women who live with their family, with a high degree of protection and help; on the other hand, young women who cannot rely on any family support, as for example lone immigrant mothers (May, 2000).

These are some of the reasons why, despite its limited quantitative incidence, early motherhood is attracting more interest from a qualitative point of view, as it represents the deep changes family patterns are going through even in a country where traditional demographic behaviours are still quite common. In Italy the marriage rate has also fallen, while the instability of marriages and the number of separations and divorces have risen, especially in the Northern part of the country. Women's employment and economic independence are steadily increasing; as a result, fertility and family behaviour are also rapidly changing. We should again mention the increased motivation of young people, especially girls, to achieve higher levels of education and training, and the greater centrality of these goals, rather than motherhood and family formation, for young women. The greatest distancing from stereotyped perceptions and also growing expectations linked to an image of autonomy and everyday and professional independence are found among young women (Leccardi, 2002; Ruspini, 2003).

Young Lone Mothers and Social Exclusion

Being a lone mother does not in itself constitute a necessary and sufficient condition to determine a situation of need. There is no causal relationship or inevitable association between lone motherhood and poverty. Their disproportionate vulnerability to poverty and social exclusion stems from the interaction between economic disadvantages and gender inequalities in the labour market, in the family, and in care and welfare systems. As has already been highlighted, young lone mothers have often not completed their education and do not have permanent work (and hence have not achieved sufficient levels of professional or social capital) or a partner and, for emergency reasons, are forced to remain with (or return to) their family of origin. We may recall that the presence of children is a negative index of social capital – seen as a system of relationship networks, bonds with the family or relatives and social membership, ascribed or acquired – in that it limits the possibility of cultivating relationships and hence to activate a synergy between the networks available which, above all, take on a particular gender form.[5]

A reading of the British Household Panel Study,[6] regarding 500 women interviewed for the first time at the age of 18 and re-interviewed the following year, examined the dynamic relationship between adolescent pregnancies and educational chances (quoted in Berthoud and Robson, 2001). What emerged is that motherhood constitutes an event able to strongly interfere with learning processes and with investment in education. Two effects in particular emerged: on the one hand, young eighteen-year-old women with low educational levels proved to be more likely to start a pregnancy in the period between the first interview and the second than more educated women (see also Kahn and Anderson, 1992). On the other hand, compared with women without children, young women who were already mothers at the age of 18 showed little likelihood (less than 50 per cent) of achieving additional educational qualifications between year t and year t+1 (and hence to invest in education and training).

Female networks are also more formed according to personal affinities and 'private relations'. While it is true that young women begin to activate 'male connections' – that is to use the networks in an instrumental way – which offer greater certainty of success in looking for a job, this happens above all with educated women, that is those who possess higher levels of human capital (Abbatecola et al., 2001; see also Schizzerotto, Bison and Zoppè, 1995).

Relating the social network with certain structural variables (gender, age, education, income and occupation), Fischer (1982) showed that education and income have important effects on the composition of the network: the greater the income. The greater the presence of individuals outside the relational group, the higher their capacity to receive help.

The problems young lone mothers face involve other types of issues, including health and the transfer of hardship along gender and generation lines. Their worsened state of health emerges from individual reports and from a greater use of health structures (Baker and North, 1999; Benzeval, 1998; Popay and Jones, 1990). They are more liable to suffer from depression and physical and psychic disturbances (see, among others, Brown and Moran, 1997), closely linked to heavy work loads in the family, lack of time and precarious economic conditions. Young lone mothers are also more exposed to pathologies during pregnancy and health complications during delivery, and their children to poor conditions of health in the years following birth (Fraser et al., 1995; Strobino, 1992; Cunnigton, 2001; Berthoud and Robson, 2001).

As far as living conditions are concerned, several comparative research studies based on European Community Household Panel[7] data show that, in all the European contexts examined, young women who become mothers during adolescence suffer much more from economic hardship than older mothers (aged twenty and above). In particular:

- many of them had no partner or no stable partner;

- regarding income sources, a large number did not work or were unemployed: help from their family of origin was often the main, or only, source of support;
- lastly, young mothers generally showed (and continue to show) decidedly lower educational levels than other groups of women.

In a second example, a study (Meadows and Dawson, 1999; Dawson and Meadows, 2001) on the features of teenage mothers and their offspring (ALSPAC – Avon Longitudinal Study of Parents and Children data) showed that, compared with mothers aged from twenty to forty years, school-age mothers more frequently come from disadvantaged families – both from the economic and social relational point of view – and, at the same time, tend to form disadvantaged nuclei.

In Italy young lone mothers also appear affected by the combination of various processes of social exclusion which, starting from education, generate economic and relational difficulties, negatively affecting the creation of human and social capital.

Table 12.3 Educational qualifications of young women (percentage values)

	15-19 years			**20-24 years**		
	Lone mothers	**Indepen. women**	**Living at home**	**Lone mothers**	**Indepen. women**	**Living at home**
Degree	-	-	-	0.5	1.0	1.9
High school leaving certificate	39.7	19.2	19.9	51.6	44.4	77.4
Middle school leaving certificate	60.3	74.9	78.8	41.7	47.3	19.6
Elementary school leaving certificate	-	5.0	1.2	6.1	7.1	1.0
Total	100.0	100.0	100.0	100.0	100.0	100.0
Absolute value	2,528	24,472	1,557,592	10,833	316,336	1,633,265

Note: Young women are classified in two main categories, 'independent' and 'living at home', according to whether they form an independent family nucleus, whatever the reason for their independence, or whether they are still living with their parents; lastly, the sub-category of young independent women is highlighted, and they are compared with the overall situation of independent women of the same age and those living at home.

Source: Boffi, 2002

Data from the Multi-Purpose Survey of Italian Families carried out by ISTAT (years 1996-1999) show that the modal education level among mothers aged from

15 to 19 is middle schooling, indicating a probable abandoning of schooling during or after their pregnancy; the employment level is very low (only a very small number is employed: about 8 per cent of 15-19-year-olds and 27 per cent of mothers aged 20-24); they have fewer friendships and social relations Boffi, 2002). In the 15-19 age group the number of those with a school leaving certificate is similar to that of young independent women and those of the same age living at home (Table 12.3); in the older group, 77 per cent of young women living with their parents have a high school leaving diploma and 2 per cent a degree – while among young independent women, 44 per cent have a medium-high level of education and the number of graduates is just over 1 per cent. This gap may be the result of an education interrupted by the transition from the parents' family to independence.[8]

Links with the family of origin however remain very strong. The majority of young mothers live with their parents and a condition of autonomy from the family prevails only in the higher age band, although the number of young lone mothers continuing to live at home remains very high (Table 12.4). From the economic point of view, younger lone mothers also have little independence, remaining supported by their family of origin, while a third of those aged from 20-24 are autonomous, also from the financial point of view (Table 12.5).

Table 12.4 Type of family cohabitation of young lone mothers

	15-19 years		20-24 years	
	Absolute	Percentage	Absolute	Percentage
Single	139	5.5	2,993	27.6
With family of origin	2,390	94.5	6,808	62.8
With friends	-	-	1,034	9.5
Total	2,529	100.0	10,835	100.0

Source: Boffi, 2002

Table 12.5 Main source of income for young lone mothers

	15-19 years		20-24 years	
	Absolute	Percentage	Absolute	Percentage
Self-supporting	-	-	2,884	28.8
Pension	-	-	381	3.8
Supported by family	2,529	100.0	6,738	67.3
Total	2,529	100.0	10,835	100.0

Source: Boffi, 2002

Regarding professional status (Table 12.6), about 38 per cent of young lone mothers (between the ages of 15 and 19) are unemployed or looking for employment; a third are housewives and a third are students. In the higher age group, the number of students falls considerably, not so much because they have completed their education but, probably, because they have dropped out of schooling; the number of housewives among young independent women increases significantly: leaving home seems to involve leaving school and taking on a dependent position inside the couple.

Table 12.6 Professional status of young women (percentage values)

	15-19 years			**20-24 years**		
	Lone mothers	**Indepen. women**	**Living with their family**	**Lone mothers**	**Indepen. women**	**Living with their family**
Employed	7.8	16.8	5.8	26.6	37.1	29.7
Unemployed	37.9	18.7	10.0	21.3	10.6	22.8
Housewives	30.1	36.7	3.5	38.3	43.9	5.0
Students	24.1	25.0	79.8	13.3	7.7	41.5
Other	-	2.7	0.8	0.6	0.7	1.0
Total	100.0	100.0	100.0	100.0	100.0	100.0
Absolute v.	2,528	24,472	1,557,592	10,833	316,336	1,633,265

Note: The young women are classified in two main categories, 'independent' and 'living at home', according to whether they form an independent family nucleus, whatever the reason for their independence, or are living with their parents; lastly, the sub-category of young lone mothers is highlighted, and compared with the overall situation of young women of the same age and those who live with their families.

Source: Boffi, 2002

To sum up, the profile of young lone mothers shows a condition of exclusion from the labour market and schooling. From the point of view of employment in domestic activities, social relations and friendships, and their economic situation, young independent women and lone mothers also appear to have lost privileges. Various indices (personal relations, meetings with friends, frequenting social venues, family income, time devoted to domestic work) show greater relational poverty in both age groups, greater commitment to domestic work and a lower income, especially in situations of independence from their family (Boffi, 2002).

These trends seem once again to underline that, in Italy, the degree of social inclusion/exclusion depends on the 'strength' and capacity for absorption of the primary solidarity networks. In general, mothers – who are mainly the parents with custody – turn to their family of origin for psychological and economic support, as confirmed by the Multi-Purpose Surveys carried out by ISTAT, even when they no longer live with their parents. In case of need, the latter continue not only to supply economic support, but also remain the main, if not only, resource. It is the parental relational network of the mother and even more of her mother (that is the grandmother) which supplies substantial help to the single-parent nucleus. Grandmothers are an indispensable source of support in the daily care and minding of children, when the mother has a job outside the home: for every young working woman there is at least one older woman (mother or mother-in-law) who may not live in the same household but who plays an active part in taking care of children (Bimbi, 2000). Thus, dependence is intergenerational rather than between men and women, and women's presence in the labour market strongly depends on the re-allocation of their care-giving work to older women. Grandfathers also, but to a lesser extent, constitute a reference point, while the more extended family networks (brothers, sisters...) do not seem to contribute in an equally significant way.

The impact of on-going social changes must not be forgotten in this context. While it is true that, for a long historical period, the organization of family reciprocity was able to maintain an equilibrium in situations on the verge of or below the poverty threshold, thanks to the combination of various incomes, today the impact of socio-economic transformations has widely undermined this ability to hold together the family, especially in Southern Italy (Mingione and Magatti, 1997). Increasingly significant phenomena of the familiarization of poverty are being revealed, 'the state of poverty in these regions might appear to be the consequence of a sort of *perverse effect* of family solidarity, and therefore of the fact that the various members of the family, jointly and severally, due to dependence or maintenance, share the economic hardship of the head of the family' (Sgritta and Innocenzi, 1993, p. 281). Furthermore, the inter-dependent relations in the family have various aspects 'in the shadow'. Some empirical evidence (Neresini, 2000) reveals that, in Italy, while lone mothers benefit considerably from the networks of family support (especially to supplement low income), some are considerably committed to help given outside, consequently reducing the positive effects of the help received (see also Giullari, 2000). Amaturo and Gambardella (2001) are moving in the same direction: to see that on the one hand, the networks surrounding poor families are often weak, that is unable to activate resources to enable leaving the poverty trap; at the same time they may constitute a factor of inequality between poor men and women. Adult women with their own family in fact often maintain relations with their family of origin providing it with care and support, and not as a network to receive help from in a situation of need.

The Labour Market and Social Policies

The trends outlined so far take on more substance if interpreted in the light of features of the Italian labour market, which is generally not advantageous for women – both regarding the supply of regular positions, and temporary or part time work – or for young people, who are a considerable percentage of those searching for work (Reyneri, 2001).

As is known, although both the activity and the employment rate of women has been increasing in the younger age groups, Italy has one of the highest levels of unemployment in Europe. The peculiarity of the Italian labour market lies, first of all, in the strong concentration of unemployment in the Southern regions of the country. According to ISTAT data (2000b), unemployment here is 20.8 per cent compared with the national level of 10.1 per cent. Secondly, there is an exceptional incidence of unemployment among young people. Again in 2000, the unemployment rate among young people aged between 15 and 24 stood at 30.3 per cent. More particularly, 26.4 per cent of men and 35 per cent of women in this age group were unemployed. Lastly, the female component is very high: in 2000, the level of women's unemployment reached 14.1 per cent. Here again the differences between the South and the Centre-North of the country are very evident: 30.6 per cent compared with 10.5 per cent in the Centre and 6.7 per cent in the North (ISTAT, 2000b). We must also mention the considerable level of long-term unemployment: 4 per cent among men and 6.7 per cent among women workers. In 2003, 58.4 per cent of unemployed men and 57.9 per cent of women had been without work for 12 months or more (Franco and Jouhette, 2004).

This situation is aggravated by other factors, such as the concentration of women in badly-paid, low prestige jobs – since their participation in paid employment is conditioned by the commitment to assistance and caring – the poor gender-sensitiveness of working hours, the inadequacy of training programmes. We must, lastly, once again bear in mind that that women heads of families with the custody of young children have fewer opportunities to find work due to their heavy care loads: bringing up children is costly both in terms of time and money, especially if these tasks cannot be shared. Caring undertaking in youth may affect opportunities for earning and hence increase the risk of poverty in later life, since young people responsible for caring are often obliged to miss school and this prevents them from completing basic schooling. Moreover, those taking on these tasks are often 'excluded' from society, since they are unable to take part in social and educational activities, unlike other young people of the same age (Olsen, 1996; Payne, 2001).

The last important element for reflection in describing the socio-economic situation of young lone mothers in Italy involves the sphere of policies. The level of adequacy/sensitivity of institutional responses to the changing risks of precariousness and social exclusion – also seen as the level of recognition of needs characterizing non-conventional family models – is a significant factor in assessment, because the welfare institutions are able to decide whether a life is regular or irregular, whether an individual has right to services, their amount and duration. In other words, to decide whether a man or a woman is deserving of assistance and whether the form of dependence is 'preferred' or 'stigmatized' (Bimbi, 2000).

Analysing the development of social assistance from Fascist legislation up to the present day, a very fragmented and complex picture emerges, marked by the absence of homogeneous standards at national level: the Italian local welfare system may be seen as an attempt at a federalist administrative model with no national co-ordination and few certainties regarding the rights of citizens.

More specifically, Italy is marked by a mosaic of local policies for minors and families in difficulty, which are mostly means-tested and whose supply strongly depends on the different local welfare models. Even Provincial and local authorities within the same Region have developed different criteria and means-tests for the allocation of benefits and services. Along with geographic heterogeneity, it appears that the few national measures are not differentiated to meet the diverse necessities of different social groups, but generically address that subpopulation labelled as the poor.

In the context of institutional policies, lone mothers remain an invisible, suppressed subject, often embarrassing from the moral point of view (Bimbi, 2000; Simoni, 2000; Terragni, 2000). They are not the object of any explicit direction of social policy, despite the fact that empirical evidence shows that they are the main beneficiaries of the social services (Sutter, 2000). Due to the crucial role played by the family in the process of social reproduction, the Italian welfare system has no particular reasons to protect them.[9]

The Provincial local authority is responsible for highly discretional and categorical policies, mainly financial assistance, to give support to un-married mothers and children born out of wedlock. Provincial policies are based on legislation to encourage population growth dating from the Fascist period.[10] Assistance from the Province requires, as *conditio sine qua non*, that there be a situation of need defined, generically, as 'a lack of adequate resources', 'belonging to a family in need ' and 'a state of poverty'. Thus no such social intervention is ever based on the recognition of a right, rather, it is based on the recognition of a situation of need. Furthermore, it is only the individual's belonging to a specific category that can legitimize the offer, or supply, of a service. A reconstruction at Provincial level of the allocation models of services (Bordin and Ruspini, 2000), has made it possible to focus on the fact that in Italy the most varied welfare models exist, whether they be residual or categorical; institutional with a universalistic nature; a stigmatizing category. The discretionary power sometimes prevails, within the same Region, regarding how to interpret competences, the definition of those entitled to them, and also the lowest and highest amounts of allocations.

The outcomes for lone mothers in such a fragmentary welfare system are extremely varied. The amounts allocated vary to a great extent, as do the requirements for means-testing; priority categories may differ; benefits may be, to a greater or lesser extent, integrated with those of the local Council or Health Authority, or delegated to these institutions. Assistance is mainly aimed at unmarried mothers, whose children may or may not be acknowledged by the father. It is mainly the child, rather than the mother, who is considered to have the right to such benefits, although it is almost always the mother who actually receives them (Bimbi, 2000). To sum up, lone mothers appear strongly segmented in social assistance intervention, since rights to benefits depend on their belonging to a very large number of categories: former illegitimate children, unmarried mothers, expectant mothers, families with children, single women with custody of children, and working mothers.

Lone mothers may however receive preferential treatment under more general provisions, such as nursery and child-care places. Lone mothers may also benefit from family and maternity allowances, from partial or total exemption from medical care costs and, until recently, from the Reddito Minimo di Inserimento (Minimum Income Support)[11] – introduced experimentally in 1998 and abolished in 2003 by the current Government. Family allowances treat single parents slightly more generously than married mothers, but only if they are workers or pensioners. In the case of lone mothers, the inadequacy of the economic support available in Italy to families with children may also be seen in the case of lone mothers. First of all, in order to receive family allowance, a lone mother must have total custody of her children[12] and must be an employee. Secondly, although the mechanism of the allowances takes the higher expenses of this type of family into account, because of the interaction between the equivalence scale adopted and the definition of income thresholds, in actual fact the income benefits provided by the allowance decreases with the increase in number of children (Toso, 1997). As for tax benefits, only unmarried women and widows are considered lone parents and therefore favoured.

Thus, the destiny of lone mothers in the Italian welfare model seems to be integration without recognition (Bimbi, 2000).

Lastly, as far as training opportunities are concerned, a survey of the educational and training policies reserved for young lone mothers in Italy – which made use of a retrieval mainly made up of structured questions sent to civil servants in charge of professional training in the 20 Italian regions – revealed that there were almost no policies specifically designed to help train lone mothers of any age. The justification (emerging during telephone interview follow-ups with various Regional directors/managers) for this lack seems to be that they are, in actual fact, an almost invisible category, and this is holding up/stopping the implementation of such policies for intervention (Trivellato, 2002).

The most important factor in assessing the level of adequacy of institutional responses to social and family change may have something to do with the processes of *social construction of dependence*. Welfare states in industrialized countries have constructed what has been described as the 'Fordist course of life' (Esping-Andersen, 1995), characterized by a particularly protective system for male adults (who formed the majority of heads of families). In other words, welfare was modelled on the life cycle of the mass industrial worker, which expected men to enter the work world at a young age and their subsequent permanence in their wage-earning area with poor prospects of changing their career (followed by compulsory pensioning); for women, a short period of gainful employment, frequently interrupted by marriage or pregnancy, followed by a remaining period devoted to the care of children, invalids, and the elderly (Esping-Andersen, 1990). Female dependence on their male partners was therefore used as a strategy to enable high levels of productivity in the Industrial era: domestic work assumed personalizing contents no longer aimed at surviving but at socializing and regenerating high productivity working potential (Mingione, 1997, 2001). In a 'familist' context such as Italy, in particular, women's dependence on male income was traditionally considered as a sort of protection from poverty. This produced some divergences: it legitimized an 'absence' and, at the same time, stigmatized dependence on state assistance and the use of social assistance systems.

The problem which now forcefully emerges involves the impact of the processes of change on the social structure, since the indispensable conditions for maintaining social and economic equilibrium in the Fordist era are rapidly disappearing in all industrialized countries. It is therefore becoming increasingly necessary to supply social policies (assistance, basic multi-purpose education, training and professional upgrading, etc.) in an organized, flexible form, able to enhance and also to guide the expansion of private social services in the production and management of support services. Training and employment policies may only be completely effective when linked intrinsically to a more comprehensive supply of help, guiding young mothers towards adulthood and enabling them to organize a 'plan for living'. For example, the growing experience of lone parenthood among immigrant women demands decisive change in intervention models. Lastly, the prevention of the 'dependency' risk must necessarily depend on a policy of support together with benefits, combining prevention and active re-inclusion. We may here quote the observation of May (2000):

> ... Training and work inclusion policies may only be completely effective when linked to and an intrinsic part of a more comprehensive supply of help enabling mothers to organise their own 'life plans'. In the case of girls continuing to live with their parents, appropriate intervention by part of family caring services will have to aim both at providing support to the parents to find a balance between ensuring help and protection, and favouring the growth and independence of their daughter; and also support to the young mother through the progressive assumption of an adult, responsible role towards her child. Within this context, the supply of consultancy and support for completing training and rapid access to the labour market may in the medium term be an absolutely crucial element in the plan. In the case of young 'single' mothers who are also 'alone' regarding their families of origin and the availability of a significant parental network, services will have the goal of favouring their growth and overall social inclusion, 'accompanying' the mother towards adulthood and independence, after coming of age, which also passes through, where possible, the recovery of or ex novo construction of a network of relations and support. In this case, since economic independence is essential to reach autonomy, suitable inclusion in the labour market and firstly a suitable programme of professional training enabling this are fundamental aspects of the intervention.

Conclusions

Young women may be considered as among the most significant protagonists of the changes in family structures and the equilibriums brought about within them, not only for their choice of postponing leaving home, but also for their strong investment in training and growing desire to enter the labour market. In this framework, lone mothers, and in particular young lone mothers, clearly embody the tension set up between tradition and modernity, social change and the response to this change, between visibility and invisibility, acceptance and stigmatization.

In a context marked by the prolonging of youth due to the growing delays in young people's acquiring the various forms of autonomy indispensable to become adults – and, therefore, by biographies which are increasingly 'blurred' and where it is difficult to identify and predict transitions between the various ages – lone mothers make up a group which is indeed small, but full of contradictions. As already said, young lone mothers mix the needs of adult life and those of youth. They overlap life events which are generally distanced in time: anticipating the event of motherhood in the absence of sufficient levels of social capital is the main cause of their vulnerability.

The impact of this anticipation may take different forms according to the different institutional and cultural contexts in which it is embedded. Specifically, young lone mothers (especially if teenagers) constitute, in Italy, a social category with high risk of social exclusion or poverty – a situation of disadvantage which may affect the lives of their children, whose welfare depends on the level of resources present in, and made available by the reference family – due to the interaction of various elements:

- the insufficient accumulation of human and professional capital which generates inability in transforming the reference networks into social capital. While the influence of individual social capital is certain in the processes of job allocation, those individuals with limited personal resources are the ones who have to most use them as a support to work (Hanson and Pratt, 1991; Bianco and Eve, 1998). This mechanism is crucial in the case of young people: the availability of high human capital, combined with the existing social networks, enables young people in search of first employment to obtain a 'better' job. Unfortunately, as far as young lone mothers are concerned, theirs is a situation where both the levels of human capital, and those of social capital are generally quite low, two factors which influence each other. Only considerable levels of human capital enable individuals to 'exploit' or 'activate' relation networks and transform them into social capital;

- the absence of targeted support by the institutional system of resource allocation: young lone mothers suffer from the lack of policies offered to both young people (in terms of job opportunities, services and housing) and lone mothers; at the same time, they do not have access to benefits reserved for particular (and more visible) categories, for example, widowed mothers. On the one hand, the delay in developing support actions able to sanction the full recognition of their right to parenthood, independence, training and assistance may be put down to their slight numerical importance. On the other hand, they are 'invisible' as far as social policies are concerned because of cultural obstacles which still prevent their needs and requests from becoming visible, in that they are clearly separate from those expressed by the 'seduced and abandoned' mother or the widow deserving assistance in traditional social policies.

- the consequent strong dependence on primary networks of solidarity, whose capacity is severely tried by the socio-democratic changes which have both diversified and complicated the needs for care and weakened the capacities for care support and economic initiative of the family and community networks. This is particularly serious if we consider that the role played by social networks (family, relations, friends, neighbours, acquaintances, work colleagues) in containing a situation of poverty is often crucial. Almost all lone mothers supplement their income with help from relations, friends, partners and the fathers of their children. The networks of parental and friendly help may radically modify the situation of a lone mother (Gambardella, 2000).

In order to improve the living conditions of young mothers, it therefore becomes of crucial importance to define the comprehensive, wide-reaching development of 'social inclusion', combining educational/training activities, assistance, the development of self-esteem, guidance towards independence, preparation for parentage and adulthood, the recovery, activation and enhancement of support networks. Indeed, lone mothers cannot be considered an homogeneous group in terms of needs; on the contrary they face very different life conditions. As already said, we have identified at least two broad categories: on one hand those women who live in their family; on the other hand those mothers who cannot rely on any family support. This deep internal differentiation should be translated into a sensible articulation of social policies, in order to offer educational and training programmes that do actually help lone mothers to enter the labour market and be economically independent. For a girl in high school still living with her family, providing support in different ways, the priority will be to complete the course of studies rather than start a vocational training programme. On the contrary, those women in a situation of social isolation should be directed into a training course to improve their chances to enter the labour market at acceptable conditions.

Notes

1   I have analysed this issue within the European Research Programme 'Education and Training for Teenage Mothers in Europe'. This study was funded by the European Union and was carried out with the support of the Commission of the European Communities under the Leonardo da Vinci research programme. The aims of the Leonardo programme are to identify educational and employment training provision for teenage mothers in Europe, to detect the barriers experienced by young mothers in their experience of education and employment training, to identify examples of good practice and, through wide dissemination of the findings, develop criteria to judge the effectiveness of such provision. The partners represent the UK, Italy, Ireland, Norway and Poland: Nona Dawson, University of Sheffield; Sara Meadows, University of Bristol; Paolo Trivellato, Elisabetta Ruspini, Mario Boffi, University of Milan-Bicocca; Evelyn Mahon, Catherine Conlon, Trinity College, University of Dublin; Bridget Penny, University of Bergen; Adam Niemczynski, Jagiellonian University, Krakow.
2   See ISTAT, 1985; Menniti and Palomba, 1988.
3   The Multi-Purpose Survey on Italian families has a complex structure. ISTAT completed an initial series of investigations which covered the period December 1987 – May 1991 and, in 1993, set off on a new course with redesigned organization of how it

operates. During the first series, because of both the complexity and the sheer quantity of different themes investigated, the survey had been split into cycles – carried out consecutively, one after the other, at approximately six-month intervals. Each of these cycles touched upon different themes/topics (with a block of questions in common) and was carried out on a new sample of about 25,000 families. The redesigned survey, launched in 1993, was based on a far simpler organizational model: data were to be collected once a year, in November, gathered using a questionnaire which changed very little from year to year and administered to a sample composed of 20,000 families (about 60,000 individuals) with a new sample chosen each year (ISTAT, 1993).

4   The fertility rate in Italy is the one of lowest of any country in the world (1.19 children per woman, according to the most recent, 1998, estimates). Indicators of this phenomenon, studied and calculated in various years, have shown that there has been a steady decrease in the fertility rate since the 1960s, a drop which began to accelerate in the 1980s and 1990s. Furthermore, there has been a clear tendency to put off reproduction until later: on average women had already had their first child by the time they were 25 in the 1960s, today, on average, women have their first child after they are 28 years old.

5   Support networks are different for men and women, as are the resources available for men and women, relating to their education level and the social class they belong to (Piselli, 2000).

6   The British Household Panel Survey (BHPS) was launched in 1991. The BHPS is being carried out by the ISER-Institute for Social and Economic Research (incorporating the ESRC Research Centre on Micro-social Change) at the University of Essex. The main objective of the survey is to further the understanding of social and economic change at the individual and household level in Britain, to identify, model and forecast such changes, their causes and their consequences, in relation to a range of socio-economic variables. It was designed as an annual survey of each adult (16+) member of a nationally representative sample of more than 5,500 households, making a total of approximately 10,200 individual interviews.

7   The European Community Household Panel (ECHP) was launched in 1994. It is a source of community and regional level statistical information. Its objective is to supply the European Commission with an instrument for observing and monitoring the standard of living of the population during the process of convergence towards monetary and political union. It presents comparable micro-level (persons/households) data on income, living conditions, housing, health and work in the EU. The ECHP is planned for a total duration of 9 years and is conducted in annual cycles. In the first wave (1994), a sample of 60,819 nationally representative households – that is approximately 127,000 adults aged 16 years and over – were interviewed in the then 12 Member States.

8   Use was made of the data relating to four Multi-Purpose Surveys (for the years 1996-1999). This made it possible to work on a population sample of about 250,000 and thus count on a higher number of young women than by using the data relating to a single survey. This was possible because the research model provides the original definition of the sample for every survey. And hence the samples coming from the different annual surveys may be compounded and used as samples of the population in the overall time period. The data reported in the text, except for a few variables retrieved in a single year, therefore show the average value relating to the four-year period 1996-1999.

9   The absence both of political debate dealing with lone mothers or of welfare policies concerning them must be seen as part of the general lack of policies for families, which is a persistent feature of post-war Italy (Saraceno, 1998; Bimbi, 2000). The reasons for this lack lie in various directions. Firstly we must recall that, for the first and only time

in Italian history, Fascism had produced policies explicitly encouraging births, centred on lone mothers. Post-war governments may have attempted to disassociate themselves from Fascist policies by neglecting this area (De Grazia, 1992). Secondly, the Mediterranean welfare model after the Second World War was marked by the essential role played by the family in caring tasks. Legislation on caring obligations was accompanied by the State's residual responsibility for family welfare. Thirdly, the presence of profound changes alongside the persistent importance of traditional and inter-generational bonds highlights the hegemony of a shared cultural model, whose characteristic feature is the importance of the family group (Bimbi, 1998).

10 Under the laws passed between 1923 and 1934, the Province is still the only public body which has direct responsibility for lone mothers as it is legally obliged to guarantee, directly or indirectly, assistance 'for illegitimate and abandoned children, for maternity and for infants in need who are abandoned or risk being abandoned'. More precisely, the Province is responsible for: a) abandoned children and minors who have only been recognized by the mother; b) maternity and infants in need; c) poor blind, deaf and dumb individuals who can be re-educated (Bordin and Ruspini, 2000).

11 http://www.reformmonitor.org/httpd-cache/doc_reports_1-29.html.

12 That is, the father must not have even formal maintenance obligations, either because he is deceased, or because the law courts have not decreed obligations on his account (Trifiletti, 1999).

References

Abbatecola, E., Alietti, A., Gambino, F., Mingione, E. and Pristinger, F. (2001), 'Generazioni, genere e capitale sociale nella riproduzione delle disuguaglianze in Veneto: il caso di Padova e Montebelluna' ('Generations, Gender and Social Capital in the Reproduction of Inequalities in the Region Veneto: The Case of Padova and Montebelluna'), in M.L. Bianco (ed.) (2001), *L'Italia delle disuguaglianze* (*Inequalities in Italy*), Carocci, Rome, pp. 167-206.

Amaturo, E. and Gambardella, D. (2001), 'Poveri e diseguali: la diversità all'interno delle fasce deboli' ('Poor and Unequal: Diversities within Weak Segments of the Population'), in M.L. Bianco (2001) (ed.), *L'Italia delle disuguaglianze* (*Inequalities in Italy*), Carocci, Rome, pp. 207-225.

Baker, D. and North K. (1999), 'Does Employment Improve the Health of Lone Mothers?', *Social Science and Medicine*, Vol. 49, pp. 121-132.

Benzeval, M. (1998), 'The Self-Reported Health Status of Lone Parents', *Social Science and Medicine*, Vol. 46, pp. 1337-1353.

Berthoud, R. and Robson, K. (2001), *The Outcomes of Teenage Motherhood in Europe*, EPAG Working Paper 22, University of Essex, Colchester.

Bianco, M.L. (1997), *Donne al lavoro. Cinque itinerari fra le diseguaglianze di genere* (*Women at Work. Five Itineraries through Gender Differences*), Scriptorium, Turin.

Bianco, M.L. and Eve, M. (1998), 'I due volti del capitale sociale. Il capitale sociale individuale nello studio delle disuguaglianze' ('Women at Work. Five Itineraries through Gender Differences'), paper presented at the European Research Conference 'European Societies or European Society?', Castelvecchio Pascoli, 3-7 April.

Bianco, M.L. (ed.) (2001), *L'Italia delle disuguaglianze* (*Inequalities in Italy*), Carocci, Rome.

Billari, F. and Ongaro, F. (1998), 'The Transition to Adulthood in Italy. Evidence from Cross-Sectional Surveys', *Espaces populations societes*, Vol. 2, pp. 165-179.

Bimbi, F. (1998), 'Family Paradigms and Women's Citizenship in the Italian Welfare State 1947-1996', paper presented at the TMR Workshop 'Family and Family Policies in Southern Europe', Turin, 20-21 November.

Bimbi, F. (2000), 'Un soggetto tacitato in un regime di welfare familistico' ('An Invisible Subject in a Familistic Welfare Regime') in F. Bimbi (ed.), *Madri sole. Metafore della famiglia ed esclusione sociale* (*Lone Mothers. Family Methapors and Social Exclusion*), Carocci, Rome, pp. 101-134.

Boffi, M. (2002), 'Il quadro statistico' ('The Statistical Picture'), in P. Trivellato (ed.), *Giovani madri sole. Percorsi formativi e politiche di welfare per l'autonomia* (*Young Lone Mothers. Educational Routes and Welfare Policies to Promote Autonomy*), Carocci, Rome, pp. 45-56.

Bonarini, F. (1999), 'L'uso della contraccezione in Italia: dalla retrospezione del 1979 a quella del 1995-96' ('Contraception in Italy: from 1979 to 1995-96'), in P. De Sandre, A. Pinnelli and A. Santini (eds.), *Nuzialità e fecondità in trasformazione: percorsi e fattori del cambiamento* (*Changing Nuptiality and Fertility: Causes and Directions*), Il Mulino, Bologna, pp. 395-411.

Bordin, M. and Ruspini, E. (2000), 'Continuità delle politiche categoriali e frammentazione del sistema di welfare. Le province' ('Categorical Policies and the Fragmentation of the Welfare State. The Provincial Local Authority in Italy'), in F. Bimbi (ed.), *Madri sole. Metafore della famiglia ed esclusione sociale* (*Lone Mothers. Family Metaphors and Social Exclusion*), Carocci, Rome, pp. 135-164.

Brown, G.W. and Moran, P.M. (1997), 'Single Mothers, Poverty and Depression', *Psychological Medicine*, Vol. 27(1), pp. 21-33.

Buzzi, C. (1998), *Giovani, affettività, sessualità. L'amore tra i giovani in una indagine IARD* (*Young People, Affectivity, Sexuality. Love among Young People. A IARD Survey*), Il Mulino, Bologna.

Buzzi, C., Cavalli, A. and de Lillo, A. (eds), (2002), *Giovani del nuovo secolo, V Rapporto IARD sulla condizione giovanile in Italia* (*Young People in the New Century. V IARD Report on Youth in Italy*), Il Mulino, Bologna.

Cavalli, A. and Galland, O. (eds),(1996), *Senza fretta di crescere. L'ingresso difficile nella vita adulta* (*No Hurry to Grow Up. The Difficult Entry into Adulthood*), Liguori, Napoli.

Cazzola, A. (1999), 'L'ingresso nella sessualità adulta' ('The Entry into Adult Sexuality'), in P. De Sandre, A. Pinnelli and A. Santini (eds.), *Nuzialità e fecondità in trasformazione: percorsi e fattori del cambiamento* (*Changing Nuptiality and Fertility: Causes and Directions*), Il Mulino, Bologna, pp. 311-326.

Cunnigton, A.J. (2001), 'What's so Bad about Teenage Pregnancy?', *Journal of Family Planning and Reproductive Health Care*, Vol. 21(1), pp. 36-41.

Dawson, N. and Meadows, S. (2001), *Education and Occupational Training for Teenage Mothers in Europe. The UK National Report*, Leonardo da Vinci Research Programme, University of Sheffield and Bristol.

De Grazia, V. (1992), *How Fascism Ruled Women 1922-1943*, University of California Press, Berkeley.

De Sandre P., Ongaro F., Rettaroli R. and Salvini S. (1997), *Matrimonio e figli: tra rinvio e rinuncia* (*Marriage and Children: Between Delay and Renounciation*), Il Mulino, Bologna.

Ditch J., Barnes H. and Bradshaw J. (eds), (1998), *Developments in National Family Policies in 1996*, European Observatory on National Family Policies, Commission of the European Communities, University of York.

Esping-Andersen, G. (1990), *The Three Worlds of Welfare Capitalism*, Polity Press, Cambridge.

Esping-Andersen, G. (1995), 'Europe's Welfare States at the End of the Century: Frozen Fordism or Postindustrial Adaptation?', paper, Instituto Juan March de Estudios e Investigaciones.

Fischer, C. (1982), *To Dwell Among Friends*, The University of Chicago Press, Chicago.

Franco, A. and Jouhette, S. (2004), *Enquete sur les forces de travail. Principaux résultats 2003*, Statistiques en bref. Population et conditions sociales, http://epp.eurostat.cec.eu.int/cache/ITY_OFFPUB/KS-NK-04-014/FR/KS-NK-04-014-FR.PDF.

Fraser, A.M., Brockert, J.E. and Ward, R.H. (1995), 'Association of Young Maternal Age with Adverse Reproductive Outcomes', *New England Journal of Medicine*, Vol. 332(17), pp. 1113-1117.

Gambardella, D. (2000), 'L'arte del packaging di risorse nelle strategie di sopravvivenza delle donne povere' ('Resource Packaging in Poor Women's Survival Strategies'), in F. Bimbi and E. Ruspini (eds), *Povertà delle donne e trasformazione dei rapporti di genere (Women's Poverty and the Transformation of Gender Relationships)*, Inchiesta, Vol. 128, April-June, pp. 56-60.

Giullari, S. (2000), 'Sostegno o (in)dipendenza? Reti di parentela e madri sole' ('Support or (In)Dependence? Kinship Networks and Lone Mothers'), in F. Bimbi and E. Ruspini (eds.), *Povertà delle donne e trasformazione dei rapporti di genere (Women's Poverty and the Transformation of Gender Relationships)*, Inchiesta, Vol. 128, April-June, pp. 91-98.

Hanson, S. and Pratt, J. (1991), 'Job Search and the Occupational Segregation of Women', *Annals of the Association of American Geographers*, Vol.81(2), pp. 229-253.

Kahn, J.R. and Anderson, K.E. (1992), 'Intergenerational Patterns of Teenage Fertility', *Demography*, Vol. 29(1), pp. 39-57.

ISTAT (1985), *Indagine sulle strutture ed i comportamenti familiari (Survey on the Structure and Behaviour of Families)*, ISTAT, Rome.

ISTAT (1993), 'Obiettivi, disegno e metodologia' ('Aims, Survey Design and Methodology'), in *Indagine Multiscopo sulle Famiglie*, Vol. 1, ISTAT, Rome.

ISTAT (2000a), 'La struttura delle famiglie e dei nuclei familiari' ('Family and Household Structure'), press release, 10 May, Rome, http://www.istat.it/Aproserv/noved/strutfam/comsta.html.

ISTAT (2000b), 'Rilevazione trimestrale sulle forze di lavoro. Luglio 2000' ('Quarterly Labour Force Survey. July 2000'), press release, 26 September, Rome.

Leccardi, C. (2002), 'Ruoli di genere ed immagini della vita di coppia' ('Gender Roles and Pictures of Life as a Couple'), in C. Buzzi, A. Cavalli and A. de Lillo (eds.), *Giovani del nuovo secolo, V Rapporto IARD sulla condizione giovanile in Italia (Young People in the New Century. V IARD Report on Youth in Italy)*, Il Mulino, Bologna, pp. 229-255.

May, M.P. (2000), Contribution to the Italian Research Group 'Education and Training for Teenage Mothers in Europe', Leonardo da Vinci Research Programme, University of Milan-Bicocca, Milan.

Meadows S. and Dawson N., (1999), 'Teenage Mothers and their Children: factors affecting their health and development', NHS 30 pages, Part of the Contribution to the Social Exclusion Unit, Publication on Teenage Pregnancy, cm 4342, June.

Menniti A. and Palomba, R. (1988), *Le famiglie con un solo genitore in Italia (One-parent Families in Italy)*, IRP, CNR, Rome.

Mingione, E. (1997), *Sociologia della vita economica (Sociology of Economic Life)*, La Nuova Italia Scientifica, Rome.

Mingione, E. (2001), 'Il lato oscuro del welfare: trasformazioni delle biografie, strategie familiari e sistemi di garanzia' ('The Dark Side of Welfare. Changing Biographies, Family Strategies and Welfare Systems'), Convegno CNR-Accademia Nazionale dei

Lincei 'Tecnologia e Società', No. 172 (Conference Proceedings, Lincei Conferences), Rome, 5-6 April, pp. 147-169.

Mingione, E. and Magatti, M. (1997), 'Strategie familiari e sviluppo: una comparazione Nord-Sud' ('Family Strategies and Development. A Comparison between North and South'), in B. Meloni (ed.), *Famiglie meridionali senza familismo. Strategie economiche, reti di relazione e parentela* (*Southern Families without Familism. Economic Strategies, Family Connections and Kinship*), Donzelli Editore, Rome.

Neresini, F. (2000), 'Madri sole, differenze di genere e processi di interdipendenza' ('Lone Mothers, Gender Differences and Interdependence Processes'), in F. Bimbi (ed.), *Madri sole. Metafore della famiglia ed esclusione sociale* (*Lone Mothers. Family Methapors and Social Exclusion*), Carocci, Rome, pp. 51-71.

Olsen, R. (1996), 'Young Carers: Challenging the Facts and Politics of Research into Children and Caring', *Disability and Society*, Vol. 11(1), pp. 41-54.

Payne, S. (2001), 'Malattia e ruoli femminili: la relazione tra dipendenza economica, responsabilità di cura e povertà' ('Illness and Women's Roles. The Relationship between Economic Dependency, Care Responsibilities and Poverty'), in C. Facchini and E. Ruspini (eds.), *Salute e disuguaglianze. Genere, condizioni sociali e corso di vita* (*Health and Inequalities. Gender, Social Conditions and Life Courses*), Franco Angeli, Milan.

Piselli, F. (2000), 'La network analysis', paper presented at the Workshop 'Genere e ricerca sociale: una sfida per la sociologia italiana' ('Gender and Social Research. A Challenge for Italian Sociology'), University of Milan-Bicocca, Milan, 1 June.

Popay, J. and Jones, G. (1990), 'Patterns of Health and Illness amongst Lone Parents', *Journal of Social Policy*, Vol. 19(4), pp. 499-534.

Rampazi, M. (2000), 'La difficile transizione delle giovani donne all'età adulta' ('The Difficult Transition of Young Women into Adulthood'), in *Economia Aziendale 2000*, http://www.ea2000.it/paper/rampazi/rampazi.htm.

Reyneri, E. (2001), *Sociologia del mercato del lavoro* (*Sociology of Labour*), Il Mulino, Bologna.

Rimoldi, S. (1999), 'A Demographic Overview On Young Lone Mothers in Italy', Intermediate Report *Education and Training for Teenage Mothers in Europe*, Part 2, Italian Research Group, University of Milan-Bicocca, June.

Ruspini, E. (2002), 'Tra visibilità e invisibilità: le madri sole in Italia' ('Between Visibility and Invisibility: Lone Mothers in Italy'), in P. Trivellato (ed.), *Giovani madri sole. Percorsi formativi e politiche di welfare per l'autonomia* (*Young Lone Mothers. Educational Routes and Welfare Policies to Promote Authonomy*), Carocci, Rome, pp. 17-44.

Ruspini, E. (2003), *Le identità di genere* (*Gender Identities*), Carocci, Rome.

Sabbadini, L.L. (1999), 'La permanenza dei giovani nella famiglia di origine. Modelli di formazione e organizzazione della famiglia' ('The Permanence of Young People at Home. Family Models and Organization'), contribution to the Conference 'Le famiglie interrogano le politiche sociali' ('Families Question Social Policies'), Bologna, 29-31 March.

Saraceno, C. (1998), *Mutamenti della famiglia e politiche sociali in Italia* (*Family Changes and Social Policies in Italy*), Il Mulino, Bologna.

Saraceno, C. and Naldini, M. (2001), *Sociologia della Famiglia* (*Sociology of the Family*), Il Mulino, Bologna.

Schizzerotto, A., Bison, I. and Zoppè, A. (1995), 'Disparità di genere nella partecipazione al mondo del lavoro e nella durata delle carriere' ('Gender Inequalities in the Labour Market and Duration of Careers'), *Polis*, Vol. IX(1), pp. 91-112.

Sgritta, G.B. and Innocenzi, G. (1993), 'La povertà' ('Poverty'), in M. Paci (ed.), *Le dimensioni della disuguaglianza. Rapporto della Fondazione Cespe sulla disuguaglianza sociale in Italia* (*The Dimensions of Inequality. Report of the Cespe Foundation on Social Inequality in Italy*), Il Mulino, Bologna, pp. 261-288.

Simoni, S. (2000), 'La costruzione di un'assenza nella storia del sistema italiano di welfare' ('The Construction of an Absence in the History of the Italian Welfare State'), in F. Bimbi (ed.), *Madri sole. Metafore della famiglia ed esclusione sociale* (*Lone Mothers. Family Methapors and Social Exclusion*), Carocci, Rome, pp. 85-100.

Singh, S. and Darroch, J.E. (2000), 'Adolescent Pregnancy and Childbearing: Levels and Trends in Developed Countries', *Family Planning Perspectives*, Vol. 32(1), pp. 14-23, http://www.agi-usa.org/pubs/journals/3201400.html.

Strobino, D.M. (1992), 'Young Motherhood and Infant Hospitalisation during the First Year of Birth', *Journal of Adolescent Health*, Vol. 13(7), pp. 553-560.

Sutter R. (2000), 'Da categoria a rischio a soggetto visibile. L'Osservatorio di Ravenna' ('From "Risk" Category to Visible Subject. The Ravenna Observatory'), in F. Bimbi (ed.), *Madri sole. Metafore della famiglia ed esclusione sociale* (*Lone Mothers. Family Methapors and Social Exclusion*), Carocci, Rome, pp. 205-214.

Terragni, L. (2000), 'Le madri nubili e i loro figli illegittimi: la ridefinizione di un ruolo sociale tra Ottocento e Novecento' ('Unmarried Mothers and their Illegitimate Children: The Construction of a Social Role between the Eighteenth and the Nineteenth Centuries'), in F. Bimbi (ed.), *Madri sole. Metafore della famiglia ed esclusione sociale* (*Lone Mothers. Family Methapors and Social Exclusion*), Carocci, Rome, pp. 75-84.

Toso, S. (1997), 'Selettività e universalismo nel ridisegno delle politiche di spesa del welfare' ('Selectivity and Universalism in the Redesign of Welfare Policies'), Ministero del Tesoro, Commissione tecnica per la spesa pubblica, Rome.

Trifiletti, R. (1999), 'Southern European Welfare Regimes and the Worsening Position of Women', *Journal of European Social Policy*, Vol. 9(1), pp. 49-64.

Trifiletti R. (2000), Contribution to the Italian Research Group 'Education and Training for Teenage Mothers in Europe', Leonardo da Vinci Research Programme, University of Milan-Bicocca, Milan.

Trivellato, P. (ed.), (2002), *Giovani madri sole. Percorsi formativi e politiche di welfare per l'autonomia* (*Young Lone Mothers. Educational Routes and Welfare Policies to Promote Authonomy*), Carocci, Rome.

UNICEF (2001), *A League Table of Teenage Births in Rich Nations*, Innocenti Report Card No. 3, UNICEF, Innocenti Research Centre, Florence.

Chapter 13

The Transitions to Adulthood of Young People with Multiple Disadvantages

Jane Parry

Introduction and Background

The transitions to adulthood debate has drawn attention to the increasingly complex and unpredictable character of young people's movements away from their families of origin, into independent housing, and in obtaining paid employment (Iacovou and Berthoud, 2001; MacDonald et al., 2001). Young people's extended transitions now frequently encompass periods of extended dependency upon their families and/or the state, a phenomenon which is to some extent attributable to the contraction of the UK's youth labour market (Furlong and Cartmel, 1997; Payne, 1998). While explanations are complex, the lengthening of the school-to-work transition in the UK appears to be, at least in part, attributable to policy decisions to prolong this period of training in response to youth unemployment (Lindley, 1996).

This chapter examines the implications of these issues for young people's expectations and self-perceptions, with reference to a group of multiply-disadvantaged young people in the UK. It draws upon qualitative research with disadvantaged young people at a stage in their lives (post-compulsory education) when they were expecting to have to made significant transitions from school to work, into their own housing, and in terms of personal relationships and family formation (Lakey et al., 2001). Semi-structured biographical interviews were employed, using a detailed topic guide. While this provided a comparable context for the research, tracking young people's progress through key transitions (Thomson et al., 2004), the format of the interviews varied, with interviewers employing probes and prompts to ensure that the research process reflected and explored the diverse and individual circumstances of young people's lives.

It is important that youth transitions studies explore both the similarities and differences in young people's experiences. As Jones (2002) has observed, while the period of the lifespan conceptualized as 'youth' has been extended in recent years, this masks considerable differences between young people, which are informed by their socio-economic backgrounds. Multiply-disadvantaged young people are particularly worth of study, since they lack a great many of the resources likely to promote the sorts of transitions typically associated with this stage of the life cycle. However, disadvantage is a complex concept, with different combinations of disadvantage producing a range of effects. By engaging with how 'normative' narratives about transitions are utilized by multiply-deprived young people as a common reference point, against which their often chaotic experiences are plotted, this chapter builds upon the transitions debate, exploring semblance amid apparent diversity. It explores how transitions narratives are deployed in combination with discourses describing 'critical' or 'fateful' moments (Giddens, 1991; Thomson et al., 2002) to explain the profound influence of particular people and events upon young people's subsequent experiences.

The following section describes the methods adopted to conduct this research. Subsequent sections outline the transitions perspective used to explore these issues, and the findings are presented in terms of school-to-work and lifestyle transitions. These are analysed with reference to 'normative' transitions which, real or apparent, served as a reference point against which multiply-deprived young people made sense of their experiences. The final section draws these issues together in terms of understanding changing patterns of transitions, and examines the meaningfulness of traditional expectations about movements towards adulthood for young people whose resources are particularly scant.

Methods and Rationale

This chapter draws upon a qualitative research project conducted at the Policy Studies Institute during 2000-2001 (Lakey et al., 2001), which was funded by the Joseph Rowntree Foundation. One element of this project was to examine the experiences of 49 'multiply-deprived' young people in the labour market. All of these young people had taken part in the New Deal for Young People (NDYP), a key component of the UK's welfare-to-work programme which aims to help young people find work and enhance their employability (Wilkinson, 2003). NDYP began in 1998 and offers young people (aged 18 to 24), who have been out of paid work for more than six months, personalized employment support (the 'Gateway' stage) and a range of training or subsidized employment opportunities. It is a mandatory programme which imposes sanctions for failure to comply. All of the young people interviewed for the project had been involved in NDYP at some point, and had therefore been unemployed for an extended period of time, although their participation in and experiences on the programme varied considerably. There was a two-year time lag between their participation on NDYP and their involvement in the research, and consequently all the young people fell into the age group 20 to 26. Interviewees' involvement in NDYP is summarized in Table 13.1.

Screening questionnaires, short survey forms addressed to young people who had taken part in an earlier survey, were sent out together with information about the study. These were used to develop an interview sample of young people in possession of two or more labour market disadvantages, who had agreed to take part in the research. This enabled us to ensure that the people we interviewed included a range of experience in terms of disadvantage, gender, ethnicity and geographical distribution. The disadvantages screened for included: time spent in local authority care, homelessness, substance dependency, being ex-offenders, possessing disabilities or long-term health problems, mental health issues, and language or literacy problems.

Table 13.1 Interviewees' involvement in NDYP

Stage in NDYP	No. of young people
Gateway only	21
Employment option	2
Environmental Task Force option	4
Voluntary sector option	6
Education option	16
Total	49

Over half of those interviewed were drawn from ethnic minority groups (some were refugees), and a significant proportion of the sample was made up of young parents, or young people who had other substantial caring responsibilities. The main characteristics of the interview sample are summarized in Table 13.2, which illustrates that particular disadvantages were strongly gendered. In particular, the young women we interviewed were more likely to have left local authority care, and the young men were more likely to have been in trouble with the police. Fieldwork was conducted in the three regions of the UK with the highest representation of minority ethnic groups: London and the South East, Yorkshire and Humberside, and the West Midlands.

Depth interviews with participants were conducted by the research team using a detailed semi-structured topic guide covering background information, experiences of paid work, training and education, periods of unemployment, different kinds of support received or desired, and hopes and expectations for the future. Interviewers and interviewees were 'matched' on the basis of gender and ethnicity as far as practicable, to promote rapport and comfort in the research process. The biographical approach to interviewing enabled us to uncover consequential social processes, transformation, structural commonalities and similarities in young people's experiences (Stanley, 1993), and to track patterns over time. Life events were necessarily explored in a broad sense, in order to identify their relative influence and meaningfulness for young people. The biographical approach also offered particular value in enabling us to analyse the range of narratives deployed by young people.

The interviews uncovered a range of problems which had not been sampled for, such as bereavement, abuse and chaotic families, suggesting that disadvantage is clustered. All interviews were taped and transcribed verbatim, and transcripts were imported onto a qualitative software package, QSR NVivo (Richards, 1999) for analysis. A detailed coding framework, covering conceptual and structural aspects of the interviews, was developed to code the interviews, and analysis followed a grounded theory approach (Glaser and Strauss, 1967). In the findings presented below young people's experiences are illustrated with examples and direct quotations from the interviews, representative of particular themes from the research. In all cases, pseudonyms are used to protect interviewees' identities.

Table 13.2   Main characteristics of sample

	Female	Male	Total
Gender	20	29	49
Substance dependency	4	7	11
Local authority care leaver	6	2	8
Disability/long-term health problems	8	11	19
Homelessness	9	11	20
Ex-offender	1	14	15
Mental health issues	7	9	16
Language/literacy problems	6	12	18
Ethnic minority group	9	12	21

A Transitions Perspective

Coles (1995) has identified three inter-related main youth transitions: the school-to-work transition, the domestic transition and the housing transition. This framework is broadly replicated in interpreting the research results below, although in recognition of the multiple transitions which comprise each of those identified by Coles, domestic and housing transitions are conflated together into 'lifestyle transitions', which are compared with school-to-work progressions. This also reflects the overlap between these social and physical relationships for multiply-disadvantaged young people.

Young people drew upon relatively linear ideas in terms of what they regarded as 'normative' or desirable transitions. These tended to be focused around concepts of independence and a particular ordering of life events, and they displayed strongly-held conventional views about their hopes and plans for the future (such as positing parenthood in the context of marriage and economically-independent households). These frequently corresponded with transitions which young people had seen or assumed to have been made by their parents, which were counterposed to their own highly class-specific and gendered experiences. Reflecting these tensions between desired, anticipated and actual experiences, in this discussion 'transitions' should not be taken to imply any particular ordering of life events. As Fergusson has stressed, a traditional transitions discourse has been superseded for deprived young people, and 'new configurations of activity may be reproducing long-established inequalities in ever more complex and subtle ways (2002, p. 184). Johnston et al. (2000), who also studied deprived young people, addressed this issue by exploring the 'diverse careers' adopted by young people in the absence of more traditional options. This chapter then, employs the language of 'transitions', but examines a broad and disparate series of events to explore the movements made by multiply-deprived young people in their journeys towards adulthood and potential independence.

School-to-Work Transitions

The roots of young people's labour market disadvantage often lay in damaging school experiences, and the same personal circumstances that made employment difficult tended also to impinge upon their educational experiences. Most interviewees described their time at school in wholly negative terms, in terms of considerable discontent, which had a lasting effect upon their self-perceptions. Frequent moves between schools, especially where these were associated with family difficulties, had severe effects on young people's educational experiences, with care-leavers experiencing a particularly large number of moves. Interviewees who moved schools often recounted difficulties establishing new social networks and catching up with missed coursework. After being taken into care Tammie's home life became characterized by instability, and she was sent to a number of schools where she found it difficult to 'fit in'. Repeatedly feeling that she was 'different' to her schoolmates, she eventually left before sitting any exams:

> After going into foster care it just all went haywire really, and I was moving about in all these different foster homes for two years. I lasted there [in one school] for two years, but all these different foster homes I kept going to, and I was like all mixed up inside as well, and really it made it difficult for me at school. And I suppose being treated differently because you're in foster care and that, you're a foster child, you get treated differently by the kids, but I don't know, it was awful really.

Many interviewees had left school prior to the statutory leaving age, and many more were poor attenders, experiences which left them with few or no qualifications. However, relatively few had experienced any interventions designed to retain them in the educational system; indeed their absence often appeared to have been normalized within their communities. The reasons interviewees gave for becoming disengaged with school included having been bullied, experiencing difficulties 'fitting in', problems with academic work or authority figures, involvement with peers who also played truant, and the lure of jobs in the informal labour market.

These experiences were often linked to young people's disadvantages, and they consequently invoked different sorts of explanations to describe their educational experiences. For example, one young women was bullied about her severe dyslexia and the coloured glasses she wore to correct this, and when the teasing turned to violence her family colluded with her decision to leave school and help in the domestic sphere, a strategy of self-defence. By contrast, a young man talked about playing truant with his friends, preferring to get involved in drug-taking, petty crime and 'cash-in-hand' work, rather than submit to what he considered to be an irrelevant educational process. While he defined himself as someone with learning difficulties, it was difficult to estimate what part this played in his experiences and subsequent strategies to create a more competent, albeit illegal, role for himself.

Many of the young people blamed themselves for the way their time at school had turned out. Notably, these young people tended to possess disadvantages which included some combination of having been in trouble with the police or involved with drugs or alcohol during their time at school. They talked about how they had correspondingly played truant, 'messed about' in class, and took on the label of 'troublemaker' assigned to them by their teachers. These young people tended to reflect upon their school experiences in terms of regret, that they had taken a path that had negative effects upon their subsequent experiences. For example, Ahmed described his dropping out of school in quite individualistic terms:

> I just went through that period in time at school when I thought, 'No, this is not me.' I suppose when my schoolwork started declining my attitude was okay, but then I just, I suppose I just lost interest really, and that's when I started doing my own thing.

This response to the educational system is comparable to that identified by sociologists, such as Clarke et al. (1976) and Willis (1976), whereby working-class students view formal schooling as alien to their experiences and respond in terms of cultural resistance, a strategy providing enhanced capital within their social networks. However, by conceptualizing their experiences in terms of individualistic agency, this response masks the ways that structural inequalities and their accompanying difficulties make school more problematic for young people who lack social, cultural and material assets. Furlong and Cartmel (1997) have termed this apparent contradiction an 'epistemological fallacy'. Thus young people with particular sorts of disadvantages became immersed in a cycle of self-blame, and found it difficult to recognize their need for, or the existence of, appropriate support mechanisms.

By contrast, some young people explicitly linked negative school experiences to a lack of support received there. This was often linked to difficulties with the English language, or to disruption associated with being moved between family members, children's homes and foster parents. Joana had moved to the UK at the age of fourteen from Africa, but found it difficult to cope with learning in a foreign language. Although she fell behind in her schoolwork and was made to feel inadequate, she conceptualized her experience as stemming from a lack of institutional support rather than personal failings:

> It was hard, because in the school I went to they never helped me, because at that time I needed help because I had just come. I didn't know anyone, I didn't know anything about the school system, and it was very disappointing for me because I didn't have any help from anywhere.

Notably, this group of young people drew on more 'naturalistic' explanations for their bad experiences at school, and through linking these to their intrinsic disadvantages, were more capable of identifying deficiencies in the support they had received.

Whatever the reason given by young people for their disengagement or difficulties at school, the result of this was that they missed out on the opportunity to sit GCSE examinations or performed disappointingly, outcomes which handicapped their subsequent labour market participation.

Difficulties experienced at school were often followed by protracted and/or unsuccessful periods at further education colleges. During this time, young people's existing problems exacerbated their educational difficulties. This trajectory was characterized by dropping out of at least one course, an experience which only confirmed young people's 'unsuccessful' self-concepts. This concurs with Meadows' work (2001), which found that school to work transitions have become increasingly complex, particularly so for multiply-deprived young people. The period when interviewees started college often coincided with a time in their lives when their disadvantages came more clearly into focus. This sometimes involved entering new social circles which introduced young people to the influences of drugs and crime, and detracted from their studies. Dennis, a young Afro-Caribbean man, had been a keen student until he began college, when exposure to these sorts of factors, and the absence of his supportive family, led to his becoming involved in an alternative culture in order to 'fit in':

> I wasn't focused, you know what I mean? So like I dropped out of college ... I was drinking see, it was a drinking problem ... I started drinking and smoking [marijuana] and all that, like night-clubbing.

Young people's personal circumstances frequently provided a very real distraction from traditional school-to-work transitions. For example, the timing of a pregnancy could lead to a disrupted or fractured education, the death of a close relative exacerbate mental health difficulties, and problems at home, such as domestic violence or being moved between foster homes, prompt young people taking time off college which set them back from their peers when they attempted to catch up with work missed. These difficulties often meant that young people left college without gaining qualifications, and that the time they had 'wasted' in this way set them upon a disadvantaged trajectory in terms of their subsequent labour market participation. This kind of trajectory is particularly significant at a time when the Labour Government has made it a policy commitment to prioritize post-16 education, since for multiply-disadvantaged young people a lengthening of this school-to-work transition is more typically associated with failure than preparation for the labour market: an effect which undoubtedly damages their self-esteem.

The process by which young people became involved in a downward spiral of events, or were correspondingly able to escape from such, can be linked to what Giddens has called 'fateful moments', at least in terms of the narratives that young people deployed to make sense of their experiences. Particular points in time took on a heightened significance, moments from when 'individuals are called on to take decisions which are particularly consequential for their ambitions, or more generally, for their future lives' (1991, p. 112). Thomson et al. (2002) have extended Gidden's concept of fateful moments, which they recognized as having particular analytical value in relating social structures and processes to biographical narratives, but which was more theoretical than descriptive. Henceforth, they developed the concept of 'critical moments' to analyse their interviews with young people: these enabled consequential periods in individual biographies to be mapped onto a continuum of agency.

From this perspective, while 'decisions' were not always freely taken, being strongly linked to the resources young people have at their disposal at particular moments, in a number of instances interviewees experienced an identifiable event or came into contact with a particular person whose influence they perceived as particularly consequential in their subsequent trajectory. So, for example, as Dennis hit rock bottom, he re-discovered Christianity, and crucially felt ready to be helped; in this sense he started accumulating resources (social capital). He subsequently spoke about his faith in terms of the focus it provided, which he considered to have been essential in overcoming his substance dependency, lack of housing, mental health difficulties, and in re-establishing contact with his family. Once he had begun to address these issues, and developed a supportive network through his church, he was able to take greater control of his life.

Notably, certain experiences lent themselves more easily to a 'fateful moments' explanation, discovering religion and moving away from substance abuse being particularly associated with a 'recovery' narrative. While these accounts essentially put young people in control of their own destinies, when no positive outcome was achieved so these types of discourses could turn into self-blame, with more detrimental and lasting effects for an already-vulnerable group of young people. Furthermore, the association of individualistic discourses with transitions masks the role of structural disadvantage in the ordering of critical life events. For example, while such explanations posit substance abuse as a social problem, it has become increasingly recognized that self-medication is also a fairly rational response to 'dull the emotional pain' of, for example, homelessness, estrangement from families, or sexual abuse (Dean et al., 2003, p. 5; Melrose, 2000).

While college attendance more broadly has risen among young people, a significant minority of our interviewees had not attended any type of college or further training. Notably care-leavers, young people with health problems or disabilities, and individuals with literacy difficulties, a group whose educational experiences and resources for coping in the labour market were particularly poor, were over-represented among non-college attenders. Some, like Sarah, had 'missed out' on college because she had her children at the time when her peers were moving from school to college, and her lack of a 'normalized' transition informed her thoughts about what to do in the future:

I feel, god, I'm twenty-two and going to college, it's going to be full of sixteen year olds. I'm not stupid and I'm a single mother, but I feel a bit embarrassed to be one because when you think of single mothers you think of scruffy little schoolgirls that the nuns taught, and I am not one of them.

While the early assumption of caring roles could negatively affect standardized educational transitions, this was counterbalanced by the ensuing responsibility, acceptance into adult networks, and intrinsic satisfactions which becoming a parent could provide for young men and women. While the former experience is discussed below, the ways in which parenting simultaneously strengthened young people's reengagement with the labour market, are taken up in the following section.

Some young people, like Abida, had been unable to sit exams at school because of a series of family problems, which led to her being placed in care and subsequently being made homeless. These problems had prevented her from attending college at a crucial life stage, since it had been necessary for her to go out to work to support herself. She had also married relatively young, and clearly derived the security she had lacked earlier on in life from her new family. Abida still thought about returning to college, but came to the conclusion that her reordered transitions ultimately offered more stability:

> I still had it a bit in my mind, maybe I'll still go on to college. But then I thought, what's the point? I'll just be doing the same, you know, just writing and writing and writing, and when I get out I've got no guarantee of a job. Even then, when I've got so many years in further education. So I found it better to just do training on the job.

Following their frustrated educational experiences, the young people we interviewed tended to experience difficulties breaking into the labour market. They frequently spoke about a lack of work where they lived and of their difficulties travelling to places where jobs were more readily available, due to public transport problems, lack of driving skills and the expense of personal transport. Most of these young people had spent their working lives in temporary, casual or part-time jobs, interspersed with periods of unemployment, and several commented that agency work was the only type available to people with their level of skills. However, this work was insecure and failed to provide opportunities for training, progression and the development of collegial workplace relationships; consequentially little occupational attachment developed in these contexts. The most frequently raised barrier to paid work was felt to be young people's lack of skills, work experience and qualifications, factors which were due in large part to their relatively poor school experiences. Many felt that unfair demands of previous experience were used to filter applicants into jobs demanding quite low levels of skill, and that this could lead to young people becoming trapped in cycles of: no job, no experience, no job.

In most instances, young people's disadvantages played a direct role in their difficulties effecting successful transitions into paid employment. Sometimes these were procedural, as with young people with literary difficulties, who experienced problems dealing with the literature associated with the jobsearch process, or in terms of the difficulties homelessness could cause through young people having no return address to give employers. Others felt that employers had become sceptical about their suitability for positions when they learnt of criminal records or periods of homelessness. In a slightly different way, disadvantages could also affect young people's 'job readiness'. For example, periods of depression or substance dependency could make young people less committed to or confident about finding work. Substance dependency in particular, frequently encompassed the adoption of 'alternative' lifestyles, which could make it difficult for young people to develop the self-discipline and routine necessary to hold down employment.

Family disruption also often constituted a barrier to labour market participation, in that young people who had experienced estrangement from their parents were unable to draw upon the sorts of familial support that would allow them to strategically take on insecure work as a stopgap while they accumulated experience. In addition, as the next section discusses, many of the young people had started their own families, and the difficulties of obtaining secure childcare arrangements in the UK, particularly when they had relatively few existing familial resources, complicated their efforts to find employment. Furthermore, there was an added pressure for young people with children to avoid the more easily attainable route of agency work and its associated insecurity, since this could place them in a difficult position in terms of benefit entitlements. Melanie, who was bringing up three children on her own and struggling with depression, explained her concerns:

> You get messed about with your money, this that and the other, and it's like, no, I don't want the hassle of it. I need to know that I'm getting constant money each week, and what I'm getting, and that's what I do know with Income Support.

In this way, the burden of caring work complicated young people's ability to effect traditional school-to-work transitions, and was revealing of gendered inequalities in the distribution of key material and symbolic resources. Young mothers' employment prospects were restricted by the cost and reliability of childcare, and forced them into extended dependency upon partners, family or the state. By contrast, young fathers often felt pressure to obtain jobs in the short-term in order to support their families, rather than to pursue the kinds of extended training and education likely to enhance their future prospects and earning power, and relied upon the unpaid work of their partners in the domestic sphere to support this strategy. Joana, a young Black woman who had moved to the UK as a teenager and experienced periods of homelessness as well as a nervous breakdown, had dropped out of college as a direct result of finding herself pregnant. A repeated theme of her interview was being 'stuck' and unable to get on because she lacked any kind of childcare support or work experience, and, living in London, she anticipated high transport costs attached to going to work and organizing childcare.

A small number of the young people interviewed had never worked. These tended to possess some form of disability, had encountered significant problems applying for employment, and received little support in this process. Of all the disadvantages used to select respondents, disability was the most varied in its consequences for labour market experience. However, the more acute instances of disability also had the most serious detrimental effects upon young people's transitions into employment. Richard had attended a mainstream school, and later graduated from a specialist residential college for blind people. Despite his ability and background, he had been unemployed for six years, and was depressed and angry at the apparent lack of opportunities for him to work. His experience on the New Deal Environmental Taskforce had been particularly inopportune. He was sent upon placements which involved picking up used syringes and felling trees, both of which he subsequently left, posing as they did serious threats to his health. The young people with disabilities who had never worked, all experienced official agencies as inflexible and having failed to provide them with the specialist help they needed to get into work.

Young people's disadvantages, often in combination with particular negative life events, could mark the beginning of a series of problems that informed their subsequent transitions. Dennis' parents had sent him to the UK from the West Indies to complete his education. At first he had settled in well, but he later developed a substance abuse problem, split up from his fiancée, dropped out of college and became homeless, factors which contributed to his growing sense of isolation and subsequent breakdown:

> I've been through a lot of darkness ... I went walkabout for two years, everything just hit me, y'know what I mean, like a train, and I was like, whoo man, my whole perception had to change. I started, I was thinking everybody's out to get me, and everybody wants to do me in, and everybody wants to beat me up, and people want to kill me, and I was real crazy, man.

Such disadvantages, and young people's associated lack of resources, often contributed to their coming into contact with others who were disadvantaged, which could lead to an exacerbation or multiplication of their disadvantages. For example, refugees who were already experiencing homelessness, language difficulties and estrangement from their families, might be placed in accommodation where drugs and alcohol were prevalent coping mechanisms.

While many of the young people we interviewed had built up a substantial portfolio of labour market experience, they tended to face difficulties acquiring the sorts of longer-term work they desired, and the work they took on was often some distance removed from the sorts of things they were interested in. These tensions became manifest in terms of a frustration that they were failing to make expected degrees of progress within the labour market, which sometimes exacerbated existing mental health problems.

Lack of confidence was a prevalent theme in many of the interviews. Difficult life experiences and histories of un- and under-employment often undermined young people's self-esteem, and had broader impacts upon their lives. They consequently failed to present themselves as capable employees, and some became half-hearted about their efforts to find work, particularly when these feelings were experienced in combination with depression. Some also felt that their physical appearance, in term of their ethnicity, physique or attractiveness, prevented potential employers from hiring them.

By contrast, a number of young people were effecting more successful transitions into work, and at the time of the interviews were employed in jobs they enjoyed and where they were developing and progressing. While these represented a minority of those interviewed, their experiences were nonetheless insightful. A prominent characteristic displayed by these young people was that they felt they had been 'given a chance' by key individuals at various crucial moments of their lives. Critically, they employed narratives which enabled them to enact a degree of *control* over their lives, which imbued a sense of progress over what might otherwise have seemed like an unmanageable random series of events. Mark, a former drug addict, explained how his employer had taken a personal interest in him, spotting his potential and taking him aside and explaining to him the opportunities he was throwing away through his constant absences from work. Mark reflected that being on the receiving end of such confidence for the first time in his life was vital in enabling him to address his addiction and throw himself into his work.

The young people who had 'succeeded' in this way tended to possess particular combinations of disadvantage, including those connected with experiences of substance dependency, homelessness, and problems with the law. This suggests that disadvantages have varied effects upon young people's longer-term trajectories, and that certain types of disadvantage, in combination with particular favourable circumstances, have a less damaging impact upon subsequent trajectories. The young people with the more successful transitions into work also tended to possess additional resources associated with particular lifestyles, having obtained at least some qualifications and living with their parents at the time of the interviews, an aspect which is explored in the following section.

Lifestyle Transitions

Young people's transitions from their families of origin to their families of destination (their domestic transitions), and from living with their parents to living independently (their housing transitions) tended to be interlinked, and correspondingly are considered here as 'lifestyle transitions'. Most strikingly, most interviewees displayed complex and non-linear lifestyle transitions, involving prolonged and often regressive movements between parental or statutory dependency and independent living. Young people who had left local authority care displayed the most chaotic transitions of all, an outcome linked to their relative scarcity of familial resources. Informants with literacy difficulties also encountered particular problems negotiating independent forms of living, reading difficulties having a detrimental effect upon their search for housing, and these young people often remained dependent upon their parents for day-to-day support. Young people's ability to effect lifestyle transitions was also undoubtedly influenced by the complex range of definitions of independence which a variety of statutory bodies employ. For example, in the UK young people may engage in limited employment at 13, leave school, pay tax, consent to sex, and marry with parents' consent at 16, and drive a car at 17 (Jones and Bell, 2000). Morrow and Richards (1996) have suggested it is this blurring of the distinctions between childhood and adult status that makes transitions to adulthood so difficult.

About half the young people interviewed had been unable to effect any degree of lifestyle transition, and were living with their parents at the time of the interviews, displaying a coincidence (and lack) of housing and domestic transitions. While this position was frequently described as a source of frustration, remaining in the family home could also provide important social support mechanisms, which young people utilized to counterbalance the difficulties they faced negotiating access to the labour market. Meadows (2001) found that young men who retained the support of their families and resided in the familial home tended to be successful in the labour market and that, as a result of difficulties establishing employment security, it has become more difficult for young men to negotiate independent living. Most of the young people we interviewed had not yet reached a point in their lives where they felt able or wanted to leave the parental home. This was partly due to an age effect amongst those interviewed, in that young people living with their parents were largely younger than those who had negotiated more independent forms of living.

However, a number had attempted to effect independent lifestyles, but their attempts had been frustrated and they returned to live with their families. Soon after Glen moved into his own flat, he was held up at gun-point, an experience which left him suffering a social phobia and unable to work, and he returned to the support of his family. Notably, Glen's experience was strongly associated with his structural disadvantage, being housed in a 'sink' estate known for its problems with crime and substance abuse. Josie, a care-leaver, had attempted to live with her mother, as well as in her own flat, and with a boyfriend (in a pattern which mirrored the frequent moves she had experienced as a child), but none of these strategies had been successful, and at the time of her interview, she had returned to live with the most 'stable' member of her family, her sister.

A high proportion of the young people who lived with their parents were disabled or suffered from learning difficulties. These sorts of disadvantages could increase young people's dependency upon their families, protracting this period of their lives. However, that young people who lived with their parents were also more likely to be in paid employment, suggests that other aspects of parental support provide an important resource facilitating labour market transitions. This support was both material and emotional, counterbalancing some of the negative effects of young people's search for employment. Tasneem described the importance of her family thus:

> I mean the thing is that you need parents. If you've got your parents or brothers, sisters, you've got every single thing, I mean you don't need money.

The practical support families could provide was particularly critical for young people with learning difficulties, who often relied heavily upon their parents to help with job applications and in improving their reading and writing skills. Furthermore, young people who lived with their parents enjoyed access to a wider set of social networks, and sometimes obtained casual work or work experience through family and friends (a phenomenon recognized in Strathdee's work (2001)). However, living with parents could also exacerbate young people's frustrations regarding their incomplete transitions, particularly where parents admonished young people about their failure to find paid work.

By contrast, some of the young people interviewed lived alone, having made a partial domestic transition in living apart from their families of origin, but not yet having formed their own families or made complete housing transitions, since these living arrangements were characterized by insecurity. Such circumstances had two distinct effects upon young people's well-being. For some individuals, they exacerbated their existing difficulties. Barry, a young unemployed man, had secured council accommodation of his own. However, this was highly unsuitable, being located in a high-rise flat, and his fear of heights meant that he spent as much time as possible away from the flat, returning to his mother's house. His largely abortive attempts to effect a housing transition had negative consequences upon his labour market experiences, as his domestic dissatisfaction prompted him to become increasingly withdrawn, under-confident and apathetic. By contrast, where young people had experienced a period of disruption and hardship, domestic transitions could be more positive, the establishment of independent households providing a source of strength and accomplishment. Kendra had recently lost a baby, and felt that the privacy afforded by her own flat played a vital part in her emotional recovery:

> Me moving into the flat had got me back in touch with myself. I can do what I want without anyone looking after me. Not like when my parents were looking over me ... I'm a lot more comfortable, I'm a lot happier. It's a lot better. I'm getting better slowly.

However, many of the young people who lived alone displayed extended domestic transitions, which had a negative impact on their ability to engage in the labour market, and only a minority of these were in paid employment. This situation tended to be a source of discontent, and young people felt that they had 'wasted' time getting to a state of relative independence in one area of their lives, only to see their labour market transitions stagnate. This phenomenon is revealing of the complex relationship between lifestyle and employment transitions among multiply-deprived young people. Although this group of young people had not yet begun to form their own families, they tended to conceptualize their futures in terms of traditional family units. Furthermore, they frequently expressed strong views about the 'correct' ordering of transitions, regarding their inability to acquire stable paid work as an obstacle to forming families of their own. A number of this group had problematic or non-existent relationships with their parents (often having been placed in care as children), and their behaviour in effecting housing transitions had been less a matter of personal choice than a pragmatic necessity. Largely, young people regarded living alone as a transitionary phase, often important in providing them with the personal space in which to examine their options and deal with troubling issues, but some distance removed from the degree of stability to which they aspired.

Some young people were living with partners, and/or also with their own or their partner's children. These households were largely organized on the basis of young people's own (rather than parental) housing, and were marked by a coincidence of domestic and housing transitions. These lifestyle transitions had a significant effect on young people's employment, in that it was only those without children who were in paid work at the time of the interviews. Partly this was the consequence of perverse benefit incentives in the UK welfare system, in that low-skilled individuals experience difficulties acquiring employment at a level of income necessary to sustain their families' quality of life. However, for some their economic status was the consequence of a more explicit decision to prioritize domestic over labour market transitions, a decision that was strongly gendered. Julie was determined that her children would benefit from full-time parenting, to the extent that she suspended her ambition to go to college until they were older. Parenting was deeply embedded in her self-identity. When asked how she felt about being a mother, the role it played in making her feel useful and needed was self-evident, and she detailed the expertise and *work* involved:

> Just the everyday things at the moment. I love the washing, the washing-up, the doing the dinners, the cleaning, playing with the kids, changing them, dressing them, bathing them and putting them to bed. I like every aspect of being a mother ... I love the challenge of it.

This strategy was facilitated by her partner taking on a relatively traditional male 'breadwinner' role, although it sat uneasily with the New Deal's labour market expectations to maximize economic activity. Critically, the capabilities Julie acquired through mothering provided an important role in enabling her to develop a self-identity as a competent and successful adult within her local community. This contrasted with her less successful experiences as a student, where her learning difficulties made her the target of sustained bullying and prompted her to leave school before sitting any exams. Julie's experience illustrates that particular transitions have more meaningful implications for young people's recognition of adulthood than others at particular times in their lives. In a few instances (and notably for men), living with a partner and children acted as an impetus to their finding paid employment, their domestic and work transitions becoming interlinked. Jack, a young man who had previously been involved in petty crime and substance abuse, described how having children had changed his attitude to work:

> It's changed me a lot, it made me pull my socks up and basically go out and look for a job. I can't stay on the dole for the rest of me life. If I've got two kids to support, I do need to start a job.

Like Julie's boyfriend, Jack drew on a conventional narrative in which he defined himself as a breadwinner and expected his girlfriend to act as homemaker. Notably both of these men earned little more than they would expect to receive from benefits, so the *role* provided by their work was clearly more important than its financial compensations.

A high proportion of care-leavers were cohabiting at the time of the interviews. One possible explanation for this is that lacking their own familial resources, these young people were particularly likely to attach importance to establishing close personal relationships and to effect domestic transitions. Emma, who had spent much of her adolescence in care, explained that her relationship with her boyfriend gave her access to the resources she associated with a caring family, and with her partner's support she tackled her substance addition, putting herself through a recovery programme:

> I've had Jake and Jake's family to help me out, you know. Before that, everything I did, I done on my own really.

However, relatively few care-leavers had been able to enact straightforward domestic transitions. This can be partly attributed to the difficulties they experienced making the transition from care to independent living, and the lack of support they received in doing so.

Relatively few of the young people who established cohabiting relationships chose to formalize these through marriage, and those who did so were either from ethnic minority backgrounds, or had married very young and since divorced. Of course, this may be in part an age effect of the sample, but it nevertheless provides a compelling contrast to other more traditional expectations they drew upon.

Of the minority of young people interviewed who had children, there was considerable diversity of domestic arrangements. Parenting took place in the same household as a partner as frequently as it did not, although the custody of children was highly gendered (female), reflecting the traditional expectations of the UK's legal framework. Arrangements included couples living together with their children, lone mothers, step-families, and fathers whose children lived with their former partners. Notably, all of these parents displayed complex and protracted lifestyle transitions. They also tended to possess few or no qualifications, which was sometimes linked to pregnancy and childbirth coinciding with school years. Partly as a consequence of missed education, few parents were in paid employment, and women in particular tended to posit themselves as full-time mothers and exempt from the labour market. In fact, Craine (1997) has identified 'the mothering option' as one of the alternative careers which takes on a greater salience in the context of high unemployment. Consequently, while domestic and housing transitions have largely occurred simultaneously for (multiply-deprived) parents, this has also tended to defer their labour market transitions.

Inertia in parents' labour market transitions was not necessarily regarded negatively, indeed having children frequently marked a relatively stable time in young people's often traumatic lives. During this period, they worked to establish a secure home for their children, and, for women in particular, housing took on an increased significance. For some, such as Becky, parenthood offered a strategy for addressing their disadvantage: she explained that becoming pregnant had provided the motivation to combat her drug dependency. Similarly, for a number of young men, fatherhood provided an important motivational force, enabling them to confront problems with drugs and alcohol, or with getting into trouble with the police. However, bringing up children, without the support of a partner could also be a stressful experience, one which exacerbated existing financial hardship or mental health difficulties. Melanie, whose husband had left her to bring up their three children alone, was finding it hard to manage, and felt frustrated that her career trajectory had been put on hold:

> I'm not happy with the way it is, nothing's happening. I've had enough of it. I want to be out there, I want to be earning money, I want to know that there is a childminder to look after my children and do a good job of it. But I can't afford even to start, it's like you need money, money, money … It's just dreary, boring and foul. It seems like you're sitting in the same rut for the rest of your life.

In such cases, the home acted as a restraint on young parents, and their workplace transitions were put on hold until their children were older. However, single parents frequently conceptualized their home simultaneously as a place of safety and as a source of restraint. This appeared to be connected to their adoption of a more complex combination of roles than co-parents, and contrasts with the experience of young people who lived with their partners, who described their homes and families as a source of comfort amid other less rewarding aspects of their lives. Parenthood offered an important and tangible aspect of hope, and gave young people the opportunity to work towards the goal of their children's future, which they often contrasted with their own difficult experiences. In one sense then, children offered them the opportunity to rewrite history and enact an alternative trajectory. Becky explained:

> My problem at school was that I didn't want to learn and didn't to go to school. Probably I'm happy to see all that, can't wait to see her [daughter] go to school in her uniform, I want her to go to college yeah, do all the things I never did.

Young people's housing transitions were strongly linked to their employment transitions. Many spoke of their hopes of 'getting my own place', but had deferred their efforts on this front until they achieved secure employment. Sometimes employment and housing transitions were experienced in tension, dependency in one context facilitating autonomy in another. Several unemployed young people explained how the high cost of housing in an area acted as a deterrent to their finding work, since the low-paid jobs they might acquire failed to match their housing costs, currently met by benefit receipts.

Notably, relatively few of the young people interviewed had made what might be regarded as traditional housing and domestic transitions, from living with parents to starting their own families and setting up their own households, sometimes interspersed with a period of living on their own. Even less had lived with friends. Amid these diverse experiences, however, interviewees' housing situations were relatively homogeneous: none were in a position to take out a mortgage, although they frequently cited this as an ambition. These findings are in large part the product of young people's disadvantage: the difficulties they faced and their relative lack of resources made it particularly difficult for them to effect anticipated transitions towards more independent forms of living. However, it is also likely to be partly a cohort effect, linked to the recent disproportionate rise in the value of UK property.

Normative Transitions Narratives and Multiply-Deprived Young People

The tension between multiply-deprived young people's actual rites of passage (or lack of) and the normative transitions framework within which these were typically posited, had one of two effects. In the first instance, their reference to normative transitions was unhelpful or detrimental, providing evidence of multiply-deprived young people's distance from 'mainstream' society. They served to illustrate the gap between our interviewees' experiences and their desired lifestyles, often prompting dissatisfaction, frustration and anger. Indeed, recent research has confirmed that the outcomes associated with differential transitions, such as early parenthood, lack of qualifications and unemployment, are linked to depression among young people (Bynner et al., 2002). By conceptualizing their experiences in terms of individualistic agency, manifested in terms of detrimental behaviour, this response masked the effects of structural inequalities and their accompanying personal difficulties upon transitions for young people – Furlong and Cartmel's 'epistemological fallacy' (1997). Thus young people with particular sorts of disadvantage become immersed in a cycle of self-blame, a reaction which Dean and MacNeill (2002) have suggested is conducive with the UK's current policy regime. However, for a second group of young people, normative transitions provided a more positive influence, offering a reference point against which their own ambitions were plotted, and a source of inspiration.

Young people's feelings about their transitions were polarized into these two groupings, with the latter group reporting a higher degree of satisfaction with their experiences. The young people most content with the way their lives were panning out were those who had developed some kind of a cost-benefits analysis of their situation, and correspondingly adopted a degree of compromise, becoming focused upon particular aspects of (a gendered and traditional) adult status, such as becoming a mother and primary caretaker, or father and breadwinner. This phenomenon is comparable to the comfort of particular gendered roles which Barnes and Parry (2004) observed offered for some older people in adjusting to retirement.

Craine (1997) has suggested that such 'options' take on a greater salience in the context of high unemployment, and Jones (2002) has considered them as 'fast-track' transitions which contrast with 'normative' (middle class) transitions, which have increasingly deferred parenthood, marriage and labour market participation. Similarly, Thomson et al. (2004) have drawn attention to the classed and gendered cultures within which young people negotiate the meanings of adulthood, with those with fewer familial and material resources experiencing more accelerated transitions. Interestingly, while such fast-track transitions may be problematic for young people, and tend to be stigmatized by broader society, they provide a role which confers adult status upon young people within their own communities. Additionally, such reordered transitions offer access to benefits, and until fairly recently have been attributed a 'respectable' position within the UK's welfare regime, and to some extent have minimized young people's risk. Alternative transitions should also be considered in the light of this group's disadvantaged circumstances, which have constrained their ability to achieve simultaneous labour market, housing and domestic transitions. Achieving independence in just one of these areas was frequently regarded by young people as a source of much-valued stability (sometimes for the first time in their lives), and had important 'soft' outcomes, building their self-confidence in their ability to manage their own lives.

The structural disadvantage of this group of young people, which includes their material poverty and the declining value of traditional forms of social capital (Strathdee, 2001), in addition to factors such as a criminal record, homelessness and disability, has increased the uncertainty of their transitions and extended the period of time for which they can expect to remain dependent. However, young people's expectations about their transitions have rarely shifted to match the environment in which they now operate, giving rise to various degrees of compromise and personal frustration.

Conclusion

While in broad terms, multiply-deprived young people's transitions to adulthood were complex and reflected the unique circumstances associated with their disadvantages, in a number of important ways their trajectories were characterized by gendered dimensions, pointing to some quite distinctive ordering of youth transitions. Primarily, the early assumption of parenthood affected men and women quite differently, with young women being particularly likely to defer occupational progression in favour of adopting a full-time caring role. While in one sense, parenthood offered up an alternative adult trajectory for investment and provided an important source of fulfilment and capability, for young mothers on their own the role encompassed particular burdens and sometimes led to depression. Secondly, amongst those interviewed, young men were more likely to remain in the family home into their early twenties, a strategy which enabled them to consolidate material and social resources; this group was particularly likely to be in sustained paid employment, but at the expense of progress in other aspects of independent living.

More broadly, early evaluation of the NDLP programme has suggested some subtle gendered effects upon young people, which mirror the experiences of the multiply-deprived young people interviewed here. Wilkinson (2003) found that NDLP led to more rapid exit from unemployment for men, although gendered effects levelled out over time; the largest effect was in terms of young people moving into government-supported training. White and Riley's (2002) consolidation of the various evaluations conducted on the NDLP concluded that the programme has had a positive effect upon participants' employment prospects. However, in terms of comparing like with like, Bonjour et al. (2001) found that the education option was the most useful element of the NDYP in terms of boosting the relative performance of young people with multiple disadvantages, a finding which reflects the disrupted trajectories experienced by this group.

The structural and intrinsic disadvantages of the young people interviewed for this research impacted in important ways upon their ability to negotiate anticipated transitions into adulthood, prolonging their dependency upon families and the state, and complicating their ability to acquire qualifications and satisfying forms of employment. These, in turn, had significant effects upon their future life chances. Furthermore, in contrast to young people's expectations about what they should be capable of at this point in their lives, and what it meant to acquire adult status, their disadvantages have made it virtually impossible for them to simultaneously effect successful transitions in more than one of these areas. Thus, successful school-to-work transitions tended to occur at the expense of lifestyle transitions, and the establishment of their own family units and independent housing hindered young people's progression within the labour market. The nature of these transitions was informed by both macroeconomic and cultural forces, but also more clearly by young people's structural disadvantage. Crucially, while their expectations reflected their parents' relatively linear transitions, their own experiences were characterized by more chaotic, drawn-out and unpredictable transitions. 'Fateful' moments had a (real or imagined) impact upon young people's transitions, the influence of particular people or events at critical moments in their experience, having a lasting influence and setting them upon certain trajectories, which were often not chosen ones. However, it is difficult to ascertain the extent to which these narratives reflect an attempt to put individualistic interpretations upon structural factors, representing an effort by young people to impose an order upon their often chaotic experiences.

Young people's difficulties in these arenas have been complicated by factors such as the contraction of the youth labour market (Furlong and Cartmel, 1997; Ryan, 2001), and the declining value of social networks and traditional forms of social capital (Strathdee, 2001). These have increased uncertainty in young people's transitions more broadly, and extended the period for which they can expect to remain dependent upon their parents, an expectation which has been underlined by the assumptions implicit in recent UK educational policy (Jones, 2002). However, young people's expectations of their transitions to adulthood rarely shifted to match the environment in which they were operating, giving rise to personal frustration at their circumstances. For multiply-disadvantaged young people, many of whom were unable to draw upon familial support, their positioning under late capitalism has frequently engendered a set of insurmountable barriers which have prevented them from acquiring various markets of adult status, and which has extended the distance between their circumstances and expectations. The young people who reported most satisfaction were those who had developed a cost-benefits analysis of their situation, and who correspondingly focused upon one particular aspect of their life, while accepting that progression in another was not currently attainable. These included those who devoted themselves to parenthood and effectively took themselves out of the labour market, or who concentrated upon early stages of their careers at the expense of acquiring their own housing.

The rub, however, is that multiply-disadvantaged young people so frequently analyse their frustrated trajectories in terms of personal failings, rather than in the light of a deprived social and material environment. Correspondingly, Wyn and White (2000) have drawn attention to the paradoxical relationship between young people's perceived agency and the structural conditions which often preclude their acquisition of adult goals. Even the relatively satisfied group of individuals identified above attained this status by placing emphasis upon personal choice, devoting little attention to the structural circumstances that restricted their ability to engage with broader range of options. Disadvantage is inter-related, clustered and henceforth reproduced; for example, Bowers et al. (1999) found that in 1996, over two-fifths of unemployed young people in the UK lived in households in which no other person was employed. Multiply-disadvantaged young people are thus forced to contend with a plurality of obstacles in attempting to make transitions into adulthood, but have relatively few resources with which to do so. Existing support mechanisms have done little to readdress the balance and enable them to effect a greater degree of choice in their lives, and this vacuum has resulted in a great deal of frustration and wasted talent.

References

Barnes, H. and Parry, J. (2004), 'Renegotiating Identity and Relationships: Men and Women's Adjustments to Retirement', *Ageing and Society*, Vol. 24(2), pp. 213-233.

Bonjour, D., Dorsett, R., Knight, G., Lissenburgh, S., Mukherjee, A., Payne, J., Range, M., Urwin, P. and White, M. (2001), *New Deal for Young People: National Survey of Participants: Stage 2*, ESR67, Employment Service, Sheffield.

Bowers, N., Sonnet, A. and Bardone, L. (1999), 'Giving Young People a Good Start: The experience of OECD countries', in OECD, *Preparing Youth for the 21st Century: The Transition from Education to the Labour Market*, OECD, Paris, pp. 7-86.

Bynner, J., Elias, P., McKnight, A., Pan, H. and Pierre, G. (2002), *Young People's Changing Routes into Independence*, Joseph Rowntree Foundation, York.

Clarke, J., Hall, S., Jefferson, R. and Roberts, B. (1976), 'Subcultures, Cultures and Class' in S. Hall and T. Jefferson (eds), *Resistance through Rituals: Youth Subcultures in Post-War Britain*, Hutchinson, London.

Coles, B. (1995), *Youth and Social Policy*, UCL Press, London.

Craine, S. (1997) 'The Black Magic Roundabout: Cyclical Transition, Social Exclusion and Alternative Careers', in R. MacDonald (ed.), *Youth, the 'Underclass' and Social Exclusion*, Routledge, London.

Dean, H. and MacNeill, V. (2002), *A Different Deal? Welfare-to-Work for People with Multiple Problems and Needs*, preliminary findings report to the ESRC, University of Luton.

Dean, H., MacNeill, V. and Melrose, M. (2003), 'Ready to Work? Understanding the Experiences of People with Multiple Problems and Needs', *Benefits*, Vol. 11(1), pp. 19-26.

Fergusson, R. (2002), 'Rethinking Youth Transitions: Policy Transfer and New Exclusions in New Labour's New Deal', *Policy Studies*, Vol. 23(3), pp. 173-190.

Furlong, A. and Cartmel, G. (1997), *Youth and Social Change: Individualisation and Risk in Late Modernity*, Open University Press, Buckingham.

Giddens, A. (1991), *Modernity and Self-Identity: Self and Society in the Late Modern Age*, Polity Press, Oxford.

Glaser, B. and Strauss, A. (1967), *The Discovery of Grounded Theory: Strategies for Qualitative Research,* Aldine, Chicago.

Iacovou, M. and Berthoud, R. (2001), *Young People's Lives: A Map of Europe*, University of Essex, ISER, Colchester.

Johnston, L., MacDonald, R., Mason, P., Ridley, L. and Webster, C. (2000), *Snakes and Ladders*, Policy Press, Bristol.

Jones, G. (2002), *The Youth Divide: Diverging Paths to Adulthood*, YPS for the Joseph Rowntree Foundation, York.

Jones, G. and Bell, R. (2000), *Balancing Acts: Youth, Parenting and Public Policy,* Joseph Rowntree Foundation, York.

Lakey, J., Barnes, H. and Parry, J. (2001), *Getting a Chance: Employment Support for Young People with Multiple Disadvantages*, Joseph Rowntree Foundation, York.

Lindley, R.M. (1996), 'The School-to-Work Transition in the United Kingdom', *International Labour Review*, Vol. 135(2), pp. 159-180.

MacDonald, R., Mason, P., Shildrick, R., Webster, C., Johnston, L. and Ridley, L. (2001), 'Snakes and Ladders: In Defence of Studies of Youth Transition', *Sociological Research Online*, Vol. 5(4), http://www.socresonline.org.uk/5/4/macdonald.html.

Meadows, P. (2001), *Young Men on the Margins of Work*, Report No. 441, Joseph Rowntree Foundation, York.

Melrose, M. (2000), *Fixing It? Young People, Drugs and Disadvantage*, Russell House, Lyme Regis.

Morrow, V. and Richards, M. (1996), *Transitions to Adulthood: A Family Matter*, Joseph Rowntree Foundation, York.

Payne, J. (1998), *Routes at Sixteen: Trends and Choices in the Nineties*, DfEE Research Report No. 55, DfEE, London.

Richards, L. (1999), *Using NVivo in Qualitative Research*, Sage, London.

Ryan, P. (2001), 'The School-to-Work Transition: A Cross-National Perspective', *Journal of Economic Literature*, Vol. XXXIX, pp. 34-92.

Stanley, L. (1993), 'On Autobiography in Sociology', *Sociology*, Vol. 27(1), pp. 41-52.

Strathdee, R. (2001) 'Changes in Social Capital and School-to-Work Transitions', *Work, Employment and Society*, Vol. 15(2), pp. 311-326.

Thomson, R., Bell, R., Holland, J., Henderson, S., McGrellis, S. and Sharpe, S. (2002), 'Critical Moments: Choice, Chance and Opportunity in Young People's Narratives of Transition', *Sociology*, Vol. 6(2), pp. 335-354.

Thomson, R., Holland, J., McGrellis, S., Bell, R., Henderson, S. and Sharpe, S. (2004), 'Inventing Adulthoods: A Biographical Approach to Understanding Youth Citizenship', *The Sociological Review*, Vol. 52(2), pp. 218-239.

White, M. and Riley, R. (2002), 'Findings from the macro evaluation of the New Deal for Young People', DWP Research Report No. 168, Corporate Document Services, Leeds.

Wilkinson, D. (2003), 'New Deal For Young People: Evaluation Of Unemployment Flows', Research Discussion Paper No. 15, Policy Studies Institute, London, http://www.psi.org.uk/docs/rdp/rdp15-new-deal-for-young-people.pdf.

Willis, P. (1977), *Learning to Labour: How Working-Class Kids get Working-Class Jobs,* Saxon House, Farnborough.

Wyn, J. and White, R. (2000), 'Negotiating Social Change: The Paradox of Youth', *Youth and Society*, Vol. 32(2), pp. 165-183.

Chapter 14

Growing Up Transgender.
Stories of an Excluded Population

Surya Monro

Introduction

The recent growth in literature concerning young people and social exclusion documents the way in which changes in social structure have made the transitions that young people go through more risky and insecure, and social exclusion more likely for those young people who are already disadvantaged (see for example Prendegast et al., 2002). Like other young people, young transgender and intersex people are affected by changing welfare regimes and family structures. However, they also face obstacles that other young people are less likely to encounter. These obstacles, concerning the social exclusion of people who do not fit neatly into 'male' or 'female' gender categories, can have profound impacts on young transgender and intersex people's lives. Whilst young transgender and intersex people are very diverse, they share the experience of living in a society where gender diversity is not fully tolerated, and where social institutions act to perpetuate the erasure of gender fluidity and non male/non female identities.

There is a limited amount of literature in the field of transgender young people, and existing literature is mostly based in the USA (for instance Stanley, 2003; Quinn, 2002; Cochran et al., 2002; Hoban et al., 2003). A considerable amount of the literature in the field is medical and/or pathologizing (Smith et al, 2002; Socarides, 1970, 1991). Another large section of the literature is autobiographical, for instance Boenke (1999) provides a series of USA-based narratives from people with transgender children or parents, Dreger's (2000) collection documents intersex people's experiences of growing up in the USA, and Rees (1996) describes his experiences as a young transsexual in the UK. There is also some autobiographical literature concerning growing up with transgender parents (Howey and Samuals, 2000; Freedman et al., 2002). Kessler's (1998) book, on intersex, is one exception to the autobiographical accounts, providing an important USA-based critique of current norms concerning the treatment of intersex children and young people. Some of the pieces in Haynes and McKenna's (2001) international collection, such as Somers and Haynes (2001), also situate transgender people's experiences of childhood and youth in the context of social analysis. In addition, authors such as Israel and Tarver (1997), Morrow (2004) and Ryan (2002) address some of the issues transgender youth face from a health and social policy perspective. There is also a trend towards the inclusion of transgender youth in the literature concerning lesbian, gay and bisexual youth (for example Quinn, 2002; Ryan and Rivers, 2003), but this may risk erasing the specificity of transgender experience. Lastly, important developments internationally have come from the transgender communities, stemming initially from the work of Stone (1991), followed by Bornstein (1994), Halberstam (1994), Feinberg (1996), Wilchins (1997), Nataf (1996), More and Whittle (1999), Prosser (1998), Namaste (2001) and Neevel (2002). However, with the exeption of Neevel (2002), these authors do not focus specifically on transgender youth.

This chapter aims to address the gap in the literature concerning transgender and intersex young people, focusing on the UK situation. It describes the social institutions and processes that act to socially exclude transgender and intersex people and to increase the risks that young intersex and transgender people may encounter.[1] I seek to move away from individualistic notions of transgender, addressing instead the structures that perpetuate young people's social exclusion, and I argue for the development of social policy and practice to support their social inclusion.

After briefly noting cross-cultural differences, and outlining the methodology, I address a number of the key issues potentially affecting young intersex and transgender people's lives. These include language, bureaucracy, legislation, economic exclusion, and the medical system. I then explore some of the issues that are particular to transgender and intersex young people, such as the family and schooling. I provide four brief case vignettes as a way of illustrating some of the relevant issues. Lastly, I outline some of the key factors facilitating young intersex and transgender people's transitions into adulthood, and explore policy recommendations concerning young transgender people. The chapter discusses the social exclusion of young transgender and intersex people rather than focusing on aspects such as the provision of services for children, or the experiences of children with transgender parents.

'Transgender' is an umbrella term covering cross-dressers, transsexuals, androgynes, intersexes (people born with a mixture of male and female physiological characteristics), drag queens and kings, third gender people and other transgender people (see Nataf, 1996). Estimates of the numbers of transsexuals in the UK range from 2,000 to 5,000 (Home Office, 2000), and intersex conditions affect between 0.15 per cent (Dreger, 1998) and 4 per cent (Nataf, 1996; Rothblatt, 1995) of individuals. The term 'transgender' is contested within the transgender communities. Initially it was developed to include and foreground people who transgress gender binaries without necessarily having surgery, but now some transsexuals are claiming it as a term for transsexuality, because transsexuality concerns gender rather than sexuality. In addition, intersex people do not necessarily change sex or gender, so that including them under the 'transgender' banner is problematic. Here, I use the terms transgender and intersex whilst acknowledging that discussions concerning these terms is ongoing, and I address issues affecting both transgender and intersex young people, whilst acknowledging differences within and between these groups.

Young transgender people's experiences are heavily structured by the norms in the societies in which they grow up. It is outside of the scope of this chapter to provide a comprehensive analysis of cross-cultural differences, but it is worth noting that levels of tolerance and inclusion vary widely across cultures.[2] Compare, for instance, some young people's experiences in Iran and Hawaai. Ghasemi (1999) describes the intolerance of gender variance in Iran and the way this impacted on her transgender child. Her child, who was born as a boy, acted in increasingly effeminate ways as he progressed through childhood. He became more and more withdrawn as he entered his teenage years, having experienced constant ridicule, violence and abuse at school. The young person's situation deteriorated into depression and they attempted suicide. In contrast, a number of the contributors to Matzner's (2001) collection discuss the place that transgender has in indigenous Hawaiian culture, and the ways in which this makes life easier for young people growing up transgender in Hawaii (although they also discuss the prejudice and exclusion that they face). For example, contributor Paige says:

> It's easy to be transgendered here in Hawai'i. People grow up with *mahus* [trangender and gay people] and know how they are, like taking care in the family. So they know what they are capable of. That's part of why my family accepts me for what I am. Because I'm there to help the family. If I were in a family that wasn't Hawaiian, I think I would have a harder time with my sexuality [sic]. I think I would probably kill myself, or run away... (2001, p. 144)

The Research

I came to the research about transgender with a commitment to supporting equality and social inclusion, and wanted to adopt a methodological approach which would be as empowering to the people who took part in the research as possible. I therefore used feminist and participative qualitative research methods (see for example Denzin, 1989; Reinharz, 1992; Maynard and Purvis, 1994), as these involve developing a relatively equal research relationship. Research contributors were involved in the research design, fieldwork and analysis as far as was possible, enabling a richer picture to be developed than would have been possible using traditional methodologies. The methodology also meant I located myself in the research as a female-bodied person who has explored a transgender identity to some extent, rather than pretending to be an objective observer.

The methodology involved 24 in-depth interviews, over 50 informal interviews, a focus group (run mostly by participants) and over 1,000 hours of participant observation with transsexuals, transvestites, cross-dressers, intersexes, an androgyne, a gender transient, drag kings and queens, other transgender people, and related professionals. Initial literature work revealed a lack of critical policy and politically oriented accounts, especially accounts which located the marginalization of transgender and intersex people at a social level, as opposed to framing transgender and intersex people in individualistic, pathologizing terms or as subjects of sociological and cultural discussion without focus on the inequities they face. I therefore sought participants who were involved in activism and/or who identified as non gender-stereotypical. Sampling and access took place through a number of transgender support and activist organizations, as well as via literature authored by a trans person (Zach Nataf) and personal contacts. The research was not intended to be representative, but I aimed to include people from a range of socio-economic backgrounds and ethnicities. In practice the sample were predominantly white, middle class, and British, reflecting the snowball sampling strategy and the difficulties of finding contributors, as well as apparent under-representation on Black and Ethnic minority people in UK transgender organizations. The participants were all adult at the time of interviewing (approximate ages ranged from 25 to 65), but some of them discussed their childhood experiences during the semi structured interviews. Findings are anonymized or named, (as requested by participants). The fieldwork has subsequently been supplemented by literature work and web material.

Transgender People and Social Exclusion

Young transgender and intersex people are subject to the social and identity changes that other young people face, but, as noted above, also face an additional set of structuring forces. These forces usually remain hidden from view when a young person is heterosexual and identifies unproblematically as male or female. I am talking here about gender binarisms, including the assumptions that there are only two genders, male and female, and that a young person's identity as female or male is determined by their birth sex. It would be impossible to understand young transgender people's transitions into adulthood without having an overview of the broader situation for transgender people and the impact of gender binarisms. I will outline, here, some of the ways in which gender binarisms are institutionally embedded and how this may affect transgender people, and I will address other aspects of the social exclusion that transgender people face, including violence and relationship difficulties. I do not address all of the forces underpinning gender binarism here; some, such as religious bigotry and homophobia, are dealt with elsewhere (Monro, 2005). It is important to point out that young people's responses to their situations vary widely, for example Blackburn (2004) in a study of lesbian, gay, bisexual and transgender youth in schools, found that three young people dealt with oppression in quite different ways.

Language

Children and young people grow up learning languages that have no socially acceptable terminology for people who are not male or female, or who move between sexes. English and many other languages automatically erase transgender, as they have no non-male or non-female prefixes or titles, and no currently acceptable nouns for people of fluid or non-male or non-female gender. This is likely to make life very difficult for transgender children, who lack words with which to conceptualize and describe themselves. It also causes problems for parents, siblings, school friends and others – if someone's gender cannot be described, how can they be socially validated? Gender categorizations in language create young transgender people as 'other', preventing them from having the option of exploring and living middle ground identities. Research contributors Zach Nataf and Christie Elan Cane saw the lack of language for transgender identities as a major problem. Authors, such as Feinberg (1996) discuss the creation of third sex pronouns, such as 'ze' and 'hir' – I will use these here, but these have not been adopted within wider society, and third sex identities remain a topic of debate within the transgender communities (see Monro, 2005).

Bureaucracy

Young transgender people grow up in a world where gender binarisms are continually reinforced via bureaucracy. Birth certificates specify whether the baby is male or female, and passports and a host of other documents require the person to state their gender, with no room for fluidity or for non-male/female identification. This forces transgender people to identify on paper as male or female, or to give up some of their social rights because they cannot be included in the current systems. This contributes to social exclusion, for instance research contributor Christie Elan Cane described the difficulties ze had had with hir passport and with all other official forms, which demand categorization as male or female. Ze is refused access to vital services unless ze compromises and accepts categorization as a woman.

Legislation

Young transgender people are, like other transgender people, excluded from citizenship via legislative rights in a number of ways. People in Britain who are diagnosed as transsexual lose a substantial part of their civil liberties (MacMullen and Whittle, 1994), for example, the right to marry and to parent or adopt (Young, 1996).[3] In the UK transsexual people's rights are in the process of being extended via a Gender Recognition Bill, which enables people who are living in the opposite gender or who are recognized as having changed gender to obtain new birth certificates, as is already the case in most of the Council of Europe states (http:www.pfc.org.uk/). Legislative discrimination is present in some other European countries, for example, legislation from several jurisdictions in countries such as Germany, Sweden, and Holland, require a transsexual person who is seeking legal recognition to be certified to be permanently sterile – a move which can only be interpreted as eugenicist, as it prevents people of diverse genders from having children (Whittle, 2002). The problems with legislation are especially marked with reference to third sex, multiple sexes, fluid and androgynous identities. Young transsexuals and intersex people face particular legal barriers to choice concerning medical treatment, as legislation in the UK generally deems people under the age of eighteen to be incapable of giving consent to treatment (with consent to some forms of treatment being legal over the age of sixteen) (Whittle, 2002).

Economic Exclusion

Young transgender people entering the employment market may be faced with a set of barriers that other young people manage to avoid. People who are gender ambiguous or going through a sex change are likely to face discrimination from employers, although there is now legislation to prevent this in some countries, including the UK (see Whittle, 2002). Employment patterns vary widely among transgender people in the UK, with various instances of supportive or tolerant employers reported in the press (for example, Pink Paper, 2000). However, economic exclusion is an issue for many transgender people. Unemployment is a major problem, particularly for transsexuals, intersexuals and androgynes, a substantial proportion of whom subsist on disability or other benefits because they are unable to find work. For example Christie Elan Cane lost hir job and cannot now get a job because of hir gender status. Needless to say, the economic exclusion of transgender affects many aspects of young transgender people's lives. For example Israel and Tarver (1997) link the exclusion of transgender people to increased rates of homelessness – something that young transgender people may be particularly vulnerable to whilst making the transition to independence.[4]

Medicine

The medical system is an important force shaping some young transgender people's lives – notably intersex and transsexual young people, who will probably have medical interventions at a number of stages. The medical system plays a crucial role in perpetuating the social exclusion of transgender people at the same time as paradoxically enabling the development of provision of treatment for transsexuals.[5] Whittle (2002) provides an important review of the medical treatment of young transsexual people. I will focus here on the difficulties facing a broader range of young transgender people concerning the pathologization of gender diversity and homophobia, whilst noting that the psychiatric pathologization of transgender is generally rejected by the transgender community (for example at the Transgender Agenda Conference, 1998 and Israel and Tarver, 1997).

Intersex children and young people face a particularly difficult set of issues concerning the pathologization of gender diversity, and the medical system plays a central role in perpetuating these difficulties. Various authors (Chase, 1988; Feinberg, 1996; Kessler, 1998) describe how the Western medical system treats the birth of an intersex infant as an emergency. The baby is assigned to male or female as soon as possible and this is enforced by surgical and hormonal intervention, with infants usually being assigned as girls and having their clitorises cut off (Kaldera, 1998). This is because intersex is viewed by the medical profession as a pathology – it is seen as socially threatening, even though many of the conditions are not in themselves harmful to the infant (Kessler, 1998). The framing of intersex conditions as abnormal even where there are no functional problems is suggested by the burgeoning medical literature (Rhind et al., 1995; Wilkinson and Greenwald, 1995). Literature (Chase, 1998; Holmes, 1998; Kaldera, 1998; Dreger,

2000) supports the wider existence of problems with infant intersex surgery. Chase (1998) has documented cases of intersex children having their sex assignment changed without being informed as many as three times whilst Dreger (2000) includes testimonies from intersex people who mourn the very severe damage to their sexual capacities due to surgery. Contributor Ann Goodley, who was born intersex and has worked within the National Health Service, said that:

> What happens in medicine regarding babies and young children who are intermediate, is that they are assigned to please the parents...some of the people I know have been mis-assigned, who were gender intermediate, and had corrective surgery in the wrong direction, taking away their physical opportunities, and stultifying them into the wrong gender.

There is diversity amongst the intersex population regarding views on gender assignment and surgery. However, a strong critique of infant surgery has been mounted by activists, for example the Intersex Society of North America argue that intersex babies should be assigned as male or female without surgery (http:www.isana.org/drupal/index.php), and they see the difficulties intersex people face as being due to trauma and stigmatization rather than the conditions themselves. The intersex critique of surgical intervention is reflected in changes concerning policy and practice in the UK, with medics becoming more cautious and less interventionist in their approach (see Channel Four, 2004).

Another way in which some transgender people are excluded via the medical system is due to the heterosexist assumptions embedded within treatment norms. This will affect non heterosexual young transgender people, especially those who are sexually active. Transgender has historically been subsumed under the category of homosexuality (Rosario, 1996), with psychiatrists such as Socarides (1970, 1991) failing to distinguish between transgender and homosexuality, and heavily pathologizing both. This has impacted on treatment methods and is reflected in transgender people's experience of the medical system. Homophobia is also related to gender stereotyping as evident in the early literature, for example young female preference for 'tomboyish' activity and male company is seen as a precursor to FTM (female to male) transsexuality (see Rosario, 1996), which negates butch lesbian and non-conformist heterosexual female development.[6]

Social Space, Violence and Abuse

Access to social space is likely to be problematic for young transgender people in a number of ways, particularly where they are visibly different from conventional women and men. This is not always the case, for example one young transvestite contributor has been out dressed up in broad daylight without experiencing harassment, but this was in an urban student environment. There is considerable evidence for the spatial exclusion of transgender people. For example, Christie Elan Cane described how hir movements are severely restricted due to lack of social acceptance of androgynous people, while John Marshall noted that he does not go out as a transvestite until after dark.

For many transgender and intersex people, being in public space is linked with experience of violence and abuse. Zach Nataf described instances of murder, for example the case of a young transsexual, Brandon Teena, in the USA. John Marshall stated the need to keep transvestism hidden because of the danger of violence and vandalization of property, while Alex Whinnom noted that the problem with coming out as transsexual was that 'all the local kids come around and put a fire bomb though your letter box'. Roz Kaveney discussed the widespread incidence of violence towards transsexuals:

> Roz: Being in transition is very difficult and people do have a desperate need to conform a lot of the time because they're trying to pass because they're trying not to get the shit kicked out of them in the street ..... I mean show me a TS [transsexual] who's never had some sort of violent incident and I'll show you someone who should probably buy a lot of lottery tickets.

> Interviewer: Yeah.

> Roz: Because they've obviously got the luck of the devil.

These findings are strongly supported by literature, including a groundbreaking study of violence against transgender people in the USA (Wilchins et al., 1997) which includes many accounts of murder and rape. Other literature documents intersex people and other transgender people being spat on, stoned, seriously beaten up (Hugill, 1998), harassment by children (Young, 1996), and many other forms of abuse (Wilchins et al., 1997). Sanctions seem particularly heavy for people with intersex or androgynous identities. Christie Elan Cane argued that many transsexuals end up settling for one sex as this is the only option available to them in the current binaried gender system: 'The bipolarized gender system; if you're not comfortable with the gender that you're born into you either have to go the whole way or change over into the opposite gender through a gender clinic, or you become, you're in a situation where you're socially excluded.' Similarly, Salmacis experienced living as intersex to be socially impossible. This forced her to adopt a female identity in a similar way to the male identity Feinberg adopted when ze found ze could not survive as a transgendered person (1996) due to the level of social stigmatization ze faced.

There are other risks facing young transgender people. Literature from the USA indicates a high incidence of homelessness and drug abuse amongst young transgender people in the USA, leaving them at risk of violence and exploitation (Israel and Tarver, 1997). Transgender people in prison (Bloomfield, 1996) and mental hospital are frequently sexually harassed and raped (Israel and Tarver, 1997). Young transgender people sometimes engage in sex work as a means of paying for treatment, potentially making them more likely to get embroiled in the criminal justice system, where they may end up being abused.

Relationships

Relationships are an area of difficulty for some young transgender people. Research suggests that most transgender youth felt that isolation is their number one problem (Hulick, 2003), and that a positive, supportive peer group is very important for identity validation. Sexual relationships may also be a challenge, although, as Prendegast et al. (2002) note, British young people face a paradoxical situation – on the one hand, there may be more opportunities for them to create alternative lifestyles and relationships, and on the other, the removal of the welfare safety net increases their dependence on their families of origin. Adult transgender people sometimes face difficulties concerning sexual relationships, for example, one contributor discussed uncertainty about his sexuality and where to find a sexual partner, given his ambiguous genitals, and another described difficulties deciding whether to have the full operation: the lack of social acceptance of in-between states, particularly amongst potential sexual partners, was the main reason in favour of having the operation in her case. Difficulties with relationships are echoed in popular and other literature. For example, the Guardian (newspaper) column (Anon, 1998) noted the problem of losing a partner when transsexual status is disclosed, and difficulties with the alternative closeting of status, whilst Somers and Haynes document one intersex person's experience:

> Relationships…are always difficult. Because I want to be honest, any prospective partner needs to know my gender and intersex history. Most people cannot deal with it. Many men have a strong sexual curiosity, but as I am not a performing seal, I refuse to be associated with them and this type of scene. (2001, p. 35)

These various challenges may impact on transgender young people's capacities to form fulfilling and healthy relationships, whether they are involved in a relationship or relationships at that time, or transitioning into an adult world where they may have future relationships.

Transgender and Intersex Young People

In addition to the wider social factors that affect transgender young people, there are issues that relate specifically to young trangender people's experience, and the ways in which this is moulded by social norms concerning gender. I will outline these issues, concerning the family, education, and other issues, first, before discussing transgender young people's transitions into adulthood, and providing some case studies of transgender people's experiences of youth as a means of illustrating my arguments.

The Family

I have already discussed some of the difficulties relating to intersex surgery. Other issues include childrearing practices, for example the colour coding of infant's clothes and toys, which makes dealing with intersex babies socially difficult. Intersex conditions may be made taboo in the family, resulting in psychological damage to the child or negative reactions. For example, Somers and Haynes (2001), describe how Somers, an intersex person, was advised by his/her father to have a double mastectomy, despite liking his/her androgynous body, and Kessler (1998) discusses difficulties and embarrassment for families of intersex children. This is also true of families with other transgender children, for example one contributor described problems in the family concerning having a transsexual child:

> Having a child who is freaking us out has an effect on the rest of the family so that actually tends to initiate things like physical abuse, and problems in the rest of the family because having a transperson, having like this well, they don't know what's going on, they can't get on with life, they get angry because nothing they will do makes this kid any better. So they start beginning to hate the kid, because it's just a drain, a constant drain. Families are in this impossible situation, where they go to experts and say 'well she keeps wanting to wear trousers all the time' and the expert says, 'well treat her like a girl, really reinforce her being like a girl' so that psychiatry becomes a means of social control, 'we must force the people even harder to build gender walls' and in actual fact what we should do is to change the walls. (Kate N Ha' Ysabet)

There may also be challenges concerning young transgender people's identity development within the family. For example, most transgender people realize very early on that they are acting 'wrongly' when they engage in cross-gender identification, and that they need to keep it secret. There are difficulties with cross-gender identification, including limited opportunities to practise, and a lack of chances to engage with all aspects of opposite-gender socialization – especially interactions that take place only within one gender group, such as the intense socializing associated with groups of girls (Gilbert, 2001).

On a wider level, the stigmatization of transgender means that family and friends of transgender and intersex young people tend to suffer from actual or perceived marginalization (see Purnell, 1998). If they are rejected by their family, this may lead to further social and economic exclusion (see above, and Israel and Tarver, 1997). Some children are taken into care, where violence or abuse may be experienced. These problems obviously increase risk, affecting young transgender people's abilities to make the transition to adulthood. For example, Dunne et al. (2002) describe UK lesbian, gay and bisexual young people's experiences of homelessness, suggesting that up to a third had been made homeless by their families because of their sexuality. Their case studies include at least one instance in which the participant linked being gay with what could be described as transgender behaviour (see also Cochran et al., 2002).

Education

Transgender and intersex young people face social exclusion in the area of education in a number of ways. Research in the UK and USA suggests that transgender youth are particularly vulnerable to victimization in schools – as well as community settings (Ryan and Rivers, 2003). As Pamela Summers said, school is a very gendered place. Somers and Haynes (2001) describe isolation as being common for intersex children, who may know nothing about intersex and who may express their distress about their situation via, for example, disruptive behaviour at school. Somers and Haynes describe Somer's experience:

> When at the age of seventeen his/her breasts began to develop, teachers and students at his/her private Catholic boy's school refused to value his/her differences. While s/he was proud of his/her androgynous body, s/he was teased mercilessly about it. (2001, p. 31)

Research contributor Alice Purnell noted that, although things have improved, single-sex schools and lessons still persist in many places, and that teachers use expressions which reinforces gender categorization, for example 'act like a man'. Sex education reinforces gender binaries, and in general taught material contains no description of the intersex body (Holmes, 1998) or hint that transgender exists. Playgrounds, toilets and so forth are usually demarcated along rigidly gendered lines, although changes are possible, for example Dillon (1999, p. 8) describes the way in which 'A very supportive (school) administrator solved the classic bathroom problem by establishing single-person rest rooms for Steve's class'. There are likely to be difficulties at school with bullying, for example research contributors Kate N' Ha Ysabet described how transgressors of the gender code are violently sanctioned at school by bullying, and Alice Purnell discussed the way that, whilst tomboys are often idolized at school, sissy boys are persecuted relentlessly. However, the literature also shows that in some cases transgender young people are positively accepted at school, for example, Evelyn (1999) describes her MTF transsexual daughter's coming out as transsexual at school – her daughter was open and proud about her identity, and although it caused a stir, she was accepted. There are a number of positive movements within the education system. For example, in the UK, anti-homophobic bullying initiatives are now taking place in some localities, for example Manchester, and these will help transgender, as well as lesbian, gay and bisexual children, because much homophobic bullying has a gendered element (for example boys are bullied because they are effeminate).

Other Issues

There are other issues of particular pertinence to some transgender and intersex young people, including the impact of the internet, increasing inclusion within the lesbian, gay and bisexual communities, changes in the area of sex work, and developments within statutory services for young people. A further issue, which I will not have space to explore here, concerns the importance of changing youth cultures to young transgender people (see for example Balzer, 2004, who documents urban German transgender subcultures in the context of paradigm shifts in youth cultures).

The internet has become increasingly important to transgender young people. There is a wide range of support organizations for transgender – and to a lesser extent, intersex – people on the world wide web.[7] These sites play a crucial role in supporting and networking young people, especially those who are geographically and socially isolated (see Pusch, 2003). They provide information concerning gender identity change, details of relevant organizations, peer support (for example 'coming out' stories) and lists of resources. Some of these sites also provide information and support for parents and professionals. There are, however, some difficulties with use of the web by young transgender people. It is dependent on resources, so that access to the internet will be limited or impossible for some young transgender people. In addition, there is a lot of transgender pornography on the net, making use of the internet by under age people difficult and problematic – searches may provide links to pornographic as well as support sites, and underage people who wish (or need) to search in privacy are likely to encounter inappropriate material, or be blocked from reaching useful sites by protective firewalls.

The increased inclusion of transgender people within the lesbian, gay, and bisexual (LGB) communities is another development with important implications for young transgender people making the transition into adulthood. Some of the sites on the world wide web are primarily aimed at lesbian and gay people, but include transgender young people in a positive way, networking them into national and international support systems.[8] This is important for both heterosexual and LGB young transgender people, as it provides links to a wider community – and those young transgender people who identify as LGB, or who are questioning their sexuality, will find these sites particularly helpful. The LGB communities have (in the UK) an established political and social base which provides affirmative discourses concerning identity and relationships, as well as social space and a sense of belonging (although not always in an unproblematic way, see Monro 2005). However, transgender tends to be 'added on' by these communities, and focus may continue in practice to be on lesbian and gay young people (see for example http://www.also.org.au/alsorts.Foreword.htm). Intersex and non transsexual transgender young people may be even less included in these communities, which tend to define 'transgender' as 'transsexual'.

There appear to be changes taking place in the area of young people and sex work. New UK legislation, via the Sex Offences Act 2003, aims to protect young people from exploitation via prostitution and pornography. At the same time, there are alterations in the way that young people do sex work. According to a London based youth project which supports sex workers[9] some of the transgender (usually preoperative MTF transsexual) sex workers whom they are in contact with are in very vulnerable positions, and selling or exchanging sex is a means of survival for some. However, the youth project also discusses significant changes in the world of sex work, which have taken place over the last five years or more. Sex workers have shifted away from work on the streets, towards contacts made via adverts/mobile phones and the internet. This is linked with a reduction in visible homelessness to hidden homelessness (for example young transgender sex workers are more likely to stay with friends) and also with an increase in young people making a choice to enter sex work, as opposed to being coerced or needing to do sex work to survive. However, the levels of agency that young transgender people are able to exercise regarding sex work remain questionable, given the lack of alternatives that some experience, and exploitation continues to be a major risk. This concern is backed up by research in Israel, where Leichtentritt and Davidson-Arad (2004) found that young transgender sex workers felt that sex work was a price to be paid for gender transformation.

A further development in the UK is taking place within the statutory sectors, where there is an increasing recognition of the needs that transgender young people have concerning making the transition into adulthood. For instance, a consultation exercise was conducted in 2002 in London with lesbian, gay, bisexual, and transgender youth workers. This has led to the initiation of a Youth Inclusion Project, including development of an LGBT Youth Parliament, a directory of LGBT youth services, and plans for a national needs assessment of Black and Ethnic Minority LGBT young people (Young, 2004). Developments in this area are linked into wider movements by New Labour to support social inclusion and to address the interests of socially marginalized groups (see Monro, 2003).

Developments affecting transgender and intersex young people in the UK are clearly complex and ongoing. As well as facing many of the issues affecting adult transgender and intersex people, young people in these groups experience specific – although varied – experiences relating to their family and education. There appear to be a number of changes taking place concerning transgender and young people's lives, including the impact of the internet, the possible effects of developments in statutory youth provision, the opportunities offered by the increasingly inclusive stance of the LGB community, and, for the young people involved in sex work, shifts in the form and context of this.

Case Vignettes

A number of research contributors discussed their childhood and adolescence in relation to transgender. These brief case studies are intended to serve as snapshots, providing an illustration of the issues that young transgender people face, as well as the diversity of their experience.

Case Vignette 1

This person identified as male and as a post-operative transsexual. He had experienced support and acceptance during his childhood regarding his gender difference:

> The fact that I had a female body would occasionally confuse them, and I did not, I didn't look particularly female. I'd, I looked very androgynous.

> Of course I was treated as a little girl as a child, and even so when I'd be out and about sometimes people would perceive me as a little boy, and erm, I just perceived myself as, you know, a human being, I knew I wasn't a girl, exactly, but I also knew I wasn't a boy. I wasn't exactly like either one. So in that sense there's a sort of otherness.

He was happy with his identity and described himself as very successful, having a professional career. He described his experience as follows:

> I don't feel that I'm any kind of victim, or that I've been pushed in direction. Erm, I think finding myself as a very young child, being, having a gender expression that was different from my body was erm, you know, posed particular challenges for me, but, erm, I was always pretty well accepted, at least by people who knew me, not necessarily by strangers, erm, people have experienced me as a human being and accepted me as a human being, or were well disposed toward me, I had the highest sense of self-esteem, and as a child and as an adult I was very successful in my life, and erm, so, you know I just feel like it's no different front having, you know, from being born with red hair.

Case Vignette 2

Salmacis, was born intersex, rejected by her family and put into care. In care she was sexually abused for several years. She is now in long-term care. She describes surgery as non-consensual genital mutilation and argues that the reasons for doing it are rarely clinical and usually cultural. She likens it to the genital mutilation that occurs in other countries and is hypocritically vilified by Western capitalist nations. For Salmacis, surgical, hormonal and psychological problems resulting at least in part from early treatment are serious and are still not resolved. She expressed anger at the way she had been treated. She described herself as asexual, due to the surgeons having 'botched up' and because of her experiences of being sexually abused while in care. She argues that certain conditions produce childhood fatalities if not treated, but says that 'that's not to do with the sexual identity, or the gender identity, that's as much of a problem as having a heart attack at that age. It is a separate issue. People make it an issue because of the gender aspect'. She sees intersex issues as different from sexual orientation ones:

> Well it is if you are say, a homosexual or a lesbian because it is part of your behavioural psychology, but in a situation like this, it's not. It is physiology that's your problem, it's not your sex, your sexuality. So when it comes to outing you can say, yes, 'oh, I'm a lesbian', or whatever, and then you are open to the mercy of the normal – whether you are accepted or not. But in many senses that seems to be far more acceptable to them, because all though it's in a sense cross-gendered behaviour, it's not cross-gendered anatomy. Cross-gendered anatomy is slightly different, because what they'll do is take you as a twelve year old child, put you in a boarding school and sexually abuse you for five years – to cry my own case.

Case Vignette 3

Kate, a pre-operative MTF transsexual describes her experiences concerning her childhood. One of the problematic ongoing issues she discusses concerning transgender is that some feminists, such as Raymond (1980), have scapegoated transsexuals, especially MTF transsexuals, partly because they see them as having enjoyed male privilege as children. However, it is clear from Kate's experience that she did not experience this privilege:

> Kate: This always thrown at transsexuals who are the next generation on by the now establishment who say 'you weren't brought up as a girl I was, you have a different experience to me' right? 'No one forces you to be a girl' right. And that's the real terror thing. And I said before about the fact that I *was* actually taught to be a girl, because my brain taught me to be a girl, because I lived in an environment which taught me how to be a girl, and I wasn't born with a cunt, and you know it doesn't make me any less of a woman. It's how, when I was four years old, I grew up thinking, when I first became aware of myself as a person, I became aware of the girl, I didn't know what the concept of a girl was, it was only later did I learn that there was a difference between boys and girls, and then later I learned what the word 'girl' meant, and that was all new stuff. But I was aware that 'I am like my body, I am like?'

> Interviewer: You didn't know...

> Kate: I didn't know. But I therefore also carried on learning how to be a girl. But when I actually found out that I had to be a boy, that's when the real tearing apart happened, massively because I was hitting like five years old in school before, and the pressure was right on me, and if you don't fit that you are beaten until you fit it. 'All the boys go here, and all the girls go there' so you go off with the girls. And the teachers give you a whack on the head and they're being nasty and 'stop, David,' and all the girls and all the boys start laughing at you. You know, 'ahaha he doesn't know what gender he is' and that's it, and that's the same stuff that happens with the feminists, it's the same sort of 'I prove that I'm a girl by my body'.

Case Vignette 4

Pamela, a MTF transsexual, describes her personality development as a child and the stereotypes she had to contend with:

> Pamela: Um, I mean there's a sense in which I can only speak for myself but in speaking for myself I am conscious that I am echoing many a discussion that I've had with friends in the community, and say that it's thought that the first step is a construction of oneself as a child, which is then denied, absolutely by the legislators and interpreters, who at that stage are typically one's parents. And certainly at school too…so I think the starting point is that the individual constructs their identity. Whether that's nature or nurture we will never know. But you know, whichever, or both, or possibly even neither, whichever the child has a sense of themselves. And that sense of themselves is then deconstructed. Is necessarily, it's opposed, it meets opposition, so the child deconstructs it. So as a child I, I would say, as a child I consciously deconstructed my identity as a girl, deliberately, to the point at which I can remember as I kind of grew older reading bits and pieces here and there or seeing bits and pieces here and there about what a girl was typically like and did and what a boy was typically like and did and noting, with horror the female characteristics, stereotypes, if you like, in myself, and correcting them. And the one, funnily enough, I don't know where I read this, or heard it, or saw it, the one that remains with me most of all is your thumb.

> Interviewer: Who?

Pamela: Your thumb, you know, your thumb on your hand.

Interviewer: Oh yeah, yeah.

Pamela: Well I don't know where that was, I don't remember at all, but what I do remember is girl's thumbs bend, and boys thumbs are straight.

Interviewer: Oh, right.

Pamela: Just check your own, Surya (laughs)...

Interviewer: Er, well it depends whether I'm bending it or not...

Pamela: Just put the hand in relaxed position...

Interviewer: It depends what position it's in. See on its back.

Pamela: Self conscious.

Interviewer: If it's on its back it bends and if it's on its front it's straight (laughs)...

Pamela: Well, you'll just have to draw your own conclusions (laughs). The thing is I can remember being very very conscious about that sort of stuff. And of course I recall that an awful lot of children's literature is highly gendered. And an awful lot of children's literature deals with um role change. So Enid Blyton is absolutely chock full with people pretending to be one thing and being another. So you get this whole sense of, 'you must be like this and there are terrible penalties but you don't know what they are' so that phase of saying, 'this is how I understand myself and this is how I construct myself and it's just a case of waiting until, and then something will happen'. And nothing does happen, and you realize that in my case I had a twin sister, and it was immediately obvious to me that the things that she did and I did were the same, but that they would meet with approval in her case and not in mine, so that's how the process goes. You have a construction of yourself which is opposed, which we then deconstruct, to the nth degree, as far as it will go and as you get older and older so you gain more and more a sense of horror and internal nonconformity so you work even harder at reconstructing this, this outer being, this social construction. And often that's very very successful. Because of course in a way again what it indicates to us is that in the end there isn't very much apart from biological functions, there isn't actually terribly much difference between men and women in terms of what people are capable of.

Analysis and Conclusion

Overall, young transgender and intersex people face a number of challenges when making the transition into adulthood, which are additional to those faced by other young people, and which may place them at a high risk of social exclusion. Transsexual young people may go through gender reassignment concurrently with adolescence and/or early adulthood, entailing an experience of two types of major life transition within the space of a few years, whilst intersex young people may also be questioning or changing their gender identity, and/or undergoing continuing medical treatment, during their transition into adulthood. Specific areas that are likely to be challenging for transgender and intersex young people during adolescence and early adulthood include family relationships, peer relationships, education, medical treatment (where relevant), and in some cases entry into the labour market. Areas in which young transgender people may face increased risk – if there is familial or economic marginalization – include vulnerability to exploitation as sex workers, homelessness, and violence. The social institutions that impact on intersex and transgender people generally, including legislation and bureaucracy, will also shape their experiences and the options open to them.

There appear to be a number of key factors facilitating transgender and intersex young people in making their transitions into adulthood. Some of these concern the general needs of young people, for example adequate economic and social support. Others are more specific, including the support, acceptance, and awareness of parents, other family members, friends/sexual partners, and professionals such as teachers, in relation to the issues that the young person is facing. This support may entail acceptance of behaviour that adults find difficult to deal with, for example Blackburn (2004) found that young people dealt with oppression in ways that were not always sanctioned by their schools. Blackburn argues that educators should recognize and value young people's agency. Affirmative life stories of young transgender people describe the challenges that they must overcome, but also highlights their agency, the acceptance and support that some young transgender people can access, and the positive contributions that they can make to their communities. For example:

> The day I decided to tell my dad, I was nervous as hell. I had just gotten into an argument with some friends, and ran home, took my jacket and shoes off in a hurry, and told my dad I had to tell him something. 'Dad, I think I'm transsexual'. Shock. He was OK with it though. He worries about me, I think. Poor sod. He thought he had a lesbian daughter, but instead he has a son, and not even a straight son…it's been a few months now, I have a boyfriend who I love more than anything in the world… (Kasper, who is Norwegian and came out to his father when he was seventeen) (http://www.outpath.taf?function=detail&mode+browse&rowid=69&cur).

> I went online and found all kinds of trans websites…It was a scary time, because the more I learned, the more I realized that I really was transgendered, and I knew I was going to have to do something about it. After a summer spent living with my partner, I came back to college and came out as female-to-male transgendered to my friends and teachers. Everyone was really supportive of me…I came out to my mother while I was home for thanksgiving in 2000, and I came out to my father in a letter…I'm doing the best I can to gently ease into transition so that they have time to process everything that's happening…I do a lot of queer youth activism…I love going out and speaking about my life to educate other people about trans issues (Kael, 21, USA) (http://www.youthresource.com/community/transtopia/stories/kael.cfm).

Models of citizenship provide one means of conceptualizing young transgender and intersex people's social inclusion (see Monro, 2003, 2004). Citizenship entails notions of rights and equality, and the participation of young people in decision making processes via, for example, consultations, youth parliaments, and research. The development of citizenship rights for transgender youth would involve support for young transgender people who wish to change sex and intersex young people who want surgery. For transgender young people involved in medical treatment, guidelines include following the preferred treatment of the patient and their parents (where possible), and developing legal mechanisms to manage issues of consent for young people under the age of eighteen (see Whittle, 2002). More generally, health risk prevention strategies could include involving young transgender and intersex people in the development of health campaigns, and ensuring that health care providers have the skills and knowledge necessary to communicate effectively with young healthcare consumers (Drabble et al., 2002). There are many other ways in which young transgender people's citizenship rights can form the basis for social policy reform, for example legislative changes and anti-discrimination initiatives. Strategies to increase social connectedness, reduce discrimination, and improve opportunities for economic participation are crucial for improving social inclusion of transgender and intersex young people (see http://www.also. org.au/alsorts/Foreword.htm). For example, Lepischak (2004) describes the development of a successful Canadian grassroots community development programme for transgender and LGB youth. Strategies in areas of particular importance to young people, such as education, should be developed and implemented (see Ryan and Rivers, 2003). Young transgender and intersex people should be encouraged to access support via the networks on the world wide web, and local support networks (sometimes linked with LGB community centres or groups) should be resourced. The development of education and support for families with young transgender and intersex members – as well as wider education programmes – will enable parents and other family members to facilitate young transgender people's transition into adulthood in a positive way. Schools, colleges, and youth services can develop and implement policies that support young people who are going through, or have been though, sex changes, who are gender ambiguous, or who cross-dress.

Acknowledgements

I would like to acknowledge the generous contributions of transgender people and organizations to this research. I would also like to acknowledge the funders of the study, the Economic and Social Research Council.

Notes

1   There are dangers involved in seeing young transgender people as victims facing discrimination – this can be disempowering. However, the issues facing young transgender people are very difficult, and before we can move beyond 'victim' models it seems important to address the forces of oppression.

2   It is important to point out that young people's experiences will be structured by other factors, such as religion, ethnicity, political stance of the family, socio-economic position, and type of transgender, and that wide variation exists within, as well as between, countries.

3   Although sexual expression, marriage and parenthood will be irrelevant to some young transgender people, there may be others who enter this phase of life early, or whose gender identity is mediated by the lack of rights in this area.

4   Prendegast et al. (2002) documents the extent of homelessness prevalent amongst young lesbian, gay and bisexual young people in the UK, often because they have been abused or rejected by their families. At the same time, levels of homophobic abuse in hostels are high, and there is little specified provision. Such difficulties are likely to also be encountered by young transgender people.

5   The medical treatment of transgender people has been criticized primarily by feminists (Raymond, 1980, 1994; Jeffreys, 1996; Hausman, 1995) and by critical theorists such as Evans (1993). These critiques argue that transsexuality is an iatrogenic, medically caused phenomenon operating in the service of patriarchy and capitalism. The general consensus among all transsexual contributors, including those who were undecided as to whether to have surgery, is that surgery should be available, and that some medical intervention may be necessary at some points. It is important to point out that there are ongoing debates and divergences of opinion concerning this matter within the transgender communities.

6   However, it is important to note that support for lesbian, gay and bisexual identities is increasing among medics, partly because of pressure from critics. For example, Watson and Hitchcock (2000) explicitly argue for professionals to support sexual diversity in response to my (2000a) paper.

7   See for example http://www.transalliancesociety.org/links/html and http:www.isna.org/drupal/index.php. Some of these include sites specifically for transgender young people (for instance http://www.transproud.com/, http://www.youthresource.com/community/transopia/index.cfm). Although there is a tendency for these networks to be USA-based, there are some European ones (for example http://www.kaffeine.freeuk.com/ korner/european.htm).

8   For example http://www.gayyouthuk.org.uk/forums/.

9   http://www.SW5.info/ourwork.htm.

References

Anonymous (1998), 'Private Lives', *Guardian*, 9 February.

Balzer, C. (2004), 'Beauty and the Beast: Reflections about the Socio-Historical and Subcultural Context of Drag Queens and "Tunten" in Berlin', *Journal of Homosexuality*, Vol. 46(3-4), pp. 55-71.

Blackburn, M.V. (2004), 'Understanding Agency Beyond School-Sanctioned Activities', *Theory and Practice*, Vol. 43(2), pp. 102-110.

Bloomfield, A. (1996), 'Discrimination in the Institution', *Gemsnews*, Vol. 25, pp. 11-15.

Boenke, M. (ed.), (1999), *Trans Forming Families: Real Stories about Transgendered Loved Ones*, Walter Trook Publishing, California.

Bornstein, K. (1994), *Gender Outlaw: On Men, Women and the Rest of Us*, Routledge Publications, New York/London.

Channel Four (2004), *Secret Intersex*, television programme.

Chase, C. (1998), 'Affronting Reason', in D. Atkins (ed.), *Looking Queer: Body Image and Identity in Lesbian, Bisexual, Gay and Transgender Communities*, Harrington Park Press, New York/London, pp. 205-219.

Cochran, B.N., Stewart, A.J., Ginzler, J.A. and Cauce, A.M. (2002), 'Challenges Faced by Homeless Sexual Minorities: Comparison of Gay, Lesbian, Bisexual, and Transgender Homeless Adolescents with their Heterosexual Counterparts', *American Journal of Public Health*, Vol. 92(5), pp. 773-777.

Denzin, N. (1989), *Collecting and Interpreting Qualitative Materials*, Sage, California/London.

Dillon, F. (1999), 'Tell Grandma I'm a Boy', in M. Boenke (ed.), *Trans Forming Families: Real Stories about Transgendered Loved Ones*, Walter Trout, California, pp. 3-8.

Drabble, L., Keatley, J. and Marcelle, G. (2002), 'Progress and Opportunities in Lesbian, Gay, Bisexual and Transgender Health Communications', *Clinical Research and Regulatory Affairs*, Vol. 20(2), pp. 205-227.

Dreger, A. (1998), '"Ambigous Sex" – or "Ambivalent Medicine"?', *The Hastings Centre Report*, Vol. 28(3), pp. 24-35.

Dreger, A. (2000), *Intersex in the Age of Ethics*, University Publishing Group, Maryland.

Dunne, G.A., Prendegast, S. and Telford, D. (2002), 'Young, Gay, Homeless and Invisible: A Growing Population?' *Culture, Health and Sexuality*, Vol. 4(1), pp. 103-115.

Evans, D. (1993), *Sexual Citizenship: The Material Construction of Sexualities*, Routledge, London/New York.

Evelyn, J. (1999), 'I Need to Be a Girl', in M., Boenke (ed.), *Trans Forming Families: Real Stories about Transgender Loved Ones*, Walter Trook Publishing, California, pp. 9-12.

Feinberg, L. (1996), *Transgender Warriors: Making History from Joan of Arc to Dennis Rodman*, Beacon Press, Boston.

Freedman, D., Tasker, F. and Di Ceglie, D. (2002), 'Children and Adolescents with Transsexual Parents Referred to a Specialist Gender Identity Development Service: A Brief Report on Key Developmental Features', *Clinical Child Psychology and Psychiatry*, Vol. 7(3), pp. 423-32.

Ghasemi, Z. (1999), 'A Transsexual in Teheran', in M. Boenke (ed.) *Trans Forming Families: Real Stories about Transgender Loved Ones*, Walter Trook Publishing, California, pp. 21-25.

Gilbert, M.A. (2001), 'A Sometime Woman: Gender Choice and Cross-Socialization', in F. Haynes and T. McKenna (eds), *Unseen Genders: Beyond the Binaries*, Peter Lang, New York, pp. 41-50.

Halberstam, J. (1994), 'F2M: The Making of Female Masculinity', in L. Doan (ed.), *The Lesbian Postmodern*, Columbia University Press, New York, pp. 210-228.

Hausman, B. (1995), *Changing Sex: Transexualism, Technology and the Idea of Gender*, Duke University Press, Durham.

Haynes, F. and McKenna, T. (eds), (2001), *Unseen Genders: Beyond the Binaries*, Peter Lang, New York.

Hoban, M.T. and Ward, R.L. (2003), 'Building Culturally Competent College Health Programmes', *Journal of American College Health*, Vol. 52(3), pp. 137-141.

Holmes, M. (1998), 'In(to) Visibility: Intersexuality in the Field of Queer', in D. Atkins (ed.), *Looking Queer: Body Image and Identity in Lesbian, Bisexual, Gay and Transgender Communities*, Harrington Park Press, New York/London, pp. 221-226.

Home Office (2000), *Report on the Interdepartmental Working Group on Transsexual People*, Home Office, London.

Howey, N. and Samuals, E. (eds), (2000), *Out of the Ordinary: Essays on Growing Up with Gay, Lesbian and Transgender Parents*, St Martins Press, New York.

Hugill, B. (1988), 'In Ancient Greece She'd Have Been a God. In Wales They Spit On Her', *The Observer*, 24 May, p. 7.

Hulick, J.L. (2003), 'A Queer Problem: Issues Facing GLBTQ Youth', *Southern Sociological Society*, 2003.

http://www.also.org.au/alsorts.Foreword.htm, last visited 22 July 2004.

http://www.gayyouthuk.org.uk/forums/, last visited 22 July 2004.

http:www.isna.org/drupal/index.php, last visited 22 July 2004.

http://www.kaffeine.freeuk.com/ korner/european.htm, last visited 19 July 2004.

http://www.outpath.taf?function=detail&mode+browse&rowid=69&cur, last visited 19 July 2004.

http:www.pfc.org.uk/, last visited 2 February 2004.

http://www.SW5.info/ourwork.htm, last visited 19 July 2004.

http:www.transalliancesociety/links/htm/, last visited 19 July 2004.

http://www.transproud.com/, last visited 19 July 2004.

http://www.youthresource.com/community/ transtopia/stories/kael.cfm, last visited 19 July 2004.

Israel, G.E. and Tarver, D.E. (1997), *Transgender Care: Recommended Guidelines, Practical Information and Personal Accounts*, Temple University Press, Philadelphia.

Jeffreys, S. (1996), 'Heterosexuality and the Desire for Gender', in D. Richardson (ed.), *Theorising Heterosexuality: Telling it Straight*, Open University Press, Buckingham/Philadelphia, pp. 91-108.

Kaldera, R. (1998), 'Agdistis' Children: Living Bi-Gendered in a Single-Gendered World', in D. Atkins (ed.), *Looking Queer: Body Image and Identity in Lesbian, Bisexual, Gay and Transgender Communities*, Harrington Park Press, New York/London, pp. 227-232.

Kessler, S.J. (1998), *Lessons from the Intersexed*, Rutgers University Press, New Brunswick, New Jersey/London.

Lepischak, B. (2004), 'Building Community for Toronto's Lesbian, Gay, Bisexual, Transsexual, and Transgender Youth', *Journal of Gay and Lesbian Social Services*, Vol. 16(3-4), pp. 81-98.

Leichtentritt, R.D. and Davidson-Arad, B. (2004), 'Adolescent and Young Male-To-Female Transsexuals: Pathways to Prostitution', *British Journal of Social Work*, Vol. 34(3), pp. 349-374.

MacMullen, M. and Whittle, S. (1994), *Transvestism, Transsexualism and the Law*, The Beaumont Trust, London.

Matzner, A. (2001), *O Au No Keia: Voices from Hawai'i's Mahu and Transgender Communities*, Xlibris, Philadelphia.

Maynard, M. and Purvis, J. (1994), *Researching Women's Lives from a Feminist Perspective*, Taylor and Francis, London.

Monro, S. (2000a), 'Theorizing Transgender Diversity: Towards a Social Model of Health', *Sexual and Relationship Therapy*, Vol. 15(1), pp. 33-45.

Monro, S. (2000b), *Transgender Politics*, unpublished thesis, Sheffield University, UK.

Monro, S. (2003), 'Transgender Citizenship in the UK', *Critical Social Policy*, Vol. 29(4), pp. 433-452.

Monro, S. (2004), 'Transgendering Citizenship', *Sexualities*, Vol. 7(3), pp. 345-362.

Monro, S. (2005), *Gender Politics: Citizenship, Activism and Diversity*, Pluto Press, London.

More, K and Whittle, S. (eds), (1999), *Reclaiming Genders: Transsexual Grammars at the Fin de Siècle*, Cassell, London.

Morrow, D.F. (2004), 'Social Work Practice with Gay, Lesbian, Bisexual, and Transgender Adolescents', *Families in Society – The Journal of Contemporary Human Services*, Vol. 85(1), pp. 91-99.

Namaste, V. (2001), *Invisible Lives: The Erasure of Transsexual and Transgender People*, Chicago University Press, Chicago.

Nataf, Z. (1996), *Lesbians Talk Transgender*, Scarlett Press, London.

Neeval, N. (2002), 'Me Boy', *Journal of Homosexuality*, Vol. 43(3-4), pp. 31-38.

Pink Paper (2000), 'Catholic School Backs Sex Change', 3 March.

Prendegast, S., Dunne, G.A. and Telford, D. (2002), 'A Story of "Difference", a Different Story: Young Homeless Lesbian, Gay and Bisexual People', *International Journal of Sociology and Social Policy*, Vol. 21(4-5-6), pp. 64-91.

Prosser, J. (1998), *Second Skins: The Body Narratives of Transsexuality*, Columbia University Press, New York.

Purnell, A. (1998), 'Exceptional People Whose Greatest Aspiration Is To Be Seen As Ordinary: A Counsellor's View', *Gendys Journal*, Vol. 1, pp. 8-14.

Pusch, R.S. (2003), 'The Bathroom and Beyond: Transgendered College Student's Perceptions of Transition', *Dissertation Abstracts International, A: The Humanities and Social Sciences*, August, pp. 456A-457A.

Quinn, T.L. (2002), 'Sexual Orientation and Gender Diversity: An Administrative Approach to Diversity', *Child Welfare*, Vol. 81(6), pp. 913-928.

Raymond, J. (1980), *The Transsexual Empire: The Making of the She-Male*, The Women's Press, London.

Raymond, J. (1994), 'The Politics of Transgender', *Feminism and Psychology*, Vol. 4(4), pp. 628-633.

Rees, M. (1996), *Dear Sir or Madam: The Autobiography of a Female-to-Male Transsexual*, Cassell, London.

Reinharz, S. (1992), *Feminist Methods in Social Research*, Oxford University Press, New York/Oxford.

Rhind, N.R., Millar, L.M. Kopczynski, J.B. and Meyer, B.J. (1995), 'Xol-1 Acts as an Early Switch in the C. Elegans', *Cell*, Vol. 80(1), pp. 71-82.

Rosario, V. (1996), 'Trans (Homo) Sexuality? Double Inversion, Psychiatric Confusion, and Hetero-Hegemony', in B. Beemyn and M. Eliason (eds.) *Queer Studies: A Lesbian, Gay, Bisexual and Transgender Anthology*, New York University Press, New York/London, pp. 36-51.

Rothblatt, M. (1995), *The Apartheid of Sex: A Manifesto for the Freedom of Gender*, Crown Publishers, New York.

Ryan, C. (2002), 'Lesbian, Gay, Bisexual and Transgender Youth: Health Concerns, Services, and Care', *Clinical Research and Regulatory Affairs*, Vol. 20(2), pp. 137-158.

Ryan, C. and Rivers, I. (2003), 'Lesbian, Gay, Bisexual and Transgender Youth: Victimisation and its Correlates in the USA and UK', *Culture, Health and Sexuality*, Vol. 5(2), pp. 103-119.

Smith, Y.L.S., Cohen, L. and Cohen-Ketteris, P.T. (2002), 'Postoperative Psychological Functioning of Adolescent Transsexuals: A Rorschach Study', *Archives of Sexual Behaviour*, Vol. 31(3), pp. 255-261.

Socarides, C.W. (1970), 'A Psychoanalytic Study of the Desire for Sexual Transformation ("Transsexualism"): The Plaster-of Paris Man', *International Journal of Psychoanalysis*, Vol. 51, p. 341.

Socarides, C.W. (ed.), (1991), *The Homosexualities and the Therapeutic Process*, International Universities Press, Madison, USA.

Somers, C. and Haynes, F. (2001), 'Intersex: Beyond Hidden A-Genders', in F. Haynes and T, McKenna (eds), *Unseen Genders:Beyond the Binaries*, Peter Lang, New York, pp. 29-40.

Stanley, J.L. (2003), 'An Applied Collaborative Training Programme for Graduate Students in Community Psychology: A Case Study of a Community Project Working with Lesbian, Gay, Bisexual, Transgender, and Questioning Youth', *American Journal of Community Psychology*, Vol. 31(3-4), pp. 253-265.

Stone, S. (1991), 'The Empire Strikes Back: A Posttranssexual Manifesto' in: J. Epstein and K. Straub (eds), *Body Guards: The Cultural Politics of Gender Ambiguity*, Routledge, London, pp. 280-304.

Transgender Agenda Conference (1998), *Transgender Agenda for the New Millenium*, Exeter College, Oxford University, 17-20 September.

Watson, J. and Hitchcock, R. (2000), 'Comment on the Paper by Surya Monro', *Sexual and Relationship Therapy*, Vol. 15(4), pp. 417-418.

Whittle, S. (2002), *Respect and Equality: Transsexual and Transgender Rights*, Cavendish, London.

Wilchins, R.A. (1997), *Read My Lips: Sexual Subversion and the End of Gender*, Firebrand Books, Ithaca, New York.

Wilchins, R.A., Lombardi, E., Preising, D. and Malouf, D. (1997), *First National Survey of Transgender Violence*, http://www.gpac.org/violence/HateCrimesSurvey97/, last visited April 2000.

Wilkinson, H.A. and Greenwald, I. (1995), 'Spatial and Temporal Patterns of lin-12 Expression During C. Elegans Hermaphrodite Development', *Genetics*, Vol. 141(2), pp. 513-526.

Young, L. (1996), 'Sometimes It's Hard to Be a Woman', *The Guardian*, 29 July, p. 6.

Young, N. (2004), 'LGBT Youth Work Forum', *Gendys Journal*, Vol. 26, p. 31.

Index